CHINA'S REGULATORY STATE

A volume in the series

CORNELL STUDIES IN POLITICAL ECONOMY

edited by PETER J. KATZENSTEIN

A list of titles in this series is available
at www.cornellpress.cornell.edu.

CHINA'S REGULATORY STATE

A NEW STRATEGY FOR GLOBALIZATION

Roselyn Hsueh

CORNELL UNIVERSITY PRESS
ITHACA AND LONDON

First published 2011 by Cornell University Press
First printing, Cornell Paperbacks, 2011

Printed in the United States of America

Library of Congress Cataloging-in-Publication Data

Hsueh, Roselyn, 1977–
    China's regulatory state : a new strategy for globalization /
Roselyn Hsueh.
        p. cm. — (Cornell studies in political economy)
    Includes bibliographical references and index.
    ISBN 978-0-8014-4995-6 (cloth : alk. paper)
    ISBN 978-0-8014-7743-0 (pbk : alk. paper)
    1. Industrial policy—China.   2. Trade regulation—
China.   3. Free trade—China.   4. Globalization—
Economic aspects—China.   I. Title.   II. Series:
Cornell studies in political economy.
    HD3616.C63H79   2011
    337.51—dc22   2011007721

Cornell University Press strives to use environmentally responsible suppliers and materials to the fullest extent possible in the publishing of its books. Such materials include vegetable-based, low-VOC inks and acid-free papers that are recycled, totally chlorine-free, or partly composed of nonwood fibers. For further information, visit our website at www.cornellpress.cornell.edu.

Cloth printing   10   9   8   7   6   5   4   3   2   1
Paperback printing   10   9   8   7   6   5   4   3   2   1

To Lee Kun-Chung

CONTENTS

TABLES AND FIGURES

TABLES

FIGURES

ACKNOWLEDGMENTS

This book would not have been possible without the support and encouragement of colleagues, friends, and mentors and the unconditional love of my family. My intellectual debts go to Steve Vogel, Kiren Chaudhry, Kevin O'Brien, and Tom Gold. Steve's commitment to scholarship and mentorship is unparalleled. I am grateful for his advocacy, close reading, friendship, and sound and pragmatic advice. Kiren's penetrating insights and questions always led to interesting findings. Kevin asked questions that sharpened my thinking on China and imparted valuable advice on professional development. Tom availed himself for support and encouragement and animated conversations on China. Steve Fish, Jeb Barnes, Bob Kagan, David Kirp, and Larry Diamond served as early mentors and teachers. David Collier, David Leonard, T. J. Pempel, and Hal Wilensky provided welcomed support and encouragement at critical points.

I received helpful feedback on the research and writing of this book during its different stages from the following people: Tim Büthe, Kiren Chaudhry, Rich Deeg, Tom Gold, Stephan Haggard, Eric Harwit, Justin Hastings, Diana Kapiszewski, Kenji Kushida, Kun-Chin Lin, Peter Lorentzen, Andy Mertha, Mike Nelson, Kevin O'Brien, Ed Steinfeld, Heiner Schulz, Joseph Stiglitz, Steve Vogel, and Hal Wilensky. Feedback received at conferences, workshops, and lectures organized by the following universities and organizations further advanced the project: American Political Science Association, Association for Asian Studies, UC Berkeley, Columbia University's Initiative for Policy Dialogue, Georgetown University, Harvard Business School, International Studies Association, University of Manchester's Brooks World Poverty Institute, Midwest Political Science Association, the Society for the Advancement of Socio-Economics, Temple University, and the University of Texas, Austin.

Several institutions and people made the research presented here possible. The Fulbright Foundation, the National Security Education Program, the UC Berkeley Graduate Division, the UC Berkeley Multi-Year Graduate Opportunity Fellowship Program, the Pacific Rim Research Program of the University of California Office of the President, and the UC Berkeley Institute of East Asian Studies financed fieldwork and writing. I am grateful to Song Hong for his support during my residency as Fulbright Visiting Scholar at the Institute of World Economics and Politics, Chinese Academy of Social Sciences. Special thanks also go to Liu Shiguo, Tian Fang, Wang Yizhou, Xi Xiaojie, and Zhang Lihua. Yi Shang served as an able research assistant. Many who opened doors, which allowed me to successfully pursue my research, and served as informants have asked to remain anonymous. Those whom I can name in Japan, China, and Taiwan include Michael Aldrich, Michael Barbalas, John Chiang, Kaiser Kao, Rocky Lee, Sheaffer Lee, Bernd Reitmeier, Bill Savadove, Toshihiko Shibuya, Hiroshi Tsukamoto, David Tullock, Craig Watts, Masaki Yabuuchi, and Anne Stevenson-Yang.

The following academic institutions and people facilitated the manuscript stage of this project. During a research fellowship at the Center for International Studies, University of Southern California, I benefited from the collegiality and constructive feedback of Carolyn Cartier, Clay Dube, Pat James, Dave Kang, Saori Katada, Dan Lynch, Stan Rosen, Jefferey Sellers, and Carol Wise. Justin Hastings, Laura Henry, and Steve Vogel gave advice and encouragement on book publishing. Constructive feedback from Roger Haydon and Peter Katzenstein, my editors at Cornell, and anonymous reviewers, improved this book. I am grateful for my Temple colleagues' friendship and mentorship: Kevin Arceneaux, Rob Brown, Rich Deeg, Orfeo Fioretos, Robin Kolodny, Gary Mucciaroni, Megan Mullin, Joe Schwartz, Hillel Soifer, Sandra Suarez, Sydney White, and Chris Wlezien.

Many good friends traveled this journey with me. From Berkeley political science are Libby Anker, Ralph Espach, Ken Foster, Jane Gingrich, Jill Greenlee, Greg Hoadley, Maiah Jaskoski, Diana Kapiszewski, Jocelyn Kiley, Min Gyo Koo, Kun-Chin Lin, Mike Nelson, Gene Park, Kirsten Rodine, and Rachel Van Sickle-Ward. Ritu Ahuja, Tonya Kim Dewey, Nonna Gorilovskaya, Jenny Larson Huang, Bonnie Henson, Lilli-Anne Suzuki, Sharon Touryan, and Peggy Sue Wright kept me company throughout and prayed with me. Mark Labberton and Sandi Hedlund encouraged me to rely on my spiritual resources.

For their camaraderie during fieldwork, I thank Jean-Noel Bonnieu, Vivian Chen, Jeannie Katsigris, Vivian Kuo, Imelda Lapthorne, Henry Lew, Gillian Li, Pattlyn Ng, Silvia Pfanner, Mintze Phua, Svenja Schlichting, Christian Sommerfeld, Lilli-Anne Suzuki, Ron Tam, Linda Tan, Calvin Tchiang, Teri Woodland, and Daniel Wong. Josie Dunning, Neil Fromer, Elly Shinohara, Tiana Tse, Rachel Van Sickle-Ward, and Yi Zhou enhanced my stay in Southern California. Delores Brisbon, Susana Fattorini, Megan Mullin, Matt Sherman, Elly Teman, Waugh Wright, and Jane Zhang help make Philadelphia home.

Without my family, there would be no book. I dedicate this book to Lee Kun-Chung, my maternal grandfather, whose life and passion inspired my pursuit of political science. Robbie Romano, my best friend and husband, and I met as undergraduates in a course on American politics; ever since, he has been my bulwark and retreat, and together our life is full of laughter and joy. I am blessed with my twin sister Lily's listening ear, prayers, and nonjudgmental advice. My dad, Tse-Huang, and my mom, Lee Pauline, inspire me in all dimensions of my life. My younger brother Peter and his family showed Robbie and me the joys of starting a family. We cannot imagine life without our son Lucas. Robbie and Lucas are why this book made it to your hands.

ABBREVIATIONS

3G	third generation telecommunications network
AQSIQ	Administration for Quality Supervision, Inspection and Quarantine
BOT	Bureau of Textiles
CAS	Chinese Academy of Sciences
CCC-T	China Chamber of Commerce for Import and Export of Textiles
CCF	China-China-Foreign joint venture
CCP	Chinese Communist Party
CDMA	Code Division Multiple Access
CHINATEX	China National Textiles Import and Export Corporation
CIC	China Investment Corporation
CNTAC	China National Textile and Apparel Council
DGT	Directorate General of Telecommunications
FDI	foreign direct investment
FIE	foreign-invested enterprise
FITE	foreign-invested telecommunications enterprise
FTC	foreign trade corporation
GIC	German Industry and Commerce
GSM	Global System for Mobile communications
HRS	household responsibility system
IC	integrated circuit
ICP	Internet content provider
ICT	information and communications technology
ISP	Internet service provider
IT	information technology
JETRO	Japan External Trade Organization
JV	joint venture
MEI	Ministry of Electronics Industry
MFA	Multi-Fiber Agreement
MII	Ministry of Information Industry
MIIT	Ministry of Industry and Information Technology
MIT	Ministry of Internal Trade

MOFCOM	Ministry of Commerce
MOFERT	Ministry of Foreign Economic Relations and Trade
MOFTEC	Ministry of Foreign Trade and Economic Cooperation
MOR	Ministry of Railways
MOST	Ministry of Science and Technology
MPT	Ministry of Post and Telecommunications
MTI	Ministry of Textile Industry
NDRC	National Development and Reform Commission
NIC	newly industrialized country
NTT	Nippon Telegraph and Telephone Corporation
PBOC	People's Bank of China
PHS	personal handy phone services
PLA	People's Liberation Army
PRC	People's Republic of China
PTA	post and telecommunications authority
RMB	renminbi
SAFE	State Administration of Foreign Exchange
SAIC	State Administration of Industry and Commerce
SARFT	State Administration of Radio, Film, and Television
SASAC	State-Owned Assets Supervision and Administration Commission
SAT	State Administration of Taxation
SATI	State Administration of Textile Industry
SDPC	State Development and Planning Commission
SETC	State Economic and Trade Commission
SLGI	State Leading Group for Informationization
SMC	supply and marketing cooperative
SMS	short message service
SOE	state-owned enterprise
SP	telecommunications service and content provider
TAB	Telecommunications Administration Bureau
TD-SCDMA	Time Division Synchronous Code Division Multiple Access
TRQ	tariff rate quota
TVE	town and village enterprise
USITO	U.S. Information Technology Office
VAS	value-added service(s)
VoIP	Voice over Internet Protocol
WFOE	wholly foreign-owned enterprise
WTO	World Trade Organization

INTRODUCTION

China's Liberalization Two-Step

When I first arrived in the People's Republic of China (PRC) in the summer of 2002, shortly after the country's accession to the World Trade Organization (WTO), I immediately confronted a paradox: the omnipresence of the state in economic activities along with genuinely capitalist practices and values. Foreign influence screamed everywhere, from neon displays of ING and Nestlé on skyscrapers lining the Bund in Shanghai, to billboards selling Motorola and LG handsets along boulevards of provincial Shandong, to foreign brands worn by China's nouveau riche in the western interior. Yet visits to town and village enterprises (TVEs), and other quasi-state–quasi-private "red hat" enterprises, revealed that the government still kept a close hand on the economy.[1] City and other local bureaucrats in Beijing, Shanghai, Shenzhen, Xian, and Yantai proudly led me on tours of government-run development and trade zones, industry and commerce bureaus, and successful local companies in retail, foodstuffs, chemicals, electronics, plastics, and textiles. Managers and their staffs beamed with pride as they spoke of working with party cadres to run their organizations, which they did according to market incentives. More often than not, although they found it difficult to explain the precise role of the state, they said that interactions with state bureaucrats to obtain requisite approvals and learn of administrative mandates and declarations were daily activities. They also sidestepped questions about the property rights of their respective enterprises and those of their competitors.

---

1. "Red hat" enterprises are companies that disguise their de facto private ownership by registering as state-owned enterprises.

Some people claimed that they rarely witnessed state intervention; in fact, they maintained that China needed more rules to better regulate corruption, other forms of rent-seeking, and overexpansion due to poor market practices. Notwithstanding contradictory depictions of the state, capitalist practices—such as production based on supply and demand and competition-driven pricing—pervaded economic life, motivating state and private entrepreneurs alike. Moreover, the apparently harmonious coexistence of state intervention and market practices provided the context for the "China strategy" of multinational corporations the world over, as well as ethnic Chinese capital, which began to flood China decades earlier.

Economic liberalization resoundingly exceeded political reform, yet the unevenness of the market capitalism I witnessed kept me questioning the scope and methods of state control and its implications for the global economy and politics in twenty-first-century China. Why has China adopted a more open strategy toward foreign capital, fundamentally breaking from the developmental state model and from its own Communist past? How do we reconcile extensive market liberalization and decentralization of economic decision making with regulatory centralization and enhanced state control? China's industrial revolution, at least this most recent attempt initiated by Deng Xiaoping, took place in thirty years, a feat few countries can boast. Certainly, Charles Tilly and Karl Polanyi would turn over in their graves if they learned how post-1978 China's process of state-building and market-building decidedly had not been a wrenching, ravaging one.[2]

The post-Deng leadership governs China today with an economic model radically different from any we have seen before. Since 1978, when the Chinese government launched the Open Door Policy as part of its integration into the international economy, it has unleashed economy-wide liberalization, including taking a much more liberal approach toward foreign direct investment (FDI) than its East Asian neighbors during an analogous stage of development.[3] Regulatory reform since the 1990s unleashed competition across the economy, and in its accession protocol to the WTO in 2001, China further committed to liberalizing previously closed industrial sectors. As China enters its fourth decade of "reform and opening up," the magnitude of foreign investment dwarfs that of many developing countries;

---

2. See Tilly (1975 and 1985) and Polanyi (1944) on the protracted and violent process of state- and market-building in early modern Europe.

3. See Lardy (2002), Guthrie (1999 and 2006), Zweig (2002), Huang (2003), Steinfeld (2004), and Gallagher (2005) on China's openness toward FDI compared to Japan, South Korea, and Taiwan during a similar stage of development. This book follows the OECD definition of FDI as "a direct investment incorporated or unincorporated enterprise in which a single foreign investor either owns 10 percent or more of the ordinary shares or voting power of an enterprise . . . or owns less than 10 percent of the ordinary shares or voting power of an enterprise, yet still maintains an effective voice in management."

as a percentage of GDP, FDI inflows outstrip China's neighbors and developing countries of comparable size.[4]

In contrast, the developmental states of Japan, South Korea, and Taiwan integrated into the international economy through policies that restricted FDI in order to promote export-oriented industrialization. Those countries helped domestic companies obtain capital and technology through foreign debt or aid and licensing. The Chinese experience also departs categorically from its post-Communist counterparts. Those governments dismantled the Communist state upon the collapse of the Soviet Union, and many pursued a liberalization program of "shock therapy" advocated by proponents of the Washington Consensus.[5] How can China possibly retain elements of a statist economic model when it has liberalized FDI more than any other developing country in recent years? How can it retain state control over critical sectors and meet its WTO commitments?

This book unravels these puzzles by demonstrating that China only appears to be a more liberal state, for it has complemented liberalization at the aggregate (macro) level with reregulation at the sectoral (micro) level.[6] Liberalization is often presented as a uniform process; yet the Chinese state has pursued a *liberalization two-step*. It has shifted from universal controls on FDI and private industry on the aggregate level across all industries to selective controls at the sectoral level.[7] It employs a *bifurcated strategy* to meet its twin goals of complying with WTO commitments and retaining some control. In strategic sectors—those important to national security and the promotion of economic and technological development—the government centralizes control of industry and strictly manages the level and direction of FDI. In less strategic sectors, the Chinese government relinquishes control over industry, decentralizes decision making to local authorities, and encourages private investment and FDI. In other words, taking a purposive orientation toward industrial and FDI policies, China permits large-scale FDI to structure foreign com-

---

4. In 2005, as a percentage of GDP, FDI inflows into China were 3.14 percent compared to Japan's 0.06, South Korea's 0.89, Taiwan's 0.45, India's 0.94, Russia's 1.68, and the United States' 0.84 percent. In terms of inward FDI stock as a percentage of GDP, China stood at 11.81 percent compared to Japan's 2.21, South Korea's 13.25, and Taiwan's 12.12 percent. India stood at 5.49 percent, Russia at 23.57, and the United States at 13.11 percent. Sources: *World Investment Report*, United Nations Conference on Trade and Development, 2009.

5. The speed and scope of market reform varied across post-Soviet countries but, in general, most adopted some variety of the neoliberal policies advocated by the Washington Consensus. See Stiglitz (2001).

6. This study uses "regulation" in the literal sense of the state formulating and creating rules to control industry, not in the sense commonly used in the developmental state literature to mean the liberal state that only regulates as a referee. See the section on conceptualizing state control in chapter 1 for more on this usage.

7. Levy (1999) employs a similar concept, "statist two-step," to describe the parallel processes of associational liberalism, whereby the French state combined more markets with German-style institutions and the transformed but continued presence of the state in policy areas.

petition in ways that allow it to transfer foreign technology, increase the national technology base, encourage indigenous technology and production capacity, and promote domestic business. By exercising this bifurcated strategy, China manages to retain political control and regulatory capacity and to modernize, industrialize, and transform its economic system in the context of international integration.

The empirical basis of this book, grounded in more than eighteen months of in-depth fieldwork in the eastern coastal and western interior provinces of China, is an analysis of industrial trajectories and government-business relations in telecommunications and textiles.[8] Across-case and within-case comparison of telecommunications and textiles, and case studies of market- and efficiency-pursuing domestic and foreign-invested companies, demonstrate that three factors shape dominant patterns of state control. First, the *strategic value of a sector* shapes sectoral variation in the state's particular approach (goals and methods) to regulation. The strategic value of a sector is defined objectively by a sector's degree of importance to national security and by its contribution to the national technology base. But government leaders define it subjectively as they prioritize political over economic objectives and vice versa, and sectoral attributes (structural and institutional) shape actual details of regulation.

Second, the *organization of state institutions* influences the state's capacity to exert central authority over industry as the state reformulates old rules and creates new ones to retain control or order competition after an initial phase of liberalization. State structures and political arrangements between the state and market actors evolve to define the incentives and constraints, which influence progressive generations of regulations and the ways in which the state enforces them in practice. Third, *critical junctures in a sector's exposure to the global economy*, including those macroeconomic fluctuations that affect the domestic sector's competitive position, shape how the state intervenes across time within an industry. The central government is more likely to loosen up during economic booms when the domestic sector is highly competitive and has the capacity to produce high-tech, value-added goods and services. In contrast, it reregulates during economic recessions and in response to critical junctures, such as WTO accession, when the domestic sector does not have the capacity to innovate and engage in technologically complex production.

The main case studies of telecommunications and textiles and mini case studies of strategic and nonstrategic industries illustrate the ways in which the strategic value of a sector and sectoral structures, the organization of institutions, and economic conditions during critical junctures together shape deregulation and reregulation across sectors and over time. These variations and details reveal the transformation of Chinese state strategy in the thirty years between China's Open

---

8. This book focuses on the regulation of domestic industry and FDI, but it does not do so exclusively because in strategic sectors the Chinese government liberalizes only foreign equity and portfolio investment and limits FDI to joint ventures.

Door Policy and the post-WTO era. Despite over three decades of liberalization, the degree of Chinese government control of the economy has not decreased. Rather, in its pursuit of the *liberalization two-step*, the state recalibrates its relationship with industry and its methods of control in sector-specific ways. The *bifurcated strategy* deployed by the Chinese government in its reregulation is part of the larger story of the state enhancing both the role of markets and the state's authority over industry as China integrates into the international economy.

China has adopted a new development model; this approach to market and industrial development varies significantly from those of its Communist past, the liberal trading state, and the developmental state, as illustrated by the mini case studies of Japan, South Korea, and Taiwan following the main ones. The standard accounts of the relationship between government and business in general, and the driving forces of regulatory reform in particular, fall short in understanding China's new economic model. This book provides a new framework to examine the significance of deregulation and reregulation in the political economy of economic change in China. By investigating in depth how China combines the introduction of competition and reregulation, this book provides the most complete picture yet of China's new regulatory state and its implications for twenty-first-century capitalism.

PART I

THE POLITICS OF
MARKET REREGULATION

1

LIBERALIZATION TWO-STEP

Understanding State Control of the Economy

The Open Door Policy in 1978 unleashed economic reforms and the liberalization of foreign direct investment in China after nearly two decades of internal economic and political upheaval and international isolation. This book investigates how China's economic statecraft has been transformed in the ensuing period as China became integrated into the international economy.[1] Because economic liberalization is not a uniform process, this book examines the different dimensions of liberalization—including regulatory challenges, the domestic business class, foreign direct investment, and intranational industrial policy—to explain the rise of China's regulatory state. By doing so, I will illuminate the relationship between the state and the market by telling the story of what happened empirically.

This book's case studies employ sectoral analysis to examine some of the core questions in comparative and international political economy about the relative capacity of the state in the face of global forces and the implications for development. By comparing industrial sectors, this book distinguishes which areas of Chinese industrial policy conform to a liberal approach toward markets, in which areas China has retained and even enhanced government control, and what methods the government has employed in these sectors to achieve its goals. Furthermore, by comparing government control in these industries across time, I explore the interaction between international economic pressures and domestic politics and impact of evolving institutional arrangements. Finally, company case studies provide

---

1. Economic integration involves trade, investment (including direct foreign, portfolio, and equity), services, migration, international standards (e.g., the World Trade Organization and the International Telecommunications Union), finance, and aid; each of these aspects has produced a rather robust literature.

evidence for this book's sectoral arguments and reveal how variations in firm-level characteristics affect the relationship between the state and market forces.

This chapter builds on existing scholarship on the Chinese state and its response to international forces to introduce the story presented in the rest of the book. This story of economic statecraft in the age of globalization reveals that China, despite a common set of pressures (outlined in chapter 2), has extensively liberalized on the aggregate level only to reregulate by exerting deliberate control in strategic industries and incidental control in less strategic industries. This chapter also outlines this study's research design, and elaborates on a typology of state control based on empirical findings. This concept of state control serves as a guide to our understanding of the dominant patterns of state control in the Chinese political economy. Moreover, combined with the analytical framework introduced in chapter 2, it explains the *bifurcated strategy*, which enables the Chinese government to increase its overall capacity by engaging in and exercising seemingly contradictory state-industry relations and economic regulation.

INTERNATIONAL MOVEMENT TO LIBERALIZE, SURGING FDI INFLOWS

Scholars of the Chinese political economy maintain that China has taken an approach toward FDI different from the East Asian developmental state because its integration into the international economy has occurred under circumstances vastly different from the context of Japanese colonialism, war, and Japanese and U.S. postwar financial support faced by the newly industrialized countries (NICs) of East Asia. The NICs entered the international economy during an auspicious moment, when international political alliances during the cold war supported their strong state and exposed them to U.S., Japanese, and European markets.[2] The state restrained politically a society (the middle class in Korea and the native Taiwanese class in Taiwan) weakened by half a century of Japanese colonial rule; and while FDI strategies varied across the NICs, in general the state restricted imports and direct foreign investments to low levels.[3] The domestic sector obtained capital for industrial investment through foreign debt and aid, which the state managed and distributed, and through exports to friendly and growing markets abroad. They obtained technology through arm's-length contracting, such as licensing and contract manufacturing, with foreign companies.[4]

---

2. Stubbs (1999 and 2005) identifies threat and eruption of and mobilization in preparation for war and internal conflict as the cause of the strong state, weak society, and ready capital critical for the pursuit of the export-oriented industrialization strategy in East Asia.

3. Similar to Japan, South Korea and Taiwan restrictively regulated FDI, whereas Singapore and Hong Kong pursued a more open FDI strategy. Among the states more restrictive of FDI, South Korea liberalized foreign portfolio and equity investment and Taiwan welcomed foreign-invested joint ventures but restricted FDI and foreign equity investment. See Haggard (1990) and E. Vogel (1991) on how FDI strategies varied across East Asia and Gold (1986) on state-society relations in Taiwan.

4. See Gereffi (1989) and Guillen (2001) on the NICs' strategies for obtaining technology.

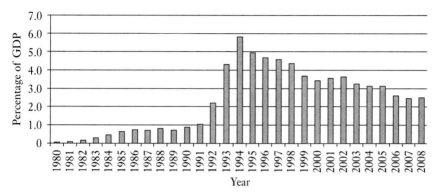

Figure 1.1. FDI inflows as percentage of GDP, 1980–2008. World Investment Report, United Nations Conference on Trade and Development, 2009.

In contrast to its East Asian neighbors, China entered the global economy at the height of an international ideological movement to export liberal reforms to developing countries.[5] Prior to 1978, the Chinese government coordinated the state-owned and collectivized economy through planning and upheld an ideology hostile to private property and market competition; thus, it is all the more surprising how open China has become toward FDI on the macro-level. Studies link bilateral and multilateral pressures to the Chinese government's conduct of sensitive economic and political reforms, including liberalizing foreign competition via special trade zones and foreign-invested joint ventures (JVs).[6] China's participation in multilateral, regional, and bilateral arrangements further obligated the Chinese government to liberalize trade and FDI.[7] Inflows of FDI surged into China beginning in 1980 (figure 1.1), and in 2005 China ranked first in FDI inflows among all countries (see also figure 1.2).[8] Moreover, in terms of trade flows, China ranked third globally in imports and exports in 2006.[9]

---

5. See Lardy (2002), Guthrie (1999 and 2006), Zweig (2002), Huang (2003), Steinfeld (2004), and Gallagher (2005) on how China's openness toward FDI contrasts with the East Asian developmental state's restrictiveness toward FDI during an analogous stage of development.

6. See Pearson (1999 and 2001), Peerenboom (2001), Yang (2004), Jacobson and Oksenberg (1990), and Fewsmith (2001). Early studies include Ho and Huenemann (1984) and Pearson (1991a and 1991b).

7. See Stiglitz (2001) on the contours and effects of the export of the "Washington Consensus," initiated by the International Monetary Fund and the World Bank, on developing countries. See also Simmons and Elkins (2004) on variations in extent of adoption of liberal economic ideas and policies across countries as a function of those exported by international institutions and hegemonic countries, such as the United States.

8. Consistent with this book's findings that China is gradually enhancing its control and tightening the market access of FDI in strategic industries, FDI inflows fell to ninth globally at the end of 2009, according to data from the CIA's World Factbook.

9. International Monetary Fund (2006). China ranked first in exports and second in imports in 2009.

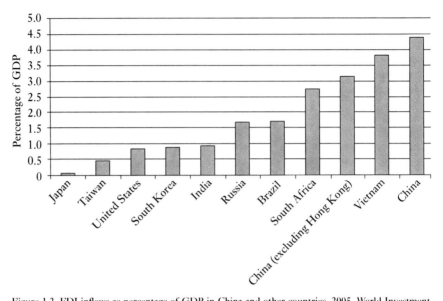

Figure 1.2. FDI inflows as percentage of GDP in China and other countries, 2005. World Investment Report, United Nations Conference on Trade and Development, 2009; World Economic Outlook, International Monetary Fund, 2010.

Throughout the reform era, FDI of Asian origin dominated the flow of FDI entering China. Figure 1.3 shows how Asian FDI exceeded those from the United States and Europe between 1997 and 2004, the period directly before and after WTO accession. In the post-WTO period, Japanese FDI ranked first, followed by Korea, Taiwan, and Singapore among FDI from Asian countries (table 1.1). The numbers for FDI via Hong Kong and the British Virgin Islands, two popular sites for corporations to register offshore, represent the high level of ethnic Chinese and domestic Chinese FDI (the latter known also as "round-tripping") entering China.

Notwithstanding the country-specific breakdown on the aggregate level, the geographic origins of FDI break down by sector. On the one hand, Asian FDI tends to be efficiency pursuing, with investments clustered in low-tech, low-value-added, and export-oriented sectors.[10] FDI from the United States and Europe, on the other hand, tend to be market pursuing and cluster in high-tech, high value-added sectors. This book's argument about China's bifurcated strategy and the evidence provided by our main and mini case studies illustrate how FDI from different origins experience different regulatory regimes. They are regulated by varying dominant patterns of state control because they cluster in different industrial

10. Table 1.3 in Huang (2003) shows that manufacturing industries with the largest FDI from Hong Kong include textiles, consumer electronics, and plastic products. Case studies of the former two nonstrategic industries can be found in this book's chapters 5 and 6 and 9, respectively.

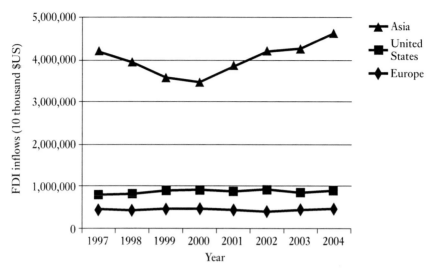

Figure 1.3. FDI inflows by country of origin, 1997–2004. Trade and External Economic Statistical Yearbook of China, National Bureau of Statistics, People's Republic of China, various years.

sectors, which are treated differently by the Chinese government based on the varying strategic value of respective sectors. In other words, government imperatives toward industrial sectors trump any concerns regarding the ethnicity of FDI or preferential treatment granted due to cultural affinities and shared language. One Taiwanese entrepreneur with several business interests in China, including consumer telecommunications, remarked, "Most Taiwanese companies are not in sensitive segments so we are less affected by government pressures and rules. But those that are experience equally strict regulations."[11] A senior investment advisor for the Ministry of Economy, Trade, and Industry-affiliated Japanese External Trade Organization (JETRO) put it plainly, "The Taiwanese and those from Hong Kong understand Chinese markets better because of less language and cultural barriers, but China's FDI policy does not differentiate by country of origin."[12]

STRONG "LOCAL" STATE, WEAK SOCIETY

The scholarship in the study of post-Mao reforms has sought to use the "developmental state model" as an analytical construct to understand the role of the state in the context of the gradual but sweeping changes in China's political economy. China scholars borrowed and attempted to refine this concept from Chalmers John-

---

11. Interview on May 14, 2010, in Taoyuan, Taiwan.
12. Interview on April 19, 2005, in Shanghai with senior investment adviser of JETRO, formerly of Deloitte Touche Tohmatsu Beijing.

TABLE 1.1. GEOGRAPHIC ORIGINS OF FDI INFLOWS (IN USD BILLIONS)				
	2000	2001	2002	2003
Hong Kong	15.5	16.7	17.9	17.7
British Virgin Islands	3.8	5.0	6.1	5.8
Japan	2.9	4.3	4.2	5.1
Korea	1.5	2.2	2.7	4.5
United States	4.4	4.4	5.4	4.2
Taiwan	2.3	3.0	4.0	3.4
Singapore	2.2	2.1	2.3	2.1
Western Samoa	0.3	0.5	0.9	1.0
Cayman Islands	0.6	1.1	1.2	0.9
Germany	1.0	1.2	0.9	0.9

Sources: Center for Research on Optimization and Control (CEIC) database and national governments; Dollar and Kraay (2006).
Note: Countries are ordered according to 2003 inflows.

son's 1982 study on the Japanese developmental state, which launched a research program that characterized and explained the origins of state-led development in East Asia. The developmental state served as a coordinator of economic growth, insulated private industry from penetration by foreign capital by decoupling technology and investment, acted as a market gatekeeper, filtered external entry into the market, and, at the same time, used market-conforming mechanisms to spur industrial development in key sectors. China scholars find the Chinese state lacks both the internal coherence and strong ties to a docile society characteristic of the "embedded" developmental state.[13] Moreover, China has extensively liberalized FDI, paralleling the more open strategy pursued by the Latin American NICs.[14]

China scholars debate the relative strength and weakness of the Chinese central government vis-à-vis the local state in regulating the market. In contrast to the "strong state, weak society" dynamic of the developmental state, the local state and diffusely dispersed institutions in China deploy developmental and predatory interventions in pursuit of local interests, which often mean they court FDI rather than seek protection.[15] Once top state elites initiated the lowering of central-level regulatory barriers, local beneficiaries began to capture and expand new chan-

---

13. Evans (1995) argues the relative success of the NICs varied according to the extent of the state's embeddedness and autonomy from society. This "synergy" between the state and private firms, including multinationals, facilitates development. Also see Haggard and Cheng (1987) and Wade (1990) on state-society relations in the East Asian NICs.

14. Evans (1979) explains the characteristic relationship that Latin American countries had with FDI, and Haggard (1990), Haggard and Cheng (1987), Evans and Stephens (1988), Balassa (1988), Wade (1990), and Evans (1995) compare variations in economic integration pursued by Latin America and East Asia.

15. Perkins (1986), Nolan and Dong (1989), Parris (1993), Oi (1992 and 1999), and Blecher and Shue (1996 and 2001).

nels of linkage with the outside world.[16] Local and regional powerbrokers are thus strengthened by formal "deregulation" and increasingly operate without much reference to formal and constitutional rules. In a "race to the bottom" manner, they court FDI based on local development goals and other local interests.

Scholars deliberate about the political and economic consequences of China's open strategy toward FDI. They argue that the state encourages FDI at the expense of the development of a dynamic domestic industry because of substantial problems in China's corporate and financial sectors. Weak institutions and uneven economic development mirror the experience of Latin America in the 1970s and 1980s.[17] More specifically, foreign investors serve as a substitute for weak domestic demand and a panacea for inefficient expansion and domestic capital misuses; they bail out state-owned enterprises (SOEs) and perpetuate poorly specified property rights.[18] Moreover, studying labor relations in foreign-invested companies, Mary Gallagher argues that the Chinese government liberalized FDI before privatization as a government strategy to sequence reforms for the purpose of retaining authoritarian control.[19] Foreign entry has changed norms and institutions in labor relations and transformed the debate on reform into one between domestic and foreign investors as opposed to one between the state and labor.

Recent studies of the Chinese political economy examine the impact of variation on the relationship between the local state and business on government policies, including privatization programs, and sector-specific outcomes.[20] Scholars analyze the state-structured impact of the diffusion of foreign practices on evolving market norms across sectors in one region and, in separate studies, variation in regional and industrial development strategies and outcomes.[21] These studies imply that increasingly nimble and sophisticated systems of control have emerged in a context of "competitive liberalization" at the subnational level to regulate the market as local governments vie for private capital by entering into calculated alliances to achieve local development goals.[22]

Other China scholars argue that developments in the last decade point toward an explicit strategy by the state to centralize its political, and therefore economic,

---

16. Zweig (1995 and 2002).

17. See Gilboy (2004).

18. See Huang (2003) and Rudolph (2006).

19. Gallagher (2005).

20. On the impact of government-business relations on policies, see Guthrie (1999), Wank (1999), Lin (2001), Wedeman (2003), and Kennedy (2005a and 2005b); on privatization programs specifically, see Liu, Sun, and Woo (2006); and on sector-specific outcomes, see Segal and Thun (200), Remick (2002), Segal (2002), and Thun (2006).

21. See Guthrie (1999) on market norms and Thun (1999), Segal and Thun (2001), and Segal (2002) on the development of the automobile and high technology sectors.

22. See Yang (1997) on regional competition in a race to the bottom to attract investment, and Naughton and Segal (2003) on how decentralization has helped the central government achieve its technonationalist goals.

power.[23] Ascension to the WTO galvanizes the government and powerful domestic interests threatened by internationalization to invent new and often sophisticated forms of authority to manage the steady flow of foreign capital.[24] To restrain companies and localities, which operate without much reference to formal and constitutional rules, and to ensure that economic opening benefits the domestic industry, the central government recentralizes control of the political economy. Furthermore, it has restricted local governments' conduct of fiscal and financial policies in order to strengthen the national revenue base and ensure financial stability.[25] The state has also restructured regulatory institutions to order competition and oversee market developments.[26] Although a "regulatory state," defined as a liberal state, might have appeared to emerge, the actual functioning of an independent regulatory structure is far from established.[27] The Chinese Communist Party (CCP) has retained oversight over these restructuring processes.[28]

LIBERALIZATION TWO-STEP: REREGULATION BY SECTOR

This book situates China's regulatory responses to internationalization before and after WTO accession and through boom-bust cycles by problematizing and extending the scholarship on the "Chinese style" developmental state. Case studies show that China differs from the developmental state and other national political-economic models of development. China has departed from the developmental state model by extensively liberalizing FDI and in other significant ways.[29] To begin, in the state-led model, an autonomous bureaucracy, which consults industry but is insulated from interest group politics (and at times the political will of state leadership), has the capacity to make and carry out government policy.[30] In contrast, central leadership in China, which consults State Council–level advisory committees, makes and approves policy for and enforces decisions on the industrial sectors and issue areas deemed most important to the state. Otherwise, decentral-

---

23. Yang (2004).

24. Zweig (2002).

25. Sheng (2007) shows that the Communist Party manipulates personnel monopoly power to enhance its control over provincial party secretaries to extract revenue, remedy interregional disparity, and maintain central rule.

26. Naughton and Yang (2004).

27. Pearson (2005 and 2007).

28. The CCP has enhanced its control over state apparatuses by streamlining vertical and horizontal controls; it also has placed tight control over the nomenklatura, placing trusted lieutenants in key positions and rotating officials to prevent them from building personal fiefdoms (Heilmann 2005).

29. The developmental state across East Asia varied in the following characteristics but I would argue they differed in matter of degrees, not type.

30. Johnson (1982) first characterized the autonomous bureaucracy in Japan. See Evans (1995) on the relationship between bureaucracy and industry. See Stubbs (2009) for a review of studies on the characteristics of the state-led development model.

ized entities—such as lower level bureaucracies, local governments, and quasi-government sectoral interests—and the politics that they generate make policy and enforce regulations. Second, key to the developmental state is the commitment to private property and markets. De facto recognition of private property has fueled economic growth in China.[31] But just as significant, central and local government intervention and specific rules and regulations, which purposively restrict or violate that right, regularly occur as a function of corruption or as the state and local governments seek to achieve political and developmental goals.[32]

Third, the East Asian developmental state intervened in select sectors by manipulating credit systems (often infused with capital from cold war-era foreign aid) to give industries and companies a comparative advantage.[33] Inefficiencies and distortion in the financial sector have forced the Chinese government, instead, to grant state-owned enterprises in priority sectors soft budget constraints and utilize foreign investment as a key channel for the capital necessary to drive industrialization.[34] This leaves the private sector, especially those in nonstrategic industries, bereft of reliable sources of finance, forcing them to rely on informal finance and locally courted FDI.[35] Fourth, scholars of the developmental state document the move from import-substitution to a winning export-oriented strategy across East Asia.[36] In contrast, China began the reform era with an export-oriented strategy, which emphasized industrial and trade zones in the eastern coastal provinces, and has since moved to combining an export-orientation with import-substitution in strategic industries. Moreover, in the post-WTO accession period, the Chinese government has focused macroeconomic policies on increasing domestic consumption to promote the growth of domestic industry.

Last but not least, scholars highlight the "market-conforming" nature of the developmental state's interventionist policies: governments intervened strongly in a manner that "followed economic principles, maintained a relatively open economic environment, and 'got prices right'" so they could be competitive in a world market.[37] On the contrary, in strategic sectors China has selectively reregulated to control the number of market players, limit competition to SOEs, prohibit FDI

31. See Oi (1992 and 1999) and Wu (2003), among others, on the role of de facto private property rights in fueling economic growth in China.

32. See Johnson (1982) on respect for private property in the developmental state.

33. Wade (1990).

34. See Huang (1996) on FDI replacing state finance in infusing the capital necessary to drive industrialization, and Steinfeld (1998) on how ownership type matters less for economic growth than a hard budget constraint, which provides the profit incentives for managers of production.

35. See Tsai (2002) on informal finance and Huang (2003) on the distortions created by a political pecking order of firms and their access to finance.

36. See Haggard (1990) on the shift from import-substitution to export-oriented industrialization.

37. Quote from Stubbs (2009). For neoclassical and statist interpretations of the NICs' market pursuits, see Balassa (1981 and 1988) and Wade (1990), respectively. Also, Stubbs (2005 and 2009) reviews the various variants of neoclassical and statist interpretations of the economically successful developmental state.

even while inviting foreign equity and portfolio investment, and/or favor domestic over foreign technology and know-how once indigenous productive capacity reached international standards. In nonstrategic industries, the Chinese government has allowed unfettered markets to reign, letting market forces determine the life and death of industrial segments and subsectors. In so doing, China engages in practices completely different from the NICs in East Asia and Latin America: it is opening up to foreign capital and allowing and enabling intense competition but retaining control through selective intervention, which varies by sector.

RESEARCH DESIGN AND METHODS

The scholarship on considerable intranational and sectoral variation in the advanced industrialized and developing countries' responses to economic globalization suggests the utility of disaggregating the Chinese "state" and investigating sectoral variation in China's economic statecraft.[38] In examining whether international economic integration diminishes the state's policy autonomy, scholars have moved to "varieties of capitalism" approaches, which stress eclectic mixtures of policies based on historical legacies and institutions, and on resources, opportunities, and costs of global integration.[39] Some scholars argue that differences in capitalist arrangements, paths to development, and national identities influence how countries respond to different types of capital flows, trade, and other forces of globalization.[40] Others contend that development paths are not inevitable but may be forged through purposive state action and that state institutional structures affect the way the private sector interacts with the state and the structure of the private sector itself.[41] In the face of globalizing changes, state activism has shifted rather

---

38. Among them, S. Vogel (1996 and 2006a), Snyder (2001), and Cammett (2007).

39. Scholars, including Strange (1996) and Rodrik (1999), have depicted the retreat of the state; others, including Gilpin (1975 and 2001), Gourevitch (1978 and 1986), Katzenstein (1978), Krasner (1991), Garrett and Lange (1995), Keohane and Milner (1996), Weiss (1998 and 2003), Kahler and Lake (2003), Paul, Ikenberry, and Hall (2003), S. Vogel (1996 and 2006a), and Levy (2006), have found the state has retained its capacity to make policy. Most agree that states today must contend with some form of integration. Building on Andrew Shonfield's (1965) classic analysis of modern capitalism, Zysman (1994), S. Vogel (1996 and 2006a), Kitschelt (1991), Reich (1989), Kitschelt et al. (1999), Hall and Soskice (2001), Guillen (2001), and Wilensky (2002) investigate national institutional structures to understand cross-national variation in the state's response to globalization.

40. In explaining divergent policy choices, see Hall and Soskice (2001), Wilensky (2002), Thelen (2004), Streeck and Thelen (2005), and S. Vogel (2006a) on varieties of capitalism; Guillen (2001) on variation in path to development; and Abdelal (2001) on variation in national identity. Attempting to understand variation in economic growth, Rodrik (2007) examines variation in national economic policies.

41. Drawing on the tradition of Gerschenkron (1962) and Polanyi (1944), Zysman (1983 and 1994) emphasizes variation in institutional mix and the state's response to the imperatives of industrialization to elucidate national patterns of state-market interactions. In explaining national patterns of regulation, S. Vogel (1996) emphasizes regime orientation and organization in relationship to industry and Reich (1989) focuses on the nature of the state in relationship to foreign and private sectors.

than fallen away; state officials have changed their goals and instruments, but they have by no means curbed their ambitions.[42] In contrast, scholars of the political economy of development argue that the state in the developing world often intervenes in a context of mobile global capital because of weak regulatory institutions and not because it eschews global pressures to liberalize.[43] Focusing on a different level of analysis and underscoring the force of microstructural factors, other scholars argue that development prospects are a function of sectors defined as forms of industrial organization and sites of global division of labor. In other words, sectoral attributes shape how the state responds to market forces by creating new institutions and mechanisms for market governance.[44]

Building on these studies' emphasis on the nation-state as one unit of analysis and the industrial sector as another, this book employs sectoral analysis to examine how macro-level state institutions and micro-level structural conditions shape the Chinese government's approach to liberalization and reregulation. This study deploys a comparative case research design, which systematically selects industry, subsector, and company cases and incorporates different dimensions (sector and time) and levels (sector and company) of analysis. This research design rigorously tests alternative expectations of state control of industry and maximizes analytical leverage to explain and document China's distinctive integration into the international economy. The increase of cases as a result of combining various comparative approaches dovetails with existing comparative studies on regulatory and policy reform, which find national, sectoral, and temporal patterns of state control.[45]

This book brings together original data from more than 250 in-depth, semi-structured interviews with local, provincial, and central-level government officials, industry experts and consultants, leaders of foreign and domestic sector and business associations, foreign trade and economic delegations, and managers and executives of domestic and foreign companies conducted during more than eighteen months of fieldwork in the eastern coastal and western interior provinces of China. I carefully selected each interviewee in each category of informants and cross-referenced them with similar questions to control for organizational, political, and economic motivations, and because developments in China are not products of a unitary actor. These interviews took place during onsite visits of factories, research

---

42. Levy (2006) includes studies on advanced industrialized countries, which find the state actively facilitating the move to the market to achieve varying state goals.

43. Chaudhry (1993 and 1997) and Stoner-Weiss (2001 and 2006).

44. Sectoral studies of the advanced industrialized world include Campbell, Hollingsworth, and Lindberg (1991), Kitschelt (1991), and Hollingsworth, Schmitter, and Streeck (1994), and studies of the developing world include Kurth (1979), Shafer (1994), Segal and Thun (2001), Gereffi and Memedovic (2003), and Cammett (2007).

45. National studies include Zysman (1983) and Vogel (1986), sectoral studies include Hollingsworth, Schmitter, and Streeck (1994), and temporal studies include Collier and Collier (1991) and Pierson (1994 and 2004). S. Vogel's 1996 and 2006 studies utilize a research design incorporating all three levels of analysis.

and development (R&D) facilities, and business and government offices. Many more follow-up conversations took place in similar settings and over the phone. Most of my interviewees have asked that they remain anonymous.

Because concerns regarding data quality and access differed between market settings of industries closely monitored by the state and those where the presence of the authoritarian state is minimal and multiple unregulated market players dominate, I also gathered other qualitative and quantitative data when available to maximize data quality and increase opportunities for triangulation.[46] Accordingly, my analysis is further supplemented by primary and secondary documentary materials, including government economy and industry reports; government- and industry-initiated rules and regulations, pronouncements, and notices; trade and industry journals; newspaper articles; company contracts and financial reports; and quantitative data from statistical yearbooks and company-level surveys collected by domestic and foreign sector and business associations.

For my primary case studies, I examine telecommunications and textiles to explore the causal significance of state agency and institutions, sectoral attributes, and economic factors in elucidating dominant patterns of reregulation.[47] A systematic comparison of these industries and subsectors within them at different extremes of capital and labor intensity and international competitiveness allows me to control for country-specific and sectoral characteristics. Any similarities in regulatory approach despite vast sectoral differences will be due to national-specific factors, and any differences will result from sectoral characteristics. Mini case studies of other industries further establish the utility of my explanatory framework, which incorporates state and sectoral characteristics to explain dominant patterns of reregulation upon economy-wide liberalization. Company case studies illustrate the state's exercise of deliberate or incidental control and how state goals, state-industry relations, and state methods of control vary by sector, in addition to revealing how firm-level characteristics shape actual control within dominant patterns. In addition to examining dominant patterns of state control, I pay close attention to the organization of state institutions and boom-bust cycles during critical junctures to explicate within-sector temporal variation in the main and mini case studies of industries. Mini case studies of telecommunications and textiles in Japan, South Korea, and

46. Hsueh (2008) discusses the relationship between environmental conditions and methodological innovations in the conduct of intensive fieldwork in reform era China.

47. Single-industry studies of Chinese telecommunications include Mueller and Tan (1997), Lu and Wong (2003), Harwit (2008), and Wu (2009). Moore (2002) and Alpermann (2010) have studied the Chinese textile and cotton industries, respectively. Murillo (2002) has examined the variations in actual implementation of privatization of basic service providers in telecommunications in Argentina, Chile, and Mexico; and Rodine (2005) and Henisz, Zelner, and Guillen (2005) have conducted large-N cross-national studies of the diffusion of market-oriented reforms in telecommunications. None of these China-specific or cross-national studies examine the interrelationship among government policies across industries and subsectors to achieve state goals.

Taiwan within the main chapters further reinforce that China is forging its own path, one distinct from the developmental state of its East Asian neighbors.

CONCEPTUALIZING STATE CONTROL

This book introduces the following analytical heuristic to understand state control. To begin, this study assumes the view that the macro-level liberalization of the Chinese economy is as much about removing barriers to competition as it is about the state actively introducing competition to meet state objectives, defy institutional constraints, and confront technological complexity. The introduction of competition can enhance as well as undermine state control and involves both deregulation and reregulation. This understanding draws on insights from Steven K. Vogel's studies on market reform in advanced industrialized countries. He contends that market reform involves the building of institutions and removing of constraints as well as changes at every level of a political-economic system, from government policies to private sector practices to social norms.[48] Promoting competition is not just about removing legal controls and then getting out of the way. It requires that state actors consciously design new markets, often with significant rules and regulations, to promote state goals, such as economic efficiency, political authority over industry, or both. The distinctiveness in which patterns of state control vary in China reveals that markets—defined here, following Vogel, as a broad range of laws, practices, and norms—are *intentional* constructs in that they are based, by design or default, on political principles and explicit choices about how individual resources, rights, aspirations, and possibilities are reconciled with collective ones.[49]

To adequately capture macro-level liberalization and micro-level reregulation, this study conceptualizes state control to systematically identify *state goals, relationship with industry*, and *methods of control*. This conceptualization incorporates ideational (state goals) and institutional (relationship with industry and methods of control) dimensions and differentiates between the central state and the local state in analysis. In the first dimension, *state goals* reveal whether the central government takes an incidental or deliberate orientation toward market players, the incumbent or the new entrant. Second, the *state's relationship with industry*—either the government level and department managing industrial development or the extent of state intervention—reveals whether the central government's control

---

48. S. Vogel (2006b) argues that "freer markets require more rules." See also S. Vogel (1996). Moreover, Snyder (2001) has observed that, to the chagrin of neoliberal reformers, the introduction of competition in Mexico has led to the formation of new institutions for market governance.

49. See Vogel (2006b) for an institutionalist definition of markets. Also, for the intentionality of market-building in advanced industrialized and developing countries, see Zysman (1983) and Chaudhry (1993), respectively. Moreover, research on developing countries has found that to defend liberalization, the state has exercised its authority to trump industrial interests, no matter how robust, advocating protectionism (Haggard and Kaufman 1992).

enhances or undermines its authority over industry. Third, *methods of state control* reveal whether central government control emphasizes liberalization (introduction of competition) or reregulation (reformulation and creation of rules). Liberalization is defined as policy- and company-level measures that introduce competition and influence and enhance the role of markets. Reregulation is defined as the reformulation of old rules and the creation of new ones to achieve state goals.[50] These definitions of regulatory reform imply that liberalization and reregulation are not dichotomous; rather, liberalization entails explicit actions taken by the state, often requiring reregulation, to undermine the role of the state and enhance markets.[51] Moreover, as a footnote in the introduction indicates, this book uses "regulate," "reregulation," and "regulatory" in the literal sense of the state formulating and creating rules to control industry and does not mean to invoke the developmental state literature's usage of a regulatory state that only exerts its control as a referee and does not intervene beyond that.[52] Measures of state control include rules on or affecting ownership, ownership and business restructuring (such as corporatization and privatization), market entry and exit, and business scope, and technical, production, and service standards.[53] State methods are differentiated by primary measures to achieve state goals or corollary measures that facilitate primary ones for functional and political reasons.[54]

We find four dominant types of state control, presented in table 1.2 in decreasing degree of central authority over industry. First, in *expansionary reregulation*, the state deliberately enhances centralized control by purposively writing new rules. The central government expands its bureaucratic discretion over industry to achieve particular goals, such as the control of information in telecommunications services. Second, in *strategic reregulation*, the state introduces competition with methods that ultimately enhance state control to achieve central goals, such as an increase in technological know-how and innovation. Government regulation of FDI in telecommunications equipment exemplifies this. Expansionary reregulation and strategic reregulation involve the central government taking a deliberate approach, with the measures taken in the former emphasizing reregulation and in the latter emphasizing liberalization.

Third, in *delegated reregulation*, the state takes a mixed orientation toward industry to write new rules that deliberately retain centralized control but assign regulatory authority over industry to a lower rank in the bureaucracy or a lower level of government. The state's regulation of less strategic subsectors of strategic industries such as value-added telecommunications services, and more strategic

---

50. See S. Vogel (1996), 3.

51. This understanding follows S. Vogel (1996)'s finding of "freer markets, more rules."

52. See Johnson (1982 and 1995).

53. The case study chapters (4–9) detail these measures and how they vary across industries.

54. S. Vogel (2006b) distinguishes between primary and corollary measures in regulation.

subsectors of less strategic industries such as textile trade and distribution, exemplifies this type of state control. This also occurs when the central government reasserts control in sectors it had previously decentralized to manage competition and promote industrial upgrading during economic downturns. Fourth, in *decentralized reregulation*, the central government takes an incidental orientation to introduce competition and deregulate, which undermines its control over industry and devolves rulemaking and enforcement to lower levels of government. This type of state control can be found in the central government's incidental control of textiles. Delegated reregulation is a mixed-orientation approach that emphasizes reregulation; and decentralized reregulation is an incidental approach that emphasizes liberalization.

In practice, these types of state control combine and emerge as dominant patterns of reregulation across industries. These distinct patterns characterize China's bifurcated strategy toward reregulation and reveal China's new economic model. Chapter 2 first shows how common forces experienced by all industries fall short in explaining why and how state control varies. It then presents a strategic value framework, which systematically identifies the dominant patterns of state control across industries following macro-level liberalization and micro-level reregulation. The strategic value logic accounts for the government's subjective assessment and the structural features of the sector in question to explain why the state exercises deliberate control in certain sectors and subsectors and incidental control in others. The organization of state institutions and the competitiveness of domestic industry during boom-bust cycles influence how state control varies across time within each sector even while the dominant patterns of state control are sector-specific. The political contexts of state control of telecommunications and textiles introduced in Chapter 3 uncover how the government deliberately enhances its control to reduce regulatory fragmentation, manage competition, and maintain infrastructural

TABLE 1.2. TYPOLOGY OF STATE CONTROL			
Type of State Control	Goals	Government-Business Relations	Methods
Expansionary	Deliberate orientation	Enhances central control	Emphasis on reregulation: new and reformulated rules increase central discretion
Strategic	Deliberate orientation	Enhances central control	Emphasis on liberalization: rules increase central discretion and achieve sector-specific goals
Delegated	Mixed orientation	Mixed outcome	Emphasis on reregulation: rules delegate regulatory enforcement to lower levels of government
Decentralized	Incidental orientation	Undermines central control	Emphasis on liberalization and deregulation: rules relinquish rulemaking and enforcement to local governments

ownership in telecommunications; and how a centrally organized textile industry at the beginning of the reform era becomes one of China's most market-oriented industries in the twenty-first century. Case studies of telecommunications and textiles before and after WTO accession in chapters 4 through 7 demonstrate the strategic value logic of China's bifurcated strategy of reregulation. Surveys of the East Asian NICs in each industry during a similar stage of development underscore China's distinct model of development. Mini case studies of other strategic industries (financial services, energy, and automobiles) in chapter 8 and nonstrategic industries (consumer electronics, food stuffs, and paper) in chapter 9 further establish the strategic value logic. Chapter 10 evaluates sectoral outcomes, assesses the Chinese state's autonomy and capacity in the face of globalization, and considers how China's emerging regulatory state varies from its Communist past and from other models of development.

2

CHINA'S STRATEGY FOR INTERNATIONAL INTEGRATION

The Logic of Reregulation

Scholars of the political economy of development have sought to explain what motivates governments to pursue particular economic policies in the face of globalization. Some look to domestic politics and institutions, others identify the role played by tradition and prevailing ideology, and still others look to exogenous factors in shaping the state's pursuit of particular policies and strategies. In three decades of reform, industrial sectors across the Chinese economy have experienced several common liberalizing forces. Although these common forces may explain macroliberalization, they only partially explain why and how reregulation, which inevitably follows, varies across industrial sectors. For example, common forces may explain state goals, state-industry relations, and state methods in one sector but not another or in one era but not the next, or they may explain state goals but not state methods. The holistic conceptualization of state control introduced in chapter 1 and the strategic value framework introduced in this chapter help us understand the whole story and appreciate how what might be seen as contradictory combinations of state goals and methods are, in fact, reconcilable patterns of reregulation in China's regime of economic governance, a new strategy for globalization.

CHINA'S PARTICIPATION IN MULTILATERAL AND BILATERAL REGIMES

China's integration into the international economy has occurred in the context of the global import of liberal ideas. Depicting China's reform trajectory as a transition to a market economy, scholars have attributed the shift away from socialist norms to China's participation in international forums.[1] These scholars contend that China's participation in the General Agreement on Tariffs and Trade and later in the World Trade Organization allowed it to internalize "free trade norms."[2] They depict institutional changes as a shift toward the liberal economic notion of the rule of law, which contributes to liberal convergence. In this understanding, liberal ideas channeled through reform-minded elites, bureaucrats, experts, and the legislature shape the nature of economic liberalization.[3] Scholars have also found that enlightened, liberal-minded reformers bargain with conservative hardliners to check local protectionism and avoid costly foreign reprisals entailed in the pursuit of economic development.[4] Margaret Pearson's 1991 study on foreign-invested joint ventures argues that international pressures compelled the state to accommodate FDI even though initial motivations for reform were based on a more conservative strategy of structured development controlled by the state. A macro-level survey of market and administrative reforms promulgated by the Chinese government reveals the gradual but progressive liberalization since the Open Door Policy in 1978.

Economy-wide market reforms since 1978 can be organized into several overlapping periods of liberalization and reregulation. Between 1978 and 1983, the Open Door Policy and the Joint Venture Law created special economic zones to accommodate foreign investment and technology. In the late 1980s, the state began to separate administrative functions from party functions. Between 1984 and 1991, the de facto recognition of town and village enterprises and other quasi-state–quasi-private enterprise forms gave rise to a domestic sector, and the issuance of laws on foreign investment enabled them to court and collaborate with FDI.

In 1992, Deng Xiaoping's Southern Tour further galvanized private and foreign investment and market activities. Between the early 1990s and 1997, the Chinese government began separating state ownership from ministerial control, and the Company Law launched the corporatization of state-owned enterprises. Further incentivizing FDI to form JVs, the government initiated exchange rate and tax and fiscal reform, which separated national and local tax administrations; and it made current accounts convertible (although it retained capital controls, including the forbidding of capital account convertibility). These reforms and the devolution of economic powers to local authorities empowered them to engage in market activities.

---

1. Pearson (1999 and 2001).

2. Peerenboom (2001) and Yang (2004).

3. Lieberthal and Okensberg (1988), Lieberthal and Lampton (1992), Shirk (1993), Tanner (1999), Fewsmith (2001), and Naughton (2002).

4. Jacobson and Oksenberg (1990), Shirk (1993), and Fewsmith (2001). Barry Naughton (1995) contrarily argues that reform in China lacks political and intellectual coherence and represents adaptive, opportunistic policies of "muddling through." Also see McMillan and Naughton (1992).

Between 1998 and China's WTO entry in 2001, state sector restructuring promoted the competitiveness of the Chinese economy. For example, the "Grab Large, Release Small" reform strategy restructured troubled SOEs through corporatization of those deemed too important to divest and elimination or privatization of those not strategic enough to retain. In the post-WTO period, state sector reform and the promulgation of rules and regulations in compliance with WTO accession agreements eased market entry. Yet reformulated and new rules sought to equalize the playing field between FDI and the domestic industry by universalizing the income tax, by making it more difficult to "hire and fire" workers, and by favoring the domestic sector vis-à-vis the foreign sector in administrative approvals of mergers and acquisitions, bankruptcy, and government procurement. These rules and administrative restructuring enhanced regulatory capacity and promoted indigenous development. The following list is an overview of key economy-wide market reforms:

1979–83 LIBERALIZATION
- Open Door Policy (1978), which initiated (agricultural) reforms
- Household responsibility system, *getihu, siren qiye*
- Joint Venture Law (1979)
- Creation of special economic zones (1980)

1984–91 REREGULATION
- Urban enterprise reforms and experimentations (1984–87)
- Fiscal reforms/revenue sharing/tax responsibility system
- Rise of quasi-state–quasi-private enterprises
- Fourteen coastal cities and island of Hainan opened to FDI
- Law on Wholly Foreign-Owned Enterprises (WFOE) (1986)
- Law on Sino-Foreign Cooperative Joint Ventures (1988)
- Separation of administrative from party functions
- State sector restructuring (1988)

1992–97 LIBERALIZATION
- Deng Xiaoping's Southern Tour (1992)
- Coastal development strategy, influx of FDI
- Administrative and state sector restructuring (1993)
- Foreign Trade Law (1994)
- Unification of official and market exchange rates (1994)
- Current account convertibility (1996)
- Company Law (1994); corporatization and privatization of SOEs
- Separation of ownership from regulatory functions
- Tax and fiscal reforms and decentralization
- Western Development Strategy (1997)

1998–2001 REREGULATION
- Administrative and state sector restructuring (incl. Grab Large, Release Small)
- Foreign market entry, business scope, and investment level recalibrated
- WTO accession protocol agreements on FDI and market liberalization (1999)
- Separation of ownership from regulatory functions

2002–05 LIBERALIZATION
- Administrative and state sector restructuring (2003)
- Foreign Trade Law (2004) and other WTO implementation rules
- "Harmonious Society" strategy (2003)

2006–10 REREGULATION
- Reformulated laws, including those on labor contract, government procurement, mergers and acquisitions, and bankruptcy
- Mergers and acquisitions liberalized to foreign investors
- Administrative and state sector restructuring (2008)

It is macroliberalization, punctuated with phases of reregulation, which unveils the Chinese state's true intent to reregulate on the sectoral and subsectoral level with a bifurcated strategy. The elimination of across-the-board protection provides a full view of how much and exactly in what form reregulation varies across sectors. Accounts of liberal convergence cannot explain why reregulation to enhance state control proceeded in some sectors even as the government introduced competition and decentralized economic governance in other sectors. Nor can these accounts explain why FDI liberalization began more than a decade before WTO accession or why reregulation to restrict FDI has happened in some sectors despite WTO commitments. If China were really fulfilling the spirit and letter of its WTO commitments, then we would not expect to find variation in the degree and nature of reregulation across industrial sectors. Liberal ideas, prevalent through the reform era and held by both domestic and international actors, may explain macroliberalization, but they do not adequately address what motivates the state to introduce competition only to follow it with sectorally calibrated reregulation. Likewise, the rise and fall of conservative hardliners within the Chinese Communist Party does not adequately account for the calibrated nature of liberalization across the political economy. Indeed, we find dominant patterns of reregulation, which vary by sector, across time despite factional politics in the PRC leadership.

POLITICAL FRAGMENTATION AND FEDERALISM, CHINESE STYLE

Fiscal policies in the reform era have decentralized economic decision making and created national and local tax administrations. These reforms, some scholars argue, have produced political fragmentation, where bargaining at lower and higher bureaucratic levels generates policies reflecting distinct cleavages between central and local levels.[5] In recent scholarship, for example, Andrew Mertha builds on earlier studies of "fragmented authoritarianism" to plot interactions across vertical hierarchies as an organizational and institutional continuum. Centralizing attempts in the 1990s, he argues, produced "soft centralization," which shifted bargaining from the lower levels to provincial levels without increasing the authority of the center.[6]

The case studies in this book show that whereas administrative decentralization and the resulting political fragmentation explain state-industry relations and mechanisms of state control in some sectors, decentralization and fragmentation do not tell the full story. In nonstrategic sectors, where the state does not apply deliberate intervention, some of these consequences occur. By and large, however, the State Council has balanced bureaucratic conflicts and retained its authority to manage developments in certain industries, such as telecommunications, that have been deemed strategic to the state. Moreover, in some cases, incomplete centralization has occurred because the government has deliberately planned it that way for economic or politically strategic reasons. The restructuring of telecommunications services exemplifies how the state has used administrative streamlining, e.g., various rounds of government downsizing, to relinquish control in some issue areas while at the same time reasserting its influence in priority areas.[7]

In studying the impact of decentralization, other scholars focus on the transitioning nature of China's market economy, arguing that the "market preserving" functions of "Chinese style" federalism explain successful economic growth. Yingyi Qian and his coauthors argue that the quasi-governmental sector has performed better than the state sector because the "appropriate" decentralization of information and state power limits state predation and associated negative incentives, reduces the soft budget constraint problem, and provides creditable commitment.[8] Such studies imply that Chinese style federalism promotes flourishing markets across the economy by providing the necessary institutional foundations.

A third related debate, described in chapter 1 in fuller detail, presents two contrasting views of the Chinese state, in the context of economic and administrative reforms launched by China's Open Door Policy. One perspective views China as having undergone decentralization, where the locus of power has devolved to local governments that are either developmental or predatory. In this view, local state-

---

5. Scholarship stressing the center-local divide includes Oksenberg and Tong (1991), Shirk (1993), Yang (1994), Walder (1995), and Huang (1996). On fragmented authoritarianism, see Barnett (1985), Lampton (1987), Lieberthal and Okensberg (1988), and Lieberthal and Lampton (1992).

6. Mertha (2005a and 2005b).

7. Chan and Drewry (2001) provide an organizational analysis of the effects of nationwide administrative restructuring.

8. These studies include Montinola, Qian, and Weingast (1995), Lau, Qian, and Roland (2000), and Qian and Weingast (1997).

society relations explain variation in local development outcomes.[9] The second perspective argues that the government has centralized in recent years in order to increase its regulatory capacity. Scholars disagree as to whether this phenomenon reflects a more liberal and efficient state or is merely "old wine in new bottles."[10]

These studies of the institutional foundations of reform provide snapshots of economic governance in China but do not exhaust explanatory theories of market liberalization and reregulation. Nor are they particularly informative regarding why decentralization, administrative and corporate restructuring, and the introduction of competition enhance state control in some cases and undermine it in others. The strategic value framework introduced here by way of a series of case studies explains the bifurcated nature of reregulation and its variance across industries. Furthermore, case studies of sectoral trajectories and companies identify the Chinese government's economic goals and regulatory methods in the pre- and post-WTO eras to more adequately illuminate the institutional foundations of the Chinese economy.

PROLIFERATION IN NONSTATE INTERESTS

The emergence of China's bifurcated strategy toward industry occurs in a context of emerging nonstate, domestic, and international interests introduced by more than three decades of economic reforms. The steady inflow of FDI across all sectors has increased the number of foreign actors in the Chinese economy (figure 2.1). What is more, FDI in value-added, high-tech sectors has increased and has dominated FDI inflows. Albert Hu and Gary Jefferson's model using data drawn from the Survey of Large- and Medium-Size Enterprises conducted annually by the PRC National Bureau of Statistics shows significantly higher levels of FDI intensity in 1995 and 1999 for the electronics industry than the textile industry. In 1999, the proportion of FDI-receiving firms in electronics was double that of the textile industry. Overall, FDI intensity in the electronics industry was nearly three times as large as that of the textile industry, and the number and proportion of majority-foreign-owned firms in the electronics industry also exceeded that of the textile industry (see figure 2.2).[11]

In the context of surging FDI across industries, scholars have identified the impact of participation in international supply chains. These chains are said to acti-

---

9. See Oi (1992) on local state corporatism and Perkins (1986), Nolan and Dong (1989), Parris (1993), Oi (1992, 1999), and Blecher and Shue (1996, 2001) for studies on the local developmental state.

10. See Pearson (2005, 2007) and Yang (2004) for varying accounts on the regulatory scope and capacity of the Chinese state. Quote from Pearson (2005).

11. Hu and Jefferson (2002), 1065–66.

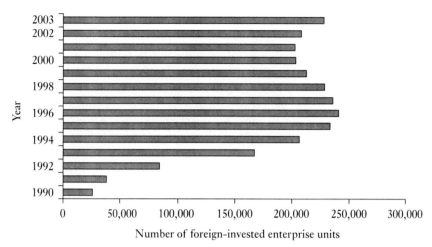

Figure 2.1. Foreign-invested enterprises in China, 1990–2003. Trade and External Economic Statistical Yearbook of China, National Bureau of Statistics, People's Republic of China, various years.

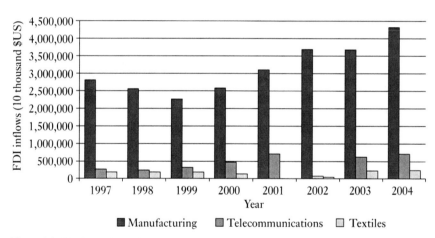

Figure 2.2. FDI in textiles, telecommunications, and manufacturing. Trade and External Economic Statistical Yearbook of China, National Bureau of Statistics, People's Republic of China, 2007.

vate the direct involvement of domestic and foreign sectors, thus affirming the role of domestic nonstate interests as factors affecting policy and institutional change.[12] David Wank, for example, elucidates commercialized clientelism in government-business relations, and other studies identify the role rent-seeking plays in obtaining policy preferences, securing bureaucratic support, and cultivating personal

---

12. Kennedy (2005a and 2005b), Zweig (2002), and Gallagher (2005).

networks, often manifesting in local protectionism.[13] Moreover, while Yi-Min Lin finds that exchange relations between economic actors and state agents occur in a marketplace embedded within state hierarchical settings, Scott Kennedy contends that domestic and foreign-invested companies gain leverage over the state by appealing frequently and directly to the government offices regulating their activities.[14] Further, in a 2008 study, Andrew Mertha affirms that an increasingly pluralistic landscape (populated by media, nongovernmental organizations, and other activist entities) positions policymaking within the context of bureaucratic infighting and bargaining. What is more, studies of the privatization of SOEs have found that the interests of local bureaucrats and other stakeholders affect ownership transfers.[15]

In addition to substantiating the embeddedness of market relationships in institutionalized hierarchies and validating the impact of nonstate actors in market settings, this book's sectoral and company case studies advance our understanding of China policy making by showcasing how the strategic value logic determines sectoral variation in government regulation and state-industry relations. By taking the study to the subsectoral level, these case studies further reveal why and how reregulation has occurred in subsectors, such as telecommunications value-added services and technical textiles, for which the state has previously liberalized market entry and lifted ownership restrictions imposed on nonstate companies.[16] The strategic value logic also explains variation in the extent of nonstate influence on policy outcomes. For example, sector and business associations affect policymaking when no government offices regulate them, but in strategic industries, such as telecommunications, central bureaucracies will always trump the lobbying power of sector associations. Moreover, my case studies disclose that high numbers of foreign actors in the political economy do not necessarily mean less government control, and low numbers of foreign actors do not necessarily mean more government control. In fact, for some industries, e.g., telecommunications, the more the state reregulated, the higher FDI surged (figure 2.2).

STRATEGIC VALUE LOGIC: HOW STATE CONTROL VARIES

The common forces discussed above help us understand the context under which China's economy has undergone liberalization. They fall short, however, in ex-

---

13. Wank (1999) and sectoral case studies of rent-seeking can be found in Ngo and Wu (2009).

14. Lin (2001) and Kennedy (2005a and 2005b).

15. For example, Liu, Sun, and Woo (2006) find that privatization programs are instituted when local governments believe that they will increase local tax revenues without sacrificing the private-control benefits of bureaucrats, and that they succeed when they satisfy managerial cooperation, workers compensation, and bank-to-debt servicing constraints.

16. Technical textiles, examined in chapters 6 and 7, are synthetic textile products manufactured primarily for functional purposes. These include nonwoven fabrics for police and fire protection and automotive, medical, construction, military, and aeronautical applications.

plaining the poles of greater liberalization and state intervention in China's political economy and hence provide an incomplete picture of the regulatory regime that has emerged in the context of global integration. This book conducts sectoral analysis to identify distinct patterns of liberalization and reregulation and introduces a strategic value framework that emphasizes state agency yet acknowledges the impact of sectoral economic and technological conditions to identify those political, economic, and structural factors that explain how, why, and with what the state has decentralized and relinquished its control in some industrial sectors while centralizing and enhancing control in others.

The Strategic Value Framework

This framework builds on the insights of scholars who have conducted sectoral analyses to examine cross-national and intranational variation in policymaking and institutionalization. Scholars have sought to combine sectoral attributes and structures and the role of the state in understanding variation in governance mechanisms. Linking industrial trajectories and national political orientation, James Kurth contends that a sector's position in the product cycle, the timing of industrialization, and an industry's fit in international market structures explain cross-national variation and variation over time in the political institutions of late and early developers.[17] Building on Kurth, D. Michael Shafer argues that the structural characteristics of the leading sector through which a country is tied to the international economy influence a country's development prospects and the role the state may play in industrial restructuring.[18] Examining industrial governance structures, John L. Campbell, J. Rogers Hollingsworth, and Leon N. Lindberg maintain that the state ultimately influences the institutional organization of the economy even though organizational actors across industrial sectors have complex motivations and interdependencies and engage in qualitatively different types of transactions.[19] In response to pressures from economic actors, the state makes political choices that manipulate property rights and takes other actions to ratify or select certain governance mechanisms.[20] The resulting modes of economic governance vary by sector, constituting a matrix of interdependent social exchange relationships.

---

17. Kurth (1979) theorizes in the Gerschenkron tradition and borrows product cycles from Vernon (1966).

18. Core variables (capital intensity and economies of scale) and composite ones (production flexibility and asset/factor flexibility) combine to create economic activities that shape distinctive state structures and capabilities, external and internal distributions of power, and sets of societal actors. See Shafer (1994).

19. Campbell, Hollingsworth, and Lindberg (1991). See also Hollingsworth, Schmitter, and Streeck (1994).

20. Campbell and Lindberg (1990).

The strategic value framework integrates an analysis of structural and institutional sectoral attributes and state agency; it argues that the Chinese state's perception of the strategic value of a sector shapes dominant patterns of reregulation in the context of macro-level liberalization.[21] Beyond that, generic and country-specific sectoral characteristics explain the actual methods of state control. The guiding expectation for the scope (degree and type) of state control corresponds to the degree of a given sector's strategic value: the higher the strategic value of a sector, the more likely the state will exercise deliberate control, and the lower the strategic value, the more likely the state will exercise incidental control. The following discussion defines the strategic value of a sector, explores its relationship to state control, and stipulates how sectoral characteristics shape actual methods of control.

Strategic Value of a Sector

We begin with an objective definition of the *strategic value of a sector*, which has political and economic dimensions. On the political dimension, strategic value is defined by a sector's importance to national security. This includes internal political and social stability, external security and foreign relations, and a sector's impact on political bargains at the highest level of the party-state.[22] On the economic dimension, strategic value is defined by a sector's contribution to the competitiveness of other sectors and the rest of the economy. It is also defined by a sector's contribution to the country's technological and infrastructural base.

The Chinese leaders and policymakers' assessment of strategic value also provides critical information about the goals and means of the Chinese state. The subjective understanding becomes salient because the boundaries between the economic and political dimensions of strategic value blur. State goals of technological advancement, infrastructural development, and competitive domestic sectors cannot be disconnected from the Chinese government's concerns regarding internal political stability and external security. Indeed, scholars have denoted the connections between security objectives and national development. Building on Charles Tilly's defining study of the relationship between war-making and state-building in early modern Europe, Richard Stubbs contends that key to understanding Northeast and Southeast Asia's economic success and the neomercantilist, export-oriented policies of the developmental state is war and geopolitics of the region.[23]

---

21. Kurth (1979), Cammett (2007), Shafer (1994), and Gereffi (2001) and Gereffi, Humphrey, and Sturgeon (2005) study sectoral variation based on these generic and country-specific sectoral characteristics.

22. Segal (2002) argues that geographic size and security concerns affect greater liberalization and state intervention in high-tech sectors; and Feigenbaum (2003), that China connects high technology acquisition with national security concerns. The strategic value framework introduced here analytically differentiates between high-tech subsectors to explain liberalization in some and enhanced state control in others.

23. See Tilly (1975 and 1985) and Stubbs (1999 and 2005).

The fighting of and preparation for war and the transfer of substantial U.S. aid and investment to specific countries as part of the U.S.'s cold war strategy in Asia have had "profound, and on the balance very positive, effect on these economies."[24] What institutional variation exists across this region is explained by the timing and scope of economic and political vulnerabilities faced by specific countries.[25]

Stubbs's emphasis on the causal primacy of real and perceived threats of war is informative for our understanding of what motivates the Chinese state to regulate in the ways that it has. Evidence introduced in this book shows that for reform-era China, preceded by the death of Mao Zedong and followed by the post–cold war environment, security imperatives have been directed, first, at political regime stability; and second, at China's status as the only major "Communist" power in the world with a regional security system positioned against it. In other words, what is considered strategic to the Chinese government involves security-related calculations that are both internally oriented and geopolitical in nature. As such, the Chinese government is predisposed to define "strategic" as that which enhances China's technology base and control over infrastructure to "make China rich and strong" in the face of perceived threats of political regime vulnerability and external offensive.[26]

The connection between economics and national security becomes apparent when government officials and bureaucrats and managers of state-owned and privately owned enterprises identify "royalties, profits, and relative economic gains" as the desired consequence of deliberate state control in civilian-based industries that contribute to the national technology base and that develop key applications for national security.[27] One state official characterizes the relationship between industrial goals and security imperatives as "the government's obsession with economic security."[28] A foreign observer of Chinese telecommunications markets maintains that "while it may be difficult to separate national security imperatives from the desire to possess strategic economic assets, national security concerns always trump money arguments."[29]

---

24. Stubbs (2005), 16.

25. Emphasizing "systemic vulnerability," Doner, Ritchie, and Slater (2005) argue that the developmental state's impressive capacities emerged from the challenges of delivering side payments to restive popular sectors experiencing extreme geopolitical insecurity and severe resource constraints.

26. Quote from interview in September 2008 with a government official working for the Research Development Center of the National Development and Reform Commission.

27. Quote from Suttmeier (2005). See Suttmeier, Yao, and Tan (2004 and 2006) for an account of the relationship between standards setting, economic goals, and national security concerns.

28. Interview on September 23, 2008, with director of a technology center under the Ministry of Science and Technology. He formerly served as a professor at the Beijing University of Posts and Telecommunications.

29. Interview on November 3, 2005, with foreign vice president of a privately owned Chinese telecommunications value-added service provider.

Relatedly, the link between security objectives and technological upgrading and product diversification is also important for our examination of the degree and type of Chinese state control over the economy. The National High Technology Development Program known as the "863" serves as a post-Mao era example of the connection between civilian-based technology initiatives, national security imperatives, and economic reform. Launched in the late 1980s, this program has financed indigenous research and development in telecommunications and other information technology sectors. Richard Suttmeier, an expert on Chinese policy toward science and technology, explains the conception of 863 as a confluence of the "perceptions of international trends, more intimate interactions with multinational corporations, the rapid growth of Chinese students and scholars studying abroad, increasingly ambitious domestic reforms, [and] influences from the strategic weapons community."[30]

On the political dimension, the Chinese government views internal security, manifested in social and political stability, as an important aspect of what is strategic. This calculation translates into such goals as control of information in telecommunications services. As illustrated in chapters 4 and 5, state ownership of telecommunications operations and the expanded regulation of value-added services in the 2000s after a decade of market liberalization and decentralized regulatory oversight exemplify how the government prioritized the control of information to ensure regime stability. For example, the government crackdown in the aftermath of the 2009 protests in Xinjiang included the blockage of the Internet and text messaging for most residents and the dissemination of political propaganda via internal websites.[31]

Citizen and worker protests of corruption and workplace and environmental safety in labor-intensive industries become strategic when the central government determines that related protests have escalated to levels that threaten social and political stability. The textile case, presented in chapters 6 and 7, reveals that the central government typically defers to local authorities in labor-related disputes and in resolving environmental and safety violations. Mediation (before reaching arbitration committees and courts at higher levels of authority) by local governments and local branches of the government-run All-China Federation of Trade Unions is the norm; this occurs even in high-profile cases, as exemplified by the labor strikes and protests involving Foxconn and Honda-invested plants in 2010.[32] All the same, updated labor laws in the 2000s increased worker job security (e.g., ensuring that full-time employees work under a contract) even while enhancing government discretion in handling labor disputes. Moreover, when regime

---

30. Suttmeier (2004).

31. See "China Nearly Doubles Security Budget for Xinjiang," *New York Times* (January 14, 2010).

32. "As China Aids Labor, Unrest Is Still Rising," *New York Times* (June 20, 2010).

stability becomes threatened, as it did after the 2008 Sichuan earthquake revealed shoddy construction and systematic corruption, the central government intervenes through administrative restructuring and criminal prosecution (chapter 7). The government also intervened when poisoning involving food and pharmaceuticals spread across the country (chapter 9).

The strategic value logic outlined here applies to strategic and nonstrategic industries, as well as subsectors within them. For example, as elaborated in chapters 6 and 7, the government retains discretion to intervene in technical textiles because of their applications in construction, transportation infrastructure, and military uses. Local and central offices of the Ministry of Science and Technology (MOST) and the Ministry of Housing and Urban Development (formerly the Ministry of Construction) routinely grant centrally funded subsidies and provide technical guidance to domestic manufacturers of technical textiles. Moreover, they collaborate with domestic manufacturers to set technical standards that minimize foreign access to domestic markets. By the same logic, the state has relinquished central regulatory control in less strategic subsectors of strategic industries. It delegates regulatory governance to provincial and local branches of central ministries even though it retains discretion to intervene. For example, the government exercises less discretion over consumer telecommunications equipment. Such products are perceived to be less politically and economically strategic than telecommunications terminal equipment, which activates the country's communications infrastructure. In addition to our main case studies, chapters 8 and 9 apply this theoretical framework to other strategic and nonstrategic industries.

Country-Specific and Generic Sectoral Attributes

The strategic value framework incorporates *structural and institutional sectoral characteristics* in understanding actual mechanisms of state control. The economic activities that take place within industrial sectors in modern economies, such as China, constitute "an enduring, coherent whole defined by distinctive combinations of capital intensity, economies of scale, production flexibility, and asset specificity."[33] They are linked to the global economy through production systems and supply chains. It is critical that we identify the structuring effects of these characteristics because industries and subsectors vary by such attributes, with implications for state control. To begin, we would expect the technological properties of a sector, including the complexity of the production system and product mix, to influence government goals and methods. The central government is more likely to use deliberate control and enhance its authority when a service or product entails complex technology and when the purpose of the product or service utilization is perceived

---

33. This definition of what constitutes a sector is from Shafer (1994), 10.

as a national security imperative.[34] To facilitate network modernization and at the same time control information, the government limits telecommunications carriers to state-owned players and retains discretionary licensing of network technology, even as it liberalizes equipment and value-added services to private players. To acquire technology, state-owned carriers procure it from foreign equipment vendors, but in an attempt to control the technology that runs the networks, the state initiates and leads the setting of technical standards. In contrast, the central government is more likely to use incidental control when the product or service in question involves linear technology and the purpose of that utilization is not associated with national security.

Research on global value chains informs us that the type of commodity chain dominant in an industry, differentiated by the degree of capital intensity and asset specificity and the nature of transactions, would also influence variations in methods of government control. We would expect that when the drivers of producer-driven commodity chains are industrial capital, when research and development and production are core competencies, and when main network links are investment-based, given China's low technology base, the central government would intervene to coordinate R&D and mobilize investment.[35] Moreover, we would expect the state to intervene in ways that would help lead or integrated firms codify transactions, such as maintaining stable suppliers, because these are sectors or subsectors with complex transactions and in which China possesses low capabilities as a supply base.[36] We find that to maximize domestic exposure to R&D in telecommunications, the state did not enforce an official ban on FDI until imperatives to control network development and manage rival ministries prompted it to do so. The government also manages the development of homegrown technical standards through state-owned equipment makers with the assistance but not the leadership of private and foreign ones. Moreover, it balances network procurement among domestic and foreign players to ensure infrastructural modernization.

In contrast, when the drivers of buyer-driven commodity chains are commercial capital, when core competencies are design and marketing, and when main network links are trade-based, given the early shift of production in such chains to China, we would expect the state to defer to local governments and for industry to govern sectoral activities. Because China tends to possess high capabilities in these sectors or subsectors, depending on the complexity of transactions and the ability to codify

---

34. Kitschelt (1991) finds that technology properties affect the choice and efficiency of governance structures and innovation strategies in different industrial sectors and that countries predisposed to particular governance structures will encounter difficulties in assimilating new technological trajectories.

35. Gereffi (2001) establishes the main characteristics of producer-driven and buyer-driven commodity chains.

36. Gereffi, Humphrey, and Sturgeon (2005) ascertain the relationship between complexity of transactions, ability to codify transactions, and capabilities in the supply base and the resultant value chain governance of hierarchy, captive, relational, modular, and market.

them, we would expect the central government to relinquish control and allow lead firms and suppliers and subcontractors or the price determine the governance structures that emerge. The textile chapters illustrate how local governments subsidize privately owned design and marketing companies through methods such as streamlined customs and trade fairs; and exercise discretionary authority in managing import and export license, quota, and tariff regimes. Moreover, it is the local government, and not the central state, that responds when labor issues on the shop floor arise in the production of buyer-driven commodities, such as garments, which typically require a high degree of labor intensity. Additionally, localities laxly enforce market entry in buyer-driven commodity chains with low asset-specificity; this encourages industrial diversification at the same time that it inadvertently promotes market saturation.

Relatedly, sectoral characteristics specific to Chinese industry—namely, the dominant ownership and user profiles of the industry in question and the industry's position in global production chains—affect the nature of reregulation. Relevant questions about China-specific sectoral attributes include the following. Is a producer or service provider state-owned, quasi state-owned, private domestic, or foreign? Are the end users domestic or foreign consumers, industrial users, or bureaucracies? Moreover, are the products or services a core component of an industry supply chain or an easily replaceable one? China Telecom's role as the incumbent carrier and China Unicom, the new entrant owned and managed by a rival ministry, had immense impact on de facto FDI liberalization in basic services throughout the 1990s. To modernize the telecommunications infrastructure, the state permitted China Unicom to compete with China Telecom by forming special foreign-invested JVs, which circumvented the formal prohibition against FDI. In another example, many global chemical processors have moved heavy polluting productive capacity away from advanced and newly industrialized countries to China and many end users of technical fabrics are local construction and transportation bureaus, which have influenced reregulation in technical textiles. Chinese technical textile manufacturers have benefited from local and central government rules, subsidies, and fiscal policies designed to promote domestic capacity and market share in the context of market liberalization. Yet another China-specific characteristic is that Chinese companies, unlike counterparts elsewhere, regularly attempt to defy technological barriers by entering subsectors with low entry requirements along their supply chain.

CHANGE ACROSS TIME AND COMPANY IN EACH SECTOR

Variation in dominant patterns of Chinese state control is best explained by the strategic value of a sector, and substantively by sectoral characteristics. The strategic value logic also applies at the subsectoral level. I now turn to the structuring impact of state institutions and global economics to understand the logical link between phases of liberalization and reregulation within industrial trajectories. I also acknowledge the effects of company level characteristics on actual bargains between the state and business within dominant patterns of regulatory transformation.

Organization of State Institutions

Scholars have argued that state structures manipulate policy formation and implementation. After all, markets are institutions embedded in society and culture.[37] More specifically, they argue that state actors and structures influence the emergence of a variety of institutional forms of economic governance. These actors and structures affect how the government responds to political entrepreneurs and societal actors, because political struggles for strategic control and power (not necessarily the search for efficiency) within economic exchange provide the dynamism required for governance transformation.[38] What is more, preexisting organization of political-economic relationships creates political interests and is predisposed to solve certain types of technologically complex problems.[39] We would expect the *organization of state institutions* to shape how government officials influence industrial reform and the manner in which government policies are enforced during phases of reform. Existing studies of China find that administrative restructuring, specifically the various rounds of reclassifying government bodies and personnel since the Open Door Policy, has transformed the Chinese government's role in governing the economy; this affects both the extent of state authority over industry and the methods available for organizing markets. These reforms not only reduced the number of personnel but also changed the roles and functions of state bureaucracies.[40]

Thus, we would expect *segmented jurisdiction* to undermine state control in one subsector even as it enhanced control in another. For example, the 1993 dismantling of the Ministry of Textile Industry undermined state control of textile manufacturing, but because the Ministry of Internal Trade and the Ministry of Foreign Economic Relations and Trade continued to manage certain issue areas within the internal and external trade and distribution of textiles, the state retained control of the marketing and distribution of raw materials critical for upstream fiber processing sectors. The central government managed the marketing and distribution of domestically produced and imported raw material inputs until after WTO accession. Moreover, *overlapping bureaucracies* would satisfy various interests but create

---

37. In his interpretation of the evolution from feudalism to market society in nineteenth-century Europe, Polanyi (1944) suggests that economic rationality is culturally conditioned and that the market system does not spontaneously arise, but that governments have to actively create national markets.

38. See Campbell, Hollingsworth, and Lindberg (1991), 5. Also, Reich (1989) argues that the degree of access granted by the state to foreign firms and the type of support it provides to domestic firms explain cross-national variation in the regulation of FDI.

39. Kitschelt (1991) argues that certain governance structures are predisposed to foster certain combinations of innovation. Moreover, Vogel (1996) finds that the organization of state actors in an industry and the relationship of those actors to the private sector structures the incorporation of interest groups, defines state capabilities, and shapes state and societal interests.

40. Chan and Drewry (2001) conduct organizational analysis to examine the effects of nationwide administrative restructuring. See also Schurmann (1968), Dittmer and Wu (2006), and Brandt and Zhu (2000) for accounts of the cyclical effects of centralization-decentralization on China's reform trajectory.

sites of political contention where early winners of the transition retain veto power and as new and old interests vie for control over industrial policy. Between 1993 and 1997, rival ministries managing incumbent and new entrant carriers courted FDI without central intervention during a period of de facto liberalization when practice diverged from formal rules. Moreover, the continued dominance of China Mobile in successive rounds of corporate restructuring illustrates how winners of previous reform hold veto power even while the central leadership retains control over the direction of reform.[41] In textiles, the elevation of the demoted textile bureaucracy to a higher level of government between 1998 and WTO accession exemplifies how retaining a bureau-level office despite abolishing the ministry in 1993 enabled the still influential textile bureaucrats to lobby patrons in the State Council to intervene in upstream sectors plagued by overexpansion. Finally, *consolidated jurisdiction* is expected to allow the state to enhance its control over industry even as it introduces competition. This is exemplified by the deliberate merger of central ministries—for example, that of electronics and post and telecommunications to create the Ministry of Information Industry in 1997.

Critical Junctures of Exposure to the International Economy

The regulatory and extractive institutions of late developers are constructed in a context of growing economic interdependence marked by highly mobile global capital and technological changes.[42] We would expect that the *macroeconomic effects of boom-bust cycles* during China's exposure to the international economy would induce subtle variations of state control across time despite dominant patterns of reregulation based on a strategic value logic. In other words, the less competitive a domestic sector is during exposures to economic reverberations, the more likely the state would exercise deliberate control; that is, the more resources the state would devote to promote industrial development and to direct market competition. Likewise, the more competitive a domestic sector is during such exposures, the more likely the state will exercise incidental control.[43] For example, during the Asian financial crisis of the late 1990s—a period of contracting export markets, slowed growth of the Chinese economy, and underemployment in the state sector—the state resurrected the textile bureaucracy to order competition in oversaturated fiber processing sectors and to promote industrial upgrading in technical ones. Senior leaders lobbied to avoid administrative cutbacks, line agencies interpreted policy

---

41. See Heilmann (2005) on the veto power of early winners in banking sector reforms.

42. See Chaudhry (1993) on capital flow effects and Newman and Zysman (2006) on those of technological changes.

43. Moore (2002) argues that international sectoral market structures force the Chinese government, in response to global competition, to compel domestic textiles to engage in industrial upgrading.

to benefit their own sectoral interests, and localities sought to pursue their own economic agenda. In contrast, when the textile industry was fairly competitive at the time of WTO accession, the state relinquished control and sector associations assumed governance of the industry. Figure 2.3 shows the state exercising incidental control in less strategic sectors and where the domestic sector tends to be more competitive, and deliberate control in more strategic sectors and where the domestic sector tends to be less competitive.

Company-Level Variation

Significantly, while dominant patterns of state control hold sway, company-level characteristics affect the precise nature of state control at the company level, influencing how bargains between the government and individual companies vary. The

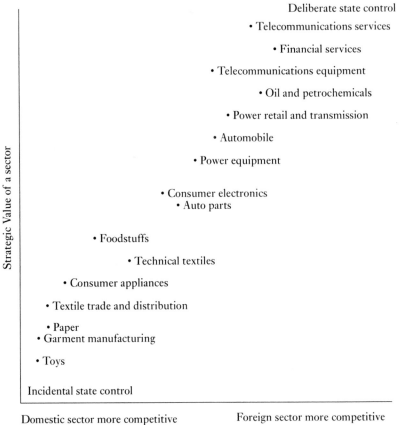

Figure 2.3. Conceptualizing sectors and state control.

home country of a firm's willingness to intervene might mean that the Chinese government allows temporary or permanent exceptions to its rules. *China's perception of the home country of firms* also influences how the state treats a foreign-invested enterprise within dominant regulatory boundaries. Finally, the *resources that each company brings to individual bargains* alter the government's treatment of particular firms, including exchanging market access for technology transfers or diplomatic favors. Figure 2.4 illustrates my basic argument.

Common forces		
Decentralizing reforms • Exert pressure to respond • Apply across time • Apply to all sectors	**Multilateral and bilateral pressures** • Exert pressure to respond • Apply immediately before and after WTO accession • Apply to all sectors (some more than others)	**Domestic and nonstate interests** • Exert pressure to respond • Apply across time • Apply to all sectors

⇩

Responses vary by sector
Strategic value logic (objective and subjective understanding of strategic value and sectoral attributes) shapes: • How the central government formulates goals and methods • Who controls industrial policy • What kinds of measures are employed **Sectoral characteristics (structural and institutional)** • How government goals are implemented • What kinds of measures are employed

Responses vary over time
Organization of state institutions in a given sector shapes: • How government officials try to shape industrial reform • How government policies are enforced **Domestic sector's competitive position during boom-bust cycles and critical junctures** shapes: • How the central government intervenes

Figure 2.4. Basic argument in diagram form.

FORCES OF VARIATION IN PATTERNS OF REREGULATION

Scholars have studied a number of common forces of change across industries in China: a concerted commitment to economic liberalization, multilateral and bilateral pressures, intended or unintended consequences of decentralizing reforms and institutional fragmentation, and emerging foreign and domestic nonstate interests. Despite these common challenges faced by all sectors across time, the government has introduced competition and reregulated with a strategic value logic. To understand the complexity of reregulation, we incorporate other economic and institutional factors that explain how state control varies across time and companies. Recognition that other factors influence temporal variation and company-level differences does not, however, replace the strategic value framework. Instead, these factors demonstrate the full range and complexity of reregulation attendant upon China's integration into the international economy. The Chinese government approaches reregulation in the industries I will examine in remarkably different ways; it has done so to reduce the costs and enhance the benefits of economic liberalization and global integration.

3

TELECOMMUNICATIONS AND TEXTILES
Two Patterns of State Control

The Third Plenum of the Fourteenth Congress of the Chinese Communist Party set the stage for macroliberalization when it adopted the Decision on Issues Concerning the Establishment of a Socialist Market Economic Structure in 1993. It officially eliminated the planning system and aimed to establish a modern market system and incorporate international institutions.[1] That year, the Chinese government abolished the Ministry of Textile Industry and formally decentralized economic decision making in subsectors of textiles to the local levels. The central government also introduced competition in telecommunications by licensing China Unicom and value-added service providers; in the ensuing decade, FDI surged to develop digital telecommunications networks. Both industries were exposed to greater competition in an environment of economic reform at home and global investors eager to pursue Chinese markets and make efficiency gains through manufacturing for exports. These two industries provide a good starting point to study the economic liberalization and the reregulation that follows because any differences in reform outcomes are likely to reflect variation in how the Chinese government has introduced market reforms across industries despite similar starting points in market liberalization.

The Chinese government has adopted successive generations of economic reforms since 1978. They range from the restructuring of state-owned enterprises and administrative bureaucracies to liberalizing FDI on the macro level. Yet these

---

1. Qian and Wu (2003) identify this 1993 decision as a "strategic shift" in the course of China's reforms, launching the country toward a modern market economy. This book recognizes this decision as de jure confirmation of the economy-wide liberalization that preceded sector-specific reregulation.

sweeping changes have been selectively applied to telecommunications and textiles. Between 1978 and 1993, one overarching sector-specific ministry supervised textile manufacturing and internal market developments across subsectors. Two ministries supervised telecommunications equipment and services, and provincial telecommunications administrations and different ministries operated telecommunications networks. Thus, if anything, the Chinese government governed textiles with more bureaucratic centralization than it governed telecommunications. In 2010, a very different regulatory regime governs textiles and telecommunications. Quasi-government sector associations have replaced the textile bureaucracy, local governments and local branches of the commerce ministry approve market entry, and FDI is completely liberalized. In telecommunications, the Ministry of Industry and Information Technology strictly regulates subsectoral developments up and down the supply chain, including ownership structure, level of investment, and business scope of market players, and state-owned national carriers operate telecommunications networks.

This divergence in reregulation cannot be explained by China's participation in liberal trade regimes, decentralization in the reform era, or the proliferation of nonstate actors in the Chinese political economy. Rather, the strategic value of these industries to the state best explains the distinct patterns of China's bifurcated strategy of reregulation. At the broadest level, the strategic value of a sector—as defined objectively and subjectively by its importance to national security and its contribution to the national technology base—influences the state goals, state-industry relations, and the methods of state control in telecommunications and textiles. The strategic value logic also explains how actual methods of state control vary based on China-specific and generic sectoral characteristics. Beyond that, the competitiveness of the domestic sector during critical junctures of China's exposure to the global economy and the organization of state institutions interact to explain within-sector temporal variation in reregulation.

Sectoral and company case studies in chapter 4 through chapter 7 more closely examine the dominant patterns of state control and the actual details of reregulation in the post-1993 era. Developments between 1978 and 1993, presented in this chapter, provide a preview of how the strategic value framework introduced in chapter 2 serves as a guide to understanding the dominant patterns of reregulation in the Chinese economy. A discussion of how the strategic value framework expects *deliberate reinforcement* to manifest in telecommunications and *decentralized engagement* in textiles follows each narrative of pre-1993 industrial trajectory.

THE POLITICAL CONTEXT OF STATE CONTROL
IN TELECOMMUNICATIONS

During the Mao era, a fragmented administrative structure governed telecommunications, with provincial, municipal, and prefectural governments controlling the planning of telecommunications in their jurisdiction. In 1978, the Ministry of Post and Telecommunications (MPT) managed the telecommunications monopoly but ceded service administration, network planning, and procurement to provincial and local post and telecommunications authorities (PTAs). The PTAs made day-to-day operating decision, with their business performance linked to a system of contractual responsibility. The Ministry of Electronics Industry (MEI) supervised the development of the telecommunications equipment industry, but the MPT also owned and operated several large equipment makers. Moreover, several ministries, including the MEI, operated special networks for government use.

Political Origins of Deliberate Control

Business reorganization, institutional reform, and government directives in the 1980s asserted central control of regulation and industrial strategy. Although the government formally separated business from bureaucracy, the MPT became the dominant administrator of nationwide post and telecommunications. These developments set the stage for China's *liberalization two-step* in the 1990s: the introduction of competition and the consolidation of state control over the entire network infrastructure.

Between 1983 and 1985, as a prelude to separating business from bureaucracy, the State Council reorganized the PTAs by creating regulatory entities and business branches. The PTAs managed provincial networks until the early 1990s, when the business branches became subsidiaries of the telecommunications monopoly and the administrative offices subsumed under the MPT. In 1988, amid economy-wide restructuring of SOEs, the State Council corporatized the Directorate General of Telecommunications (DGT), legally transforming it from a bureaucracy to a business entity specializing in services. The restructuring eliminated the DGT's manufacturing functions but empowered provincial subsidiaries with decision making regarding equipment procurement, operations, and network development and financing. The MPT retained management and regulatory control of the DGT, but the dedicated networks owned and managed by several ministries remained outside the MPT's control.

Accompanying these institutional and corporate reforms, government policies and pronouncements, including a fifteen-year plan released in 1985 by the MPT, designated telecommunications a national strategic priority.[2] The Group for the Revitalization of the Electronics Industry, which was composed of technocrats within the State Council and was led by Li Peng, also championed the development of a domestic telecommunications industry.[3] To promote infrastructural development, in 1988 the government inaugurated the "Three 90 Percents" strategy. The

2. Harwit (1998), 184.

3. The Group for the Revitalization of the Electronics Industry drafted development priorities for computers, telecommunications, software, integrated circuits, and sensors. Zita (1989), 18–24.

strategy forgave 90 percent of central government loans for telecommunications, excused 90 percent of the PTAs' taxable profits, and allowed the MPT to keep 90 percent of its foreign currency earnings from international traffic.[4]

The liberalization of equipment imports in the mid-1980s further promoted infrastructural modernization. Up to that time, to protect domestic equipment producers the Chinese government resisted the importation of analog technology, allowing only foreign exchange purchases of digital technology.[5] In 1985, the Chinese government began accepting older generation crossbar and step-by-step analog switching technology, some donated by Japan's NTT, Singapore's Telecommis, and Hong Kong Telecom, and some purchased at a lower price from foreign equipment vendors.[6] Later in the decade, the central government granted preferential tariff treatment for equipment imports to encourage network development. Moreover, the MPT introduced a licensing scheme that permitted the PTAs to choose among competing suppliers.

Regulation before 1989 scarcely formally addressed FDI. By the end of the 1980s, however, foreign concessional loans, which enabled the PTAs to sign contracts with foreign equipment makers, had tapered off, accelerated by the Tiananmen Square Incident.[7] In response to the diminishing foreign exchange, and hoping to reduce the cost of high-quality products and potential collusion among foreign equipment makers, the State Council promulgated several regulations that sanctioned limited FDI liberalization in equipment.[8] Directive 56, issued in 1989 after the United States imposed trade sanctions in response to Tiananmen, allowed three foreign equipment makers to participate in JVs manufacturing terminal equipment and sought to enhance government management of network infrastructure through minimizing incompatible equipment purchases.[9] These companies, Alcatel, Siemens, and NEC, participated in technology transfers and invested in local production to build their market share. Shanghai Bell Telephone Equipment Manufacturing Co., a partnership between Alcatel and the MPT's Post and Telecommunications Industry Corporation, which had operated China's only operational digital switching facility throughout the 1980s, benefited in particular from this directive.[10] This set the stage for the strategic utilization of FDI to modernize infrastructure and maximize foreign technology acquisition, which became a hallmark of reregulation in the 1990s and through the 2000s.

---

4. Harwit (1998), 185 and 187.

5. Zita (1989), 18–19.

6. See Zita (1989), 18–19, and Sprafkin and O'Brien (1989), 25.

7. Gorham and Chadran (1993), 19, and Sprafkin and O'Brien (1989), 26. In 1987, foreign loans accounted for 12 percent of total financing in telecommunications.

8. Harwit (2005).

9. Luo (2000), 94.

10. SBTEMC, established in 1983, is now known as Putian, the domestic partner for several foreign equipment manufacturers. See Mueller and Tan (1997) for more on the development of Putian.

Foreshadowing the higher extent of state control that the government now exerts on telecommunications services, in contrast to limited market opening in equipment, an internal rule circulated to the PTAs in 1989 prohibited FDI in services. Moreover, in 1991, in an effort to curtail overexpansion, the MPT banned PTAs from pursuing soft loans, which, along with toll tariffs and stiff subscription fees, funded massive investment programs.[11] Shortly before the breakup of the telecommunications monopoly in 1993, the Restatement on Forbidding Joint Operation of Postal and Telecommunications Business with Foreign Companies, issued in June 1992, officially prohibited FDI in services.

Toward Deliberate Reinforcement in Telecommunications

The narrative of the strategic value context of telecommunications prior to macroliberalization reveals that a fragmented regulatory regime governed the industry, but the Open Door Policy commenced the government's deliberate orientation toward market reforms in telecommunications. The discussion below evaluates the strategic value of telecommunications and the impact of sectoral structures on regulatory reform, providing a preview of *deliberate reinforcement*, the dominant pattern of reregulation in telecommunications detailed in chapters 4 and 5. It also previews how the strategic value framework applies at the subsectoral level.

State Goals

The state views telecommunications carriers and the backbone network infrastructure they operate as important for the development of the national technology base and national security imperatives. To enhance the national technology base, the state seeks to modernize carriers and network infrastructure, maximize technology transfers, and strengthen domestic industry. To achieve security requirements, such as retaining control of information dissemination and technology, the state seeks to control the development and operation of the physical infrastructure on which telecommunications networks function, including the technology that runs the networks, and the development of the carriers that operate these networks. To accomplish these goals, we would expect the state to retain, if not also enhance, its authority over the ownership, management, and operation of basic and mobile carriers and the networks they operate; at the same time, the state would willingly relinquish some control to nonstate forces in certain issue areas in order to achieve network modernization and development.

State-Industry Relations and State Methods

Consistent with these expectations, the government has shifted the means of control from crude overall limits to more fine-tuned regulations. The dominant methods of

---

11. Gorham and Chadran (1993), 19.

state control in telecommunications are not the standard neutral regulation of price and entry to ensure an equal playing field or free competition but the introduction of competition combined with deliberate reregulation to achieve state goals. Control methods include sector-specific rules on ownership structures; market entry and exit and business scope; and technical standards. Sectoral attributes, including sectoral organization and technological constraints, determine the precise ways in which control methods translate across subsectors.

Telecommunications Services

The strategic value logic would expect the state to exert the most control over basic services because network carriers own and manage the operation of communications infrastructure. By prohibiting FDI and private entry, the state maximizes its ability to take control of telecommunications networks to achieve security imperatives, including political and social stability. Yet to modernize infrastructure and maximize technology and knowledge transfers, the government introduces state-owned competition and allows foreign participation but calibrates collaboration to retain majority ownership and discretion to intervene in operations and to control the technology running the networks.

In contrast, we would expect the state to exert less control over value-added services (VAS); VAS providers function on top of the backbone infrastructure already owned and managed by the state. To facilitate the modernization of the country's technology base, the state exposes VAS markets to competition and liberalizes non-state and foreign entry. Though the state prioritizes VAS development, because end users utilize VAS services to communicate and disseminate information, to ensure overall political control and social order the state exerts bureaucratic authority to restrict business scope and content dissemination.

Telecommunications Equipment

We would expect market entry and exit in equipment markets to be substantially less restrictive than in service markets because equipment makers do not operate communications networks and their products are installed into the network infrastructure already owned and managed by the state. Rather than restrict market entry, ownership type, and business scope, as it does in telecommunications services, the state seeks to enhance the national technology base through reregulation, which maximizes technology acquisition and the development of the domestic sector. Early in the reform period, the Chinese government recognized the need to acquire foreign technology to modernize network infrastructure and expressed a desire to cultivate indigenous research and development.[12]

---

12. Zita (1989), 18.

The strategic value logic explicates variation in the state's control of terminal and consumer telecommunications equipment. Because terminal equipment makers supply the network infrastructure critical for national security, which represents a substantive increase in the national technology base, the state utilizes control mechanisms that maximize technology transfers, control the deployment of technology, and invest in indigenous innovation. The state exploits the technologies possessed by foreign manufacturers through the extensive liberalization of equipment markets. However, the complexity of transactions and the difficulty in codifying them (including that imported equipment could not be guaranteed to operate networks and that foreign-made equipment may be difficult to operate), combined with an underdeveloped domestic sector, motivate the state to control which technologies are deployed, and how and when. It does so through discretionary licensing and the equipment procurement of state-owned carriers. Moreover, it promotes the domestic sector and the national technology base through technical standards setting.

In contrast, the state intervenes less in the manufacturing and distribution of consumer telecommunications equipment because end users of consumer products are many steps removed from the technologies that activate network infrastructure. The state's limited control over the distribution of such equipment includes requiring equipment makers and users to register with state-owned carriers. However, the resources the state exerts to enforce such rules remain minimal relative to the sector-specific and micro-level control experienced by terminal equipment manufacturers and service providers. The state control experienced by telecommunications consumer equipment makers mirrors the experience of consumer electronics manufacturers (see chapter 9).

Notwithstanding the dominant pattern of deliberate control in telecommunications, the organization of state institutions and the competitiveness of the domestic sector during boom-bust cycles shape temporal variation in reregulation. That a sector-specific ministry governs sector developments implies that the scope of state control in the least strategic of telecommunications subsectors still exceeds the extent of control the state exercises in textiles, a nonstrategic industry regulated by the commerce ministry and lower levels of government. What is more, to retain strategic economic assets in Chinese hands and ensure state dominance over the direction of infrastructural development and technology adoption, the government intervenes periodically to bolster the competitiveness of state-owned carriers during economic downturns or critical junctures of exposure to the international economy.

Company-level variation in state control exists in telecommunications, but much more subtly than in nonstrategic industries where the state has relinquished regulatory authority and more extensively deregulated. For example, case studies reveal that when a more liberal approach is taken toward a company, such as in the licensing of AT&T's joint venture in Shanghai to operate a broadband network normally restricted to FDI, it is usually for a strategic reason, whether political or economic in nature.

THE POLITICAL CONTEXT OF STATE
CONTROL IN TEXTILES

In contrast to the decentralized nature of economic governance in telecommunications during the Mao era and through most of the 1980s, centralization marked the state's governance of the textile industry. From the founding of the PRC until 1993, the Ministry of Textile Industry (MTI) dominated the industry.[13] The MTI owned textile mills that processed raw and manmade materials and manufactured fabric, supervised the distribution of raw materials and domestically produced inputs, and controlled the China Textile Resources Group Company, an importer of textile inputs.[14] In addition to managing the textile supply chain and coordinating internal trade and distribution, the MTI intervened on the company level, exercising bureaucratic influence on issues ranging from the allocation of capital and equipment to decisions involving pricing, which the planning ministry also supervised.

The Political Origins of Incidental Control

In spite of the high level of centralization and state monopoly across subsectors, the dominant pattern of incidental reregulation in textiles witnessed today emerged in the 1980s. Formal and de facto economic reform permitted market entry of nonstate producers in industries less important to national security imperatives and that do not contribute to the country's technology base. Nonstate textile manufacturers began to flourish alongside the state sector, and institutional restructuring decreased the power of trade bureaucracies.

The MTI did not possess regulatory monopoly over the entire textile industry. Overlapping jurisdictions governed textile subsectors and segments of the supply chain. Supply and marketing cooperatives (SMCs) under the Ministry of Commerce managed the marketing and procurement of raw inputs, such as cotton and wool, distributed by the MTI to processing mills.[15] The MTI shared supervision of the processing of raw and manmade materials with government departments, such as the Ministry of Light Industry, the Ministry of Agriculture, the Ministry of Chemical Industry, and the Ministry of Construction. Additionally, the light ministry oversaw garment factories, and the Ministry of Commerce distributed the finished products to consumers. In 1987, however, the State Council, responding to restrictive export quotas imposed by the Multi-Fiber Agreement (MFA), which China joined in 1983, moved garment production under MTI jurisdiction to improve production coordination between garment and other textile subsectors.

---

13. The MTI ceded control to provincial and city-level authorities during the Great Leap Forward, but regained the power to operate and tax textile factories in the 1960s.

14. The textile and foreign trade ministries competed in controlling textile imports.

15. Administrative restructuring reorganized the commerce ministry several times; it became the Ministry of Internal Trade before merging with the foreign trade ministry in 2003. See Zheng (2004), 83–108.

Importantly, the Ministry of Foreign Economic Relations and Trade (MOFERT) monopolized textile imports and exports, including distribution to factories, through the China National Textiles Import and Export Corporation (CHINA-TEX) and other foreign trade corporations (FTCs). The first Sino-American Textile Agreement in 1980 and China's participation in the MFA further augmented the power of these trading agencies as they controlled the distribution of export quotas and increased the central government's prerogative to control the procurement and distribution of imports and exports.[16] The CHINATEX's administration of export quotas, along with market developments discussed below, contributed to the diminishing of the MTI's authority over industry.

In the mid-1980s, the government separated regulation from the business of trade and decentralized the enforcement of quota allocations, effectively ending state-owned import and export companies' de facto monopoly over textile trade. It reasserted MOFERT's authority to allocate quotas, which curbed CHINATEX's allocations with political rather than performance-based criteria. It also established the China Chamber of Commerce for Imports and Exports of Textiles (CCC-T) in 1988 to supervise the utilization of quotas and export licenses and make recommendations for their allocation. Soon thereafter, the State Council, at the urging of the MTI, granted autonomous export rights to textile manufacturers, which ended the FTCs' monopoly over quota utilization.[17] Even before that, Shanghai, Tianjin, Guangzhou, Jiangsu, and other regional centers of textile manufacturing had already granted greater autonomy to textile-exporting enterprises to improve their performance in world markets.

The MTI, CHINATEX, and related ministries wielded considerable influence over the manufacturing, marketing, and trade and distribution of textiles throughout the 1980s, but politics between competing ministries and market developments undermined the power of these central-level government offices. Moreover, de facto market practices, including the operation of TVEs with unclear property rights, the liberalization of private entry, and the devolution of economic decision making to local governments gave rise to a vibrant nonstate, private textile industry.

The private sector began small scale as the government's adoption of the household responsibility system (HRS) in 1980 introduced the *getihu* (individual household enterprises) and *siren qiye* (private enterprises).[18] Throughout the 1980s and

---

16. China signed the first Sino-American Textiles Agreement (SATA) in 1980 and SATA V in 1997 (1997–2008). In parallel, China participated in negotiations for the fourth MFA and became a signatory in 1986.

17. Unsurprisingly, CHINATEX and the FTCs strongly resisted export rights for textile factories. See Moore (2002), 146–49, on their declining influence in textiles.

18. Under the HRS, households were free to work the land and to dispose of the surplus after fulfilling government obligations. Many went into business as a *getihu*, whose policy limited it to seven nonfamily employees, or a *siren qiye*, which comprised eight or more nonfamily employees. See Meisner (1999), 461–64. For more on the *siren qiye*, see Gold (1989), 187–200.

1990s, private entrepreneurs, local governments, and SOEs entered textile production as the government lifted more restrictions on market entry along the fabric and garment manufacturing supply chain and in the subsectors of industrial and technical textiles. Many textile businesses operated as "red hat" enterprises, adaptive informal institutions that escape legal restrictions and the vagaries of informal control by collaborating with reflexively strategic local officials to operate as TVEs.[19] Parallel to the surging domestic private market entry in the mid-1980s, foreign investors, beginning with ethnic Chinese from Hong Kong, Taiwan, and Singapore, set up garment, furniture, and shoe textile manufacturing capacity in southeastern provinces.[20] These institutional and market developments set the stage for the incidental control of the post-Deng era and local government-initiated FDI surge and private sector development in textile manufacturing and trade.

By the early 1990s, the government had deprioritized textiles. The textile industry's low strategic value did not warrant the resources required to arbitrate between overlapping bureaucracies and micromanage the sector. Underscoring the strategic value of sectors with high contribution to the national technology base and national security implications, however, the central government policies prioritized the development of technical textiles even as it deregulated other subsectors of textiles. The five-year plans regularly granted select state-owned, export-oriented textile manufacturers in value-added and technical sectors preferential access to raw materials, transportation, and energy resources. To spur consumption in downstream subsectors and increase value-added production, the government set prices on imported raw materials and high-tech fibers and fabrics. The Eighth Five-Year Plan (1990–95) prioritized the development of synthetic fiber sectors and high-tech equipment for apparel production. Furthermore, the government created special foreign exchange funds to help textile manufacturers finance technology imports.

Toward Decentralized Engagement in Textiles

Although the Chinese government regulated textiles with a fairly centralized regime in the prereform era, the dawn of reform commenced the state's incidental control of textiles. The following outlines the driving forces behind *decentralized engagement*, the dominant pattern of reregulation in textiles presented in chapters 6 and 7. It evaluates the strategic value of textiles and discusses the impact of sectoral structures on actual methods of control.

---

19. TVEs are commercial enterprises initiated by local governments or private entrepreneurs and legally owned by the local state. See Tsai (2003) on the scholarship on the vagaries of the local state and variation in its impact on the local economy. On the relationship between TVEs and marketization, see Nee (1989), Parris (1993), Unger and Chan (1999), and Whiting (1999). See also Pearson (1997) and Tsai (2007).

20. Hsing (1998).

State Goals

The textile industry's relatively low contribution to national security and infrastructural development shapes the central government's goals for the industry, state-industry relations, and methods of state control. We would expect the state to adopt an incidental orientation toward textiles. All the same, within textiles we would expect the central government to assume a more deliberate orientation toward technical textiles and textile trade and distribution because of its concern for indigenous technological development and the importance of textile exports in foreign economic relations.

State-Industry Relations and State Methods

Consistent with these expectations, the state eliminated a sector-specific ministry to supervise industry developments, devolved licensing powers to local branches of the commerce ministry, and completely liberalized market entry across textile subsectors. When decentralized authorities exert regulatory control in manufacturing to achieve local and private goals, textile subsectors' varying levels of capital and labor intensity and positions in the global supply chain influence the nature of state control.

Textile Manufacturing

Given the low strategic value of textiles, we would expect the central government to rarely intervene in textile manufacturing. It has decentralized regulatory enforcement to lower levels of government; the locus of intervention occurs at the local level. But textile manufacturing subsectors—from fiber processing to garments to technical textiles—are labor intensive, contribute to local employment, enhance the local industrial base, have low capital requirements and relatively less complex transactions that are easy to codify, and belong to predominately buyer-driven commodity chains. Thus, local branches of the commerce ministry and local governments introduce fiscal incentives and other subsidies, such as accelerated customs, to maximize investment and value-added production and to satisfy local economic and political interests. The central government rarely intervenes; it does so only to adjudicate escalating conflicts that threaten political and social stability.

The strategic value framework would expect the central government to intervene in industrial and technical subsectors of textiles. Industrial and technical textiles have a high technology content and some product categories are inputs for construction, space, and aviation sectors, which have military applications. Compared to telecommunications, the textile industry falls on the low end of the technological ladder, but because of potential military and aeronautical applications, related central ministries intervene to promote industrial upgrading and FDI in high-tech, high-value-added subsectors. Central and local governments also introduce fiscal and other subsidies to promote the development of high-tech textile equipment and fabrics, which are sometimes unavailable as imports because of other countries' export restrictions.

The decentralized nature of state control in textiles, however, means that, depending on the political acumen of the locality and company in question, government subsidies and collaboration are often illusive. Furthermore, because market entry in industrial and technical sectors is completely liberalized and asset specificity and sunk costs are still relatively low, what government intervention does exist contributes as much to industrial upgrading as it does to market overexpansion.

Textile Trade and Distribution

The external trade in textiles is strategic because of its economic contribution to the rest of the economy and its significance to China's foreign economic relations. Textile exports have become particularly important because trade relations have become strained in recent years; Chinese exports of low-end, low-value-added products regularly exceed the volume ceilings negotiated in bilateral agreements. Thus, although the state has completely decentralized the regulation of textiles to the local levels, the central government regulates textile exports through voluntary export restraints, quota allocation regimes, and a highly calibrated currency regime. The Ministry of Commerce, though not a sector-specific office, retains discretionary authority over the allocation of textile export and import quotas and licenses in order to balance industrial prerogatives with the demands of multilateral and bilateral trade agreements. Moreover, to maximize the contribution of value-added, export-oriented textile sectors to the rest of the economy, the state uses macroeconomic levers to manipulate China's currency. Notably, Chinese textiles' important position in the global production chain and the potential economic gains reaped from it have induced manufacturers, subcontractors, traders, and brand marketers to collaboratively engage economic and trade authorities to meet the demands of this buyer-driven industry.

In the governance of internal trade, local and central-level market practices favor domestic producers and distributors over FDI and brand marketers. Central ministries, local governments, business and sector associations, and private actors set technical standards that protect local markets and impede the internal access of market- and efficiency-pursuing foreign-invested technical textile manufacturers. Local governments and branches of the Ministry of Commerce also regularly issue import, retail, and distribution licenses to promote local industry. On the one hand, these efforts persist despite China's WTO commitment to national treatment in internal trade. On the other hand, the implementation of WTO commitments on internal trade has tackled local protectionism, especially in extensively decentralized sectors.

The incidental, less deliberate orientation of state control in textiles foreshadows the politics generated by the organization of government institutions, which interact with the domestic sector's competitive position during boom-bust cycles to affect variation in actual control methods across time. A loose collection of overlapping central ministries and local governments enforce the commercial rules and macroeconomic policies that regulate business activities in textiles. This multilayered institutional landscape and diversity of state and private actors in textiles routinely impede state capacity, particularly during critical junctures of state intervention.

The decentralized nature of textiles translates to more firm-level variation in state control. The experiences of foreign-invested companies, such as apparel brand marketer Bestseller (Denmark), illustrate how in extensively liberalized sectors where the central government intervenes less purposively over market developments, local governments, driven by local goals and interests, respond first and foremost to the resources that companies bring to the table. Moreover, in subsectors where centralized oversight remains, the willingness of a company's home country to intervene influences the nature of government-business relations. Finally, the Chinese government's perception of the home country of firms plays little or no role in influencing the nature of state control in nonstrategic industries. Local governments, eager to attract investment, do not discriminate by country of origin.

ARGUMENT IN BRIEF

The strategic value framework helps us understand why and how reregulation varies despite common forces of change, detailed in chapter 2. China's participation in liberal trade regimes might explain the initial motivation to liberalize but cannot explain why, prior to economy-wide liberalization in the 1990s, the state separated regulation and business in both industries, but state control was reinforced after administrative and business restructuring in the more strategic telecommunications industry and diminished in the less strategic textile industry. Both industries underwent decentralization, yet institutional restructuring after initial devolution of economic decision making increased centralized oversight of industrial developments in telecommunications and further relinquished state control in textiles (table 3.1). Furthermore, the increase of nonstate actors helps to achieve state goals in telecommunications even as it contributes to a pluralistic market landscape in textiles.

The same common conditions hold after macroliberalization in the early 1990s, but the divergence in dominant patterns of state control becomes even more pronounced and enduring. Exercising *deliberate reinforcement* in telecommunications, the Chinese government not only preserves but enhances control over telecommunications, a sector strategic to national security and economic and technological advancement. In the pre-WTO era, the state tolerated foreign investment to promote network development; however, when rival ministries, with the assistance of FDI, began to construct what central state leaders viewed as redundant telecommunications networks that affected infrastructural control and the carriers' competitiveness directly before WTO accession, the state consolidated ministerial authority and divested FDI between 1998 and 2001. In the post-WTO era, the state delayed meeting WTO commitments to liberalize basic services and expanded bureaucratic discretion over value-added services to retain control of information dissemination. Moreover, the government's setting of technical standards impeded the market access of foreign equipment makers.

TABLE 3.1. DOMINANT PATTERNS OF STATE CONTROL		
	Telecommunications	Textiles
Perceived strategic value	Strategic	Nonstrategic
Dominant pattern of state control	Deliberate reinforcement	Decentralized engagement
State goals	Modernization of networks, control of information, control of technology and infrastructure	Local goals: maximization of employment, FDI, tax revenue Central goals: Foreign economic relations
State-industry relations	Enhance central government control	Undermine central government control
State methods	Sector-specific rules and regulations on ownership structure, market entry, product certification, and technical standards	Economy-wide rules on market entry, macroeconomic policies, and local rules and regulations

In contrast, the state relinquished control of textiles, an industry less strategic to the central government. *Decentralized engagement* combines the liberalization of market entry with the decentralization of economic decision making to local governments and branches of the commerce ministry. Administrative decentralization and extensive market liberalization stymied state efforts when the central government intervened immediately before WTO accession to manage overexpansion in fiber processing and promote industrial upgrading in what it perceived as globally uncompetitive domestic textiles. In the post-WTO era, sector and business associations and local governments courted private domestic and foreign investment with fiscal and infrastructural incentives and collaborated with local companies to set technical standards.

PART II

STATE CONTROL OF TELECOMMUNICATIONS

4

CONSOLIDATING CENTRAL
CONTROL OF TELECOMMUNICATIONS
IN THE PRE-WTO ERA

China in the 1990s was a playground for foreign companies interested in tapping into the potential of reaching 1.2 billion customers through telecommunications. Technological advances—more efficient use of the spectrum available for wireless communication and fiber-optic technology, which dramatically increased the capacity for data transmission—also propelled FDI inflows. Foreign institutional investors and private entrepreneurs alike, hoping to maximize first-mover advantage, teamed with local governments and provincial branches of Chinese carriers to build second-generation telecommunications networks. The issuance of an operating license to China United Telecommunications Corporation (China Unicom) in 1994 created history. The subsequent breakup of the telecommunications monopoly owned and managed by the Ministry of Post and Telecommunications (MPT) officially sanctioned competition for the first time. Despite formal restrictions barring FDI in the period leading up to China's accession to the World Trade Organization in 2001, state-owned carriers courted FDI in practice. Foreign investment also flooded value-added services (VAS) without state intervention. To win market share, foreign equipment makers formed joint ventures with state-owned equipment makers and contracted to transfer technology.

But the fun and games lasted less than a decade. In 1998, the central government intervened to break up the joint ventures in basic services; it instructed the divestment of nonstate interests. "Every one interpreted what happened as an antiforeign game," explained a former executive of one of those foreign-invested JVs. "I saw things as they were. This 'China telecom play' was simply the desire to not introduce competition that could not be controlled by the government."[1] Even as

---

1. Interview in Beijing on September 15, 2006, with former executive of Metromedia China.

the state introduced competition and adopted a policy of de facto FDI liberalization to modernize network infrastructure and develop the domestic sector, the state reregulated to check rival ministries and new stakeholders created by liberalizing policies. On the eve of WTO accession in 2001, the unleashing of competition had not undermined state control.

Market reform through the 1990s reinforced the state's increasingly deliberate orientation toward telecommunications. With limited resources and capacity, the government chose its battles carefully; it reregulated according to a strategic value logic. On the one hand, the state exercised *strategic reregulation* in telecommunications services; it permitted competition to modernize infrastructure and promote the growth of value-added services, and reregulated to retain monopoly over infrastructure and control the direction of network development. The government's actions created the "re-enforcing phenomena of increasing liberalization of sectors, increasing regulatory capacity."[2] The government permitted "competition to reform domestic industry, including state-owned enterprises, to force them to work at higher profit margins, to be more efficient, leaner, to innovate more, etc. The losers are not always foreigners," explained the managing director of a domestic information technology business association.[3]

On the other hand, *delegated reregulation* dominated telecommunications equipment. The government took a mixed orientation toward industry to write new rules, which deregulated market entry and assigned regulatory authority to provincial branches of the telecommunications ministry. The merger of the formerly separate equipment and service ministries and the competitiveness of Chinese telecommunications during the WTO accession protocol negotiations further influenced the nature of reregulation. These developments set the stage for state retrenchment in the post-WTO accession era (examined in chapter 5) despite China's WTO commitments to liberalize.

The developmental states of Japan, South Korea, and Taiwan, on the contrary, pursued a different strategy consistent with the state-led model to develop telecommunications. Chapter 5's mini case studies of countries illustrate how, with some variation, instead of exploiting greater competition to achieve state goals, the developmental state closely managed competition to protect the incumbent and promote the expansion of subsectors. Moreover, rather than strategically utilize FDI to maximize technology and knowledge transfers, the developmental state restricted foreign capital and technology penetration and worked closely with domestic business to promote sectoral development.

---

2. Interview in Beijing on October 13, 2005, with China-based Asia chairman of a global consulting firm.

3. Interview on April 29, 2005, in Shanghai.

TELECOMMUNICATIONS SERVICES: STRATEGIC
REREGULATION

The Directive on Strengthening Regulations in the Management of Telecommunications Sector ("Directive"), formally approved in October 1993, linked the introduction of competition to the modernization of infrastructure. It directed the MPT to license mobile and value-added service providers operated by rival ministries. The MTP's monopoly over telecommunications ended in 1994 when China Unicom, a carrier established and operated by the Ministry of Electronic Industry (MEI) and other central bureaucracies, received an operating license.[4] In addition to having non-MPT affiliated founders, China Unicom positioned itself under the administration of the State Economics and Trade Commission (SETC), a predecessor to the present-day Ministry of Commerce. The government also licensed Jitong Communications, a VAS provider established by MEI-affiliated equipment makers and research institutes.[5]

The licensure of China Unicom and Jitong authorized and encouraged large users within the government to set up new networks and modernize existing dedicated networks that the MPT had prohibited from offering public access.[6] By the end of 1995, the MPT licensed 2,136 paging service providers and sixty-eight interprovincial value-added service providers. Moreover, the MEI and other ministries launched the Golden Projects, linking the MEI's equipment manufacturing capabilities to the construction of non-MPT-controlled data networks. They justified these "Internet" projects because of their role in collecting and sending information to the State Council to be "used to make scientific macro control decisions."[7] On the eve of WTO accession, non-MPT-affiliated basic service providers, namely China Unicom, Jitong, China Netcom, and China Railcom, emerged as competitors to the incumbent China Telecom (known as the Directorate General of Telecommunications, DGT, until 1995).[8]

---

4. The MEI, Ministry of Railways, and Ministry of Electric Power and thirteen major SOEs founded China Unicom. See Lu and Wong (2003).

5. Jitong's shareholders included thirty central and local SOEs and research institutes in Beijing, Guangzhou, Shanghai, and Shenzhen. See Mueller and Tan (1997), 45–64.

6. Beginning in the 1960s, central bureaucracies, including the Chinese Academy of Science (CAS), constructed dedicated networks outside the control of the MPT. The largest of these were owned and operated by the People's Liberation Army (PLA), the ministries of Railways, Electric Power, Transportation, Petroleum, and Foreign Trade, and the People's Bank of China. See Mueller and Tan (1997), 46–47, and Gorham and Chadran (1993), 24.

7. Through Jitong, the MEI launched the Golden Bridge, Golden Customs, and Golden Card. Other bureaucracies and SOEs created Golden Taxation, Golden Agriculture, and Golden Macro-Economic Supporting System. See Mueller and Tan (1997), 52–58, and J. Wang (1999), 12–14.

8. China Netcom, founded by CAS, the Shanghai government, the State Administration of Radio, Film and Television (SARFT), and the Ministry of Railways (MOR) and licensed in 1999, leased from the incumbent to offer an Internet Protocol (IP) telephone service. China Railcom, under MOR jurisdiction, received a license in January 2001 to provide fixed-line service, Internet access, and IP telephony.

The Directive's two follow-up measures issued in September 1994 granted the incumbent and non-MPT affiliated investors procurement authority and the economic incentives required to modernize network infrastructure. China Telecom's branch offices were permitted to establish a capital account system to manage infrastructure funds and seek investment from local governments and other local interests. Non-MPT affiliated investors in trial projects received a fixed-rate remuneration and dividend distribution.

Despite sanctioning domestic competition, the Directive reinforced the Restatement on Forbidding Joint Operation of Postal and Telecommunications Business with Foreign Companies of 1992, which explicitly stated that foreigners could neither invest in nor participate in the operation of telecommunications services.[9] Regulatory and market developments, however, tabled enforcement of the FDI ban until the end of the decade.

Liberalization Phase (1993–1997)

The introduction of competition weakened the regulatory authority of the MPT and the market power of the telecommunications incumbent. The MEI's confidence in mobilizing support from higher authorities for its network activities gained strength and the MPT and MEI's rivalry over the telecommunications regime intensified. The MPT still held regulatory authority over the industry, but it now competed with other bureaucracies for grants, loans, and investments to subsidize the incumbent. China Unicom's bureaucratic backers, with the SETC's political clout, used their coequal status with the MPT to veto a draft Telecommunications Law, which would have given the MPT "too much power."[10] The corporatization of China Telecom in 1995, which separated the DGT from a government agency, further weakened the MPT's authority.[11]

To compensate for its weakened authority and raise funds for the incumbent, in late November 1994 the MPT issued a regulation that encouraged China Telecom branches to find innovative ways to absorb foreign capital and compete with China Unicom and other networks.[12] Contradicting the 1993 Directive, the regulation

---

9. The Directive states that "no organization, enterprise, or individual outside China may engage in the management of China's broadcasting networks, special wire or wireless services, or become a shareholder in a telecommunications business."

10. Chapter 5 discusses why, as of 2010, China has not released a Telecommunications Law. See "The Real Telecom Battleground in China Is Multimedia," *Chinaonline.com* (April 5, 1999), on an earlier battle.

11. Shortly thereafter, provincial-level postal and telecommunications enterprises corporatized as subsidiaries of China Telecom and other carriers. China Telecom had its first international public offering in Hong Kong in October 1997. The listed subsidiary was formed from several provincial GSM networks, with China Telecom holding 51 percent of shares. See Lu and Wong (2003), 116.

12. In 1994, China Telecom became the borrower of a World Bank loan obtained by the Ministry of Finance. After a series of innovations, the loan came under the possession of China Telecom's listed arm in mid-2002. Papers obtained from the Stock Exchange of Hong Kong reported that the loan was repaid in 2003.

contained nebulous language suggesting that foreign capital could be absorbed.[13] Using the MPT regulation as a guide, carriers with patrons outside the traditional telecommunications establishment and tacit support of the State Council also courted foreign participation in network development.

Foreign investors responded eagerly.[14] In their excitement over the licensing of a service provider, the separation of China Telecom from the MPT, and the incumbent's 1997 initial public offering (IPO) in Hong Kong, they paid little attention to the 1993 Directive's FDI ban. They also ignored the Catalogue for the Guidance of Foreign Investment Industries of 1995 ("First Catalogue"), which reiterated the FDI ban and backpedaled from the liberalization language used in the 1994 MPT regulation.[15]

For its part, the State Council did not enforce the 1993 Directive or the First Catalogue, permitting the burgeoning FDI activity in network development to continue. In this liberal climate, the MEI encouraged China Unicom to raise start-up capital through creative means, foregoing government approval for foreign exchange loans and contracting with international banks and paying market interest rates. Through the China-China-Foreign (CCF) structure, a technically illegal property rights and fund-raising arrangement, China Unicom and its president, Zhao Weichen, sought foreign investors for the rollout of GSM (Global System for Mobile communications) networks. China Telecom and other network operators also formed extralegal ventures.[16] For example, Guangdong Telecom collaborated with equipment vendors, including Sweden's Ericsson, to construct trial networks.[17]

Typically, a wholly foreign-owned enterprise (WFOE) and a local company would form a JV, which would then form another JV with a network subsidiary. Bell Canada, for example, formed a JV in 1995 with the Yantai Industry and Trade Corporation in Shandong Province to provide cellular phone service; this JV then formed a JV with Yantai Unicom.[18] The contractual terms of the CCF ventures varied; in general, foreign investors transferred technical knowledge through joint operations and officially earned "installation and consulting fees." Local and foreign partners justified the financial arrangement as a contractual relationship and not as an equity investment. In reality, CCFs often served as holding companies without government approval and foreign partners received an after-tax return on

13. The MPT regulation suggested that officially sanctioned FDI liberalization might be under way; some international lawyers, however, believed the regulation indicated disagreement within the government concerning FDI and, therefore, it did not trump the 1993 Directive. Interview on September 21, 2006, with Michael Aldrich, managing partner at Lovells Beijing.

14. Interviews between 2006 and 2008 with foreign investors that entered China during this time.

15. Subsequent catalogues have guided FDI investment based on sector-specific goals.

16. Interviews with industry insiders between 2005 and 2006. See also Chan and Goldsmith (1999).

17. J. Wang (1999), 10.

18. Harwit (1998), 190.

investment. Moreover, CCFs engaged in activities including "importation and the resale of telecom products, outside of legally permitted parameters, which required special approvals."[19]

One executive explained that CCFs benefited Chinese partners and the government's goal of modernizing infrastructure: instead of the Build-Operate-Transfer schemes envisioned by foreign investors, CCFs typically fell in the category of "Build, Transfer, Thank You Very Much."[20] McCaw International confronted this attitude after providing $22 million for a 25 percent share of net proceeds to build a GSM network in Shanghai. McCaw's Chinese partners threatened to reduce its share if it did not invest an additional $80 million to expand the network. Hoping to retain a market foothold, McCaw did not immediately exit the CCF; however, as fate would have it, events forced McCaw to walk away shortly thereafter.[21]

Between 1993 and 1997, CCF ventures soared as the MPT- and MEI-controlled carriers competed for foreign investment and fought fierce price wars to gain market share. During this time, at least forty-five foreign-invested companies invested US$1.4 billion through CCFs to develop and operate wireless and fixed-line networks; de facto foreign equity reached as high as 90 percent.[22] For many foreign companies, CCFs represented one of many ventures abroad; others, such as Wel-Com, a consortium of thirty U.S. and Taiwanese investors, were "formed . . . for these particular JVs."[23]

Reregulation Phase (1998–2000)

The formal separation of carriers from ministerial ownership and management, the breakup of the telecommunications monopoly, and the nonenforcement of the prohibition against FDI helped to modernize telecommunications infrastructure and maximize technology transfers. Between 1998 and 2000, in light of China's impending WTO accession, however, the central government reregulated in ways that enhanced the state's authority over network development and market coordination of state-owned carriers. To arbitrate between state-owned carriers and their feuding bureaucratic patrons, the State Council centralized regulatory authority over equipment and services through administrative restructuring. Next, the government divested FDI in basic services to stem what it perceived as runaway network development and private domination of state-owned physical and financial assets. Subsequently, the government restructured the incumbent and its competi-

---

19. Interview on September 15, 2006, with Anne Stevenson-Yang, former vice president of business development, Metromedia China Corporation, a CCF partner of China Unicom.

20. Harwit (1998), 191.

21. "The Wireless World Tour," *Telephony Online* (April 21, 1997).

22. "Beijing Sets Deadline on Unicom CCF Resolution," *CNET.com* (September 3, 1999), and Lu and Wong (2003), 72.

23. "Sorry Wrong Number," *CFO Asia* (April 2000).

tors, which created competitive telecommunications duopolies on the eve of WTO accession.

Creation of the Ministry of Information Industry
In the half decade after the 1993 breakup of the telecommunications monopoly a fierce competition for market share and FDI developed between the telecommunications carriers under the aegis of rival bureaucracies. By 1998, however, during the economic slowdown of the Asian financial crisis, state leadership began to feel that the growing number of nonstate stakeholders threatened its control of telecommunications. To more effectively manage the equipment and service sectors to allow competition but retain its control, in late 1995 the State Council created the State Leading Group for Informationization (SLGI), a supraministerial panel in the State Office of Informationization, to study the problem. The SLGI, which was composed of high-ranking officials, immediately set out to find a solution to resolve competing ministerial ambitions and to check the growing number of sectoral stakeholders. As a first step, the State Council merged the MPT, the MEI, and the Radio Regulatory Commission to create the Ministry of Information Industry (MII) in March 1998.[24] Yet signaling that MEI bureaucrats, the chief patrons of China Unicom, had lost their turf war against the MPT, the State Council appointed former MPT head Wu Jichuan as the first MII minister.[25] Shortly after consolidating its control over rival bureaucratic stakeholders, the State Council questioned the legality of CCF ventures.[26]

Mandating Divestment of FDI
Immediately after the MII's establishment, word spread quickly that the State Council and the State Development and Planning Commission (SDPC) had issued a notice backed by Premier Zhu Rongji that questioned the legality of the CCFs.[27] After half a decade of unofficially sanctioning de facto FDI liberalization, the State Council forcefully intervened to divest FDI (and other undesirable investments). The newly created ministry formally declared in October 1998 that the CCFs violated the ban on foreign investment in telecommunications services, and decreed in February 1999 that the carriers must terminate CCF contracts by the end of

---

24. SARFT had supervised the Radio Regulatory Commission. Administrative restructuring in 1998 demoted the remaining departments to bureaus. See Chan and Drewry (2001), 563–64.

25. Former MPT bureaucrats dominated telecommunications policy and rulemaking long after the MPT's dissolution. Interviews with J.M. Chen, director of government relations, Motorola China in Beijing, on September 19, 2006, and with former MEI and MPT officials between 2005 and 2008.

26. Some analysts contend that administrative restructuring in 1998 failed to centralize control (Mertha 2005a and 2005b). This study finds that the state achieved centralization in strategic industries where it prioritized resources to enhance its control.

27. See Chan and Goldsmith (1999), 18–19. Previously the State Planning Commission, the SDPC merged with the State Council Office for Restructuring the Economic System and part of the SETC in 2003 to form the National Development and Reform Commission (NDRC).

September.[28] The MII threatened to prohibit those foreign investors who refused to end their contracts from participation in the China market, and attempted to lure those willing to negotiate with better compensation.[29] With its government patron, the MEI, subsumed under the MII bureaucracy, China Unicom terminated CCF contracts by July 1999 and stopped distributing payments to JV partners in October. Shortly thereafter, China Unicom secured state approval to list in stock markets in Hong Kong and overseas.

Foreign investors initially responded by banding together to demand that China Unicom and other carriers honor their equity contracts. But they disagreed on strategy, and the foreign embassies remained silent on what many considered anti-foreign actions.[30] Metromedia soon broke ranks to negotiate a divestment agreement with the Chinese government.[31] "We reached an agreement to bring the deal to an end," explained Mark Hauf, president of Metromedia. "We got less than we wanted; they paid more than they wanted. But we walked away friends."[32] Some industry insiders believe Hauf's shift proved instrumental in persuading Zhu Rongji to compromise and allow foreign investors to negotiate individually for equity owed to them.[33] After a prolonged process of individual negotiations, in summer 2000 China Unicom issued warrants pledging shares from its Hong Kong listing equal to a certain proportion of equity owed to thirty of the foreign companies involved in CCFs.

Foreign companies could have pursued China Unicom both through international arbitration and within China based on fraudulent representation and breach of contract. But because they did not receive support from home governments, many took substantial losses. For example, the U.S. Embassy advised U.S. companies "to take it by the chin or else they may never be able to return to China" or will "be denied future market access."[34] Moreover, some industry insiders speculate that the forced divestment of FDI in China did not lead to more industry protests because of booming telecommunications in the United States and elsewhere at that time. In the mid-1990s, a combination of deregulated markets for telecommunications services with the passage of the Telecommunications Act of 1996 and

---

28. Interview on October 30, 2005, in Beijing with Patrick Powers, former China managing director of the U.S.-China Business Council. Also see *South China Morning Post* (September 2, 1999).

29. Harwit (2008), 64.

30. *Far Eastern Economic Review* (September 30, 1999); "Beijing Sets Deadline on Unicom CCF Resolution," *CNET.com* (September 3, 1999); Lu and Wong (2003), 72; and Harwit (2008), 64.

31. See "Metromedia China Corporation and China United Telecommunications Executive Definitive Agreements," SEC File 1–05706, Accession Number 912057–99–9310 (December 14, 1999).

32. "Sorry Wrong Number," *CFO Asia* (April 2000).

33. Interview with Stevenson-Yang (September 15, 2006). These companies included Ameritech, Bell Canada, CCT Holdings, Deutsche Telekom, France Telecom, McCaw International, Metromedia International, NTT International, Siemens, Singapore Telecom, Sprint, Tomin, and WelCom.

34. Interviews with Aldrich (September 21, 2006) and Stevenson-Yang (September 15, 2006).

improvements in technology for data transmission led to greater market demand in the United States and investment in intercity and transoceanic fiber-optic infrastructure around the world. In 2001, massive overinvestment began to plague global telecommunications, contributing to the tech bust and economic recession in the United States.

The strategic value framework explains the lax enforcement of the prohibition against foreign investment and the eventual abrupt crackdown on China Unicom's CCFs as exemplifying the state's willingness to exercise its authority when and where it sees fit to achieve state goals. It is not in the interest of the state to introduce foreign or domestic competition in basic services that the state cannot straightforwardly control and which it believed would ultimately hinder Chinese success in domestic and international markets. The divestment of "illegal" foreign investment and China Unicom's public listing presented opportunities for the State Council to clean house and exert its control over both China Unicom's domestic stakeholders and foreign investors. The State Council had also mandated the divestment of domestic stakeholders, including the Ministry of Electric Power, which owned Chongqing Unicom, and companies operated by local governments involved in CCFs. Hauf of Metromedia elucidated, "The pressure to compete made it necessary to abandon this [market] approach."[35]

Restructuring State-Owned Carriers

The forced divestment of FDI allowed the government to reclaim control of network infrastructure and made way for the State Council's ambitious project to restructure and internationally list the incumbent and other carriers before WTO accession.[36] In several rounds, the state restructured the carriers to solidify its control of the direction of network development and create more modern, globally competitive carriers. It shifted ownership of network assets and assigned service specialties and geographical responsibilities to the carriers. By WTO accession, in December 2001, the State Council had created duopolies in fixed-line (China Telecom and China Netcom) and mobile services (China Unicom and China Mobile) and had again strategically utilized foreign investment without lifting the ban.

The organization of state institutions and the political interests that it generates, and the state leadership's perception of the competitiveness of domestic carriers, shaped variation in reregulation across several rounds of restructuring. During the first round of restructuring, former MPT bureaucrats sought to maintain their control of network development and promote the interests of those closely connected to the former telecommunications ministry within China Telecom.[37] In

---

35. "Sorry Wrong Number," *CFO Asia* (April 2000).

36. Conversation on February 26, 2006, in Beijing with William Li, vice president of Greater Asia, Accenture, and former vice president of China Unicom.

37. Studying Spain and Latin America, Etchemendy (2001 and 2004) finds that established interests, bypassing other groups, can craft policies to protect their rents in the new market setting.

spring 1999, the MPT-dominated MII proposed a vertical divestiture to create incumbent carriers across several business lines; in practice, China Telecom had already operated under a framework of four businesses and dominated the market for
basic, long distance, and mobile services. In contrast, China Unicom had less than a
5 percent market share since founding in 1994.[38] With the State Council's official approval, this first divestiture created basic, mobile, paging, and satellite incumbents,
respectively: China Telecom Group, China Mobile Telecom Group, Guoxin Paging
Telecom Group, and China Satellite Telecom Group.[39] In May 2000, China Mobile
Telecom Group acquired at no cost China Telecom Group's stake in the internationally listed China Telecom (HK) Company Limited. Five months later (elaborated in greater detail in chapter 5), British telecommunications operator Vodafone
invested a 2 percent stake in China Mobile's internationally listed vehicle.

Next, the State Council set about pressuring the MII to take measures to ensure
the competitiveness of new entrant carriers: China Unicom and China Netcom, a
fixed-line operator. The MII mandated that China Telecom and China Mobile sign
interconnection agreements with China Unicom, officially approving Unicom's expansion into mobile and Internet telephony and domestic and international long
distance. The MII also created network access points (NAPs) overseen by China
Telecom to eliminate bottlenecks, which had adversely affected competition and
network traffic.[40] It further permitted Unicom to grant up to 10 percent discounts
on GSM services to compete with China Mobile.[41] The MII also permitted Unicom to raise funds via an IPO in June 2000.[42]

Notwithstanding these measures to create a competitive playing field between
the mobile carriers, the MII transferred China Telecom's CDMA (Code Division
Multiple Access) network operated by Great Wall to China Unicom in October
2000.[43] This transfer followed the Chinese government's commitment to roll out a
CDMA network in its WTO accession protocol agreement with the United States.
Industry insiders maintained that the MPT-dominated MII leadership purposely
saddled Unicom with CDMA, making it a permanent laggard to China Mobile. In
another signal of the state's willingness to intervene on the company level to achieve
its goals, the MII replaced China Unicom's executives with former executives of

---

38. J. Wang (1999), 9.

39. China Satcom officially incorporated in December 2001.

40. Up until the interconnection agreements and creation of NAPs in 1999, traffic was often routed
through a foreign country rather than directly between the carriers. See Dean (2001), 23–24.

41. The NDRC's Pricing Office continues to possess regulatory authority over telecommunications
pricing, including determining minimum tariff rates and arbitrating issues, such as directional charges
on calls.

42. China Unicom's represented, at the time, the largest IPO by a PRC company and the largest
Asian IPO outside of Japan.

43. The MPT, the PLA, and Guoxin Paging Company jointly operated and managed Great Wall.
The 1998 government order that the PLA withdraw from commercial activities also set the transfer in
motion. See Chan and Goldsmith (1999) and J. Wang (1999), 9.

China Telecom. (Chapter 5 details how this practice of rotating executives among the carriers continues in spite of WTO accession and international public listings.)

To create a viable fixed-line competitor to China Telecom, the SLGI next halted the MII's second IPO plan for China Telecom by pursuing a second restructuring of the incumbent. The State Council rejected restructuring strategies advocated by prominent telecommunications experts, favoring a horizontal divestiture along geographical lines, backed by non-MPT-dominated carriers as they anticipated gains from the weakened China Telecom.[44] The second divestiture divided the incumbent with a north-south division plan. Leading the second divestiture was the founder of China Netcom, Jiang Mianheng, President Jiang Zemin's son and the head of the Chinese Academy of Science. He played a critical role in securing for his company the merger of Jitong and China Telecom's ten northern provincial networks.[45] Moreover, despite the prohibition against FDI, China Netcom received high-level political sponsorship in 2000 to raise funds from a consortium of foreign investors to construct a broadband network to provide high-speed voice and data service in seventeen cities and connect with seven countries.[46] The newly restructured China Netcom and China Telecom officially launched in May 2002. In November, China Telecom relaunched its IPO in Hong Kong and New York. By 2003, the fixed-line and mobile duopolies were incorporated and publicly listed, in time to confront post-WTO competition.

Value-Added Services

Even as the Chinese government divested FDI in basic services and intervened several times to restructure the state-owned carriers directly before WTO accession, it did not take the same approach toward value-added services. The nature of state control in VAS differed from basic services according to a strategic value logic. Because VAS providers operate on network infrastructure owned and controlled by the state-owned carriers, the state extended less oversight over VAS providers, and the scope of state control did not include ownership or direct company-level intervention. After the state liberalized paging operations and VAS to nonstate players in 1993, thousands of domestic and foreign players entered VAS markets. VAS markets flourished and foreign entry took on forms similar to the CCFs.[47] Foreign-invested

---

44. See Lu and Wong (2003), 97–98, for a discussion of the different plans suggested by domestic experts, including Han Kaili, Zhou Qiren, and Wang Xiaoqiang, and international ones, including Morgan Stanley.

45. The new China Telecom operated fixed-line services in twenty-one provinces, autonomous regions, and municipalities in southern China.

46. U.S. (Dell Computer, Goldman Sachs, and News Corporation) and Hong Kong companies (Sun Hung Kai, Henderson Land, and the Kerry Group) participated. See Dean (2001), 24.

47. Interview in Shanghai on November 9, 2005, with Walker Wallace, partner, O'Melveny & Myers LLP.

VAS providers successfully listed in Hong Kong and other jurisdictions with prospectuses that clearly identified the "illegal" method of their participation.[48] Several of China's most successful foreign-invested JVs, including Sina.com and Sohu.com, launched in May 1999.[49] TOM Online, another Internet content provider (ICP) with a large market share, launched in 2001.[50]

Based on a strategic value logic, the government, however, restricted the business scope of market players in select VAS subsectors through China-specific service definitions. Classified as offering a basic service at the time of market liberalization in 1993, paging providers had to compete with state-owned carriers for spectrum allocation.[51] Rules on basic services also governed Internet service providers (ISPs). Moreover, the state defined value-added services to include Internet content provision, as it continues to do in 2010, a practice that departs from most advanced industrialized countries. These definitions foreshadowed the state's expansion of bureaucratic authority to control information and order what it believed were chaotic markets.

WTO Accession Negotiations

After four years of negotiations with the United States, the Chinese government signed a WTO accession protocol in November 1999. Six months later, in May 2000, China and the European Union signed a similar accord that further solidified a phased liberalization timetable for China's industries. Given the strategic value of telecommunications to the Chinese, the fate of the Sino-U.S. WTO protocol agreement rested on terms related to this industry. During the negotiations, the U.S. government requested two major concessions in telecommunications; while one went unmet, the Chinese government accepted the other one. The State Council's enhanced authority over industry developments through the creation of the MII, the elimination of foreign participation in basic services, and the state-orchestrated restructuring of carriers enabled the Chinese government to grant concessions during WTO negotiations without undermining its control of telecommunications assets and network development. In the end, the U.S. and the EU agreements failed

---

48. CCFs remain popular among foreign-invested enterprises (FIEs) in VAS and other strictly regulated sectors, including real estate. Because of licensing delays, most FIEs entered the market via contracts with Chinese companies holding operating licenses. One informant describes this as "regulatory obsolescence."

49. Sina.com, for example, operates a NASDAQ-listed parent company based in the Cayman Islands, a PRC company holding an ICP license, and a WFOE of the Cayman parent, which provides Sina's Chinese "contractor" with various services. Interview in Beijing with Mary Yu, Beijing general manager of Walden International, a venture capital investor of Sina.com (October 6, 2005).

50. Hong Kong's Li Ka-shing–invested TOM Online indirectly participated as an ICP by forming a WFOE, which operated with licenses of PRC companies owned by the company through complex shareholding arrangements. Interviews in Beijing on November 3 and December 3, 2005, with Craig Watts, former director of International Business at TOM Online.

51. See Sterling (1999), 33–34.

to win major concessions on telecommunications market access or FDI levels even while the Chinese government budged on less strategic issue areas, including the elimination of tariffs on information technology (IT) electronics by 2005 and the limited adoption of a U.S. network technology.[52]

In its first request, the U.S. government sought up to 51 percent foreign ownership in basic and value-added services.[53] To avoid committing China to majority foreign ownership in an industrial sector strategic to national security, the Chinese government offered a "compromise." The Chinese government pitted the U.S. insistence on a 51 percent ownership ceiling against a Chinese demand to end restrictions on textiles in 2005, as outlined in the WTO's Agreement on Textiles and Clothing (ATC), rather than in 2010, the U.S. government's preferred expiration date and the timeline China had already agreed to in the fifth Sino–American textiles agreement.[54] In the end, the two sides agreed to a four-year safeguard mechanism after the ATC expired in 2005 and a 49 percent ceiling on foreign equity in basic services and a 50 percent ceiling in value-added services. The protocol also bound China to the principles outlined in the 1996 WTO Agreement on Basic Telecommunications, and it detailed the equity caps and foreign investment levels across subsectors to be phased in geographically and over six years, starting with China's WTO accession in 2001 and ending in December 2007.

Next, the U.S. government successfully lobbied China to adopt CDMA, a second-generation network standard, on behalf of Qualcomm Corporation, the chief owner of the intellectual property associated with the CDMA technology.[55] In November 1999, the State Council mandated that China Unicom adopt China Telecom's CDMA network.[56] China Unicom initially resisted, having recently experienced the forced divestment of FDI. By October 2000, however, four months after China Unicom's IPO and under State Council pressure, China Unicom announced it would deploy the CDMA standard and adopt China Telecom's existing CDMA network.[57] Soon thereafter, the MII transferred the assets of China Telecom's

---

52. Lapres (2000), 8–14, and the "WTO Special Report: The Real Work Begins," *China Business Review* (January–February 2000), 17–27.

53. Interviews in Beijing on October 26, 2005, with an official from the U.S. Commercial Service, and on February 25, 2006, with an official from the Economic Section of the U.S. Embassy.

54. The fifth Sino–American textiles agreement, signed in February 1997, provided for twelve years of total coverage: four years (1997–2000) formally covered by the accord; four years (2001–04) under the terms of the ATC; and four years (2005–08) *beyond* ATC's expiration. Under the ATC, the United States also reserves the right to treat China as a nonmarket economy in monitoring the dumping of textiles and can trigger a second safeguard mechanism in force for twelve years after China's WTO accession. See Moore (2002), 59–70, and Jacobs (1997).

55. Interviews in Beijing on October 24 and November 7, 2005, with Ted Dean, managing director at BDA Consulting Research, and on February 17, 2006, with Dan Carini, manager, Norson Telecom Consulting.

56. Interview in Beijing on September 20, 2006, with Robert Tanner, manager of Technology Business Development, CDMA, Nokia China.

57. Conversation with Li (February 26, 2006).

Great Wall network to China Unicom. This commenced China Unicom's operation of two incompatible network technologies—GSM, a European-initiated standard, and CDMA, an American standard. The following list is an overview of the WTO commitments for basic and value-added services that China negotiated with the United States and the EU:

PAGING SERVICES

No more than 30 percent foreign investment in JVs in Beijing, Shanghai, and Guangzhou in the first year; within one year, no more than 49 percent, with the area expanded to include Chengdu, Chongqing, Dalian, Fuzhou, Hangzhou, Nanjing, Ningbo, Qingdao, Shenyang, Shenzhen, Xiamen, Xi'an, Taiyuan, and Wuhan; and after two years, no geographic restrictions.

MOBILE VOICE/DATA SERVICES

No more than 25 percent foreign investment in JVs in Beijing, Shanghai, and Guangzhou in the first year in the following services: analogue, digital, and cellular; within one year, no more than 35 percent, with the area expanded to include Chengdu, Chongqing, Dalian, Fuzhou, Hangzhou, Nanjing, Ningbo, Qingdao, Shenyang, Shenzhen, Xiamen, Xi'an, Taiyuan, and Wuhan; within three years, no more than 49 percent; and after five years, no geographic restrictions.

FIXED-LINE SERVICES

Within three years, no more than 25 percent foreign investment in JVs in Beijing, Shanghai, and Guangzhou in the following services: domestic services and international services; after five years, no more than 35 percent, with the area expanded to include Chengdu, Chongqing, Dalian, Fuzhou, Hangzhou, Nanjing, Ningbo, Qingdao, Shenyang, Shenzhen, Xiamen, Xi'an, Taiyuan, and Wuhan; and within six years, no more than 49 percent and no geographic restrictions.

VALUE-ADDED SERVICES

E-mail, voice mail, online information, database retrieval, electronic data interchange, enhanced value-added facsimile services (including store and forward, store and retrieve), code and protocol conversion and online information and/or data processing (including transaction processing)

No more than 30 percent in foreign investment in Beijing, Shanghai, and Guangzhou in the first year; within the first year, no more than 49 percent, with the area expanded to include Chengdu, Chongqing, Dalian, Fuzhou, Hangzhou, Nanjing, Ningbo, Qingdao, Shenyang, Shenzhen, Xiamen, Xi'an, Taiyuan, and Wuhan; within two years, no more than 50 percent and no geographic restrictions.

The assignment of CDMA to China Unicom represented the State Council's continued influence over the operators in spite of the formal separation of ownership and regulation, international listing, and increased competition in telecommunications. Moreover, during this period, at the behest of the State Council, the MII regularly intervened to halt price wars in response to China's imminent WTO entry. The MII also permitted China Unicom to grant 10 percent discounts on prices offered by China Mobile to stave off competition from the incumbent.[58] All the same, Unicom's saddling with CDMA, rather than the mobile incumbent, China Mobile, revealed the MPT faction's influence within the MII.

Codification of State Control

Regulations promulgated to enshrine into law China's international treaty obligations emphasized reregulation that enhanced state control, rather than liberalization, and legalized variations in state control across subsectors. The State Council issued the Administrative Regulations for Telecommunications Services ("Telecommunications Regulations") in September 2000 as a first step toward enshrining China's WTO obligations into law. Replacing the 1993 Directive prohibiting FDI in telecommunications services with a liberalization timetable that China had committed to during WTO negotiations, the Telecommunications Regulations legally designated the telecommunications service industry as open to foreign investment with varying restrictions on business scope and level of foreign equity across subsectors.[59] Departing from WTO requirements, however, the Telecommunications Regulations identified the "department in charge of information industry under the State Council" as the regulatory authority, but did not specify whether the MII, at that time the department in charge of the information industry, is an independent impartial regulatory body. Nor did the Telecommunications Regulations specify whether the SLGI, which had orchestrated the second and geographical divestiture of China Telecom, trumped the authority of the MII.

The Telecommunications Regulations also centralized the enforcement of regulations concerning the construction of telecommunications facilities in the provinces by placing provincial Telecommunications Administration Bureaus (TABs), formally separated from network carriers, under the dual control of provincial governments and the MII. At the same time, it delegated the authority to license VAS providers and plan and manage public telecommunications facilities, special-purpose telecommunications networks, and radio and TV transmission networks in their own areas to the TABs. In practice, the centralization of the MII's authority over the provincial TABs is incomplete, but deliberately so. As the unfolding story of state control of telecommunications reveals, a strategic value logic shapes how

---

58. Price regulation did not relax until the catalog of services promulgated by the SDPC and MII in 2002 allowed the carriers to set rates based on the market within the catalog's specified range of businesses.

59. Interview with Aldrich (September 21, 2006).

state control varies across subsectors. If central oversight of a particular subsector appears to be lacking, it is very likely that the center has adopted a less deliberate orientation toward that subsector.

The Telecommunications Regulations legalized the government practice of differentiating between two main types of telecommunications operators (basic and value-added service providers) and specified their business scope and licensing authorities.[60] Under China-specific definitions, basic services refer to the fixed-line and mobile operations. The MII and the SLGI closely manage the networks owned and operated by state-owned carriers upon which VAS providers operate. The state retains final authority to approve operating licenses and the level of foreign participation in basic services, which it has limited to equity investment and strategic partnerships. In contrast, value-added services refer to the non-carrier-provided services that operate on top of the backbone infrastructure. The TABs possess the regulatory authority to license value-added services if the service scope does not cover two or more provincial territories, and to enforce pricing policy.[61] They supervise the fees of basic and VAS providers and a system for companies to apply for pricing changes. The Beijing Telecommunications Administration, for example, routinely fined China Unicom for tariff violations.[62]

The Telecommunications Regulations also enhanced the state's control of technology in equipment sectors. It required networking equipment makers to obtain network access permits for imported and China-manufactured equipment, including terminal, wireless communications, and interconnections equipment.[63] The Arrangements for the Approval of Network Access of Telecommunications Equipment issued by the MII in 1998 also stipulated this provision.

State-Company Bargains

Two bargains between the state and a private firm ("state-company bargains") illustrate how the willingness of the home country to represent corporate interests

---

60. They are not inconsistent with the WTO's General Agreement on Trade in Services or the Agreement on Basic Telecommunications because neither agreement defines these subsectors. See Horsley (2001).

61. Chapter 5 elaborates on the impact of this geographical distinction on ICPs, which as a technical reality must come under ministerial-level authority. When service scope covers two or more provinces, the "department in charge of information industry under the State Council" (DII-SC) has final approval authority. DII-SC is also designated as the licensing authority for basic services. Lawyers interpreted DII-SC as the MII because China's WTO accession protocols instructed that China conform to the WTO Basic Telecom Agreement. The SLGI's management of ministerial disputes reveals the State Council's intention to retain discretionary authority. Interviews in Beijing with Andrew Starger, legal counsel, AT&T China (December 6, 2005, and September 13, 2006), and Aldrich (September 21, 2006).

62. Laperrouza (2006).

63. Horsley (2001), 68.

and the actual resources commanded by a company influenced how the Chinese government, in order to achieve its ultimate goals, willingly stretched rules without violating dominant modes of state control at the intermediate stage. The deft enforcement of China-specific service definitions on a company-by-company basis allowed the government to maximize the benefits of nonstate investment and minimize its costs to the state's overall control of telecommunications markets and network technology. In the first example, the State Council redefined what constitutes a VAS when it granted permission in 1999 to allow UNISITI, a JV between the U.S. company AT&T, Shanghai Telecom, and Shanghai Information Investment, to build and operate an IP network to serve the international business community in Pudong, Shanghai.[64] By redefining broadband network operation from a basic service to a VAS, the state differentiated UNISITI from the illegal CCFs in basic services. This allowed the MII to continue to observe the FDI ban in basic services, and scored a foreign relations victory by satisfying the U.S. State Department, which had lobbied aggressively on behalf of AT&T. Despite the high hopes of foreign investors, who touted this deal as a breakthrough agreement, the Chinese government has not approved another project of similar business scope involving a nonstate-owned carrier.[65]

UT Starcom's introduction of personal handy phone services (PHS), also known as "Xiao Ling Tong," in collaboration with fixed-line carriers in the late 1990s exemplifies another state-company bargain, which granted exceptions to the rule to serve a strategic purpose. Initially unsure whether PHS represented an attempt by fixed-line carriers to operate mobile services without permission, the MII halted PHS and instituted a ban against the unapproved construction and operation of PHS. When China Telecom and China Netcom failed to cease PHS trials, and UT Starcom, a promising equipment upstart owned and operated by an overseas Chinese businessman, lobbied on behalf of the fixed-line carriers to license PHS networks, the MII relented in June 2000 with the promulgation of the Notice on Regulating PHS Development and Operation.[66] The Notice sanctioned PHS as a "supplement to and extension of fixed-line telephony with small-scope, slow-mobility and wireless connections to the network," arguing that PHS served as a

---

64. The Framework Opinions about Opening Broadband Customer Premise Network (CPN) Market issued in June 2001 redefined broadband network operation. Interviews with Starger. See also Lu and Wong (2003), 72.

65. By the time the MII licensed UNISITI, domestic cable and broadband access companies, ISPs, and real estate companies, some of which are owned by other bureaucracies, including SARFT, had entered the broadband market as VAS providers. See Liu (2006), 112–13.

66. Interview in Beijing on December 6, 2005, with Zhe Zhang, government relations manager, UT Starcom. In late December 2009, the Securities and Exchange Commission charged UT Starcom under the Foreign Corrupt Practices Act for authorizing "millions of dollars in unlawful payments to foreign government officials in Asia," including China, between 2002 ad 2007. See SEC Press Release 2009–277 (December 31, 2009).

fixed-line alternative for users unable to afford more expensive mobile services.[67] The definition of PHS as fixed-line service subsidized fixed-line operators' revenues in the face of tremendous market gains by the mobile carriers, satisfying the government's imperative of maintaining competitive carriers.

TELECOMMUNICATIONS EQUIPMENT: DELEGATED REREGULATION

The Chinese government did not fully liberalize telecommunications equipment until the early 1990s, but when it did the gates opened widely. In contrast to the state's policy in telecommunication services, the state did not limit competition to state-owned players or the business scope of market players. Rather, the government unleashed competition to domestic private and foreign equipment makers alike and granted them access to terminal and consumer equipment markets. Taking a mixed orientation, the state introduced competition, assigned regulatory enforcement to provincial branch offices of the MII, and focused capacity on exploiting the technology possessed by foreign network equipment makers. The government used informal and formal methods to encourage technology transfers and promote domestic innovation and manufacturing, including partnerships with FDI to develop a homegrown networking standard. End users of consumer-based telecommunications products are further removed from the technology that activates networks; thus, the state expended fewer resources to regulate them. In general, regulatory measures in telecommunications equipment involved less state control than in services, but they exhibited a deliberate, not laissez-faire, approach to regulation.

Liberalization Phase (1993–1997)

By the early 1990s, many foreign telecommunications equipment makers had supplied China's telecommunications monopoly, its many branches, and the country's many dedicated networks for nearly a decade. These foreign equipment makers first entered Chinese markets as imports and after-sales support. Directive 56, issued in 1989, limited domestic production to three foreign equipment makers (Alcatel, Siemens, and NEC), but by 1993, in an effort to maximize local production and technology acquisition, the MPT began encouraging FDI and key component imports through low trade barriers and preferential tariff treatment. When the MPT licensed China Unicom and other service providers, the government also liberalized the equipment market and abolished the JV requirement. Foreign equipment makers interested in manufacturing domestically, however, were required to obtain approval from the state-owned Posts and Telecommunications Industry Corpora-

---

67. Dean (November 7, 2005) and Watts (November 3 and December 3, 2005) interviews.

tion (renamed as Putian).[68] Through its approval authority, Putian courted FDI and controlled the number of producers of fiber optic equipment. Motorola soon became the fourth foreign manufacturer approved by Putian to localize production and the only one to produce cellular equipment in the first few years of its entry.[69]

Foreign and domestic telecommunications equipment makers benefited from the licensing of network providers and the de facto entry of FDI in services between 1993 and 1998. A State Council study conducted in 2005 attributed the development of the domestic telecommunications equipment sector to the entry of China Unicom.[70] The "illegal" FDI flooding telecommunications services facilitated the construction of GSM networks, creating markets for equipment. Moreover, the fragmented and decentralized regulatory regime before the merger of the MEI and the MPT provided market opportunities for equipment makers serving public and dedicated networks as well as provincial telecommunications administrations.[71] By the late 1990s, major foreign telecommunications equipment makers, including Motorola, Nokia, Ericsson, Siemens, NEC, and Philips, had built production lines in joint ventures with Putian and other state-owned telecommunications equipment makers. In 2000, seventeen JVs and wholly foreign-owned networking equipment makers produced nearly 94 percent of China's telecommunications equipment; ten domestic companies manufactured the remaining 6.4 percent.[72]

Formal and Informal State Control

The government exercised a variety of formal and informal methods to balance the effects of market liberalization with its authority to promote sectoral development. To maximize technology spillovers, the state strongly encouraged FDI to form JVs with state-owned telecommunications equipment manufacturers.[73] The informal requirement helped transfer technology, financial resources, and management expertise to the fledgling domestic sector. To prepare state-owned telecommunications equipment makers for competition, the state corporatized and separated many of them from the bureaucracy through the 1990s.

The state also instituted a local content policy and issued rules on imports, exports, and production. In 1993, the MPT's investment guidelines required that production ventures supplying the domestic market source 60 to 70 percent of all their inputs locally.[74] Moreover, to maximize technology transfers in high-tech

---

68. Horsley (2001), 67.

69. Gorham and Chadran (1993), 22.

70. See Wu (2005).

71. Interview in Shanghai on April 26, 2005, with Robert Chen, former general manager for National Semiconductor's JV with Hong Kong Sunrise.

72. Horsley (2001), 66.

73. Interviews in Beijing on March 2 and September 14 and 21, 2006, with a former professor of post and telecommunications at Beijing University, now an official in the Ministry of Science and Technology, and with J. M. Chen (on September 19, 2006).

74. Gorham and Chadran (1993), 20.

products and market segments dominated by foreign equipment makers, the pre-WTO local content policy emphasized products with low technology content, placing few restrictions on high-tech imports. Restrictions on imports and production in low-tech product categories, including traditional telephone sets and switch equipment, protected domestic equipment makers.[75]

To control the technology that operates China's network infrastructure, government standards and quality certification bodies for the inspection of imports complicated market access in this formally liberalized sector. Networking and mobile equipment imports required type approval before they could be sold domestically; domestically manufactured equipment was not subject to the same approval process. Though the Chinese government signed the APEC Mutual Recognition Agreement for Conformity Assessment of Telecommunications Equipment in 1998, China-specific standards plagued the conformity assessment process, enhancing state control rather than streamlining regulation. Additionally, licensing schemes required equipment makers selling imported or domestically produced equipment, which connects to public networks, to register with the telecommunications ministry. To protect the domestic sector, the MII routinely used these permits to bar imported products that were also manufactured by domestic equipment makers.

Complementing these policies, export quotas limited FDI's access to the domestic market.[76] The MII's annual production goals show that, of the number of units targeted for production, 50 percent are expected for export and of the 50 percent targeted for domestic consumption only 40 percent are allocated to foreign-invested manufacturers. The sales figures for 2000 confirm that foreign-invested handset producers' exports comprised 46.7 percent of their total sales and 99 percent of total exports.[77]

Investment incentives further promoted domestic electronic and telecommunications equipment makers. They enjoyed discounts on sales-related taxes, including those on city maintenance and construction, consumption, and resources, and subsidies for education and community development. Manufacturers of telecommunications equipment also paid lower sales-related taxes than producers of other special purpose equipment and instruments, meters, and machinery used by the government.

Throughout the 1990s, the electronics and telecommunications equipment subsectors demonstrated the fastest growth in sales revenue within manufacturing.[78] China's top telecommunications equipment maker, Huawei, came of age in this investment and regulatory climate. Huawei's rise was also greatly assisted by the provincial telecommunications administrations' authority over procurement.[79] In 1988, Ren Zhengfei, a former director of the agency of the People's Liberation Army

75. Horsley (2001), 66.

76. Interview in Beijing on December 1, 2005, with John Chiang, former vice president of R&D, Motorola.

77. Horsley (2001), 66–67.

78. Lu and Wong (2003), 34.

79. Interview with Chiang (December 1, 2005).

responsible for telecommunications research, the PLA General Staff Department's Information Engineering Academy, founded Huawei to distribute business-based telephone exchanges.[80] Five years later, at around the same time the MPT licensed China Unicom, Huawei introduced C&C08, making it the first domestic telecommunications equipment maker to build a digital telephone switch. Today, Huawei sells branded networking equipment in Chinese and foreign markets, competing with other top mobile equipment makers. Huawei took advantage of the procurement authority of local governments and the PTAs by deploying its switches in small cities and rural areas, where it gained market share before tapping into city switch offices and toll service. Huawei also solicited investment from municipal governments and local telecommunications agencies to operate its sales branches. It further benefited from the introduction of competition in basic services as it supplied newly licensed networks. Furthermore, Huawei's close connection to the military meant that in addition to public networks, it supplied equipment to dedicated networks operated by the PLA. Huawei's corporate structure "is a matter of constant debate. Its equity is held by a number of state players, including the telecommunications operators, and it is widely believed that individuals at Huawei are nominees for other interests. Whether you call it state or private, Huawei is a fascinating example of the adaptability of the Chinese corporate model, among whose formative events are the invention of government venture capitalists in the late 1980s, of the 'group corporation' format, and of the 'limited shares' entity," explained Anne Stevenson-Yang, a telecommunications industry expert based in China.[81]

A Homegrown Networking Standard
In 1993, the China Academy of Telecommunications Technology (CATT), under the MPT, initiated the idea of China developing a global standard to showcase the modernization of the Chinese telecommunications industry as well as to offset the licensing fees that Chinese mobile carriers and equipment makers paid to foreign telecommunications equipment makers.[82] When the MPT proved unable to convince the National Development and Reform Commission of the merits of developing a homegrown standard, it appealed to the 863 Program administered by the Ministry of Science and Technology (MOST) for initial capital.[83] MPT also began searching for foreign partners to develop radio-based technologies, particularly high-capacity digital microwave and TDMA systems.[84]

---

80. See Medeiros et al. (2005).

81. Huawei's corporate board includes members of the Chinese Communist Party, according to the company's public affairs managers.

82. Interviews with former and current officials of the MII, MOST, and MPT in spring and October 2006.

83. For more on the role of the MOST's 863 program in China's "state-centric, highly nationalistic approach to technology indigenization," see Feigenbaum (1999 and 2003).

84. Gorham and Chadran (1993), 20, and interview in Beijing on September 16, 2006, with a former bureaucrat at the Ministry of Electronic Industry.

The MPT targeted Siemens AG, AT&T, Harris Corporation, and TRT Communications as potential partners; in the end, the resources that German equipment maker Siemens brought to the table jump-started efforts to develop a technical standard for third-generation telecommunications networks. After the EU adopted the WCDMA standard, Siemens jumped at another chance to take its TDD technology globally.[85] In the mid-1990s, Datang, owned and operated by the CATT, and Siemens began integrating the CATT's research on the SCDMA "smart antenna" technology and Siemens' TDD to develop TD-SCDMA. They formally submitted TD-SCDMA to the International Telecommunications Union (ITU) in 1998 for acceptance as an international 3G standard. The ITU's International Mobile Telecommunications–2000 and the Third Generation Partnership Project (3GPP) approved TD-SCDMA as a global standard two years later.

The development of TD-SCDMA took nearly a decade, and its commercialization took another decade. Chapter 5 details how the government exercised licensing powers to delay the introduction of other network technologies and restructured state-owned carriers yet again to maximize the market adoption of TD-SCDMA. Meanwhile, Siemens's "bargain" with the Chinese reaped rewards even though it divested most of its telecommunications business in 2007.[86] Siemens's contribution of initial network technology garnered it preferential market access across many electrical and electronic sectors, from automotive to transportation systems to power generation. In the transportation sector, Siemens helped build the high-speed train in Pudong and secured the bid to build another such train between Shanghai and Hangzhou. Siemens also contributed technology to the world's longest railway electrification from Harbin in Heilongjiang province to Dalian in Liaoning province. The government has also been slow in prosecuting Siemens for a bribery probe, which began in Europe but also implicated Siemens Information and Communication Mobile (ICM) unit's business in China. "Entry number 7277 in [Siemens] ICM's books shows that money from the mobile communications business was also sent to China, among other places," explained Christian Schmidt-Sommerfeld, a lawyer involved in the probe.[87] Moreover, KPMG auditors found that several million euros worth of consulting contracts were paid to PRC companies.[88]

---

85. Interview in Beijing on December 5, 2005, with Peter Weiss, president of Communications Group, Siemens Limited China.

86. Siemens divested its handset division to Taiwanese-owned BenQ in 2005, and in April 2007 it established a JV with Nokia in networking equipment. See "Silent Hands behind the iPhone," *New York Times* (July 18, 2007), and "Nokia Siemens Network Struggles Out the Gate," *CNET News.com* (April 2, 2007).

87. See "Siemens' Companies in China Involved in Bribery Scandal," *China TechNews* (May 20, 2007).

88. See "New Report Details Far-Reaching Corruption," *Spiegel Online* (January 29, 2007).

Reregulation Phase (1998–WTO Accession)

The creation of the SLGI and the MII enhanced state management of telecommunications. Between 1998 and 2000, the government reinforced some of the informal and formal mechanisms it already exercised to promote the domestic equipment sector before WTO accession unleashed more competition. Moreover, upon the divestiture of CCFs, the State Council issued a directive asking local operators of GSM networks (at that time, branches of China Telecom and China Unicom) to favor locally produced telephone equipment over imports. The directive coincided with the introduction of new mobile systems produced by state-owned Datang and Huawei, the PLA-backed equipment maker.[89] The merger of the MEI and MPT also granted all previously MEI-owned and affiliated equipment makers access to the procurement of MII-managed carriers. In addition to overseeing the carriers' procurement patterns and managing infrastructural development, the MII exercised its licensing authority over equipment makers to enhance its control over technology and calibrate the market share of foreign manufacturers. In December 1998, the Arrangements for the Approval of Network Access of Telecommunications Equipment required manufacturers to obtain a Network Access License and Network Access Identifier.

The MII also granted domestic equipment makers direct financial support, ranging from interest-free loans to R&D awards.[90] Direct financial subsidies, regulatory favoritism, including lax enforcement of quality standards and import processes, and the increasing availability of merchant wireless chipsets in the late 1990s, enabled relatively inexperienced but aggressive domestic entrants to enter handset manufacturing.[91] Direct financial subsidies are estimated to have reached $169 million in 1999.[92] In November 2000, the CCP created a 6 billion renminbi R&D fund under the control of the MII to support domestic firms involved in producing GSM, CDMA, and base-station equipment.[93] Additionally, public statements by MII and foreign trade ministry officials declared that no new foreign suppliers would be permitted to manufacture mobile phones before WTO entry.[94]

The government did not pick winners; rather, the MII supported aggressive competitors once they emerged.[95] Much like industrial textiles producers who tweaked their machines to produce nonwoven fabric (further elaborated on in chapter 7), many domestic handset producers originally specialized in consumer

89. Chan and Goldsmith (1999), 17.

90. In 1999, domestic handset companies had less than a 5 percent market share. See "Global Ambitions," *Far Eastern Economic Review* (June 15, 2000).

91. For more on the development of Chinese handset makers, see Cheung (2004), 70–74.

92. Naughton and Segal (2003), 181.

93. "China to Impose Quotas on Foreign-Funded Mobile Phone Manufacturing," *China Online* (November 6, 2000).

94. Horsley (2001), 66.

95. Naughton and Segal (2003), 181.

electronics, especially color televisions, and not telecommunications equipment. The majority of these handset manufacturers initially acquired technology through purchasing handset modules from foreign suppliers. As technical barriers to entry fell, more handset manufacturers entered the market and some began to invest in domestic R&D and rely less on modules and more on integrating purchased chipsets.[96] Charging low prices helped them seek comparative advantage in assembly, design, and systems engineering.

Notwithstanding the state's enhanced control over equipment makers and interventions to promote domestic industry, between 1998 and 2001 foreign equipment makers continued to enjoy relatively free markets. State-owned carriers carefully balanced procurement orders among foreign and domestic equipment makers. Moreover, the MII issued a rule in 2001 requiring formalized bidding processes for telecommunications procurement. The Chinese government also agreed not to treat the equipment purchases of state-owned carriers as government procurement in its WTO accession protocol agreement.[97] It also agreed to guarantee national treatment and loosen investment restrictions by implementing a "technology neutral" policy whereby service providers and their vendors can freely use and produce any technology and equipment. In this regulatory environment, "everyone enjoys a share of the pie," explained an executive at a foreign equipment maker.[98] Another former manager of foreign-invested manufacturers of networking and consumer equipment explained it a bit differently: "Everyone has food to eat, but no one is ever full."[99] We shall find in the post-WTO era that to promote domestic equipment makers and technology, procurement increasingly favored domestic equipment makers, state-owned equipment makers strategically utilized FDI to set China-specific standards, and the further consolidation of regulatory regimes to eliminate overlapping authorities offset liberalization and national treatment.

State-Company Bargains

In the context of market liberalization in telecommunications equipment and the adoption of varying formal and informal measures to compensate for it, foreign equipment makers' experiences in structuring market entry and gaining market share vary according to the willingness of their home countries to intervene, the resources that these companies bring to China, and the perceptions of the Chinese government at the highest levels. An example of home country influence is the

---

96. Suppliers included Motorola and Texas Instruments. See Dean (2003), 28–31.

97. China did not, however, commit to the WTO's voluntary Agreement on Government Procurement.

98. Quote from interview in Chongqing on May 19, 2006, with James Xi, vice president of Chongqing Ericsson Communications China. Xi previously served as executive of several other Ericsson JVs.

99. Robert Chen interview (April 26, 2005).

U.S. government's intervention during WTO negotiations on behalf of Qualcomm, which assured market share. A case of the impact of company resources is Siemens AG's collaboration with the Chinese government to develop an indigenous networking standard in exchange for unprecedented market access and another opportunity to contribute technology for a global standard. Moreover, the following story shows how, despite existing laws, the perception of the Chinese government at the highest levels influences equipment makers' investment structures.

Motorola became the first foreign company to invest in China as a WFOE when it received "tremendous good will" from the government for returning to China six months after the Tiananmen Square incident. The government initially balked when Motorola first proposed to invest without a domestic partner in 1992. However, the State Council relented after the Tianjin Economic Development Area (TEDA) signed a memorandum of understanding with Motorola shortly after the government publicly informed the equipment maker that China "is a free country with no government control."[100] The TEDA sealed the WFOE plan when Li Renhuan, a member of the Political Consultative Committee of the National People's Congress, met with TEDA and Motorola officials, who had their business proposal in hand. Li described the investment as a "win-win" proposition for all parties and said TEDA and Motorola's efforts were part of Deng Xiaoping's development initiative.

Other foreign equipment makers at that time were required to form JVs with state-owned equipment makers. Nokia formed a complicated investment structure with its state-owned partner, Putian.[101] Ericsson also partnered with Putian and other SOEs, including China Mobile, to operate in China.[102] In 2010, to leverage Putian's government and carrier connections, Nokia and Ericsson continue this practice though the law no longer requires them to do so and Putian's myriad subsidiaries produce and sell networking equipment and handsets that compete with its foreign partners. To enhance its relations with the government, Ericsson also invested in production capacity in the western interior in response to the Western Development Strategy.[103]

CONSOLIDATION OF STATE CONTROL
FOLLOWED LIBERALIZATION

The State Council introduced competition in telecommunications in 1993 by licensing state-owned carriers outside the ownership and management of the Ministry of

---

100. Interview with Chiang (December 1, 2005).
101. Interview in Beijing on April 20, 2006, with a manager at Nokia Capitel Telecom, which operated handset and networking equipment factories in Beijing, Dongguan, and Suzhou.
102. Interview with Xi (May 19, 2006).
103. Interview with Xi (May 19, 2006).

Post and Telecommunications. Between 1993 and 1998, to modernize the telecommunications infrastructure and create competitive carriers, the State Council did not enforce the official policy prohibiting FDI in basic services. Rather, provincial subsidiaries of the state-owned carriers courted FDI to construct new generation networks. The laissez-faire climate did not last long; the State Council created the Ministry of Information Industry in 1998 to consolidate state control of service and equipment subsectors. This enabled the state to proficiently and decisively intervene when government control of new entrants outside the traditional telecommunications hierarchy, preparation of state-owned carriers for international listing, and management of network development became state imperatives directly before WTO accession.

The nature of state intervention varied across subsectors according to a strategic value logic and structural sector characteristics. Believing that FDI undermined its ability to intervene in the carriers' operations when it sees fit and to maximize state returns from IPOs, the State Council terminated the "don't ask, don't tell" FDI policy in basic services and ordered the dismantling of special investment vehicles designed to circumvent the law. Foreign investors exited telecommunications services with individually negotiated compensation packages when their home countries chose not to intervene and the companies themselves lacked the resources to bring their cases to international courts.

The following is a list of the economy-wide and sector-specific rules that regulated telecommunications in the pre-WTO era:

- Law on Sino-Foreign Equity Joint Ventures (National People's Congress [NPC] 1979, revised 1990, 2001)
- Implementation rules on Law on Sino-Foreign Equity Joint Ventures (State Council [SC], 1983, 1986, 1987, 2001)
- Law on Wholly Foreign-Owned Enterprises (NPC, 1986, revised 2000)
- Three 90 Percents (SC, 1988)
- Directive 56 (on FDI in telecommunications equipment) (SC, 1989)
- Law on Sino-Foreign Cooperative Joint Ventures (NPC, 1988, 2000)
- Re-statement on Forbidding Joint Operation of Postal and Telecommunications Business with Foreign Companies (Ministry of Post and Telecommunications [MPT], 1992)
- Directive on Strengthening Regulations in the Management of Telecommunications Sector (SC, 1993)
- MPT regulation, which contained language that suggested foreign capital could be absorbed (MPT, 1994)
- Corporation Law (SC, 1994)
- Catalogue for the Guidance of Foreign Investment Industries (approved by SC and promulgated by Decree No. 5 of State Planning Commission [SPC], State Economic and Trade Commission [SETC], and Ministry of Foreign Trade and Economic Cooperation [MOFTEC] in 1995) (Revised edition approved by the State Council and promulgated by SPC, SETC and MOFTEC in 1997)

- Arrangements for the Approval of Network Access of Telecommunications Equipment (MII, 1998)
- Administrative Regulations for Telecommunications Services (SC, 2000)
- Notice on Regulating PHS Development and Operation (MII, 2000)
- Framework Opinions about Opening Broadband Customer Premise Network (CPN) Market (MII, 2001)

In contrast, reregulation in the VAS and equipment sectors varied from state entrenchment in network development. Because VAS providers operate on backbone infrastructure already owned and managed by the government, to promote domestic industry the State Council introduced competition, separated business from bureaucracy, corporatized state-owned players, and delegated regulatory enforcement to MII's provincial bureaus. It also permitted the de facto liberalization of FDI in progress in value-added services. The introduction of competition in services and market liberalization in equipment beginning in the late 1980s gave nonstate equipment makers unprecedented market access. The divestiture of FDI in basic services in 1998 did not terminate the state-owned carriers' need for equipment to modernize network infrastructure. In this environment, domestic and foreign equipment makers supplied and helped build new generation networks and set network standards. This gave the Chinese government a glimpse at the power over markets that ownership of technical standards entailed. To ensure market access, however, FDI remained in JVs with domestic equipment makers.

5

STATE-OWNED CARRIERS AND CENTRALLY LED REREGULATION OF TELECOMMUNICATIONS IN THE WTO ERA

China became the 143rd member of the World Trade Organization on December 11, 2001. The global telecommunications industry expected China, a signatory of the WTO Basic Telecommunications Agreement, to open its markets and erect liberal regulatory institutions. The Chinese government had other goals in mind, and the regulatory regime set up immediately prior to WTO accession laid the institutional foundations for government-business relations in the post-WTO period. Prior to WTO accession, the government's deliberate utilization of foreign direct investment after the initial introduction of competition and consolidation of regulatory control helped modernize telecommunications infrastructure and corporatize and restructure state-owned carriers in the span of less than a decade. Market and institutional reform also promoted domestic sector development in value-added services and telecommunications equipment. But China's telecommunications regime did not include competitive safeguards, streamlined interconnection, public availability of licensing criteria, regulatory independence, or transparent allocation and utilization of scarce resources.

The shift from universal to selective controls on the sectoral level and the divide between policy and practice became even more apparent in the post-WTO era when international law supposedly dictated market developments. Based on a strategic value logic and structured by sectoral characteristics, market liberalization and subsequent reregulation in telecommunications expanded the state's regulatory scope and enhanced its overall ability to meet sectoral goals. Having achieved network modernization, by exercising *strategic reregulation* the Chinese government moved to control, through administrative and corporate restructuring, the development of new generation networks and the technology that runs them. Moreover, to control information dissemination, curtail oversaturated markets, and develop

the domestic sector, the government exercised *expansionary reregulation* to supervise value-added services with China-specific definitions and a reinterpretation of
WTO commitments. FDI that enjoyed a de facto free market began to experience
state encroachment on their ownership structure and business scope. Sergey Brin,
Google's cofounder, noted that the "Chinese government is large, with millions of
officials, and varying points of view. But in matters of censorship, political speech
and Internet communications, . . . a totalitarian mentality . . . controls policy."[1]

Institutional and carrier restructuring in 2008 further reinforced the centralized, sector-specific regulatory regime, which governs Chinese telecommunications

TABLE 5.1. TEMPORAL VARIATION IN TELECOMMUNICATIONS REREGULATION		
	Emphasis	Year
Telecommunications basic services	Liberalization	1993–97: The government issued licenses to state-owned carriers outside of the telecommunications regime and legally prohibited but permitted FDI in practice.
	Reregulation	1998–2000: The government forced the divestment of FDI.
	Liberalization	2001: In WTO accession protocols, the government committed to a 49 percent ceiling in foreign equity investment.
	Reregulation	2002–10: The government managed and restructured state-owned carriers and limited FDI to less than 10 percent.
Telecommunications value-added services	Liberalization	1993–2000: The government legally prohibited FDI but, in practice, permitted them.
		2001: In WTO accession protocols, the government committed to a 50 percent FDI ceiling in foreign-invested joint ventures.
		2002–05: The government required special licenses but permitted FDI to operate as domestic companies in practice.
	Reregulation	2006–09: New rules threatened to regulate FDI business scope and ownership structure.
Telecommunications networking equipment	Liberalization	1993–97: The government extensively liberalized market entry.
	Reregulation	1998–2000: The government issued new equipment licensing rules.
	Liberalization	2001: WTO accession
	Reregulation	2002–10: The government controlled standards setting and network licenses.

---

1. "Interview: Sergey Brin on Google's China Move," *New York Times Bits Blog* (March 22, 2010).

with *deliberate reinforcement*. It possesses the consolidated power to direct and enforce policy and regularly intervene in sectoral development and on the company
level when national security imperatives dictate and when exposure to the international economy threatened the competitiveness of domestic industry. Table 5.1
charts the various phases of market liberalization and reregulation between the
breakup of the telecommunications monopoly in 1994 and the creation of integrated carriers through government-mandated restructuring in 2008. The East
Asian developmental state took a strikingly different approach to promote domestic
telecommunications, as illustrated by the mini case studies at the end of this chapter. In spite of important differences between Japan, South Korea, and Taiwan,
these countries limited competition rather than embraced it; they restricted FDI
and nurtured close relationships with domestic industry to achieve sectoral development rather than strategically utilizing both to accomplish national imperatives.

TELECOMMUNICATIONS SERVICES: EXPANSIONARY REREGULATION

The Telecommunications Regulations of 2000, issued shortly after the signing of
the WTO accession protocol agreements, provided the legal foundation for China's
interpretation of its WTO commitments in telecommunications. Upon WTO accession in 2001, the Chinese government issued four regulations that specifically
addressed market entry and business scope in telecommunications services. These
rules and their enforcement expanded regulatory authority and bureaucratic discretion to control information dissemination and technology and promote the
fledging domestic sector. By confining FDI to services specified in the WTO accession agreements and introducing market barriers, these new rules confirmed the
scope of liberalization as well as limited the salience of WTO commitments. The
Administrative Regulations on Foreign-Invested Telecommunications Enterprises
("Administrative Regulations") and Administrative Procedures for Telecommunications Business Operating Permits ("MII Decree 19") codified the phased liberalization of FDI with a 50 percent equity cap for the value-added services identified
in the WTO accession protocols.[2] MII Decree 19 also prohibited foreign investors from illegally providing telecommunications velue-added services by specifying licensing rules, including imposing minimum registered capital requirements
and limiting an industry-specific operating permit to the licensee and prohibiting
its transfer to third parties.[3] By so doing, it discredited the CCF model popular

---

2. WTO commitments obliged China to phase-in increases in foreign equity ownership in value-
added services over a period of two years ending on December 11, 2003. Foreign equity caps increased
to 50 percent after that date.

3. "The MII VAS Circular: A Summer of Uncertainty to Be followed by a Winter of Discontent?"
Lovell Client Bulletin (September 2006), 10.

between 1993 and 1998 in basic services and since the early 1990s among foreign-invested VAS providers to circumvent bureaucratic discretion.

The 2002 Catalogue for the Guidance of Foreign Investment Industries ("Second Catalogue") reiterated the phased liberalization of telecommunications sectors specified in the WTO agreements in addition to listing other subsectors open to foreign investment.[4] But the February before the complete phase-in of the WTO commitments, which was set for December 11, 2003, the MII departed from China's accession protocols and the Second Catalogue with the promulgation of the Notice Regarding Adjustment to the Catalogue of the Classification for Telecommunications Services ("Telecoms Catalogue"), which listed only the services specified in the Sino-U.S. WTO accession protocol as those subsectors open to FDI. A subsequent MII commentary, also excluding subsectors listed in the Second Catalogue, reiterated that China's liberalization obligations extended only to those services expressly listed in its WTO commitments. This distinction, in effect, barred FDI from the most attractive VAS sectors.

The Telecoms Catalogue also limited FDI to up to 50 percent of registered capital and required that investors obtain a foreign-invested telecommunications enterprise (FITE) license.[5] To operate legally, a FITE must "personally" obtain an operating license for each service provided to Chinese subscribers. In other words, foreign participation in VAS activities requires the incorporation of a Chinese legal entity with a Chinese JV partner and the completion of a discretionary approval process before the MII and the commerce ministry. The Telecoms Catalogue also reiterated China-specific service definitions stipulated in the Telecommunications Regulations.[6] The implications of these definitions soon became apparent.

Basic Services

In its WTO accession protocols, the Chinese government committed to a 49 percent foreign equity ceiling in basic services. Despite this commitment, foreign carriers attempted with varying success to enter Chinese markets by developing strategic relationships with state-owned carriers. FDI secured equity shares that do not constitute direct investment by international standards and engaged in technology and knowledge transfers in exchange for limited business scope in its market

---

4. The NDRC and the Ministry of Commerce issued subsequent editions of the *Catalogue for the Guidance of Foreign Investment Industries* in 2004 and 2007.

5. The MII exempted foreign investors who invest through a qualifying Hong Kong entity under the Closer Economic Partnership Arrangement from these restrictions. Presumably under this exemption, Hong Kong-invested companies, such as TOM Online, would be safe from a government crackdown on violators of these rules.

6. It defines basic services as the "provision of public network infrastructure and public data and voice transmission services," and value-added services as the use of a "public network to provide telecommunications and information services."

activities.[7] The Chinese government denied requests to increase equity investments beyond 9 percent and expand business scope beyond cross-border interconnection and joint marketing.

Notwithstanding these de facto restrictions, the state-owned carriers negotiated bargains with foreign carriers, which varied in investment structure, business scope, and level of influence. On the one hand, first movers did not have an advantage in obtaining better contractual terms or more influence in the direction of market liberalization.[8] In 2009, the business scope of Vodafone and AT&T had not changed since their pre-WTO entry. Through Vodafone's 3.2 percent equity stake in China Mobile, it provided international mobile voice and data services to its global customers operating within China and jointly marketed Vodafone-branded services to China Mobile's domestic customers.[9] The government also had not granted AT&T permission to expand its business scope beyond contracting with Chinese carriers and VAS providers to offer similarly limited mobile voice and data services to global customers.[10] Though the U.S. government helped secure the approval during WTO negotiations of UNISITI, AT&T's Sino-foreign JV, to operate a broadband network in Pudong, Shanghai, the Chinese government made UNISITI the norm and not the exception by defining UNISITI's business as value-added services. UNISITI remained, in 2010, the only foreign-invested JV to operate a telecommunications network in China.[11]

On the other hand, later entrants secured bargains that FDI hoped would presage market footholds. Industry insiders intimated that fixed-line carrier China Netcom had ceded a comparatively high 9.9 percent equity stake to Telefónica in exchange for the Spanish carrier's vast experience in foreign markets and Telefónica's willingness to share its outside assets to help achieve Netcom's interests.[12] For example, Telefónica operates in Latin America, where the Chinese government and companies have been busy forging strategic links. Additionally, not long after its foray into China's telecommunications market, Telefónica became a proxy in China's interference in Hong Kong's business affairs when Hong Kong business tycoons attempted to trade ownership stakes for market share in China. Although

---

7. The global standard distinguishes FDI from foreign equity investment at 10 percent or more ownership or voting power of an enterprise by a single foreign investor.

8. China's first foreign-invested investment bank, CICC, did not secure the most lucrative investment deals. Conversation on March 12, 2007, in San Francisco with Jack Wadsworth, former Chairman of Morgan Stanley Asia. See also the survey of reregulation in financial services in chapter 8.

9. Interview in Beijing on April 16, 2006, with project manager of Vodafone China. Vodafone planned to sell its China stakes to possibly one or more institutional investors in late 2010 according to "Vodafone Selling China Mobile Stake for £4.3bn," *Financial Times* (September 7, 2010).

10. Starger interviews (December 6, 2005, and September 13, 2006).

11. See also Harwit (2004 and 2005).

12. Telefónica's stake, which it increased from 5 percent in 2005, represented the highest foreign interest in a Chinese carrier. The Spanish carrier gained a seat on the board of Netcom's listed subsidiary. See "Telefónica Raises Stake in China Netcom," *Computer Business Review* (November 16, 2005).

China Netcom opposed the bids of Australia's Macquarie Bank and U.S.-based Texas Pacific Group for PCCW, Hong Kong's largest carrier, on the grounds that strategic telecommunications assets should not be controlled by foreign investors, it attempted to control PCCW by pooling its existing 2 percent stake in PCCW with Telefónica's 8 percent stake in a special purpose vehicle set up by a consortium led by Hong Kong financiers Francis Leung and Li Ka-shing, the father of Richard Li, the chairman and executive director of PCCW Limited. With 28 percent control of PCCW, China Netcom would have been just short of the 30 percent required by the Hong Kong authorities for triggering a formal takeover. In the end, however, the intriguing behind-the-scenes political maneuver concluded when Netcom failed to take over PCCW.[13]

For Telefónica's part, though regulation and business practice limited its equity to 9 percent and its business scope to collaboration in equipment purchasing, research and development, marketing, and business strategies, China Netcom's listed arm had the largest number of independent directors and non-Chinese board members among the state-owned carriers and appeared more open to nonstate influence.[14] Before the issuance of third generation (3G) network licenses in 2009, industry insiders had anticipated that MII would award China Netcom, which merged with China Unicom in the 2008 restructuring, a 3G license that would garner Telefónica a foothold in China's 3G markets.[15]

In June 2006 another later entrant, SK Telecom, purchased convertible bonds that transferred into a 6.7 percent stake in China Unicom in exchange for "a strategic alliance" between the two companies in introducing handsets and developing China Unicom's CDMA and 3G networks. In 2008, Telefónica and SK Telecom's equity shares became diluted, however, when China Netcom merged with China Unicom in a state-mandated industry-wide restructuring to create globally competitive integrated carriers and maintain control of network development so that it favored homegrown technology.

Intervention to Achieve Sectoral and Political Goals
Further eroding its liberalizing commitments in telecommunications, the government regularly intervened in service markets to achieve sectoral and political goals. Discretionary licensing, personnel rotation, and corporate and industry restructuring directed from the very top reveal the embeddedness of the state in a strategic industry. The strategic value logic explains the dominant approach of state con-

---

13. "Banker Blames Media for PCCW Takeover Deal Collapse," *Teleogeography* (November 30, 2006).

14. Of China Netcom's thirteen directors, seven were outsiders; China Telecom had four.

15. See "Telefónica to Buy China Netcom Stake for $290m," *Financial Times* (July 7, 2005), and "Rumor: Telecom Restructuring to Result in Two Operators," *China Business News* (March 4, 2008). In 2010, Telefónica held 8.37 percent of the public shares of China Unicom, which received a license to operate a 3G WCDMA network.

trol in telecommunications and subsectoral variation within it. The organization of central-level bureaucracies, including the MOST, National Development and Reform Commission (NDRC), State-Owned Assets Supervision and Administration Commission (SASAC), and MII, shaped the actual timing and outcome of state intervention.

The Chinese government exercised discretionary licensing to fulfill bilateral commitments, balance competition between state-owned carriers, and control network development. It licensed the CDMA network technology and obliged one of its carriers to adopt the technology after the Sino-U.S. WTO accession protocol negotiations. Moreover, to balance fierce competition between carriers, which decreased state sector revenue growth and profits, the government permitted less competitive new-entrant carriers to introduce select services outside the business scope of their original operating licenses.[16] Furthermore, to control network development in favor of homegrown technology, the MII withheld licensing from 3G networks for nearly a decade.

The central government also mandated personnel changes and pressured the carriers to share revenue in order to balance competition and retain final management control. Dubbed playing "musical chairs," the State Council rotated the executives of the carriers during periodic personnel changes. The government also required the carriers, along with other central-level SOEs, to submit budgets along with the government's share of their profits.[17]

The frequency of corporate reorganization throughout the 2000s reveals the growing bureaucratic influence of SASAC, the legal owner of the corporatized parent carriers and majority shareholder in the carriers' listed subsidiaries. As the bureaucracy most sensitive to the revenue windfalls that Chinese companies lose from imports, foreign competition in domestic markets, and royalty fees for the licensing of foreign technology, SASAC orchestrated periodic leadership changes to halt the fierce price wars between the carriers and to "remind foreign investors of the strength of the government's hand in China's strategic industries."[18] Calling SASAC the "mother-in-law and protector of SOEs," one former Unicom executive observed, "The SASAC does not want to see competition and would be happy if the operators merged together because it means more money for the government." He also interpreted the shuffling of corporate management as the SASAC's attempt to unseat the MPT faction within the telecommunications regime. The majority of the carriers' executives served in the former telecommunications bureaucracy, although the balance of power between the two factions shifted in 2003 with the appointment of Wang Xudong, a former MEI official, as MII minister.[19]

---

16. Chapter 4 examines episodes related to the introduction of these services in greater detail.
17. See "Telecoms Operators to Share Profit with State," *Communications Weekly* (June 15, 2007).
18. Li interview (February 27, 2006).
19. Wang served as the CCP secretary of Hebei immediately prior to becoming head of MII. He became the head of the State Electricity Regulatory Commission when the MII became the MIIT.

In the post-WTO era, the central government once again employed institutional and industry-wide restructuring in order to create more competitive carriers and to ensure the smooth implementation of homegrown technology. The actual restructuring took years to reach fruition because the MII, SASAC, and NDRC disagreed about whether carriers should provide integrated services and how to maximize the interests of all stakeholders, and importantly, they waited for the technical maturity of TD-SCDMA.[20] In March 2008, consolidating bureaucratic and industrial interests, the government created the Ministry of Industry and Information Technology (MIIT), which merged the MII and other industry-specific departments. Shortly thereafter, on May 24, 2008, the MIIT, the NDRC, and the Ministry of Finance announced the creation of three integrated carriers and the government's plan to grant 3G licenses upon the completion of carrier restructuring.[21] According to plan, China Telecom purchased China Unicom's CDMA network and took control of China Satellite Communications' fixed-line network. The remnant of China Unicom, including its GSM network, joined with China Netcom. China Mobile took control of China Railcom's fixed-line network and was assigned the commercialization of TD-SCDMA. Industry insiders speculated that, for its troubles, the government would allow China Mobile to operate broadband services.[22]

The principal goals of the carrier restructuring reflected the deliberate orientation of the dominant pattern of reregulation in telecommunications. The restructuring created three market competitors, owned and managed by the government, of comparable strength and scale with regard to nationwide network resources and service operation capabilities. It also accomplished the commercialization of TD-SCDMA. In recent years, China Telecom and China Netcom had both suffered as consumers defected to mobile phones for local calls and to cheap Internet-based services for long-distance calls. Moreover, aggressive marketing, network expansion, and price competition through innovative tariff schemes, which subsidized users and skirted NDRC's pricing regulation, led to a decrease in the usage of outgoing minutes on the fixed-lined networks and an increase in the number of mobile users. Of the two mobile carriers, China Mobile, the incumbent, emerged as the stronger competitor; unsurprisingly, the state assigned the rollout of TD-SCDMA to it. "Operators are out for themselves," as one informant explained. "There is redundant infrastructure everywhere because the carriers do not share towers for their base stations. In China, they not only don't share, they cut each other's wires!"[23] In this "chaotic" market landscape, the creation of the MIIT, a supramin-

20. Li conversation (February 26, 2006).

21. They issued the Circular on Three Ministries' Plan to Deepen the Reform of Telecommunications Restructuring. See "China Orders 6 Telecoms to Merge Their Assets," *Bloomberg News* (May 26, 2008).

22. Dean interview (September 23, 2008), Aldrich interview (September 24, 2008), and Chiang interview (September 29, 2008).

23. Li conversation (February 26, 2006).

istry, which incorporates the Commission of Science, Technology, and Industry for National Defense and the State Council Informatization Office, further ensured the governance of telecommunications according to a strategic value logic. Price controls became among one of MIIT's priority actions. To promote TD-SCDMA, it decided on a preferential policy for its inter-network fee settlement (e.g., calls made from a TD-SCDMA phone to another TD-SCDMA subscriber will be as much as 80 percent lower than calls made by China Mobile's non-TD-SCDMA subscribers). Moreover, to ensure that fixed-line networks remain competitive, the MIIT further lowered settlement fees for fixed-line phones.[24]

Value-Added Services

For the first half decade after WTO accession, state control in VAS sectors varied from the multifaceted state encroachment witnessed in basic services. For the first five years after WTO accession, the state did not differentiate between domestic and foreign-invested VAS enterprises nor did it micromanage their business scope. Notably, the MII did not enforce the requirement that foreign-invested VAS providers enter into a JV with a domestic provider, among other requirements, to obtain a foreign-invested telecommunications enterprise license. Few bothered to apply for a FITE license because of long wait times and the discretionary nature of approvals.[25] The MII also did not enforce the prohibition against FDI in Internet content provision. In short, the state did not scrutinize ownership and business scope until policing information flows and ordering competition became state imperatives in 2004.

Most foreign-invested VAS providers entered China by eschewing legal procedures. To skirt the Administrative Regulations and the MII Decree 19, many foreign-invested VAS providers adopted the holding company structure, a popular market entry model widely referred to as the "Sina.com Model." They entered VAS markets using the license of their registered WFOE's domestic contractor.[26] For example, using the license of a Chinese contractor, NTT Communications solved Japanese-invested companies' IT-related problems, such as Internet security, a case where algorithms require approval from the MII.[27] NTT Communications developed alliances with domestic VAS providers to expand its business scope

24. "MIIT Sets TD-SCDMA Inter-Network Settlement Fees," *Marbridge Daily* (December 27, 2009).

25. The Regulations on the License for Operation of Telecommunications Business and Regulations on Foreign-Invested Telecommunications Enterprises specified up to ninety days for the review of VAS licenses. In practice, the wait time was much longer.

26. IPO documents reveal that companies commonly use the holding company structure to circumvent entry rules in China. Also Walker interview (November 9, 2005).

27. Interview in Shanghai on May 24, 2005, with Qi Wei, vice president, NTT Communications China.

without actually obtaining a FITE.[28] In addition to NTT Communications, high-profile American-owned foreign-invested VAS providers, such as E-Bay, Yahoo, and Google, also operated using the licenses of Chinese contractors. Google, for example, operated using the license of its domestic partner, Ganji.com, with the full awareness of the MII until June 2007 when the MII issued a FITE to the company.[29] Smaller, less high-profile companies, such as 21 Communications and Blue Bamboo, formed with the express purpose of targeting Chinese markets and operated with a similar market entry model. The government did not enforce the rules until state imperatives shifted from sectoral development to information control.

The Telecommunications Regulations' relinquishment of regulatory authority of VAS markets to the MII's provincial branches influenced the manner in which VAS markets proliferated. The TABs' exercise of their discretionary licensing authority resulted in overcrowded and saturated markets; this is a common phenomenon in nonstrategic sectors, such as cotton and chemical fiber processing (investigated in chapters 6 and 7), which experienced even less or no central oversight. Adding to the exploding market are complex business relationships between VAS providers and the carriers.[30] This has created a symbiotic situation where VAS providers were at the mercy of the carriers, and the carriers, in turn, increasingly became reliant on the revenue generated from the data services offered by service and content providers (SPs).[31] One industry insider described VAS markets as the "wild, wild West."[32]

Reregulation Phase (2004–2009)

The State Council and the MII did not intervene to regulate VAS markets until controlling information to maintain social stability and ensuring healthy sectoral development became state imperatives.[33] The exploding number of VAS providers and SP agreements gave rise to an influx of subscriber complaints about overbilling, inability to cancel service subscriptions, inappropriate content, and wireless spam. Also disruptive to the state were a series of large anti-Japanese, anti–industrial pollution, and anti–political corruption protests in 2004 and 2005, which were swiftly organized and publicized via Internet chat rooms, instant and text messages, and

---

28. See "NTT Communications, Chinacache Partner for CDN Services," *Digital Media Asia* (February 6, 2007).

29. See "Google Secures Own ICP License," *21st Century Business Herald* (June 17, 2007). Google's ICP license, which officially expires in 2012, requires annual review.

30. Because service and content providers market their products and services through the carriers, websites, and traditional media, they come under the regulatory purview of the carriers, MII, and SARFT.

31. *Deutsch Bank Report* (2005), 9.

32. Interview in Beijing on March 2, 2006, with a government bureaucrat at MOST.

33. Interviews between October 2005 and 2006 with former and current MII and MOST officials.

other forms of mobile communication. The state believed that information dissemination via wireless VAS fomented citizen discontent and mobilized social protest. In addition, these protests created demonstration effects that the state ultimately felt were detrimental to foreign economic relations and internal political stability. For example, a labor strike in a Japanese company in the Pearl River delta originally organized in response to unfair wages expanded the company-specific grievances to embrace the dispute over Japanese history book's coverage of China, which mobilized the anti-Japanese protests in April 2005.[34] "Frustrated that it lacked control over the membership of the social organizations active on Internet sites and wireless platforms, the government concluded that controlling the business of VAS is a critical component of restricting information dissemination and, therefore, social organization."[35]

In a shift in how information dissemination had been controlled, the MII began focusing bureaucratic energies on enhancing its regulatory authority in restricting the market entry of VAS providers through centralizing license approvals, enforcing licensing rules, regulating business scope and interactions with consumers, and expanding carrier oversight of SPs.[36] Press and publication administration director Long Xinmin remarked that "advanced network technologies, such as blogging and webcasting, have been mounting new challenges to the government's ability to supervise the Internet."[37] These new rules allowed the state to restrict content *before* it was created. "It is quicker, more efficient, and a better use of limited resources to control the business operating the technology media on which the content is delivered," said a former MII official.[38]

Exercising Licensing Powers

Reinterpreting a geographical distinction stipulated in the Telecommunications Regulations, the MII began enforcing VAS licensing rules in 2004. The MII issued a rule that refined the principle to mean that an intraprovincial VAS provider delivers services to subscribers located in one province while an interprovincial VAS provider delivers services distributed to subscribers in more than one province.

---

34. Interview in Shanghai on April 19, 2005, with Xu Zhang, Milan Zhu, and Zhi Zhang, assistant directors of JETRO-Shanghai.

35. Interview on September 15, 2006, in Beijing, with the chief executive officer of a value-added service provider.

36. The state typically employs myriad security agencies, including an Internet police task force to monitor and censor content in an Internet monitoring system known as the "Great Firewall of China." Moreover, fourteen government organizations, including the MII, the Ministry of Culture, the Ministry of Public Security, and the People's Bank of China, regulate Internet cafés and online games. Content rules also targeted the Internet.

37. Quote from "China to Expand 'Great Internet Firewall,'" *Agence France-Presse* (March 13, 2007).

38. Interview in Beijing on September 21, 2006, with former official at the Ministry of Information Industry.

The rule obligated Internet content providers operating in more than one province to acquire a nationwide ICP license before entering a SP agreement with a carrier. In practice and as a technical reality, all mobile services extend nationwide; thus, all VAS providers by default must apply for a national license. To qualify, ICPs register 10 million renminbi (RMB) in capital, present evidence of six branch offices in at least two provinces, and submit a business plan deemed convincing by the MII. Additionally, the MII used a long waiting list to delay approvals.

One foreign observer described the geographical distinction as a "bricks and mortar" view of telecommunications that has "flummoxed industry observers already reeling from the news that ICP activities necessitate a telecommunications license."[39] The CEO of a foreign-invested VAS provider interpreted these requirements as the state's attempt to promote domestic industry and attract FDI to less developed regions.[40]

Proliferation of Rules Governing Service Providers

"Consumer dissatisfaction" justified the expansion of regulatory control over the activities of service and content providers in 2005.[41] New rules directly regulated SPs and increased the carriers' authority over them. The MII standardized fees in mobile information services and set up systems of rewards and punishments based on discretionary evaluation of SPs' income and trustworthiness on matters such as unclear tariffs and forced subscriptions. The Special Governing Program on Wireless Information Services, a central complaint-processing center, enabled users to report SPs directly to the MII, which reviewed the level of complaints periodically and used the complaints as a basis for assessing fines or recalling licenses. The MII also began requiring that carriers provide itemized billing to customers, so they could easily contact SPs or identify SPs for complaints. Furthermore, the MII created a database of provider codes, which it unified under a four-code system, making it easier to terminate an SP's service.[42] It also began to regularly publish blacklists of offending service providers.[43]

Not to be outdone, the state issued new rules regulating business scope that required that VAS providers submit detailed information for every service introduced and endure a lengthy approval period. Under this strict regime, low-performing

---

39. Aldrich (2006), 11.

40. Interview in Shanghai on October 29, 2008.

41. Interviews with Watts (November 3 and December 3, 2005).

42. According to a Beijing-based wireless VAS provider, the MII and mobile operators launched a nationwide investigation of SP tariffs for SMS, mobile Internet, and IVR services. See also "MII to Regulate SPs Again in March," *Beijing News* (March 8, 2007).

43. Domestic media predicted as much as 30 percent of China's VAS providers would fail due to this policy shift. See "China Publishes Blacklist of 102 Wireless Service Providers," *ChinaCSR.com* (July 28, 2006).

SPs were subject to removal from the market. Importantly, these rules empowered provincial TAB administrators to scrutinize the justification for each service included in the business plan each applicant must submit. Many TAB administrators exercised this and other discretionary powers to achieve personal or local goals.[44] For example, Xiamen in Fujian Province considered banning anonymous Internet postings when a demonstration prevented the construction of a $1.4 billion chemical plant.[45]

Further reinforcing its control of information dissemination, the State Council and the MII, one of eight government departments involved in regulating content, released the Notice Concerning the Special Project for the Development, Administration, and Standardization of Charging for and Collection of Fees for Mobile Information Services Business (the June 2006 Notice). The June 2006 Notice officially assigned the carriers regulatory authority over their SPs and further reinforced and legitimized the MII and the carriers' dual regulation of VAS providers.[46] It also authorized the carriers to conduct a review of SP activities and to standardize the SPs' fee collection. This expanded authority provided the carriers opportunities for financial gain, more avenues to compete with one another, and incentives to assist the state in enhancing control over VAS.

Eager to use the state-mandated cultural cleanup as a pretext for strengthening their hand against content subcontractors, the carriers acted quickly.[47] The carriers introduced policies and technology to improve their subscribers' "customer service." China Mobile introduced a new technical platform, which enhanced its control of the VAS providers operating on its network.[48] China Mobile and China Unicom also imposed increasingly strict rules, which fined and suspended SPs as they found necessary.[49] Moreover, China Mobile and China Unicom, without consent from their SPs, notified subscribers of the carriers' plan to provide them with a one-month free trial period for "packaged information services." China Mobile further allowed subscribers to opt out of previously subscribed content services via a short message service (SMS) notification. It also issued a policy specifying that if two or more provincial TABs have banned an SP's services, it would end that SP's operation over its entire network. China Telecom also established similar rules to regulate PHS value-added services, including double-confirmation rules

---

44. Interviews in Shanghai and Beijing with general managers of VAS providers between 2005 and 2008.

45. See "China: City Weighs Ban on Online Anonymity," Associated Press (July 7, 2007).

46. Interview with Watts (November 3, 2005).

47. Interviews with Dean (October 24 and November 7, 2005).

48. The software also has the capability of stopping user-generated content from being proliferated. Also see "China Internet Wireless VAS: The Second Coming; Initiating with Overweight," *Deutsch Bank Technology Software and Services Report* (July 14, 2005).

49. According to the MII, the carriers fined SPs a total of RMB 4.3 million during a three-month period in spring 2006. See *Marbridge Weekly* (May 12, 2006).

for monthly subscriptions and SMS packages, and a tariff ceiling for monthly SMS fees.[50]

The carriers' regulatory authority over the SPs also led to allegations of corruption among general managers of the data departments of the carriers. Zhang Chunjiang, who served as party secretary and general manager of China Netcom before the 2008 telecommunications restructuring assigned him as party secretary and deputy general manager of China Mobile, became the highest ranking senior telecommunications official to fall from grace. The relationship between Zhang's personal connections to the founder of Ultrapower Software, a China Mobile SP, and financial wrongdoing came under scrutiny as Ultrapower prepared to list on the Shenzhen stock exchange.[51] The National Audit Office also investigated other data department heads; they allegedly abused their authority by participating in SP operations and investing in or owning shares in SPs.[52]

The carriers' unilateral revision of the subscription agreement terms provoked strong complaints from domestic and foreign-invested VAS providers alike, which stood to see their revenues sharply cut by these measures. Foreign-invested VAS providers found their business models incapacitated as revenue sharing arrangements with domestic license holders suffered from decreased subscription fees.[53] In response to the enhancement of the state's bureaucratic authority and the carriers' encroachment on SP activities, domestic and foreign-invested VAS providers engaged in self-censorship, entered into bargains with the state and government-affiliated organizations to stay in operation, and collectively petitioned the state. "All Chinese blog-hosting companies are required by government regulators to censor their users' content in order to keep their business licenses. . . . They all make different choices not only about how to implement censorship requirements, but also how to treat the users who get censored," explained Rebecca MacKinnon, assistant professor of journalism and media studies at the University of Hong Kong, who conducted a study of Chinese blog censorship.[54]

Cracking Down on "Illegal" Ownership Structures

In July 2006, the state further enhanced its control over VAS markets with the release of the Circular on Strengthening the Administration of the Provision of

---

50. "Shanghai Telecom Toughens SP Service Regulations," *Pacific Epoch Newswires* (July 14, 2006).

51. See "Old Chums and a Troubled Telecom Chief," *Caixin* (February 3, 2010). Industry insiders claim that the "serious disciplinary breach," a euphemism for corruption, investigated by SASAC began during Zhang's tenure as chairman of China Netcom Group before its merger with China Unicom.

52. "Rumor: Sichuan Mobile Data GM Disappears in Investigation," *Marbridge Daily* (March 31, 2010) and "Rumor: China's Audit Office Investigating SPs," *Marbridge Daily* (March 30, 2010).

53. Interview with Aldrich (September 21, 2006).

54. MacKinnon and her team found that the government outsources domestic web censorship to the private sector, and the system of managing user-generated Web content appears to follow a similar logic and approach as the system for controlling news media.

Value-Added Telecommunications Services Involving Foreign Investment ("VAS Circular"). The VAS Circular signaled the government's intention to crack down on illegal forms of investment, officially centralized the VAS licensure process, and favored the domestic over the foreign sector. Several stipulations in the VAS Circular questioned the legality of the CCF model, the preferred market entry model among foreign investors, and a final provision retained licensure approval at the ministerial level. The VAS Circular reiterated the principle, going back to MII Decree 19, which stipulated that domestic VAS providers may not "lease, lend, transfer, or resell operating permits to foreign investors in any disguised form." Underscoring that a holder of an operating permit cannot transfer its license to a third party, the VAS Circular affected FDI the most; as of the VAS Circular's issuance, the MII had approved only five FITE licenses.

Moreover, violating the WTO Basic Telecommunications Agreement's requirement of fair allocation and use of scarce allocations, the VAS Circular expressly limited the domain names and registered trademarks used by a VAS provider to those belonging to the subject company or its shareholders and required that the VAS provider set up premises and facilities in a manner consistent with its approved business scope.[55] Up until that point, the MII rarely enforced the rule that each Internet website register its owners, IP address, domain, and host.[56] Foreign investors interpreted the new limits on the use of domain and trademark registration and the requirement of facilities consistent with approved business scope as the government purposely restricting foreign investors to providing technical services, which existing laws severely curtailed. They further interpreted these rules as attempts to control intellectual property and technology so as to retain economic margins in Chinese hands.[57]

The VAS Circular also invoked the Telecommunications Regulations' geographical distinction and expanded upon Decree 19 by defining "premises and facilities" to mean that the applicant must set them up in accordance with the geographical areas covered by its operating permit.[58] Foreign investors viewed the requirement that a VAS provider set up premises and facilities in a manner consistent with its approved business scope as unreasonable for those VAS providers that held nationwide SP contracts with carriers that had little knowledge of local conditions and few local connections. This stipulation further invoked the requirement of nationwide

---

55. *Wilmer Hale Briefing Series* (September 2006), 2.

56. In June 2007, the MII claimed that 90 percent of China's 840,000 websites had complied. See "Website Real Name Registration System Nears Completion," *XinhuaNet* (June 20, 2007). New rules, such as the Communications Short Message Service Management Measure, also required mobile phone users to register phones with their real names.

57. Conversations in Beijing in September 2006 with Anne Stevenson-Yang and Tom Melcher, executives of Blue Bamboo Ventures, a foreign-invested ICP, now a subsidiary of the media and trading company Global Sources.

58. The reference to intraprovincial and interprovincial value-added services has always struck foreign observers as a counterintuitive description of mobile telecommunications services.

offices, or at least extensive offices, for the interprovincial operating permit, which VAS providers wishing to operate across more than two provinces must acquire.[59] Given that most VAS providers conducted their business from one location, this requirement worried participants of CCFs. If enforced, the nationwide license would likely be a precondition for nationwide SP agreements with the carriers. To preempt contractual problems with the carriers, many foreign-invested VAS providers responded to the 2004 rule on nationwide operating licenses by working with their Chinese partners to obtain a license. After expending resources and time, the owners of the foreign-invested 21 Communications gained approval for the nationwide operating license in late 2005. Its CEO remarked, "The national license is worth a lot of money because ICPs that cannot meet the odious requirements are otherwise 'landlocked'." ICPs feared that if they did not comply, they would be confined to signing SP contracts that geographically restricted their services.

Furthermore, the VAS Circular required VAS providers planning to list offshore (such as with a holding company) to undergo examination for consent by, and to obtain approval from, the State Council's department in charge of information industry (presumably the MII) in accordance with relevant state regulations.[60] The VAS Circular did not clarify whether VAS providers would be required to demonstrate full compliance with the rule before obtaining approval for the holding company structure. Industry experts speculated that this ambiguity may have been the state's attempt to retain discretionary control, leaving open the possibility of making exceptions that would allow Chinese-founded companies to continue full or partial utilization of this parallel ownership structure in order to preserve their ability to attract foreign investment and list overseas.[61] If these exceptions favored Chinese companies, YeePay, an electronic payment company started by Chinese returnees from the United States, would be able to continue its market practice while Blue Bamboo Ventures, founded by Americans living in Beijing and now a subsidiary of the media and trading company Global Sources, would have to restructure. Chen Yu, the vice president of marketing at YeePay, did not expect the rule changes to affect its business in the near future.[62]

Uneven Enforcement of New Rules
The lower strategic value of value-added services meant that even though the VAS Circular's crackdown on illegal FDI mirrored the steps taken between 1998 and

---

59. The interprovincial operating permit involves a discretionary approval process, a capital requirement of RMB 10 million, proof of six branch offices, and a "convincing" business plan.

60. Similar to the Telecommunications Regulations, the VAS Circular does not specify whether this office is the MII or the State Leading Group on Informationization or some other group.

61. *Wilmer Hale Briefing Series* (September 2006), 2.

62. Interview on February 22, 2006, in Beijing, with Chen Yu, vice president of marketing for YeePay. YeePay's business model straddled two regulatory environments, value-added services in telecommunications and financial services.

2001 to eradicate illegal FDI in basic services, the state failed to use similar resolve and bureaucratic resources to enforce these measures. The government's control of VAS markets was not primarily about the MII taking steps to shut out foreign investment indefinitely. Rather, rules on licensing, business scope, and owner- ship structure aimed to control information dissemination and ensure the orderly development of VAS markets. The VAS Circular left open that "noncompliance with the investment procedures provides, at least theoretically, the opportunity to restructure a project so as to be compliant with the regulatory regime," ex- plained Michael Aldrich, a Beijing-based lawyer who had advised foreign-invested VAS providers.[63] Another industry insider observed that the MII sought "to put the house in order, taking the opportunity to slap around ICPs it want[ed] to order" and "[would] issue operating permits when Sina and Sohu restructure into JVs . . . if that even happens."[64] Evidently, the VAS Circular assigned the supervi- sion of self-examination and self-correction by noncompliant companies to TABs and required that they focus only on VAS providers that receive a large number of complaints from consumers.

That no major public cases of government crackdown resulted from the VAS Circular further confirms that the government never intended to eradicate FDI in VAS. The privatization of TOM Online provided fodder for rumors, but "it's more likely a business decision on the part of the Li Ka-shing empire to shift its fast and loose approach" and not a company-initiated restructuring decision affected by the VAS Circular.[65] "The VAS Circular served as a warning only of the government's capacity to crack down," remarked the CEO of a foreign-invested VAS provider. "At the end, the government closed down only VAS providers that engaged in offensive spamming, which it views as detrimental to domestic sector development."[66] For example, in March 2008, following the CCTV's broadcast of its World Consumer Rights Day program, which exposed mobile spam creators, China Mobile revoked its SP contract with Focus Wireless.[67] In 2010, foreign-invested VAS providers con- tinued to operate as WFOEs with business permits held by its Chinese contractors. "The WTO model is used very rarely except by big and high-profile companies with resources to pay legal fees to wait for a license. Still, though the government has lowered the capital requirement and not cracked down on CCFs, it has not eliminated its posturing on FITE licenses," explained Ted Dean, cofounder and managing director of BDA Consulting in Beijing.[68]

---

63. Aldrich interview (September 21, 2006).

64. Interview in Shanghai in September 2006 with an executive of a foreign-invested VAS provider.

65. Interview with Aldrich (September 24, 2008).

66. Interview on October 29, 2008, with the CEO of a Shanghai-based foreign-invested VAS provider.

67. See "Rumor: Focus Wireless Will Disband; Dismiss Chinese Employees," *China TechNews* (June 30, 2008).

68. Interview with Dean (September 23, 2008).

State-Company Bargains

All VAS providers, domestic and foreign-invested, experienced greater scrutiny of their model of market entry and the expansion of regulatory authority over their business scope. But how VAS providers responded to the expansion of regulatory authority and the state-owned carriers' control over their business activities varied at the company level. The extent to which a VAS provider self-censored and catered to the government's wishes varied according to the resources it brought to its bargains, which secured the company's commercial distance from the state. Moreover, SPs interpreted their space to maneuver according to the regulatory boundaries set by penalties the government inflicted on other SPs. One American executive described as routine the lengths ICPs take in order to guarantee bureaucratic distance from the MII:

> Censorship is the baseline in this business, and it is about learning from the experiences of others so we don't get shut down. The government is not phantom about this; there is no bogey man behind this. We make sure to avoid hardcore porn, gambling, and politics, including content on Taiwan and Tibet, and the other 90 percent of content is fine. Operators are motivated by money, not humanistic reasons, so as long as we don't touch the above-mentioned topics, everything is fine.[69]

High-profile foreign-invested ICPs, such as Yahoo, Google, MySpace China, and Microsoft's MSN, all of which operated using the business license of a Chinese partner, functioned without state interference by filtering Internet content that the government deemed offensive and subversive, including the Tiananmen Square massacre, the Dalai Lama, and Taiwan independence.[70] They sought to avoid the fate of the hundreds of websites shut down in 2009 by the government in its campaign to eradicate pornography and piracy; the SPs whose services were used by those suspected of transmitting unhealthy content were suspended by the carriers in early 2010 while the police evaluated the users' messages.[71] They routinely signed a Public Pledge on Self-Discipline for the Chinese Internet Industry.[72] Steps taken by TOM Online's to control content and respond to customers typified corporate

---

69. Interview in Shanghai (December 9, 2005).

70. Google registered as a FITE and operated as "google.cn" after its domestic competitors filed complaints of pornography stored in its cache function. Interview on September 15, 2006, in Beijing with a manager of a foreign-invested value-added service provider.

71. See "Text Messages in China to Be Scanned for 'Illegal Content'," *New York Times* (January 19, 2010).

72. Sina.com, Sohu.com, NEtease.com, and Tom Online all signed self-discipline agreements. See also "The Great Firewall of China," *Business Week* (January 12, 2006), and "MII Announces Ways to Protect Consumers," *ChinaCSR.com* (June 26, 2006).

adjustment.[73] TOM Online employed full-time self-censors and operated a call center that attempted to contain customer complaints to internal affairs. Sometimes, however, customers went straight to the MII, which raised the possibility of TOM Online losing its SP agreement with China Mobile.[74]

Foreign-invested VAS providers have also cooperated with state authorities to stop users engaging in prohibited or criminal online activities. In a highly publicized case, MSN shut down Chinese blogger Michael Anti's site at the end of 2005. When "the order comes from the appropriate regulatory authority," explained Brooke Richardson, a group product manager for MSN, "the company removes the content."[75] Going a step further, Yahoo submitted personal information of users on the government's blacklists. Not to be outdone, MySpace China, a foreign-invested venture that licensed its trademark to a local consortium of investors to circumvent the FITE process, abided by censorship laws and the self-discipline regime by placing a link on every page of its site to allow users or government monitors to "report inappropriate information."[76]

Companies with the most *guanxi* (personal relationships, which can include bribery) with the authorities tested the boundaries of the new regulations. This made VAS providers that did not have deeply entrenched local connections particularly susceptible to disparate treatment in the review process. As a survival strategy, companies that did not have an existing relationship with the government often relied on Chinese partners or more experienced foreign-invested VAS providers to show them the ropes. For example, Skype Technologies' partner TOM Online recommended that Skype install filters to screen out words in text messages deemed offensive to the state. "No filtering, no service" functions as the modus operandi.[77] Still, despite steps taken to self-censor, Skype faced difficulty entering the Voice over Internet Protocol (VoIP) market because of internal disputes between government bureaucracies and carriers on how convergence technologies should be defined according to existing China-specific service definitions.[78] Until state leaders

73. Interviews with Watts (November 3 and December 4, 2005) and on December 5, 2005, in Beijing with Tony Xi, senior counsel, TOM Online.

74. The China Consumers' Association and the National Telecommunications User Commission, both quasi-government organizations, along with the carriers periodically pledge to provide better service.

75. Quoted in "The Great Firewall of China," *Business Week* (January 12, 2006).

76. News Corporation's JV partners include U.S.-based International Data Group and China Broadband Capital Partners, an investment company founded by Edward Tian, the former head of China Netcom. News Corporation had invested in Netcom before WTO accession during the period of de facto FDI liberalization. See "Murdoch's Dealings in China: It's Business, and It's Personal," *New York Times* (June 26, 2006).

77. See "The Great Firewall of China," *Newsweek* (January 16, 2006).

78. In September 2005, the MII designated computer-to-computer VoIP a VAS, a shift from its policy that voice and fax services could flow over the public network but not the Internet. Conversation on October 24, 2005, in Beijing with John Liu, Interfax's telecommunications journalist. Also see J. Wang (1999), 11.

approved a regulatory scheme for VoIP, the state-owned carriers and their provincial branches would continue to regulate such technologies according to local goals and interests. In 2006, the Beijing branches of China Telecom and China Netcom blocked Skype with an "anti-Skype filtering system."[79]

Though the government did not enforce rules requiring foreign-invested VAS providers to register as a FITE, it treated foreign-invested VAS providers differently from domestic ones as it enhanced government control of information flows. For example, state-owned media and news producers required foreign-invested Internet content providers to enter into contracts to use their content. In fall 2006, *Beijing News* brought a copyright infringement suit against TOM Online.[80] *Beijing News* targeted only TOM Online for copyright infringement even though other Internet portals, including the Web sites of *Xinhua*, *People's Daily*, and *China Daily*, routinely practiced *zhuanzai* (the copying and pasting of entire articles) without obtaining permission.[81] Citing IP lawyers and other experts that "*zhuanzai* is to an extent protected by Chinese copyright law," TOM argued that legal ambiguity and market practice permitted its practice. Despite TOM's justification, backed by interpretation of existing law, *Beijing News* claimed that TOM stood out as an exception because its competitors had already signed licensing agreements in compliance with state control over information flows. In a published memo, an international intellectual property lawyer practicing in China explained: "Extra-legal considerations, which are conceivable particularly in China, where the filing of a lawsuit often indicates the breakdown rather than the apotheosis of the conflict resolution process, have come into play. The range of extra-legal political actions includes political lobbying, other actions by TOM's competitors and other business considerations, and possible upcoming changes in the law, which explain why *Beijing News* was emboldened to act now."[82] Foreign investors observed the case closely because its resolution could be a legal precedent for online copyright issues.[83]

In general, domestic and foreign companies as a collective adjusted differently to government regulation. On the one hand, American- and European-invested

79. Interviews in November and December 2006 with Watts and Xi of TOM Online. See also "China Said to Be Ready to Block Skype until 2008," *Computer Business Review* (March 21, 2006).

80. The claim of *Beijing News* that TOM Online republished its articles without permission between 2003 and 2006 coincided with increased regulation of information flows. See "The Media Environment behind the Case of Beijing News vs. TOM," *Southern Weekend* (December 22, 2006).

81. The practice of *zhuanzai* is the lifeblood of popular Internet forums, such as Tianya and Xici.

82. Maya Alexandri quoted in "Republishing: Protected by China Law?" posted by Jeremy Goldkorn on *Danwei.com* (December 24, 2006). Also conversations between 2005 and 2006 and interview on March 2, 2006, in Beijing with Alexandri, legal consultant based in China.

83. Judges in China can interpret statutes differently from case to case, which makes the discretionary power that policy and regulations often leave to bureaucracies all the more unpredictable. See "The Media Environment behind the Case of Beijing News versus TOM.com," *Southern Weekend* (December 22, 2006).

high technology companies formed lobbying groups and coalitions to interface with the relevant government and quasi-state authorities. These included the U.S. Information Technology Office, the IT subcommittees of the American Chamber of Commerce (in Shanghai and Beijing), and the various issue and sector-specific committees of the European Union Chamber of Commerce. Their campaigns facilitated friendly interactions between foreign investors and central bureaucracies and influenced policy enforcement outcomes but garnered little concrete regulatory change in strategic sectors and issue areas.

Business associations from coordinated market economies such as Japan and Germany did not formally engage in lobbying activities. Rather, the China branch offices of the Japan External Trade Organization (JETRO), an arm of the Ministry of Economy, Trade, and Industry, advised small and medium-sized Japanese companies about entering Chinese markets, including holding roundtable discussions, conferences, and briefings in China and Japan whereby Japanese companies, local governments, and central bureaucracies discuss commercial and investment issues.[84] The U.S. Commercial Service, under the interagency management of the U.S. Department of State and Department of Commerce, represented U.S. business interests to "bring to the table the U.S. government perspective"; yet it did not interface with central bureaucracies and local governments on behalf of American companies, as did JETRO and the German Industry and Commerce (GIC).[85] The GIC, under the umbrella of the Association of German Chambers of Industry and Commerce that German law requires all commercial businesses registered in Germany to join, "gives practical assistance to small and medium-sized enterprises wishing to tap into the Chinese market, holding their hands through the process of setting up shop in China, with consulting services, such as site search, legal set-up, and contract drafting."[86]

On the other hand, domestic quasi-government telecommunications associations embedded in the state bureaucracy generally initiated collective forms of corporate adjustment at the behest of the state to achieve sectoral goals. Domestic VAS providers, at the behest of quasi-government sector and business associations, routinely promoted self-discipline in response to government-initiated crackdowns on prohibited Internet and wireless content. Unlike the quasi-government sector and business associations in less regulated industries that operated with more autonomy, these organizations, known as *siye danwei*, acted as appendages of state-owned carriers and related central ministries, such as the MII and MOST. In 2006, in what could be erroneously interpreted as civil society vibrancy, the Internet So-

---

84. Interviews on April 12, 2005, with Masaki Yabuuchi, the president of JETRO Shanghai, and on December 2, 2005, with Yoichi Maie, deputy director general of JETRO Beijing.

85. Interview on May 25, 2005, with Jonathan Heimer, director of the Commercial Center of the U.S. consulate general in Shanghai.

86. Interview in Shanghai on April 29, 2005, with Bernd Reitmeier, deputy managing director, GIC Shanghai.

ciety of China (ISC) and China Communications Association initiated a Mobile Information Services Companies Self Discipline Agreement signed by more than fifty domestic and foreign-invested VAS providers, including Sina, Sohu, Netease, TOM Online, Tencent, and Shanda.[87] These VAS providers agreed to seek approval for content and refrain from holding misleading promotions, overcharging users, or charging users without first receiving user confirmation. In another initiative, the ISC and China Communications Standards Association, in conjunction with the MII, launched a national "anti-spam campaign." The MII set up a hotline for spam-related tip-offs and engaged in spamming by sending antispam notices.[88]

The chaotic nature of a saturated market in telecommunications value-added services and the varieties of corporate adjustment in response to state intervention to regulate content and business conduct made the outcomes of state retrenchment difficult to measure. The expanded regulatory authority over telecommunications prompted at least two foreign-invested businesses to adjust their business models. On the one hand, the TOM Group, the Hong Kong-based media company controlled by billionaire Li Ka-shing, claimed that restrictions on marketing to VAS subscribers had influenced its decision to privatize TOM Online in late August 2007 and reorganize its China businesses.[89] On the other hand, Google stated that Internet censorship and the government's requirement of filtered searches had led to it giving serious consideration in January 2010 to leaving the telecommunications market in China. It further linked its decision to "sophisticated cyberattacks on its computer systems that it suspected originated in China" and China's attempts to "limit free speech on the Web."[90] Google eventually decided to offer limited services in China and direct users to its uncensored Hong Kong-based Chinese language search engine.[91] For its part, the State Council is expected to establish a National Internet Management Office in 2011 to consolidate Internet regulation.

TELECOMMUNICATIONS EQUIPMENT: STRATEGIC REREGULATION

In the post-WTO era, the Chinese government enhanced its control of technology and promoted domestic sector development in a liberalized context. As we observed

---

87. "Operators, SPs Form WVAS Self-Discipline Agreement," *Beijing Star Daily* (June 20, 2006)

88. "MII Organizes Anti-Spam Activity," *Nanfang Daily* (June 22, 2006).

89. TOM Online's mainstay business in mobile phone ring tones and music downloads suffered; its net revenue fell 15 percent and profit dropped 59 percent in the third quarter of 2006, compared to the same period a year earlier. Its shares fell 42 percent from July through March 2007.

90. Quotes from "Google, Citing Attack, Threatens to Exit China," *New York Times* (January 12, 2010). In June 2009, the Chinese government forced Google to disable a function that allows the search engine to suggest terms and required the company to remove links to any obscene, pornographic, or vulgar content. Moreover, the 2009 report of the United States–China Economic and Security Review Commission described the cyber attacks originating from China as "a vast electronic spying operation," involving Internet documents stolen from around the world by computer systems based in China.

91. "Beijing Renews Google's License in China," *New York Times* (July 9, 2010).

in previous chapters, the strategic value of telecommunications equipment sectors centers on the ways that China can obtain and utilize technology to increase its national technology base and control the operation of technology for national security purposes. In the 1990s, the Chinese government found it could achieve technology acquisition and domestic sector development through FDI liberalization and the use of formal and informal control mechanisms in a liberal environment. In the 2000s, the government sought to control technology and engage in industrial upgrading through the commercialization of its homegrown network standard, discretionary licensing of network technology, carrier-controlled equipment distribution and procurement, a local content policy, and Chinese deviations in technical conformity certification. The corporate restructuring of the state-owned carriers enabled the rollout of indigenous technology in addition to creating more competitive carriers.

Networking Equipment

By WTO accession, top Chinese leadership had made the commercialization of TD-SCDMA, its homegrown telecommunications network standard, a priority in its efforts to manage technology standardization and implementation in a liberal environment.[92] The NDRC, which had initially balked at the MII and MOST for initiating the setting of technical standards to promote the development of a domestic telecommunications industry, directed the research and development behind the commercialization of TD-SCDMA. Not to be outdone, the NDRC conducted studies that concluded that investment in 3G technologies enhanced economic development, employment opportunities, exports, and economic "competition and fairness."[93]

To the chagrin of the MII and NDRC, Datang's poor corporate performance and technical problems delayed TD-SCDMA's development and complicated its market rollout. Taking corrective steps, the state withheld the licensing of other third generation telecommunications networks to manage the direction of network development, control the operation of network infrastructure, and assure market share for TD-SCDMA.[94] To speed the commercialization of TD-SCDMA, the government recruited the collaboration of other domestic and foreign-invested companies, including Huawei and Motorola.[95] The government created the TD

92. Other efforts include wireless local area networks, product tracking and remote identification, digital audio-video coding and decoding, audio-video disc formats, and digital home networking and next generation Internet protocols. See Suttmeier, Yao, and Tan (2004 and 2006).

93. See Zhou (2006) and Zhang (2005).

94. Interview on April 28, 2006, in Beijing with Wenjie Gu, vice president, U.S. Information Technology Office.

95. Interview in Beijing with J. M. Chen, director, Motorola China Electronics (September 19, 2006).

Tech Alliance in 2006 in partnership with domestic and foreign companies, including Nortel, Huawei, and state-owned ZTE and Putian to further promote product
development. Shortly thereafter, in anticipation of future market share, a proliferation of small domestic equipment makers entered the market to produce consumer
products based on the TD-SCDMA standard.

Throughout the 2000s, the TD-SCDMA's commercialization happened in fits
and starts. China Telecom, China Netcom, and China Mobile began conducting
TD-SCDMA trials in 2005 but which carrier would carry the financial burden of
rolling out TD-SCDMA remained unclear for several years.[96] The state intended
to restructure the carriers to ensure rollout but disagreements between central-
level agencies (the MII, the SASAC, and the NDRC) prompted the government
to scrap plans to issue 3G licenses before the 2008 Olympics. Yet despite nearly a
decade delay and bureaucratic conflicts, the government remained committed to
implementing the technology and "making sure that foreign equipment makers
pay their dues."[97] An industry insider intimated that during intellectual property
discussions in May 2007, the United States and China agreed on a 4.2 percent royalty for the commercialization of TD-SCDMA.[98] Moreover, as the official Olympic
sponsor for wireless communications equipment, Samsung, in partnership with
Datang, developed TD-SCDMA handsets for China Mobile during the Beijing
Olympics.[99] In January 2009, the MIIT finally issued 3G licenses; China Mobile
bore the responsibility for market rollout. In 2010, many domestic handset producers have invested in production but few global ones have done so despite verbal
commitments. Finnish equipment maker Nokia joined Samsung when it unveiled
its first TD-SCDMA handset in September 2009.

China-Specific Deviations in Technology Conformity

In 2003, the government introduced the new unified China Compulsory Certification (CCC) standard and reorganized and merged its standards enforcement bureaucracies to enhance implementation. The government justified these changes as
WTO compliance to eliminate separate certification processes for domestic and foreign equipment makers (the Great Wall and CCIB marks, respectively) and streamline market access for importers and foreign-invested manufacturers.[100] In fact, the
new compulsory certification and its accompanying enforcement infrastructure
enhanced the government's control of a broader range of technologies incorporated within component inputs, affecting market access in a liberalized context.

---

96. "Telecoms in China: Olympic Hurdle," *Economist* (June 14, 2007).

97. Quote from interview on September 25, 2008, in Beijing with a MOST bureau-level official.

98. See report in *Marbridge Weekly* (June 8, 2007).

99. "Samsung Gives TD-SCDMA an Olympic Run Out," *PC World* (July 14, 2008).

100. They are China Commission for Conformity Certification of Electrical Equipment (CCEE)
and China Commodity Inspection Bureau (CCIB).

The CCC mark introduced China-specific deviations in production specifications and created new electromagnetic compatibility and safety certification procedures. Moreover, confusing rules regulated the introduction of new products that meet CCC mark standards and the process for converting the previous certifications into CCC marks.[101]

Domestic Sector Development and Chinese Technology

The organization of state institutions and the politics within which homegrown technical standards were initiated and commercialized affected the relative success of China's technical standards regime and sectoral modernization. The experience of Andrew Corporation, a U.S. producer of telecommunications components, illustrates how domestic companies worked with local governments and research institutes to set technical standards that favored the domestic sector at the expense of technological advancement. Andrew Corporation faced exclusion from the Chinese market for RF (radio frequency) cables when a domestic competitor initiated a technical standard based on older technology that was written to exclude Andrew's product. China Electronics Technology Group Corporation (CETGC), Andrew's competitor, successfully excluded Andrew's product because of the government agencies and companies that continued to overlap in ownership and management interests despite having undergone corporatization and separation from the state. CETGC's owner, the No. 23 Research Institute, operated the testing labs for cable certification, owned companies that produced cable, and dominated the national technical committee that set standards for RF subsystems.

Michael Barbalas, a former managing director of Andrew's Suzhou factory, explained: "The top leadership probably did not know the standard they chose happened to be based on older technology. How to write a standard that meets their objective of protecting the domestic industry likely drove them instead."[102] Other equipment makers have found that often "it is about struggling to bring technology backwards to meet government-chosen standards set at a lower technological threshold to protect the domestic market for domestic players."[103] This and similar experiences drove Andrew to request a presence on and to "push its way into technical boards." Andrew and other equipment makers found that although "foreigners can't lead the process, they can vie for a seat at the table and contribute to the process if they possess technical competence."[104] Media reports emphasizing the high number of patents filed by Japanese and Korean companies, however, nega-

---

101. Interview in Shanghai on October 31, 2005, with Leslie Bai, general manager of Siemic, a consulting company specializing in certification compliance. See also Chen (2003).

102. Interview on December 8, 2005, in Suzhou with Michael Barbalas.

103. Interview in Shanghai on April 12, 2006, with Jeff Albright, general manager, Briggs & Stratton.

104. Interview with Barbalas (December 8, 2005); Kaitai Chen, standards consultant for Rockwell Automation, expressed similar sentiments in interviews in March and April 2006 in Shanghai.

tively affected domestic companies and bureaucracies' receptiveness toward foreign participation on technical committees.[105]

In another standards setting episode, government leadership at the highest levels attempted to set a technical standard, which represented an attempt to impose a nontariff barrier for new entrants and unofficially acquire technology. In 2004, Xian Xidian Jietong Wireless Network Communications, Shenzhen Minghua Aohan Technology, the Founder Group, and twenty-one other state-owned or state-affiliated vendors proposed WAPI (Wired Authentication and Privacy Infrastructure), a wireless LAN standard that required foreign producers selling WiFi in China to transfer technology to government-designated domestic companies that owned the intellectual property and held requisite licenses. The WAPI standard included a "back door" that would allow the government access to encrypted data.[106] To the relief of foreign investors, in spite of ministerial-level intervention, establishing the WAPI as a requirement for domestic market entry ultimately failed.[107] The State Council abandoned support for WAPI after a public campaign led by foreign-integrated circuit manufacturers, including Intel, whose Centrio chips were in jeopardy, and Broadcom, prompted the United States to pressure China during trade discussions.[108] In 2006, attempting to push the standard via market means rather than state mandate, the state-owned carriers, Huawei, Lenovo, Haier, and fifteen other domestic companies, with ministerial-level guidance, established the WAPI Industrial Union.[109] Market acceptance of WAPI never caught on; in 2010, equipment makers conformed to global standards.

The government found other ways to strengthen the domestic encryption industry and its control over information dissemination by imposing rules on telecommunications and IT electronics equipment makers. For example, rules allowed "the government easy access to decryption codes—while withholding the government certification that foreign-owned encryption companies in China need to sell their products to many users."[110] Furthermore, the government did not permit open source hardware security solutions; it only authorized international standards certified by the Chinese government. "Companies cannot use open encryption standards because the Chinese government could more easily monitor [information] and decode encryption using known standards," explained the director of a

---

105. Interview on March 2, 2006, in Beijing with Masayoshi Miki, general manager, intellectual property department, Panasonic China.

106. Interview on October 26, 2005, in Beijing with Kaiser Kuo, IT consultant and journalist based in China.

107. Interview on September 21, 2006, in Beijing with an official at the MOST.

108. See "China Agrees to Drop WAPI Standards," *IDG News Service* (April 22, 2004) and "Intel to Miss China Deadline on Standard for Wireless," *New York Times* (March 11, 2003).

109. See "China Forms WAPI Alliance," *Beijing Morning Post* (March 8, 2006).

110. "Google Is Not Alone in Discontent, but Its Threat to Leave Stands Out," *New York Times* (January 14, 2010).

foreign-invested IT consulting company based in Shanghai.[111] Not to be outdone, in 2009 the MIIT announced a rule that required personal computers sold in China after July 1 to preinstall a filter software, Green-Dam Youth Escort, that would protect against unhealthy information on the Internet. But after meeting fierce resistance from computer makers, the MIIT claimed that the installation of the software was "always intended to be optional and not mandatory."[112]

Restructuring the Telecommunications Carriers

In March 2008, the State Council created the Ministry of Industry and Information Technology, a supraministry that subsumed the MII and other sector-specific bureaucracies, and restructured the state-owned carriers. Industry insiders attributed the restructuring, in addition to ensuring that fixed-line carriers remained competitive vis-à-vis their mobile counterparts, to the government's promotion of homegrown technology, epitomized in the goal of reaching one hundred million subscribers for TD-SCDMA.[113] "This is a policy-oriented, not performance-oriented, restructuring. TD has become so political that the decision must be made on high," explained John Chiang, the former head of R&D at Motorola China, now director of the Beijing-based United States Information Technology Office and vice chair of the China Association of Standards.[114]

To lay the groundwork for deploying TD, the government created integrated carriers. The actual mergers and acquisitions contained imprints of the carriers' behind-the-scenes aggressive lobbying efforts. Most insiders believed that China Netcom emerged as the winner because of its past connection with Jiang Zemin's son and that China Unicom lost major battles. All the same, state imperatives rose to the forefront. Prioritizing domestic technology but recognizing the technological shortcomings of TD-SCDMA, the government assigned the deployment of TD-SCDMA to China Mobile, the strongest of the carriers. It also continued the trend of balancing procurement among foreign and domestic equipment makers, and in 2009, after nearly a decade of delay, licensed the other carriers to deploy other 3G networks.

According to industry insiders, though the government continued its policy of balanced procurement and competition, it would not too aggressively equalize competition; rather it would prioritize the development of domestic technology, including longer-term evolution technologies, such as TDMD, a TD-based mobile TV standard developed by Datang.[115] "The government [was] clearly not supporting balanced competition by delaying 3G licenses to other carriers. This [resulted]

111. Interview on May 24, 2005.
112. "China Pulls Back from Edict on Web-Filtering Software," *Wall Street Journal* (August 14, 2009).
113. Interviews with Dean (September 23, 2008) and Chiang (September 29, 2008).
114. Interview with Chiang (September 29, 2008).
115. Interview in Beijing on September 23, 2008, with former MII official.

in asymmetric competition because by not making 3G licenses available to other carriers, China Mobile continued to make money off GSM as they showed patriotism by promoting TD-SCDMA," explained the general manager of a foreign equipment maker.[116] Notwithstanding protectionist measures to promote TD-SCDMA, the government for a long time had been incubating new generation wireless technology, which it listed as a priority in the fifteen-year Medium-to-Long-Term Plan for Science and Technology (2006–20). The MOST and the Shanghai Research Center for Wireless Communications convened an academic panel to head China's 4G initiative, which established dialogue with Korea and Japan through the 4G Forum in 2004, and the China National Institute of Standardization started discussion in 2008 on 4G standards slated for deployment after 2010.[117]

Consumer Telecommunications Equipment

In the post-WTO era, in contrast to interventionist measures in networking equipment, market-oriented measures promoted the development of the domestic sector in consumer telecommunications equipment. The MII liberally licensed domestic handset makers, and local governments and TABs promoted them through R&D grants, investments, and procurement orders. The government did not necessarily intend to expand the sector, which happened inadvertently; it accelerated market entry (and restructured the carriers) for the purpose of technology implementation and not promotion of domestic industry. Domestic equipment makers received licenses and procurement orders to manufacture TD-SCDMA handsets and equipment without regulatory hassles.

Decentralized regulatory enforcement and subsectoral imperatives produced varied company-level outcomes. On the one hand, the introduction of competition, ease of market entry, and local subsidies promoted the development of domestic manufacturers of consumer telecommunications. In the 2000s, handset makers gradually won domestic market share through price competition made possible by chipsets and software solutions sold cheaply by foreign-invested companies, such as the Taiwan-owned Mediatech. Through what is called the "sanzhai" handset phenomenon, they entered the market "dressed in jeans, not in suits."[118] They also expanded globally: Ningbo Bird and TCL, two of China's largest handset makers, tapped developing markets, Europe, and the United States.

On the other hand, hypercompetition plagued saturated consumer telecommunications equipment markets, marked by increases in inventory, falling average

---

116. Interview on September 23, 2008, in Beijing with China general manager of a foreign equipment maker.

117. Interview with MOST official (September 23, 2008).

118. Interview on May 14, 2010, in Taoyuan, Taiwan, with board director of a Taiwanese telecommunications equipment maker.

prices, and depressed prices.[119] Additionally, due to the subsector's less strategic value, rarely did the state explicitly favor domestic handset makers over foreign ones and, when it did, its goals were rarely developmental in nature. The experience of Japanese equipment maker Panasonic provides a case in point. In 2001, the MII threatened to terminate Panasonic's license after domestic media reported that Panasonic used software that referred to Taiwan as the Republic of China.[120] Other handset makers, including Nokia, Ericsson, and state-owned TCL, also used the European-made software but did not experience similar scrutiny; the local media had associated Panasonic with China's disputes with Japan over interpretations of history. Soon thereafter, Panasonic established a strategic alliance with TCL to develop and market consumer handsets.[121]

Notwithstanding the largely equal treatment of producers of consumer-oriented telecommunications products, when national security or economic strategic value implications emerged, the government did not hesitate to issue rules to circumvent the potential threats posed by such products. For example, makers of smart phones sold in China are required to disable WiFi functions. "The government is afraid information will leak through this channel. It can track information dissemination via central control of telecommunications networks but it is more difficult to do so through WiFi," explained a former director of a smart phone producer and brand marketer.[122] The following lists the sector-specific rules promulgated in the post-WTO era:

WTO ACCESSION, 1999–2001
- US-China WTO Market Access Agreement (November 17, 1999)
- EU-China Agreement on WTO (May 19, 2000)
- Annex on Telecommunications of the Fourth Protocol to the General Agreement on Trade in Services (adopted April 30, 1996; entry into force February 5, 1998)
- GATS/SC 135 (Schedule of Commitments in Services, which includes telecommunications)
- Administrative Regulations for Telecommunications Services (State Council, 2000)

POST-WTO, 2002–08
- Administrative Regulations on Foreign-Invested Telecom Enterprises (State Council, 2001)
- Administrative Procedures for Telecommunications Business Operating Permits ("MII Decree 19," 2001)

---

119. Dean interview (November 7, 2005).

120. Interviews on March 2, March 13, and April 27, 2006, in Beijing with Toshihoko Shibuya, deputy general manager for Public Relations Section, Corporate Planning Department, Panasonic China.

121. Interviews on January 7, 2005, in Tokyo with Masaki Yabuuchi, then senior coordinator of planning, JETRO, and with Koji Sako and Yoji Okano.

122. Interview on May 17, 2010, in Taipei, Taiwan.

- Catalogue for the Guidance of Foreign Investment Industries (MOFTEC), 2002
- Notice Regarding Adjustment to the Catalogue of the Classification for Telecoms Services (MII, 2003)
- China Compulsory Certification (State Council, 2003)
- Catalogue for the Guidance of Foreign Investment Industries (NDRC and MOF-COM, 2004)
- Notice Concerning the Special Project for the Development, Administration and Standardization of Charging for and Collection of Fees for Mobile Information Services Business (MII, 2006)
- Circular on Strengthening the Administration of the Provision of Value-Added Telecommunication Services Involving Foreign Investment (MII, 2006)

REREGULATION TO ACHIEVE
DELIBERATE REINFORCEMENT

In the pre-WTO era, the Chinese government structured competition and strategically utilized FDI despite a formal ban to modernize network infrastructure and promote technology and knowledge transfers. Overall developments in the post-WTO era reveal that the dominant pattern of state control of telecommunications enhanced government control over industry, emphasized reregulation, and remained deliberate in orientation. The government followed the WTO liberalization schedule with reregulation, which reinforced *deliberate reinforcement* as the dominant pattern of state control in telecommunications. The Chinese government introduced new rules and employed control mechanisms that enhanced the state's control over network development, technology, and information dissemination and promoted domestic sector development (see table 5.2). The extent and nature of liberalization and reregulation continued to vary across subsectors. The Telecommunications Law, which promises to transparently enshrine China's regulatory regime of market liberalization and on which the government "diligently" worked the past two decades, remains in draft form. When asked about the Chinese government's liberalization efforts of the last fifteen years, a foreign telecommunications networking equipment executive explained, "The Chinese bureaucrats have no basic understanding of the liberal political economic model. China's telecoms policy process is very Soviet; very top-down Soviet-style decision making with nationalistic impulses, protectionism, and a desire to create national champions."[123]

---

123. Interview in Suzhou on December 8, 2005, with the general manager of a foreign-invested telecommunications equipment maker.

TABLE 5.2. STATE CONTROL IN TELECOMMUNICATIONS

Control pattern	Deliberate Reinforcement			
Timing	Pre–WTO Accession (1993–2001)		Post–WTO Accession (2002–10)	
Subsector	Services	Equipment	Services	Equipment
Reregulation	Strategic	Delegated	Expansionary	Strategic
Scope of control (central government's goals)	Introduce competition to modernize infrastructure; maximize technology transfers; strengthen carrier competitiveness	Introduce competition to promote development of domestic industry; maximize technology transfers	Order service markets; control network infrastructure and information; promote domestic industry	Promote development of domestic industry via initiating and controlling standards; maximize technology transfers
Extent of control (central government's relationship with industry)	Central ministries and provincial branches regulate industry and make policy.	Central ministries and provincial branches regulate industry and make policy.	Central ministries and provincial branches regulate industry and make policy.	Central ministries and provincial branches regulate industry and make policy.
Methods (nature of state control) *Macroeconomic levers*	Low interest rates; foreign exchange regime; currency control; quantitative measures, such as loan controls, rules on bank reserves, quotas, tariffs, and fiscal incentives	Low interest rates; foreign exchange regime; currency control; quantitative measures, such as loan controls, rules on bank reserves, quotas, tariffs, and fiscal incentives	Low interest rates; foreign exchange regime; currency control; quantitative measures, such as loan controls, rules on bank reserves, quotas, tariffs, and fiscal incentives	Low interest rates; foreign exchange regime; currency control; quantitative measures, such as loan controls, rules on bank reserves, quotas, tariffs, and fiscal incentives
Methods (nature of state control) *Micro (sector) levers*	Market entry limited to state-owned carriers; Chinese-style corporate restructuring of state-owned companies; de facto FDI liberalization but forced divestment of FDI in basic services	Liberal entry but, in practice, FDI forms JVs with SOEs; discretionary licensing regime; local content policy; corporatization, mergers and acquisitions, and corporate restructuring of SOEs; fiscal and infrastructural incentives for domestic sector	China-specific definitions; committed to 49% ceiling in foreign equity in basic services but permitted <10%; in VAS, liberal entry with FDI ceiling of 50% but FDI entered via special structures; discretionary licensing; state sanctioned increase in carriers' oversight of service providers; restrictions on VAS business scope	Liberal entry; discretionary licensure and certification; network licensing regime; state-led setting of technical standards; local content policy; corporatization, mergers and acquisitions, and corporate restructuring of SOEs; fiscal and infrastructural incentives for domestic sector

TELECOMMUNICATIONS AND THE
DEVELOPMENTAL STATE

The Chinese government's employment of deliberate reinforcement, which combined the introduction of competition and administrative and corporate restructuring to enhance state control of telecommunications, contrasts with the carefully managed competition and bureaucratic bargains and interaction with private domestic industry that typified the regulation of telecommunications in the developmental states of Japan, South Korea, and Taiwan. In telecommunications services, Japan, South Korea, and Taiwan privatized the telecommunications monopoly but protected the incumbent basic and value-added service providers from competition with formal and informal rules and regulations. China, on the contrary, permitted fierce competition between state-owned carriers and promoted the development of VAS markets through market and FDI liberalization. In telecommunications equipment, with variation in the actual methods used and the density of public-private industry networks, the developmental state strictly regulated FDI and initiated R&D that brought together private manufacturers to develop indigenously designed terminal and consumer-based equipment. The close relationship between carriers and their suppliers controlled the development and use of technology. As we have learned in the last two chapters, the Chinese government maximized technology and knowledge transfers and promoted sector development by extensively liberalizing telecommunications equipment and balancing procurement among foreign and private equipment makers. But instead of working collaboratively with domestic industry to develop indigenous technology as was done in the development state, the Chinese government led the development of a homegrown networking standard through SOEs and foreign technology transfers and guaranteed its commercialization through assigning network rollout to its most competitive state-owned carrier and licensing equipment upstarts.

Japan

Up until the 2000s, regulatory control of telecommunications in Japan conformed to the traditional Japanese model of state-led growth with bureaucracies managing competition between market players and working closely with domestic private industry to achieve bureaucratic imperatives and developmental goals. In the 2000s, even while Japan deregulated and reregulated to introduce competition (across different market segments and subsectors), it also took steps to protect the incumbent (due to political influence). China, in contrast, broke up the monopoly, introduced competition, and restructured state-owned fixed-line and mobile carriers to modernize network infrastructure and create competitive carriers and value-added service providers that were disconnected from the original monopoly and telecommunications bureaucracy.

In the postwar period, "they put a high priority on rebuilding the telecommunications infrastructure . . . They would both support the telecommunications equipment industry and enhance the productivity of corporate users."[124] In contrast, central imperatives in China, whether those pertaining to national security or technological upgrading, always took precedence over bureaucratic and sectoral goals. Importantly, unlike China, where fierce competition characterized the relationship between state-owned carriers, the Japanese "[tended] to coddle the telecommunications incumbent" to achieve goals such as "the development of certain [domestic] technologies."[125]

Between the end of U.S. occupation in 1952 and the 1980s, the Nippon Telegraph and Telephone (NTT) dominated the telecommunications regime.[126] The NTT developed a strong cooperative relationship with a group of domestic manufacturers; it provided a stable market and worked closely with these companies in designing, manufacturing, and testing telecommunications equipment. This relationship and the general protection of domestic equipment makers from foreign competition through standards setting, product certification, and procurement remained intact after regulatory reform in the 1980s.[127] Quite the reverse, Chinese carriers balanced procurement among a competitive group of foreign and domestic equipment makers supplying various networking standards.

Regulatory reform in the 1980s introduced competition and increased the authority of the Ministry of Post and Telecommunications (MPT). The Telecommunications Business Law of 1985 privatized NTT but on most issues of market management, including NTT's budget and personnel, investment in R&D and supply of services, the regulation of prices and business scope, and the direction of technology, the MPT prevailed.[128] The MPT created the Japan-specific classification scheme for telecommunications services and wrote rules on entry, prices, and foreign equity to "tightly control the terms of competition."[129] Moreover, it used "administrative guidance" to regulate business scope and prices and organize mergers and assemble consortia of firms to enter market segments.[130]

In equipment, the MPT licensed foreign standards and technology, which gave rise to new entrants in mobile services. Yet it delayed opening Japanese standards, such as PHS, to foreign firms in order to give Japanese manufacturers an advantage.[131] The failure to require appropriate connection charges and "the NTT

124. Vogel (1996), 140.
125. Tilton and Choi (2007), 23.
126. Vogel (1996), 138.
127. Tilton and Choi (2007) and Fransman (1995).
128. The MPT also "maintained the ability to intervene" on other issues. See S. Vogel (1996), 156.
129. Vogel (1996), 166.
130. Vogel (1996), 161–66.
131. Funk (2006), 71–77.

and its suppliers' long-term reluctance to abandon domestic technology in favor of [global] standards," have, however, compromised the development of domestic equipment makers.[132] In contrast, the Chinese invited foreign equipment makers to participate in standards setting while retaining the lead, and wooed them with market share to manufacture products based on TD-SCDMA to speed and expand the commercialization of the indigenous standard.

In the late 1990s, Japan's prolonged economic crisis, combined with a series of political and bureaucratic scandals, challenged the authority of the ruling party and the bureaucracy, prompting calls for bold reform. Thus, fifteen years after the NTT Law of 1984 first proposed it, the NTT "reorganized" in 1999 into one company for long-distance and international services and two regional companies but maintained unified ownership through a holding company structure.[133] The "[MPT officials] now feel some responsibility to make sure that NTT [local service providers] survive" and "have come to accept the reality of NTT's political clout, so clearly manifested in the breakup settlement."[134] At the same time, the MPT allowed FDI into the market and began to support the use of non-NTT controlled Internet protocol technologies. In 2001, legal changes introduced "asymmetric regulations to allow smaller firms to compete more effectively with NTT" and entry and price changes required registration rather than MPT approval.[135] Moreover, notwithstanding the continued dominance of NTT and ministerial guidance, foreign pressure through trade agreements and Japan's WTO membership have influenced subsectoral liberalization, including mobile services, and changes in NTT's interconnection and procurement policies.[136]

In the 2000s, an empowered Cabinet Office and the Ministry of Internal Affairs and Communications (MIC, formerly the MPT) combined "liberalization of the telecommunications market, heavy investment in telecommunications infrastructure, improvements in the legal apparatus to support electronic commerce, and measures to promote electronic government" to support a national strategy for ICT (information and communications technology) development and protect the incumbent NTT.[137] Targeting broadband development, the MIC pressed NTT to lower collocation and voice interconnection charges and to lease unused copper and fiber-optic lines. As new carriers began offering DSL services, a price war exploded; in response, NTT delayed access, demanded higher interconnection charges, and issued restrictions on access to its fiber-optic network. When

---

132. Quote from Anchordoguy (2005), 118–26.
133. Negotiations, in the midst of the Asian financial crisis, involved NTT's union and family of equipment vendors, among others, and ended with the holding company compromise. See Vogel (2000), 7. Kushida and Oh (2007), 18, lists the many stakeholders involved.
134. S. Vogel (2000), 11.
135. Quote from Anchordoguy (2005), 116.
136. See Vogel (2000), 8–9; Kushida and Oh (2007), 498–99; and Funk (2006), 69–72.
137. Vogel (2006), 101.

the government sided with NTT and allowed it to raise prices on interconnection rates for fixed-line (voice) services not identified as strategically important, NTT's competitors challenged the decision in court in 2003. The government eventually dismissed the first-of-its-kind lawsuit filed by five companies, including two foreign-owned ones. But it scrapped plans to delay measures forcing NTT to lease out its fiber infrastructure.[138]

South Korea

Similar to Japan, the Korean government also restricted FDI and micromanaged competition between market players in telecommunications. What is more, it nurtured the development of telecommunications equipment makers and service providers (typically part of *chaebol*, or large business conglomerates) through initiating and investing in R&D and infrastructural development. In the 1980s, the Korean government initiated telecommunications reform amid rising demand, technological innovations, and worldwide telecommunications reform. It separated regulation from business and established the Korea Telecommunications Authority (KTA), a monopoly carrier, and DACOM, a data communications provider, was launched with majority private equity.

Market liberalization followed but the Ministry of Communications (MOC) supervised it in a calculated and gradual manner to protect the incumbent, develop subsectors, and strengthen its status as the lead bureaucracy. The Korean government gradually divested ownership of KTA (from 1987 to 2002) and did not loosen its management of competition in basic services until the realization of three competing carriers.[139] To stem societal opposition, "an accord was reached with KTA's labor union to limit foreign ownership in order to protect employment, in line with Korea's restrictive overall strategy toward foreign investment."[140] Moreover, the government licensed new competitors across international, long-distance, and domestic segments in stages; until 1997, it accepted new applications only during a preannounced window. The government also "set fixed ceilings on dominant firms' market share and onerous licensing requirements for new firms, sought to guarantee minimal market shares for and offered relatively cheap bandwidth licenses to selected marginal operators, and actively encouraged consolidation among small firms."[141]

---

138. Anchordoguy (2005), 119, on the lawsuit, and Kushida (2009) on this issue in relation to his study of sectoral variations in the political strategies of foreign investors in Japan.

139. In 1997, the government abolished the Korea Telecommunications Business Law that governed KTA's activities; in 2002, KTA was renamed Korea Telecom.

140. Quote from Kushida and Oh (2007), 11. See Guillen (2001), 141–47, on Korean labor and the "arm's-length" collaboration between FDI and *chaebol*.

141. Pirie (2008), 121.

Throughout, the MOC expanded telecommunications infrastructure. In the 1980s, it financed new switching equipment with revenues from KTA, most of it produced by foreign equipment makers. To shift to indigenously designed equipment, the MOC assembled a "formidable institutional structure," which provided incentives for *chaebol*, such as Samsung and Goldstar, to design and produce electronic switching systems.[142] The MOC allocated three percent of KTA revenue to R&D, guaranteed future markets through a massive procurement budget, and through government-run research centers, such as the Electronics and Telecommunications Research Institute, coordinated R&D, including technology collaborations between Korean equipment makers and foreign ones. "The result was extension of telecommunications infrastructure to new areas at less foreign exchange cost, new indigenous technology with export potential, and a strengthened R&D infrastructure."[143]

In 1994, to coordinate the expansion of the information communications technology sector in Korea, the Kim Young Sam administration created the Ministry of Information and Communications (MIC), which merged regulatory authority with industrial policy functions in one ministry. The Framework Act on Informatization Promotion in 1995 and an Information Promotion Fund in 1996 strengthened MIC's legal and financial tools. The newly created MIC held effective control of the entire telecommunications industry, not unlike China's Ministry of Information Technology after the merger of MEI and MPT. The MIC spearheaded the Korea Information Infrastructure Initiative (KII) between 1995 and 2005. The KII combined public financing to build infrastructure and facilitate R&D with fiscal incentives and loan guarantees to encourage carriers to invest in network construction. The government did not regulate entry and pricing, nor did it require telephone carriers and cable TV companies to provide network access. The result was fierce facilities-based competition, which spurred broadband development.[144] To further promote broadband development, the government designed "demand magnification" programs to encourage computer use in schools and homes, offer computer-based assistance, and educate housewives about the Internet. One program embedded computer literacy in Korea's university entrance exams, which increased demand for broadband subscriptions among homes with school-age children.[145]

142. Evans (1995), 140–46. On the relationship between government promotion of semiconductors and the development of telecommunications equipment, see Wade (1990), 312–19.

143. Evans (1995), 143.

144. Chung (2006), 97–98.

145. Kushida and Oh (2007), 24–25.

Taiwan

Before 1996, the Ministry of Transportation and Communications (MOTC) assumed regulatory and operational responsibilities of Taiwan's Directorate General of Telecommunications (DGT). The Telecommunications Act of 1977 technically allowed domestic private and public companies to enter the local telephone service; in practice, the government permitted only special networks limited strictly to internal communication set up by a few SOEs and value-added services operated by six international news agencies to communicate with their global news networks.[146] The Telecommunications Act of 1996, stimulated by critical development policies related to becoming a Asia–Pacific Regional Operations Center and building the National Information Infrastructure, partially privatized the DGT. These acts introduced private competition, separated operation from regulation, and distinguished fixed versus nonfixed services. Mobile phone and data communication services were deregulated the same year; fixed-line services in 2000. The DGT became Chunghwa Telecom Company (CHT) and entered as the incumbent in most market segments. The MOTC issued eight mobile licenses to six service providers in 1997, and three licenses to fixed-line carriers in 2000. In 2002, MOTC issued 3G licenses to five mobile carriers. The ceiling for FDI, in the form of JVs, was raised to 40 percent from 20 percent in 2004.[147] Incumbent service providers continued to lead the market in the 2000s; they charge high tariffs on interconnection and control the allocation and portability of numbers.[148]

Unlike the Japanese and Korean counterparts' close ties with domestic private companies, which spurred the development of a domestic telecommunications equipment industry, until the late 1980s Taiwan's telecommunications equipment industry was composed of joint ventures—producing terminal equipment and in which the DGT held stakes—between Alcatel, Siemens, and AT&T and local minority partners closely connected to the émigré KMT government. These three companies served as regional monopolies as part of the "three systems, three suppliers" policy.[149] Equipment liberalization began gradually in the late 1980s with consumer premises equipment; but in the 2000s, the "three systems, three suppliers" policy continued to be out of reach of most local telecommunications manufacturers.

In the late 1970s, "the government had begun to envisage an integrated information technology industry for Taiwan, linking semiconductors, computers, computer software, and telecommunications."[150] But the relatively well-developed policy networks between economic bureaucracy and private industry, in particular

146. Chen (2000), 328.
147. Boulton (2002), 61.
148. Chen (2000), 340–41.
149. Chen (2000), 328–29 and 342–43.
150. Quote from Wade (1990), 104.

large conglomerates and group companies, and the financial system of patient capital (long-term capital willing to take major hits in profitability to achieve particular goals) typical of Japan and Korea did not exist in Taiwan. Rather, "the Taiwan government . . . relied more on arm's length incentives to steer private firms and often used public enterprises or public laboratories to undertake big pushes in new fields," such as industrial sectors with high barriers to entry, including telecommunications networking equipment.[151] Replacing the massive investment in patient capital is "an institutional system [of industrial innovation] built around public research institutions–led R&D science-and-technology industrial policy and a policy goal of attaining a defined position within the IT industry's global production network."[152] Still, these state initiatives, typical of the public-private collaboration of the developmental state, ultimately promoted the development of private domestic industry. In China, the private sector took a backseat to other state imperatives and state-owned enterprises.

State-owned experimental integrated circuit facilities were more successful in founding private domestic computer and networked semiconductor industries, including spurring the development of integrated circuit design, and not telecommunications.[153] Nevertheless, though a late entrant to consumer telecommunications equipment, with R&D investment and coordination from government labs and other facilities, such as the Hsinchu Science–based Industrial Park, Taiwan "is now using its experience in [integrated circuit design and manufacturing] to move into the telecommunications industry. . . . Taiwan has been developing the supply chain required for producing wireless products as was done previously for PCs and ICs [integrated circuits]."[154] In the 2000s, Taiwanese equipment makers started to develop chipsets for 3G standards and design and manufacture handsets, including smart phones, for global manufacturers.[155]

---

151. Quote from Wade (1990), 321. Taiwan under the KMT had one of the largest state-owned sectors in the non-Communist world in part because the government did not find palatable "increasing the power of an ethnically distinct, politically hostile private elite." See Evans (1995), 54–57.

152. Breznitz (2007), 99, which also discusses the successes and shortcomings of this industrial development strategy.

153. For example, UMC and TSMC, two world-class semiconductor manufacturers, were both initiated by the government-run Electronic Research and Service Organization of the Industrial Technology Research Institute in response to the demand for a local specialized foundry. See Amsden and Chu (2003), 107–9. Also Wade (1990), 102–6.

154. Boulton (2002), 58.

155. Interview on May 14, 2010, in Taipei, Taiwan, with board director for a Taiwanese telecommunications equipment maker.

PART III

STATE CONTROL OF TEXTILES

6

DISMANTLING CENTRAL CONTROL
OF TEXTILES IN THE PRE-WTO ERA

"The numerous central incentives are policies of the past. Government support to encourage MNCs to source and procure in China has all but stopped. Any encouragement of manufacturing, which are dominated by private Chinese firms, are done on the local level," explained a former China general manager for Liz Claiborne, an American apparel brand marketer.[1] The dismantling of the Ministry of Textile Industry in 1993, forty-four years after its creation, represented a milestone in post-Mao market liberalization and foreshadowed the relinquishing of state control in textiles, a nonstrategic industry. The elimination of the textile ministry followed fifteen years of market reform and devolution of economic decision making. Less strategic to national security and technological development in the post-1978 era, and thus not associated with state goals of enhancing government control of infrastructural and financial assets and technology, the textile industry along with other nonstrategic industries constituted a playground for China's market experiments.[2] Administrative restructuring and regulatory reform further undermined state control between 1993 and WTO accession in 2001. The Chinese government completely liberalized FDI and private entry. Local governments and business stakeholders governed textile manufacturing, creating a vibrant private sector. These developments contrast with those in telecommunications; reregulation there enhanced state control. "China does not have an industrial policy in clothing manufacturing. China's attitudes toward

---

1. Interview in Shanghai on May 23, 2005.
2. See chapter 9 for regulatory developments and state-industry relations in nonstrategic sectors.

textiles, particularly clothing production, and telecommunications differ like day and night," explained an industry consultant who previously oversaw the EU-China WTO Project.[3]

Demonstrative of how economic cycles and the organization of institutions shaped temporal variation in state control, however, former textile bureaucrats convinced central leadership to reassert its control during the Asian financial crisis. Between 1998 and 2001, the central government curbed overexpansion, ordered competition in upstream subsectors, and promoted industrial upgrading ahead of impending global competition unleashed by membership in the WTO. But these interventions did not prove permanent; shortly before WTO accession, the state eliminated government textile offices altogether.

Though the central government relinquished regulatory control of textiles, state control varied across subsectors according to a strategic value logic and shaped by textiles' structural sectoral attributes. Related central ministries intervened to promote technical subsectors that contribute to construction, aviation, and high technology industries and have military applications. Moreover, the government retained centralized management of raw material inputs and apparel exports because of their impact on the rest of the economy and China's foreign economic relations, respectively. Textiles' lower strategic value, however, meant that the state delegated licensing and quota distribution authority to provincial branches of the trade bureaucracy. Also, although formal rules forbade FDI in apparel retail, in practice select foreign-invested companies entered the domestic market. Significantly, the state's overall incidental orientation toward textiles led China during WTO accession negotiations to agree to keep textiles under trade agreements for additional years in return for more favorable terms in more strategic industries.

These pre-WTO state-industry relations and methods of control, shaped by textile's low strategic value and sectoral characteristics, foreshadowed the decentralized and incidental nature of reregulation in the post-WTO period, explored in chapter 7. The East Asian developmental state took a vastly different attitude toward textiles during a similar stage of economic and industrial development. Despite some variation in extent of state control, these countries intervened strongly, rather than relinquish control to market forces, to develop textile industries during the import-substitution stage of development, and to promote textile exports in the subsequent export-orientation phase. Later, Japan, South Korea, and Taiwan cushioned industrial adjustment in the face of competition from one another and from developing countries, including China. The mini case studies of countries in chapter 7 illuminate the divergent path toward textile development, thereby illustrating how China is paving its own path.

---

3. Interview on February 24, 2006, in Beijing with Julio Arias, EU-China WTO Project.

TEXTILE MANUFACTURING:
DECENTRALIZED REREGULATION

The elimination of the Ministry of Textile Industry in 1993 formalized a path of industrial development that began a decade earlier. Taking an incidental orientation, the state introduced competition and devolved economic decision making to lower levels of the central bureaucracy. The demoted bureaucracy became the Bureau of Textiles (BOT), officially an enterprise level unit, under the supervision of the newly created State Economic and Trade Commission.[4] Many of the MTI and provincial-level textile bureau personnel, who jealously guarded their eroding supervisory roles and resisted the abolishment of the ministry, transferred to the BOT. They remained government employees but lost their discretionary power in licensure approvals and regulatory authority along different stages of the textile supply chain.[5] Lower-level bureaucrats transferred to the state-owned assets corporations that held the property of former textile offices. Others joined textile SOEs, officially separated from the textile bureaucracy in 1992 when the state affirmed the fourteen "autonomies" granted to textile producers.[6]

Liberalization Phase (1993–1997)

The MTI's dissolution eliminated rules on market entry and exit and business scope in most subsectors of textile manufacturing and terminated central-level supervision of fabric and garment production. It also commenced the corporatization of abolished local textile offices permitted by the State Council's 1992 Direction on Regulation for Transforming the Operational Mechanism of State-Owned Enterprises. In the *shouquan* process, the state divested the assets of a given government department to an SOE.[7] Furthermore, the state introduced limited state-owned competition in the internal distribution of raw and processed materials along the textile supply chain. External trade and distribution, however, remained under centralized control and under the export restraints imposed by the Multi-Fiber Agreement.

---

4. In 2003, the SETC's internal trade departments, which joined it in 1998, merged with the foreign trade ministry to form the Ministry of Commerce. Its industrial management departments merged with the State Development and Planning Commission to create the National Development and Reform Commission.

5. Most former MTI bureaucrats did not stray too far from government circles. Though the State Council demoted the MTI's status, former minister Wu Wenying retained her ministerial-level status to head the BOT and the State Administration of Textile Industry (SATI), and sat on the twelfth through fourteenth CCP central committees between 1982 and 1997. She retired in 2000 when the government dismantled SATI. See Rosen (1995), 326. In 2010, sixteen years after the dissolution of the MTI, many former midlevel bureaucrats held positions in the China National Textile and Apparel Council (CNTAC).

6. Moore (2002), 151.

7. McNally and Lee (1998).

Liberalization of Market Entry and
Chinese-Style Privatization

The reduction of market entry rules and elimination of centralized oversight, combined with fiscal reforms and state sector restructuring, introduced private and foreign competition and gave rise to a dynamic private textile industry. Institutional reform transferred the supervision of industrial development and licensing of textile manufacturers to local commerce bureaus and local governments. Moreover, administrative restructuring and fiscal reforms vested significant financial responsibility in local governments to manage state-owned textile assets and invest in the emerging quasi-private sector. Following national guidelines for industrial reform and pursuing local political and economic interests, local governments became active in implementing economic reform and carrying out industrial adjustment. They also became especially agile in negotiating FDI–local state bargains and setting local rules on production, trade, and investment. Local governments frequently courted FDI and private investment with free land and electricity, even without the legal authority to do so. As one entrepreneur explained, "The rules of the new economy are made on the ground as we go."[8]

To promote the local economy and address local employment needs, local authorities, undermining overall state control, orchestrated mergers, privatization, and foreclosures during several rounds of SOE reform.[9] Corporate restructuring in telecommunications, in contrast, took a different path to enhance state control. State leaders, including Premier Zhu Rongji, specifically identified the textile industry as being at the forefront of state sector reform. Mergers of SOEs introduced leaner and more agile companies, and although the number of factories decreased, production increased.[10] For SOEs and TVEs in more desperate financial straits, central and local governments either closed down factories altogether or engaged in the "privatization, Chinese style" typical of nonstrategic industries. In these situations "so dire that a wolf without gloves becomes the caretaker of rabbits" (*kong soutao bailiang*), central and local authorities assigned ailing SOEs and TVEs to former managers in a divestiture process of distressed companies known as *chengbao*. Factories became "private" overnight without any exchange of capital. Rather, the new owners, in exchange for management control, promised to assume welfare responsibilities and employ laid-off and *xiagang*

---

8. Moore (2002), 159.

9. In a 1997 policy known as "grasp the large, let go of the small" (*zhuada, fangxiao*), the government merged companies to create large enterprise groups with extensive cross-ownership.

10. The state afforded these "national champions" preferential treatment in trade quotas, and referred to them when "Chinese industry" interests became relevant in trade talks. Interview on October 25, 2005, in Beijing with Zhu Lei, lawyer, King & Wood, and on March 28, 2006, in Davis, California, with Ning Pan, professor of textile engineering and former MTI official who worked in Shandong textile mills.

workers.[11] Enterprising entrepreneurs soon learned to shirk welfare responsibilities by using the newly privatized factories as collateral to obtain bank loans and dismissing workers after giving them a small compensation.[12] One former MTI official lamented that such practices reflected the dark side of China's reform process and represented market reform without proper rules, compelling people to "cross the river by feeling the stones" (*mozhe sitou guohe*).

The introduction of the Company Law in 1994 provided qualified, privately initiated enterprises under the aegis of local governments that were interested in entering textile manufacturing and other liberalized sectors with the opportunity to restructure and corporatize their assets without relying on localized, piecemeal legislation. The liberalization of FDI further promoted the growth and development of domestic textiles.

Courting FDI, Benefiting Emerging Private Sector

By the mid- to late 1980s, FDI became free to enter most textile manufacturing sectors and investors were legally permitted to structure as wholly foreign-owned enterprises. Local governments, empowered by the abolition of the MTI and fiscal decentralization and motivated by revenue generation and other interests, used their licensing authority to aggressively court FDI. They attracted FDI with local fiscal and infrastructural incentives, including local development zones and special economic areas.[13] They purchased ads in international papers advertising investment opportunities and JV collaborations in high-tech, value-added subsectors such as textile machinery.[14]

The central government also promulgated policies and regulations and granted investment incentives favorable to FDI while benefiting industrial development. Labor laws attracted FDI in garment manufacturing and other labor-intensive textile subsectors and helped localities solve unemployment. For example, the 1994 labor contract law allowed employers to terminate contracts without notice, withhold workers' wages, and refuse contract renewals.[15] Rules regulating JVs further ensured that technology and knowledge would be transferred from foreign-invested factories to local stakeholders.[16] Moreover, policies attracted

---

11. *Xiagang* workers are those who have stepped down from their post without pay but are still officially retained by their work units. See Lee (2000) for more on the Chinese government's approach of reconciling its social obligations with the economic logic of reform.

12. Pan interview (March 28, 2006).

13. Such efforts included China's biggest furniture textile industrial park in Shandong. See "Shandong to Build Biggest Household Textile Industrial Park," *Comtex News Network* (August 1, 2003).

14. Ads included "Qinhuangdao Seeks Overseas Investment, Cooperation," *Asia Pulse* (January 8, 1998).

15. Labor activists described abuses ranging from poor working conditions to labor-management disputes to unstable labor markets as a consequence of flexible labor laws and lax enforcement. The 2008 revised Labor Contract Law more strictly protects workers and regulates employers.

16. Ho and Huenemann (1984).

ethnic Chinese business entrepreneurs to invest in their ancestral homeland.[17] Macroeconomic policies, including currency manipulations, also sustained FDI inflows.

In this liberal and market-enhancing regulatory context, FDI flourished, especially in apparel and textile sectors, which have low start-up costs and a plethora of foreign brand marketers and manufacturers eager to outsource and/or shift production to China. These efforts attracted, in particular, apparel and textile manufacturers from Taiwan, Hong Kong, Macao, and Southeast Asia. These countries underwent cross-border industrial restructuring and shifted production of low-value-added, labor-intensive sectors overseas from the 1980s through the 1990s.[18] Moreover, to take advantage of incentives by the central and local governments, enterprising domestic entrepreneurs circumvented rules in order to incorporate offshore and enter China disguised as FDI.[19] Before WTO accession, this "round-tripping" phenomenon reportedly comprised 30 to 50 percent of total FDI, based on an analysis of 1999 and 2000 data.[20]

Market-Oriented Industrial Structure in the Making

The decentralized regulatory environment in textiles created an industrial structure that by official and unofficial accounting is China's most extensively privatized and liberalized industry. In 2005, the nonstate sector comprised 96 percent of textile enterprises. In the apparel sector, privately owned producers reached 99 percent. Many of these companies were foreign-invested. In the 1980s and early 1990s, the majority of FDI originated from Hong Kong, Taiwan, and Macao.[21] By 1999, FDI in textiles from Hong Kong, Macao, Taiwan, and OECD countries became more balanced.[22]

---

17. These policies included the 1986 Provisions for the Encouragement of Foreign Investment, which encouraged investment from Hong Kong, Macao, and Taiwan, and the 1988 Regulations on Encouraging the Investment of Taiwan Compatriots. See Fu (2000), Naughton (1997), and Hsing (1998).

18. Prior to China's entry into the global production chain, these countries enjoyed considerable comparative advantage because of low-cost labor and solid production infrastructure. See Tao (2005).

19. Circulars 11 and 29 issued by the State Administration of Foreign Exchange in 2005 sought to restrict "round-tripping." A separate circular retained regulatory jurisdiction over offshore transactions involving the establishment of special-purpose companies owned or controlled by PRC residents and enterprises and acquisitions of shares or assets by such vehicles in China by way of "round-tripping." See *Lovells Corporate Bulletin* (September 2005) and 2005 conversations in Beijing with Rocky Lee, counsel, Lovells.

20. Guy Pfeffermann, chief economist of International Finance Corporation, presented this estimation. See *European Commission Report* (2005). Also "China's FDI Merry-go-round," *fDi Magazine* (April 2, 2003).

21. See Gu (1999) on the structure of China's textile industry.

22. See a report by Hu and Jefferson (2002), 1066–67, using data drawn from the Survey of Large- and Medium-Size Enterprises of the PRC Bureau of Statistics.

The structure of FDI varied across domestic and export-oriented textile manu-facturers. Until the late 1990s, FDI consisted mainly of export-oriented producers of fabrics, garments, and home furnishings. Quasi-private collective and foreign-invested enterprises made up 46 percent and 50 percent, respectively, of the value exported in textiles and clothing.[23] Foreign-invested manufacturers entered the domestic market in the mid-1990s. They previously had produced only for export markets or entered the Chinese market indirectly through imports distributed by domestic agents.

Runaway Investment and Overproduction

In the mid-1990s, runaway investments, a result of overzealous local stakehold-ers empowered by administrative restructuring and decentralization, gave rise to overcapacity in cotton processing and other subsectors up and down the tex-tile supply chain, which had low barriers to entry. Many state-owned and quasi-private factories, cushioned by soft-budget constraints and less accustomed to market signals, manufactured regardless of demand. Increased demand in cotton processing drove up prices of domestic and imported cotton and other fibers, de-creasing profit margins for cotton processors and fabric manufacturers further downstream.[24]

Concerned that overproduction in fiber processing was harming the overall competitiveness of the textile supply chain, the Bureau of Textiles began a spindle cutting program to retire spindles and to discourage cotton processors from fur-ther investment. Around the same time, the BOT issued a call for a large-scale relocation of textile mills to western interior provinces and to Xinjiang, a major production base for domestic cotton.[25] The central government attributed the in-land transfer of 100,000–200,000 spindles to an insufficient cotton supply, which domestically grown cotton would fulfill, and rising labor costs.[26] Local regula-tors, empowered by decentralization, largely ignored the center's edicts. Besides, sensitivities surrounding local unemployment and development made the BOT's demands difficult to accomplish. In 1997, in spite of the spindle elimination cam-paign, the number of spindles in production increased.[27]

---

23. See "Study on China's Textiles and Clothing Industry and Its Market Expansion Strategy," *Report of the European Commission* (January 2005), 23–24.

24. Steinfeld (1998) examines the soft budget constraints, which prevent SOEs from operating as efficient, profit-driven companies that properly respond to market signals.

25. In 2007, Xinjing produced the majority of the country's domestic cotton. See "China Reviewing Textile Strategy as Going Gets Tough," *Journal of Commerce* (February 29, 1996), and "China: Spindle Production Transformation Project Seeking Cooperation," *Enterprise Information News* (October 07, 1997).

26. See "Textile Mills in China to Move from East to West," *China News Digest* (March 22–23, 1995).

27. Interviews on March 1, 2006, in Beijing with Zhao Hong, former official in the Ministry of Textile Industry, and March 8, 2006, in Shanghai with professor Qingliang Gu, Donghua University.

Reregulation Phase (1998–2001)

Between 1998 and WTO accession, a period of economic downturn during the Asian financial crisis, the central government took a more deliberate approach toward market players in its reregulation. By 1997, Premier Zhu Rongji and other central leaders, including Hao Jianxiu, a former MTI minister who served as vice minister of the State Development Planning Commission between 1998 and 2001, had become concerned about overexpansion along the textile supply chain. Recently demoted textile bureaucrats argued that the competitiveness of the Chinese textile industry vis-à-vis global industry was at stake, especially as demand slowed due to the financial crisis.[28] In February 1997, at the tail end of negotiations concerning the fifth Sino-American textiles agreement, the CCP's Central Economic Working Committee proposed a restructuring of the textile sector as a solution to overexpansion and to force industrial upgrading before WTO accession. Former MTI bureaucrats, including those on the CCP Central Committee, began to lobby Zhu to resuscitate some of the functions of the former textile ministry, which they characterized as the "only" option available. In November 1997, Zhu remarked that despite its myriad problems, textiles could provide "a breakthrough for state sector reform."[29] "Like wild grass, bad roots needed to be cut," explained a former MTI bureaucrat.[30]

Soon thereafter, the state upgraded the BOT and created the State Administration of Textile Industry (SATI), which held government agency status (*guojia jiguan*).[31] To stem overproduction in fiber processing and reduce low-value and low-tech production and equipment, the state practiced what it did best: it resorted to heavy-handed tactics, a legacy of Communist rule. The SATI mandated lower levels of government to regulate "out-of-control" markets, going as far as sending central bureaucrats to state-owned cotton processors to supervise spindle cutting.[32] SATI bureaucrats stood watch as factories destroyed equipment and spindles. During this period, the SATI also delegated restructuring to local governments, which

---

28. See "Zhu Rongji Urges Reforming State-Run Textile Firms," *Xinhua* (November 3, 1997). State leaders believed that with a healthy cotton textile industry the domestic sector would be able to secure lower-cost fabric, inputs for downstream subsectors. See Abernathy, Volpe, and Weil (2006), 2207–32, on the impact of geographical proximity on cost differentials and replenishment dynamics that confer competitive advantages. See also Abernathy et al. (1999), chapter 11, on different uses of textiles.

29. "Zhu Rongji Urges Reforming State-Run Textile Firms," *Xinhua* (November 3, 1997), cited in Moore (2002), 130.

30. Interview on March 1, 2006, with former MTI bureaucrat now employed by the China National Textiles and Apparel Council, the enterprise-level successor organization to SATI.

31. The head of the BOT, former MTI minister Wu Wenying, headed the SATI until 2001, when the government abolished the textile bureaucracy.

32. Between 1998 and 2001, the SATI targeted spindles in the processing of fibers, including cotton and wool. See "China: Spindle Reduction for First Quarter Reported," *Xinhua* (April 6, 1998), and "Spindle-Decreasing Task Fulfilled," *Asian Info Daily China News* (December 4, 1998).

orchestrated mergers, privatization, and foreclosures across textile subsectors "to eliminate poor producers and create local industrial champions."[33]

The SATI declared immediately before China's WTO accession in December 2001 that it had accomplished its goal of destroying ten million spindles, a quarter of the total during that period, and had laid off 1.16 million textile workers.[34] Foreign industry analysts affirmed the SATI's success by attributing the export competitiveness of the Chinese apparel sector to the qualitative and quantitative gains of China's fiber processing industries made by the SATI's restructuring efforts between 1998 and 2001.[35] The SATI's efforts, however, did not permanently enhance government control of textiles. Though the State Council elevated the textile bureaucracy during this period, the central government's authority over the industry continued to be undermined by local authorities because decentralization initiated during the liberal phase shaped reregulation, and regulatory control of the textile supply chain remained fragmented. The demotion of the Ministry of Internal Trade, which had supervised the internal distribution of raw materials, to the State Administration of Internal Trade in 1998 contributed to the undermining of the state's control of developments in the fiber processing sector.

Local Variation in Reregulation
Regulatory capacity and the interpretation of central edicts to eliminate spindles varied by locality. Earlier efforts to decentralize the regulation of textiles meant that in the face of central edicts to destroy millions of obsolete spindles, local governments and stakeholders, empowered by market reforms and administrative restructuring, exploited central-level mandates for their own interests. What is more, local measures to promote local interests and development goals coexisted with the interventionist efforts of the SATI. Local fiscal and infrastructural incentives and local production standards courted FDI, encouraged industrial upgrading, restructured, privatized, or eliminated SOEs, and provided employment for those who lost their jobs.

During the spindle cutting campaign, the Shanghai Municipal government destroyed spindles not to quell rampant overproduction but in response to local economic and financial interests. Shanghai needed to "clean house" because, at that time, Shanghai was falling behind Guangdong in development; thus, under pressure to raise gross domestic product and respond to foreign investors' demands for land and space, the Shanghai government eagerly complied with the mandate to destroy spindles. By 2000, Shanghai shuttered 185 cotton mills and reduced its

---

33. Interview on March 1, 2006, with a former MTI bureaucrat, now a vice president of CNTAC.

34. "Sharpen Competitive Edge to Meet New Challenges: China's Textile Industry Will Further Accelerate Its Restructuring Step," *Report of the State Administration of Textile Industry* (March 31, 2000).

35. See "Study on China's Textiles and Clothing Industry and Its Market Expansion Strategy," *Report of the European Commission* (January 2005), 1–87.

number of spindles from 2.5 million to fewer than one million.[36] The high-tech, high-value orientation of Japanese FDI since 1995 represented Shanghai's aggressive attempts to recalibrate the special administrative region's industrial structure.[37] Also taking the opportunity to reorganize its local industrial structure, local authorities in Wuhan, Hubei Province, eliminated 100 state-owned textile enterprises and replaced them with JVs, which released large numbers of former workers. Other plants simply collapsed, unable to tackle competitive pressures.[38]

In contrast, local governments in Shandong Province protected textile mills as much as they could from the spindle-cutting campaign. To minimize unemployment, they created sixty group companies out of more than three hundred enterprises.[39] In other localities, for every spindle destroyed in state-owned mills, local state entrepreneurs invested in more spindles. In Jiangsu, the Jintan government divested its silk farms and fiber processing factories to local entrepreneurs.[40]

Garment Manufacturing

By 1998, extensive deregulation made the garment sector one of China's most liberalized. Many garment manufacturers owed their establishment to market entry liberalization in textiles and economy-wide market reform, including the devolution of economic decision making to local governments and de facto recognition of private property. They operated as quasi-private collective enterprises and served as contract manufacturers working closely with foreign brand marketers and foreign-invested manufacturers. Typically, foreign partners managed the supply chain, helped set up production processes, and dictated production standards. The central government encouraged value-added production in garment production, but it did not support that policy with concrete industrial programs or financial resources. In fact, in 1994 and 1997 the Chinese government signed bilateral textile agreements that granted unprecedented market access to foreign textile producers and preserved quotas on China-made textile products until 2008, four years after the phasing out of the MFA.[41] Nevertheless, reregulation between 1998 and 2001 proved a critical juncture for the development of a private domestic sector in garment manufacturing. The parallel transformations of Bosideng Corporation, from

36. "Shanghai Restructuring Textile Industry," *Xinhua* (January 26, 2000).

37. Interview in Shanghai on April 19, 2005, with Masayuki Nakatani, senior investment advisor, JETRO.

38. See June 27, 2002 interview, "Will China's Workers Benefit from This 'Win-Win' Deal?" with Dorothy Solinger on WTO entry, published on the website of Human Rights in China: http://www.hrichina.org/public/contents/article?revision%5fid=1846&item%5fid=1845.

39. Qingliang Gu (March 8, 2006) and Ning Pan (March 28, 2006) interviews. See also "Shandong Restructuring Textile Industry," *Xinhua* (June 27, 2001).

40. Interviews on May 16, 2006, in Jiangsu with Jintan government officials and factory visit and interviews with managers of Chenfeng Apparel.

41. Jacobs (1997), 30–37. See also section on textile trade and distribution in this chapter.

a *getihu*, comprising less than seven people in a business, into one of China's largest producers of branded winter coat apparel, and Chenfeng Apparel, from a SOE into a privately owned fashion garment manufacturer, illustrate the government's goals and methods and company-level variation in a nonstrategic industry.

Travelers on Shanghai Airlines, China Eastern, and long distance buses across provinces would recognize the Bosideng logo plastered on seat covers.[42] In 1976, during the early days of the household responsibility system, Gao Dekang, equipped with five sewing machines, founded Bosideng in Changshu, Jiangsu Province, with several family members. From the beginning, Gao exchanged de facto recognition of his private property rights for a transfer of social welfare burdens to Bosideng. Working closely with local officials, Gao registered Bosideng officially as a town and village enterprise, employed local workers, provided them with housing and insurance, and set up a union and a Communist Party branch in his factory. In 2006, Bosideng employed more than twelve thousand workers and operated forty-four subsidiaries nationwide, including factories in Jiangsu and Shandong, an automobile mechanics' shop and wholesales stores in Changshu, and three trading offices in Shanghai.[43] In 2001, Changshu was renamed Kangbor to honor Gao's "revolutionary spirit," and the Ministry of Agriculture designated Kangbor as a *xiaokang*, a designation as one of the most modern, livable villages in China. Moreover, Gao served as a delegate to the National People's Congress as part of Jiang Zemin's Three Represents campaign, a member and president of several national and local sector associations, and the Communist Party secretary for his home village.

Gao attributed Bosideng's success today to operating in the decentralized regulatory context of the textile industry, the intervention of the central government during the 1998 and 2001 phases of reregulation, and Bosideng's strategic alliances and JVs with foreign investors. Between 1976 and 1989, Bosideng engaged mainly in contract work, but in 1989 it began to produce branded apparel. In 1994, Bosideng suffered overproduction when it struggled to understand regional markets for winter coats in China's different climates. With financial assistance from the local government, Bosideng regained market share quickly; between 1995 and 1997, Chinese hikers on Mount Everest wore Bosideng jackets. Between 1998 and 2001, during a period of state retrenchment to restructure the industry and advance industrial upgrading, the central government mandated that Bosideng merge with the Hualian Group in Shenzhen, which held 51 percent of Bosideng when it went public. According to Gao, though both quasi-private companies initially objected to the merger, the state-initiated merger made Bosideng more competitive.

---

42. Factory visit and interviews on March 10, 2006, in Changshu with Bosideng's factory managers and Gao Meizheng, vice general secretary of the Communist Party branch and union, form the basis of this case study.

43. An additional one hundred thousand employees worked for Bosideng's three hundred original equipment manufacturers (OEMs) and two hundred suppliers.

In 2005, Gao purchased Hualian's shares to regain management control, and in 2007 Bosideng successfully listed on the Hong Kong Stock Exchange after ranking second in profit among China's top one hundred garment manufacturers.[44]

Bosideng also benefited over the years from financial incentives granted by local authorities to invest in key services, such as overall product definition, branding, and marketing. Local commerce and inspection bureaus and the local government supported Bosideng through inspection exemptions and business awards to pay for tariffs and duties. These subsidies contributed to Bosideng's success in branding domestically, which prompted one national sector association to designate Bosideng as a promising top China brand to "go global." Moreover, Bosideng formed joint ventures with foreign manufacturers and engaged in contract manufacturing, both of which increased Bosideng's manufacturing and branding capabilities. Bosideng's JV partners included Tyvek (Plus Dorm), a subsidiary of Dupont, which produced cloth used for goose-down clothing and bedding. In addition to its own brands, Bosideng manufactured garments for Gap, Liz Claiborne, Victoria's Secret, and other global brands.

Taking a different path of market-oriented development in the same decentralized, regulatory context, Chenfeng, a contract manufacturer for top global fashion brands, began life as a town and village enterprise operated by the city of Jintan in Jiangsu Province.[45] Chenfeng restructured into a private company during the 1998 to 2001 phase of textile restructuring. In 1997, after suffering from the effects of overexpansion up and down the supply chain, Jintan and the Ministry of Agriculture presented Chenfeng's general manager with the opportunity to own and operate Chenfeng at a discounted price in exchange for guaranteed employment for the garment factory's workers and management of the local farm bureau's mulberry farm and bankrupted silk worm cocoon processing factories. Yin Guoxin, CEO of Chenfeng Group and a delegate to the National People's Congress who actively participated in local and national garment and apparel associations, responded by purchasing the company from Jintan. In 1998, Chenfeng became the first company in China to acquire silk farming assets from the Ministry of Agriculture and set about operating the mulberry farm and investing in the vertical supply and manufacturing chain for silk production. It grew cocoons, spun and dyed silk pieces, subcontracted weaving to local enterprises, and laundered silk fabric. In 2006, Chenfeng, which employed ten thousand workers, had become so successful that local banks routinely offered special loans; moreover, it

---

44. Bosideng raised USD 500 million with help from Morgan Stanley and Goldman Sachs. See Sundeep Tucker, "Global Banks Shift Focus to China's Smaller Companies," *Financial Times* (May 18, 2007).

45. Factory visit in Jintan and interviews on April 23, May 16, and September 8, 2006, with Enock Mundia, general manager of Shanghai Liberty International Trade; Yuzhen Wu, administrative coordinator; and Guohua Yin, president and general manager of Chenfeng Clothing, form the basis of this case study.

received the annual China National Garment Industry Prize awarded by the National Garment Association.

Ineligible for the investment incentives that Bosideng received because it did not brand, retail, and distribute domestically, and tired of producing low-value-added garments, Chenfeng actively engaged in "self-reform," made possible by the extensively liberalized context in textiles. According to Yin Guohua, general manager of one of Chenfeng's factories, Chenfeng's self-reform involved working in close association with foreign clients.[46] Cognizant that the textile industry is a buyer-driven industry in the world market, Chenfeng learned from foreign manufacturers sourcing in China; this induced wide-ranging changes at the factory level, including imparting specifications for the latest fashion garments. Chenfeng worked closely with foreign brand marketers to initiate supplier roundtables. Through several JVs with Japanese trading conglomerates, including Sumitomo, Mitsubishi, and Marubeni, Chenfeng perfected the garment manufacturing process preferred by Japanese companies.[47] Moreover, to maximize its collaboration with brand marketers and fashion designers, and hoping to tap new markets in the post-MFA era, Chenfeng established a subsidiary in 2003 that produced strictly high-end apparel. Moreover, it established the Shanghai Liberty Trading Company to exploit export rights granted to individuals by the Foreign Trade Law of 2004.

INDUSTRIAL AND TECHNICAL TEXTILES

Liu Heng, an official in charge of the machinery sector in the Bureau of Textiles, maintained in 1995 that "our products are badly in need of transformation from low-grade to high-grade to reduce the distinction from advanced world standards. We must devote a lot of time and energy to the unification of machinery and electronics and to adaptability, high efficiency, automation, and consistency."[48] Notwithstanding economic liberalization and subsequent market developments in textiles, because the technical and industrial textile subsectors contribute to military applications and infrastructural and technological development, the central government promoted industrial upgrading, value-added production, and market entry in technical and industrial textiles, and dissuaded investment in low-value, oversaturated subsectors. State leadership emphasized that domestic industry in these subsectors would increase consumption of domestic production (as opposed

---

46. Chenfeng's clients include Liz Claiborne, Juicy Couture, City Line, DKNY, Dana Buckman, and Uniqlo.

47. Export to Japan involved Japanese trading companies, which posted staff in factories for quality assurance. In the post-WTO era, most JVs established for this purpose closed because Japanese retailers operated WFOEs. But Chenfeng continued to do business with them, including Fast Retailing Company.

48. Quoted in "The Chinese Textile Industry: Treating the Dragon's Toothache," *ITS Textile Leader* (Autumn 1995).

to relying on imported inputs).[49] Export restrictions placed on high-tech fabrics in advanced industrialized countries further persuaded the Chinese leadership to promote technical textiles and value-added production.[50]

The higher capital intensity and asset specificity and complexity of production and market transactions of technical textiles influenced the actual methods of intervention. China's five-year plans included provisions specifically aimed at increasing technology transfers, product diversification, and value-added production in technical and industrial textiles. During the period of state intervention in response to impending WTO accession and the Asian financial crisis, the State Development and Planning Commission and the State Economic and Trade Commission under the framework of the Ninth Five-Year Plan (1996–2000) created funds to establish new textile mills, upgrade existing ones with high-tech equipment, and to subsidize the growth of technical textiles and other textiles for industrial uses. These funds focused on increasing efficiency in the production of manmade fibers and upgrading cotton spinning and weaving facilities.[51] They also augmented efforts made in the Eighth Five-Year Plan (1991–95) to promote synthetic fiber production; during that period, the state directed 80 percent of government investment in the textile industry to the construction of synthetic fiber plants.[52]

Between 1998 and 2001, the central government also had at its perusal regulatory instruments available to related ministries, such as the Ministry of Construction and the Ministry of Chemistry Industry, to promote technical and industrial subsectors.[53] The construction ministry used its authority to approve national standards and specifications for infrastructural projects, which helped domestic companies gain market share. Moreover, state-owned petroleum and gas companies controlled the internal trade and distribution of raw material inputs for chemical fiber processing sectors.[54] Furthermore, in line with the "grasp the large, let go of the small" (*zhuada, fangxiao*) guiding principles of SOE reform, the SATI declared bankruptcy and wrote off debt, shut down small, inefficient SOEs with low-value

---

49. See "Chemical Fiber Industry to Be Given Priority," *BBC Summary of World Broadcasts* (September 18, 1996). Military applications include sacks, bulletproof vests, composite textiles, lightweight materials, insulation for aircraft and aerospace, and paramilitary purposes.

50. Pan interview (March 28, 2006).

51. These funds included USD 1.5 billion to subsidize the SATI-directed scrapping of obsolete spindles and related job losses. See "Study on China's Textiles and Clothing Industry and Its Market Expansion Strategy," *Report of the European Commission* (January 2005), 13–15, and "Good Prospects for Textiles for Industrial Use," *China Chemical Fiber* (June 26, 1997).

52. See "China Plans to Revamp Its Textile Industry," *Daily News Record* (October 18, 1990).

53. The Ministry of Construction underwent several rounds (1998, 2003, and 2008) of administrative restructuring, and the State Council downgraded the Ministry of Chemical Industry in 1998 and merged it with ten other government departments to create the State Economic and Trade Commission.

54. The China Petroleum and Chemical Industry Association replaced a government agency in 2001, when the state also corporatized SOEs that controlled the sourcing of raw materials in chemical fiber processing. For more on administrative restructuring in energy subsectors, see chapter 8.

production, and privatized others. It also compelled vertical consolidation to create group companies.[55] Finally, it encouraged localities to court FDI in new product areas and market segments of technical textiles.[56]

Notwithstanding these central efforts aimed at developing value-added and technical subsectors, because of the textile industry's low strategic value, and the already decentralized nature of textile regulation, the central government delegated the authority to approve and allocate central funds earmarked for these subsectors to local governments. Local governments responded en masse with capital allocation and regulatory support.

Geosynthetics and Nonwoven Sectors

The period between 1998 and 2001 witnessed tremendous growth in technical sectors, such as geosynthetics. In addition to state intervention to encourage investment, nonwoven sectors grew overnight after Zhu Rongji visited flood sites along the Yangtze in 1998 and commented that "shoddy dike construction and levees made of bean curd and turtle eggs" had exacerbated the crisis.[57] The MTI created the Association of Nonwoven Manufacturers in 1984, but the nonwoven sector did not receive mass attention until Zhu's 1998 visits. Hao Jianxiu, a former MTI minister and vice minister of the State Development and Planning Commission, further encouraged investments in geotextiles when she became vice chairwoman of the China International Committee for Natural Disaster in 2000. Equipped with central and local capital, local governments responded by providing investment incentives and subsidies for the production of chemical fiber and nonwoven synthetic fabrics.[58] Local authorities offered free land, tax rebates, bank loans, and ad hoc technical standards dictated by major domestic players in the fledgling industry.

Textile producers, both those already in technical and industrial sectors and those not, rushed to enter construction fabrics and related subsectors of geosynthetics.[59] Though higher in capital intensity and asset specificity compared to low-tech fabric and garment subsectors, China-specific sectoral characteristics influenced the development of technical and industrial textiles. It is uncommon globally for

55. See "China Petrochemical Merger Okayed," *China Daily* (August 21, 1997), and interview on September 6, 2006, in Shanghai with Sherry Wu, executive account manager, Cotton Incorporated.

56. Interview on January 7, 2005, in Tokyo with Hiroshi Tsukamoto, president of JETRO.

57. Quote from Lawrence (1998), 19. Nonwoven fibers are inputs for geotextiles, which have applications in construction. That summer, extreme rains flooded the valleys of the Yangtze, Nenjiang, and Songhua rivers and the government sent PLA troops to assist after embankment bursts along the Yangtze River in Jiangxi and Hebei provinces.

58. Interviews on April 15 and September 7 and 8, 2006, with Yimin Wang, professor of material science, Donghua University.

59. These included woven and nonwoven polymers, geogrids, synthetics, pipes, composites, and clay liners.

producers of one technical subsector to manufacture products in other subsectors; but many Chinese manufacturers of geotextiles began in other subsectors, producing such products as carpets, sacks, and building insulation. Other companies began in sectors unrelated to nonwoven products, such as clothing fabric. It also became commonplace for a textile manufacturer to produce construction fabric for road use and other high-grade textiles (for space age, medical, and security applications).[60] Not to be outdone, Shenzhen-based Ocean Power, for example, produced mixes for soft-serve ice cream before entering R&D in geosynthetics (see chapter 7).[61] A 2005 State Council study attributed differences in motivation, timing, and "enterprise diversification" to differences between Chinese market orientation and the market orientation predicted by Western theories.[62]

Despite a booming industry and government subsidies during this period, Chinese companies mainly produced low- and middle-value technical and industrial products for the domestic market. Market saturation and overcapacity in low-end segments became common as factories tweaked existing equipment to enter new markets without considering market demand. Meanwhile, the domestic market continued to rely on foreign imports of high-end technical textiles. All the same, central efforts in formulating industrial policy goals and directing the restructuring of the industry in favor of value-added market segments and technical and industrial sectors, along with local government and firm-level initiatives between 1998 and 2001, created domestic producers that in 2005 accounted for a majority of domestic sales.[63]

Chemical Fiber Processing

Between 1998 and 2001, the central government deployed a similar approach in restructuring and compelling industrial upgrading in other subsectors of technical textiles. Chemical fiber processing serves as a good case study of such efforts. The government focused on developing domestic productive capacity for raw materials since overexpansion in chemical fiber processing drove up demand for purified terephthalic acid (PTA), biocide, polyethylene terephthalate (PET) chips, polyester fiber, and other raw material imports.[64] It directed the construction of chemical fiber manufacturing bases and encouraged foreign-invested JVs and FDI in high-value-added product areas and market segments.[65] In Shanghai, even as the govern-

60. Globally, technical textiles are considered distinct from woven sectors. Equipment configuration constraints and specialization make it difficult to branch into technical textiles. Very seldom do companies producing construction textiles also produce carpets and apparel, as is commonly done in China. Interview on February 9, 2006, in Beijing with a former general manager for PolyFelt China.

61. Interview on April 20, 2006, in Shenzhen with Polo He, CEO and general manager of Ocean Power.

62. See Jia et al. (2005).

63. *European Commission Report* (2005).

64. "PET Seeks Scale Economy," *AsiaInfo Daily China News* (September 2, 1997).

65. See "China Polyester JV Receives Approval," *China Daily* (August 22, 1997); "Investors Consider More Wholly Owned Projects," *Chemical Week* (September 3, 1997).

ment pushed out apparel manufacturers, it encouraged foreign manufacturers to build productive capacity for value-added subsectors.[66] Moreover, the government mandated mergers and acquisitions to create economies of scale and the closure of companies producing low-value-added products.[67]

Not to be outdone, in a move to protect domestic chemical fiber and other raw material processing sectors, the SATI and the SETC led antismuggling and antidumping drives against South Korean and Taiwanese companies, major producers of PET chips and polyester staple fibers. The government claimed that foreign-invested processing companies violated the rule requiring raw materials imports be reexported after value-added processing.[68] "Many textile plants in the region have suffered from mounting stockpiles, resulting from frustration in exports," a SATI official said at the time.[69] The government further attributed the ongoing Asian financial crisis to the illegal dumping. As restitution, SOEs petitioned for a bailout, and the China Chemical Fiber Association under the SATI represented domestic companies at meetings with Taiwanese and South Korean producers. In the end, the foreign producers agreed to lower their export price to below 92 percent of the domestic price.[70] The central government used similar measures, including imposing tariffs, in 2002 and 2003 against South Korean PET chip and polyester staple fiber producers.[71]

State-Company Bargains

The following experiences of foreign-invested manufacturers of garment and technical textiles demonstrate how a strategic value logic shaped subsectoral variation in state control. On the one hand, in low-tech sectors, such as garment manufacturing, local interests to maximize FDI and encourage local development and employment prevailed. In 1992, local investment incentives attracted Taiwanese-invested Joy You, a contract manufacturer of home furnishing products, to relocate its manufacturing capacity from Taiwan to Changping Township in Dongguan County in Guangdong Province. With few sector-specific rules to contend, Joy You, incorporated in the British Virgin Islands, easily obtained a business license from the local commerce department to operate as a wholly foreign-owned enterprise. In 2003, when a local government in Zhejiang Province offered attractive investment incentives, Joy You increased its manufacturing capacity in China by starting a factory there. Similar to other apparel and home furnishing manufacturers that

---

66. Interview on April 19, 2005, with Masaki Yabuuchi, president of JETRO Shanghai.
67. "China Petrochemical Merger Okayed," *China Daily* (August 21, 1997).
68. "China Chemical Fiber Smuggling Hurts Earnings," *Associated Press* (November 30, 1998).
69. "Action Urged to Bail Out Chemical Fibre Firms," *China Daily* (December 8, 1998).
70. "Asian Chemical News: Antidumping Disputes over Polyester Staple Fiber; China PSF Claim Spurs Talks," *Chemical Business NewsBase* (February 4, 2000).
71. "China SETC Proposes Antidumping Measures on South Korean Short Polyester Fibre," *AFX–Asia* (May 30, 2002), and "Punitive Taxes on ROK Imports," *China Daily* (February 11, 2003).

produced predominantly for export, Joy You followed global standards and specifications, ignoring noncompulsory local and national standards set by sector associations. To maintain good relations with local stakeholders, Joy You employed sewing line workers and managers from surrounding towns, cities, and provinces and occasionally wined and dined local officials. In exchange, local commerce departments awarded Joy You with streamlined inspections, and local public security bureaus immediately responded when managers complained of conflicts with workers.[72]

On the other hand, FDI in technical sectors experienced more state intervention than those in apparel manufacturing. Performance Fibers, a U.S.-based producer of high-performance polyester fibers and fabrics, entered China in 1995 as a JV, as was required by law.[73] At that time, Honeywell International, Performance Fibers' former parent company, partnered with Shanghai Chunhui, a state-owned producer of industrial fabrics for neon signs.[74] Because Performance Fibers operated at the intersection of the processing of raw material inputs such as petrochemicals and polyester chips and the manufacturing of technical fabrics used on roads and related to automobiles, it had to obtain requisite permissions and licenses from the Ministry of Chemical Industry, Ministry of Construction, the BOT, and local branches of foreign trade and internal trade departments. Moreover, Performance Fibers had to abide by the rule, designed to protect domestic technical textile producers and generate foreign exchange, that required foreign-invested manufacturers to export 20 to 25 percent of their Chinese production.[75]

Eve of WTO Accession

The marginal contribution of the textile industry to national security and technological advancement meant that the 1998 to 2001 round of reregulation did not represent permanent recentralization or portend future recentralization in textile manufacturing. The promotion of the SATI did not signal the state's intention to permanently enhance its authority over industrial developments in the manufacturing sectors of the textile supply chain. Though the SATI intervened dramatically in cotton processing, and the central government exerted more control over raw materials processing and technical textiles immediately before WTO acces-

---

72. Conversations between February and April 2006 in Taipei with Amy Tsai, managing executive of Joy You.

73. Sun Capital Partners purchased Performance Fibers in 2004. The state had also restricted FDI to JVs in other sectors related to the automobile industry, including automotive parts and engines. Like Performance Fibers, many of these companies restructured to wholly foreign-owned enterprises (WFOEs) as soon as it became legal for subsectors of the automobile supply chain to do so. See Thun (2006) and chapter 8 for a survey of state control of FDI in the automotive industry.

74. In the 2000s, Performance Fibers operated as a WFOE but collaborated with Shanghai Chunhui, a raw material supplier. Interview in Shanghai on September 9, 2006, with Hongjian Sha, general manager of Performance Fibers (Asia).

75. The 25–50 percent export ratio pales in comparison to the 50 percent export rule in the manufacturing of telecommunications equipment detailed in chapter 4.

sion, the government gave limited financial and regulatory resources to the SATI and other related bureaucracies. The SATI did not regulate the level of production or investment, or the market entry and exit of the nonstate sector, and it did not have the capacity to monitor enforcement of central-level edicts. Thus, the SATI represented more the state's attempt to minimize the costs of liberalization than it did deliberate reregulation to enhance state control permanently or even temporarily. The manner in which the state conducted the spindle-cutting campaign represented residual forms of intervention from a Communist party-state no longer concerned with managing the development of nonstrategic industries, such as textiles. What is more, administrative decentralization in previous phases of liberalization permitted local variation in enforcement of central edicts between 1998 and 2001. The textile industry's major contribution to local employment and to economic growth drove local authorities to enforce central edicts according to local interests.

Additionally, the low strategic value of textiles explains the state's decision in its reregulation to retain administrative segmentation in the governance of the textile manufacturing, as opposed to the regulatory consolidation in telecommunications. Before WTO accession, the ministries and departments that regulated textile subsectors operated independently of each other, without coordination, frequently conflicting over how best to regulate. In contrast, during the same period, to achieve state goals, the central government merged ministries that managed subsectors of telecommunications to enhance its control of the telecommunications supply chain.

By the turn of the twenty-first century, with the exception of the processing of natural fibers and other raw materials, the State Council had lifted all sector-specific restrictions on market entry in textile manufacturing. In October 2000, on the eve of WTO accession, the People's National Congress revised the 1979 law on foreign capital enterprises and Chinese-foreign contractual JVs to abolish rules on foreign exchange balances and stipulations requiring foreign-funded enterprises to give priority to Chinese-processed raw materials. At that time, soon-to-retire textile official Liu Heng explained, "Even with such protective measures as local purchase of raw materials, foreign clothiers in China still have to import a large quantity of cloths due to the poor quality of Chinese materials."[76] Revealing the central government's incidental orientation toward the domestic sector, he added, "After years of efforts, Chinese weavers have made tremendous breakthroughs in improving the quality of their products, which are now very competitive. Even the garment industry that insiders say would be hardest hit will be able to survive the revisions [on imports and the business scope of FDI]." All the same, because of the strategic value of textile trade and distribution to foreign economic relations, the rest of this chapter discusses the state's centralized supervision there.

---

76. "China Massively Cuts Restrictions on Foreign Investors," *People's Daily* (October 31, 2000).

TEXTILE TRADE AND DISTRIBUTION: DELEGATED REREGULATION

In the pre-WTO period, the central government retained a deliberate orientation toward textile trade and distribution but delegated regulation to provincial and local branches of the internal and foreign trade ministries. The central government gradually relinquished control of internal trade, but it did not relinquish centralized allocation of import and export licenses and trade quotas. Retaining centralized control of external trade enabled the state to address issues arising from foreign economic relations when it saw fit, which it did during WTO accession negotiations.

Reregulation Phase (1993–1997)

The dismantling of the Ministry of Textile Industry in 1993 ended sector-specific micromanagement of textile manufacturing and empowered local governments and stakeholders to seize influence over local markets and the textile supply chain. The government, however, treated the administration of textile trade with a more deliberate orientation. On the one hand, the overlapping administration of internal trade maintained government control of the internal distribution of raw and processed inputs. To begin, it merged the Ministry of Materials and the Ministry of Commerce to create the Ministry of Internal Trade (MIT). The supply and marketing cooperatives under the MIT dominated the procurement and marketing of domestically produced raw and processed inputs until their abolishment in 2001. The more a raw materials sector contributed to value-added production, the more likely an SMC monopolized procurement and marketing. Moreover, the Ministry of Agriculture and the Ministry of Chemical Industry supervised the internal trade of raw inputs in the natural fiber and chemical fiber processing sectors. The Price Bureau of the State Planning Commission continued to price raw material commodities.

While the state gradually relinquished monopoly of the internal trade of most processed inputs, it did not begin to liberalize natural fibers until WTO accession. As chapter 7 shows, because the domestic production and import of raw materials, including cotton, wool, and petrochemicals, affected the competitiveness of many economic sectors, the state continued to exert more control over the processing and trade of raw materials in the post-WTO era. Even so, the Chinese government delegated the implementation of internal trade supervision, with the exception of FDI, to lower levels of government, making monitoring less likely. Trade rules promulgated upon the MIT's creation limited FDI to equity or cooperative retail JVs in six cities and five special economic zones. To obtain market entry approval, a prospective foreign retail investor had to submit a project proposal and feasibility study to the State Council, which then solicited the MIT's opinion. Only after obtaining State Council approval could an investor apply to the foreign trade ministry for a JV license.[77] Once approved, joint retail ventures had unlimited export privileges but could import only 30 percent of their total retail sales without going through a state-owned foreign trade corporation. In 1995, only fourteen foreign-invested enterprises had received approvals from the State Council and the MIT.

The Chinese government's view of the external trade of textiles as a critical aspect of foreign economic relations influenced how the government allocated trade quotas and licensed those engaged in trade. To retain leverage over trade partners in negotiations, including cross-sector dialogues to join the WTO, the government maintained centralized control of external trade despite a growing domestic textile sector and the high number of local stakeholders created by decentralization. Notably, to enhance its control and increase regulatory capacity, the state reorganized the textile quota allocation system to introduce transparency, limit the power of foreign trade corporations, and eliminate the speculation and profiteering that plagued the black market. The 1994 Regulations on the Management of Textile Export Quotas streamlined quotas distribution and limited transfers between companies; they also favored exporters of value-added products with domestic content. The Committee on Textile Quota Auctions in 1996 expanded the number of products under quotas and reserved quotas for previously disadvantaged private companies and FDI. The state also issued Tentative Measures on the Establishment of Sino-Foreign Joint Venture Trading Enterprises on an Experimental Basis. These measures permitted select FDI to directly import raw materials and semimanufactured goods for their own use and export self-manufactured products without going through FTCs, which monopolized trade at the expense of central imperatives.

The reformed external trade system enabled the state to intervene in 1994 to revoke business licenses and arrest offenders at nine trading companies for violating China's commitment in bilateral agreements against the transshipment of textiles through a third country to circumvent China's allocation of quotas.[78] It also acquiesced to a particularly restrictive Sino-American textile treaty that year. The 1994 accord capped annual export growth in all categories to levels much lower than before; placed tighter restrictions on export amounts for quota violation disputes; and imposed new penalties, including U.S. unilateral action, for transshipment on both China and individual shippers. This accord foreshadowed the 1997 agreement that extended China's tenure on the export quota system for four years after the expiration of the MFA and four years beyond the terms of the WTO Agreement on Textiles and Clothing.[79] Despite what might appear to be harsh terms, the Chinese government made the best of the unfolding WTO accession negotiations by trading

---

77. Lam (1995), 23–24.

78. See Martin (1994), 9–12.

79. Under the 1997 agreement, the United States also reserved the right to treat China as a nonmarket economy in monitoring dumping and could trigger a second safeguard mechanism, which applied to all products in force for twelve years after WTO accession. See Moore (2002) and Jacobs (1997).

more years under textile quotas to protect telecommunications, a more strategic industry.

Liberalization Phase (1998–2001)

The 1998 round of administrative restructuring undermined state control of internal trade. The State Council downgraded the MIT and certain sector-specific ministries, including the Ministry of Chemical Industry. They became the State Administration of Internal Trade and the State Administration of Petroleum and Chemical Industries.[80] These actions reflected the steady shift away from microeconomic controls in sectors and issue areas less strategic to national security and technological advancement.[81] The state did not formally liberalize the marketing and procurement of wool and cotton until 2001 and the Ministry of Agriculture remained; however, the demotion of MIT affected market developments in the manufacturing and marketing of raw and processed materials.[82] It rendered the government's spindle-cutting campaign in fiber processing ineffective as trade in inputs flowed without difficulty even as the State Administration of Textile Industry temporarily raised the Bureau of Textiles' status. Moreover, although foreign brand marketers remained formally prohibited from engaging in internal trade and distribution, a period of de facto liberalization of FDI in apparel retail commenced. Foreign-invested retailers, such as Denmark's Bestseller and Hong Kong's Esprit, circumvented rules prohibiting FDI in retail and distribution. They formed special enterprise structures and engaged in a series of contractual agreements, which were also common among foreign-invested telecommunications service providers, that circumvented market entry rules to invest in internal markets.

Local State-Company Bargains

State control of FDI in retail and distribution during this period of de facto liberalization in the already decentralized textiles varied across companies. Bestseller Fashion Group took advantage of the rules permitting foreign-invested companies to trade "self-manufactured" products by establishing bargains with the local state to engage in domestic retail. The founding of Bestseller Fashion Group China

---

80. These downgraded offices, along with eight other departments, including the State Administration of Textile Industry, came under the supervision of the State Economic and Trade Commission. The China Petroleum and Chemical Industry Association replaced the state agency in 2001. In 2003, to better regulate internal and external trade, the State Council created the Ministry of Commerce.

81. For example, in abolishing the first Ministry of Commerce and Ministry of Materials in 1993, the state relinquished the administrative allocation of production, an authority it held under the command economy, to move toward sectoral guidance, the scope and nature of which this book argues varies across industries.

82. See Brown, Waldron, and Longworth (2005). See also Alpermann (2006), 33–61.

began in 1996 when longtime expatriates Allan Warburg and Dan Friis successfully convinced Troels Holch Poulsen, owner of Bestseller, to enter the Chinese market to source for export and to sell domestically.[83] From there, Bestseller China easily obtained a license to operate as a WFOE that outsourced garment manufacturing for exports. However, to sell in the domestic market, Bestseller had to engage in creative handiwork. To circumvent rules that required licensing Bestseller's trademarks (including Only, Jack & Jones, and Vera Moda) and technology to a domestic company, Bestseller Denmark and Bestseller China signed contracts that granted Bestseller China the rights to Bestseller Denmark's brands, trademarks, and other technology and intellectual property. Next, nearly a decade before the 2004 rules on trade and distribution (promulgated as part of China's timetable of WTO commitments) permitted foreign retailers to distribute products not manufactured domestically, Bestseller China broadly interpreted in its favor trade laws that permitted foreign-invested manufacturers that engaged in domestic production to distribute domestically. To independently market and distribute garments produced by its contract manufacturers, Bestseller engaged in "value-added production" by adding stickers and tags and repackaging the already manufactured garments to bear Bestseller's brands.

Moreover, taking advantage of the abolishment of sector-specific control of the internal supply chain and relaxed enforcement of the prohibition against FDI in apparel retail, Bestseller China distributed its apparel products via Bestseller-owned retail centers and franchises by building good relationships with local authorities across the country. Bestseller China began operating in department stores and stand-alone shops in 1996 by renting spaces stocked with its own inventories and staffed with its own salespeople. Customers paid department stores, which then paid Bestseller China after deducting rent and issued Bestseller China VAT invoices each month. Stand-alone stores, in contrast, operated as Bestseller China's branch offices. The establishment of each branch office required that Bestseller China interact with local commerce and tax bureaus to obtain business licenses and rental contracts; this process, repeated in each location, proved cumbersome and exposed Bestseller to the vagaries of local state protectionism.

Since 1997, Bestseller China also operated franchises with a *"one brand, one city, and one franchise taker"* strategy to minimize competition between franchisees. Because a law on franchises did not exist prior to 1997's Interim Measures for Administration of Commercial Franchise Operations for domestic enterprises and prior to 2004 for FDI, Bestseller set its own contractual terms with franchisees. Bestseller China set sales targets, waived franchise fees, and earned revenue when franchisees bought its products. In 2008, Bestseller China operated fifteen hundred retail outlets in more than 130 cities and led the midmarket fashion segment

---

83. Interview on April 26, 2006, in Beijing with Allan Warburg, general manager of Bestseller Fashion Group (China).

in China. Bestseller directly employed more than eighty-five hundred people and indirectly employed another five thousand through franchises. Bestseller did not plan to change its franchise model despite rules promulgated in 2004 that permitted FDI in franchising. According to Warburg, "The new rules enhance bureaucratic oversight and introduce competition in ways that include cumbersome entry requirements."

In the same regulatory context, other foreign-invested fashion retailers adopted a different strategy. Hong Kong-based Esprit Corporation joined forces with China Resources Enterprises, the Hong Kong subsidiary of state-controlled China Resources Holdings, to open Esprit outlets in China five years after performing poorly with a market entry model similar to that of Bestseller China. Seeking to maximize China Resources Holdings' central and local state connections, Esprit set up the JV after the promulgation of Tentative Measures on Establishment of Sino-Foreign Joint Venture Trading Enterprises on an Experimental Basis. At around the same time, a subsidiary of the State Council's China Everbright IHC Pacific joined forces with Theme International under a similar business model. Esprit and Theme formed these alliances in the hope that potential franchisees would favor companies with the implicit blessings of Beijing.[84] In the mid-1990s, Giordano International, another Hong Kong retailer, had to dramatically scale back its expansion plans because its founder, Jimmy Lai, who has since resigned from the company, made insulting comments about Premier Li Peng.[85]

Reregulation Phase: WTO Accession

It became evident during WTO accession negotiations that textile manufacturing and trade pales in strategic value to other industries more critical for national security and technological advancement. The central government's enhanced management of external textile trade enabled it to exchange more years of textile quotas under bilateral agreements for less openness toward foreign competition in telecommunications services and a restrictive schedule on tariff rate quotas (TRQs) for the import of natural fibers. To begin, to avoid committing China to majority foreign ownership in telecommunications, the Chinese government negotiated a "compromise" involving "sacrifices" in apparel textiles.[86] To convince the U.S. government to relax its insistence on the up-to-51 percent foreign ownership in

84. "Taking an Alternate Route to the Mainland: Esprit's Red-Chip Joint Venture Will Speed Its Expansion in China," *Business Week International Edition* (August 11, 1997).

85. In 2008, despite being penalized a decade earlier, Giordano owned 741 outlets compared to Esprit Holdings' 450 stores, 49 percent of which owned are by Esprit and 51 percent of which are franchised.

86. Interviews on March 1 and April 24, 2006, in Beijing with former textile bureaucrats and current sector association officials, and on February 20 and February 24, 2006, with EU and American embassy officials.

telecommunications services, the Chinese government insisted upon an end to textile restrictions in 2005 as provided by the ATC rather than meet the U.S. demand
for the maintenance of formal textile quotas until 2010 as a condition for American
support of China's WTO membership. Its insistence triggered intense negotiations
in search of a compromise; in the end, the two sides reached an agreement that entailed a 49 percent ceiling on foreign equity ownership in telecommunications basic
services, a 50 percent limit on FDI in value-added services, and a four-year safeguard mechanism for textiles after the ATC expired in 2005. The Chinese government did not lose ground because the textile terms of the bargain simply reiterated
what it had already agreed to in the fifth Sino–American textile agreement.[87]

Moreover, the Chinese government negotiated a tariff rate quota schedule that
expired in 2005, which allowed the government to gain generous revenue from
tariffs imposed on imports of raw commodities, including natural fibers, such as
cotton and wool, and petrochemicals. The WTO accession protocols committed
China to specify annual quantities of grain and fiber imports that pay only 1 percent tariff rate through 2005.[88] However, although China specified a low in-quota
tariff rate of 1 percent, relative to other agricultural commodities, the quantities
considered within the quota for both cotton and wool remained well below a million metric tons annually between WTO accession and 2005 compared to the one-
to-ten million metric tons tariff rate quotas for other commodities. Moreover, the
central government imposed relatively high over-quota tariffs, between 40 percent
and 50 percent for cotton and wool for those years. For example, the TRQ regime set the quantity of cotton imports that pay 1 percent tariff at 818,000 tons
or below in 2002 and increased it to 894,000 tons in 2004. Not until 2006, when
the TRQ regime expired, did the 1 percent rate cover cotton imports under 9.8
million tons; a 5 to 40 percent floating tariff, which varied according to the gap
between market prices and a government-set benchmark price, applied to imports
over that quantity.[89] Additionally, import licensure and quota distribution under
the TRQ subsidized state-owned raw material distributors while farmers received
near zero subsidies. Receiving low priority in import quota allocation and, by default, subjected to higher tariff rates, were nonstate distributors and small and
medium textile enterprises, whose cumulative cotton consumption outpaced domestic supply by four million tons in 2005 and represented the largest consumers
of U.S. cotton.

---

87. See chapters 4 and 5 on the relationship between the strategic value of a sector and reregulation
in telecommunications. The WTO timetable for telecommunications liberalization is outlined in a list
in chapter 4.

88. U.S. Department of Agriculture briefing on China's TRQs for agricultural commodities:
http://www.ers.usda.gov/Briefing/China/wtotrq.htm.

89. "WTO Commitments and Its Implications on Cotton Trade in China," *Research Center for
Rural Economy* (PRC Ministry of Agriculture, 2003), and U.S. Department of Agriculture's China
Tariff Rate Quota information pages, http://www.ers.usda.gov/Briefing/China/wtotrq.htm.

THE FORESHADOWING OF MARKET-ORIENTED
REREGULATION

The dismantling of the Ministry of Textile Industry in 1993 officially commenced the market-oriented development of textile manufacturing. The central government introduced competition and adopted an incidental approach toward market players and significantly reduced deliberate intervention in textile manufacturing. The strategic value and the organization of institutions in a given sector shaped how reregulation varied across manufacturing subsectors between 1993 and WTO accession. Because of existing regulatory overlap, the dismantling of the MTI did not remove regulatory supervision of several subsectors along the textile supply chain. The garment sector became extensively liberalized while the natural and manmade fiber processing sectors contended with other related government offices, including the ministries of Agriculture, Chemical Industry, and Construction. For several years after its creation in 1998 to prepare the textile industry for global competition upon WTO accession, the State Administration of Textile Industry enhanced the central government's authority to promote industrial restructuring and upgrading and value-added production. Moreover, the government intervened more in technical and industrial textiles because of their contribution to infrastructural development and military applications. Structural and China-specific sectoral characteristics influenced actual methods of control in those high-tech, high-value-added subsectors marked with complex production and market transactions. All the same, textile manufacturers operated in a liberal context and contended with local bureaucrats and their interests, not the central government, because of previously launched market reforms and decentralization.

The following list itemizes the economy-wide and sector-specific rules regulating textiles in the pre-WTO era:

INTERNAL TRADE AND DISTRIBUTION
- Tentative Measures on Establishment of Sino-Foreign Joint Venture Trading Enterprises on an Experimental Basis (MOFTEC, 1996)
- Interim Measures for Administration of Commercial Franchise Operations (MIT, 1997)
- Foreign-Invested Commercial Enterprise Pilot Measures (MOFCOM, 1999)

INVESTMENT/MANUFACTURING
- Law on Sino-Foreign Equity Joint Ventures (NPC, 1979, revised 1990, 2001)
- Regulations for the implementation of Law on Sino-Foreign Equity Joint Ventures (SC, 1983, revised, 1986, 1987, 2001)
- Law on Wholly Foreign-Owned Enterprises (NPC, 1986, revised 2000)
- Article 20 of Provisions for the Encouragement of Foreign Investment, which encouraged investment from Hong Kong, Macao, and Taiwan (SC, 1986)
- Regulations on Encouraging the Investment of Taiwan Compatriots (SC, 1988)

- Law on Sino-Foreign Cooperative Joint Ventures (NPC, 1988, revised 2000)
- Eighth (1991–95) and Ninth Five-Year (1996–2000) Plans
- Direction on Regulation for Transforming the Operational Mechanism of State-Owned Enterprises (SC, 1992)
- Company Law (SC, 1994)
- Catalogue for the Guidance of Foreign Investment Industries (State Council, SPC, SETC, MOFTEC, 1995, revised 1997)

EXTERNAL TRADE AND DISTRIBUTION

- Sino-American Textiles Agreements (SATA) (SATA I covered 1980–82; SATA II, 1983–87; SATA III, 1987–93; SATA IV, 1994–96; and SATA V, 1997–2008)
- Multi-Fiber Agreement (China joined MFA III in December 1983 and signed MFA IV in 1986 and signed WTO's Agreement on Textiles and Clothing, which replaced MFA in December 1994)
- Foreign Trade Law (1994)
- Regulations on the Management of Textile Export Quotas (State Council, 1994)
- Committee on Textile Quota Auctions (MOFTEC, 1996)
- Tentative Measures on Establishment of Sino-Foreign Joint Venture Trading Enterprises on an Experimental Basis (MOFTEC, 1996)

The central government's regulatory approach toward textile trade and distribution differed from the goals, state-industry relations, and control methods found in manufacturing. To maintain control of the internal trade of raw materials and preserve leverage in foreign economic relations, the central government retained centralized management of trade licenses and production quotas set by bilateral and multilateral agreements. It delegated implementation, however, to local commerce bureaus. When it counted the most, enhanced control over textile trade allowed the state during WTO accession protocol negotiations to bargain continued trade restrictions on textiles for concessions in more strategic sectors and issue areas.

7

SECTOR ASSOCIATIONS AND LOCALLY LED REREGULATION OF TEXTILES IN THE WTO ERA

To join the World Trade Organization, China committed to extending bilaterally negotiated export restraints in textiles in exchange for a lower ceiling on foreign direct investment in telecommunications. This trade-off revealed the low strategic value of textile manufacturing and the Chinese government's purposive orientation toward market reform to achieve paramount goals of national security and technological advancement. According to an official at the National Development and Reform Commission, "China has a tendency to represent 'national' interests over industry interests; basically, the interests of the textile industry have not been on the top of the state's agenda."[1]

In 2001, immediately before WTO accession, the Chinese government completely eliminated administrative guidance of textile manufacturing and shifted to utilizing macroeconomic policies to influence industry developments. Sector and business associations replaced industry-specific government offices, and local authorities administrated textiles to further local interests. As one local government official explained, "Universal commercial regulations apply to the textile industry, but localities have their own regulations, controls, and practices."[2]

Decentralized engagement characterized the overall pattern of state control in the post-WTO era but the extent and nature of reregulation varied across textile subsectors according to a strategic value logic and China-specific and structural sectoral characteristics. The organization of institutions and global economic

---

1. Conversation in Beijing on January 16, 2006.
2. Interview on March 10, 2006, with local commerce bureau official in Changshu, Jiangsu Province.

reverberations elucidate reregulation across time. Garment and woven fabric manufacturers, which were not critical for national security or technological advancement, faced few regulatory entry barriers and operated in liberal markets. But as an important part of the international textile supply chain, they contended with the ups and downs of the worldwide industry and the licensing and quota allocation regime. The regime was established by the state in response to global protectionism, and implemented by local governments according to local interests.

Industrial and technical textiles faced a different institutional environment. Although few sector-specific rules persisted, related central ministries collaborated with local governments and companies to promote domestic industry and soften the impact of global oil and resource prices. To control what the state considered as strategic raw materials and high-tech inputs, the newly consolidated trade bureaucracy imposed nontariff barriers despite meeting WTO commitments. The delegation of implementation to decentralized actors, however, meant that regulatory outcomes varied according to locality and company. Industrial attributes structured actual methods of intervention. Company case studies reveal the dominant regulatory pattern in textiles and illustrate subsectoral and overtime developments.

Table 7.1 charts the various phases of market liberalization and reregulation across subsectors between 1993 and 2010. By relinquishing state control of textiles, China decidedly departs from the pronounced role of the state and the intimate alliance between government and private domestic industry in textiles that is characteristic of the East Asian developmental state. The mini case studies of countries at the end of this chapter reveal the strikingly different approach toward textiles taken by Japan, South Korea, and Taiwan.

BUSINESS ASSOCIATIONS AND
MACROECONOMIC RULES

The State Council eliminated administrative guidance and supervision of the textile industry on the eve of China's WTO accession in 2001. It abolished the State Administration of Textile Industry (SATI) and overnight quasi-government sector associations, enterprise-level organizations created throughout the 1980s and 1990s, became industry representatives at the national level.[3] The China National Textile and Apparel Council (CNTAC) quickly occupied the former ministry's offices on Beijing's Changan Road, where commanding ministries traditionally stood.

---

3. Sector and business associations functioned as informal appendages of ministries and research institutes as retired bureaucrats, "reassigned" civil servants, and "victims" of administrative reforms worked in them. For more on the varying nature of associations in China, see Foster (2001).

TABLE 7.1. TEMPORAL VARIATION IN TEXTILES REREGULATION

	Emphasis	Year
Textile manufacturing	Liberalization	1993–97: The government dismantled the Ministry of Textile Industry.
	Reregulation	1998–2001: The creation of the State Administration of Textile Industry reasserted state control.
	Liberalization	2001–09: Sector and business associations replaced the textile bureaucracy.
	Reregulation	2002–09: Local stakeholders reformulated old, and created new rules to favor local interests.
		2004–06: Central government and sector associations encouraged restructuring in chemical fiber processors in response to global oil and resource price hikes; upgrading in technical textiles.
Textile trade and distribution	Reregulation	1993–97: The Ministry of Internal Trade was created.
	Liberalization	1998–2001: The government downgraded the Ministry of Internal Trade.
	Reregulation	WTO Accession: China's WTO protocol agreement traded textile export restrictions for a lower foreign investment ceiling in strategic industries, established tariff rate quotas to protect domestic raw material producers, and committed to liberalizing retail and distribution.
		2003–05: The creation of the Ministry of Commerce consolidated management of internal and external trade and distribution and created new rules that liberalized internal trade and distribution while favoring the domestic sector.
		2006–08: Export taxes were recalibrated to shelter the domestic sector during global slowdown.

The following list itemizes the economy-wide and sector-specific rules regulating textiles in the post-WTO era:

WTO ACCESSION 1999–2001
- Agreement on Textiles and Clothing (ACT) with the founding of WTO (January 1, 1995, to December 31, 2004)
- US-China WTO Market Access Agreement (November 17, 1999) (four-year safe-guard mechanism for textiles after ATC expires in 2005, which confirmed the fifth Sino-American Textiles Agreement)

POST-WTO 2002–2007
INTERNAL TRADE AND DISTRIBUTION
- Protocol on the Accession of the PRC, Part 1, Section 5 (1999)
- Interim Provisions on the Establishment of Chinese-Foreign Trading Joint Ventures (MOFCOM, 2003)

- Foreign Trade Law (amendments 2004) and Measures on Registration of Foreign Trade Operators (2004)
- Administrative Measures on Foreign Investment in the Commercial Sector (MOFCOM, 2004)
- Administrative Measures on Commercial Franchise Business (MOFCOM, 2004, revised 2007)

INVESTMENT
- Opinion on Further Deepening Reform of the Cotton Circulation System (State Council, 2001)
- Catalogue for the Guidance of Foreign Investment Industries (MOFTEC, 2002)
- Government Procurement Law (GPL) (MOFCOM, 2003)
- Catalogue for the Guidance of Foreign Investment Industries (NDRC and MOFCOM, 2004)

EXTERNAL TRADE AND DISTRIBUTION
- US-China WTO Market Access Agreement (November 17, 1999) (four-year safeguard mechanism for textiles after ATC expires in 2005, which basically confirmed the fifth Sino-American Textiles Agreement)
- Foreign Trade Law (amended and adopted by 10th National People's Congress, 2004)
- Circular on Relevant Policies to Promote Chinese Textile Industry to Shift to New Ways of Growth in Foreign Trade and Support Chinese Textile Enterprises to Go Global (MOFCOM, Ministry of Finance, and NDRC, 2006)

Staffed by former textile bureaucrats, the CNTAC functioned as a business federation, representing textile associations and serving as a liaison between government and business.[4] It also provided nonbinding guidance, supervision, and coordination of industry performance and subsectoral development. The State Economic and Trade Commission oversaw the CNTAC and other textile associations until 2003. Administrative restructuring ended bureaucratic oversight and the State-Owned Assets Supervision and Administration Commission became owner and manager of the associations' assets. Although technically state-owned enterprises, the CNTAC and its member associations received little funding from the central government. To cover administrative overhead and finance its activities, the CNTAC operated as a consultancy, published trade journals, and organized trade fairs.

Most local textile offices operated as SOEs. Some local governments continued to operate textile bureaus supervised by local branches of the NDRC, due to tradition and not government mandate. Shanghai's former textile bureau, for example, operated as an SOE with assets managed by the municipal SASAC. "The CNTAC

---

4. Former MTI officials, including the last textile minister Wu Wenying, headed sector associations.

interacts with these local textile departments in an exchange-based and not *guanli* (management-based) relationship. The CNTAC does not exert *chuanli* (authority)," explained Li Jinbao, director of the Department of Science and Technical Development at the CNTAC.[5]

Sector associations' role as liaison between government and business became salient in the more strategic subsectors of textiles. These decentralized actors worked closely with central and local government agencies to promote domestic industry in technical textile sectors and assisted in central administration of textile trade and distribution. Sector associations representing technical textiles partnered with the Ministry of Housing and Urban-Rural Development (formerly the Ministry of Construction), the Textile Industry Standardization Institute, oil and petrochemical bureaucracies, and other central and local government agencies to set national standards and promote technological upgrading through subsidies, research grants, and fiscal and investment incentives. The China Chamber of Commerce for Import and Export of Textiles (CCC-T) and its member business associations allocated export quotas on behalf of the Ministry of Commerce and the State Administration of Industry and Commerce (SAIC). They also distributed import and export licenses approved by the NDRC and the Customs Administration and assisted the Administration for Quality Supervision, Inspection, and Quarantine (AQSIQ) in conducting import and export inspections. Additionally, the CCC-T and other sector associations represented domestic industry at international forums during trade disputes and foreign economic exchanges.

Economy-Wide Rules and Macroeconomic Policies

The elimination of a textile-specific central bureaucracy illustrates China's move away from microeconomic controls in nonstrategic industries. It undermined the center's authority over textiles and reduced the likelihood the state would again assume the deliberate approach it took between 1998 and 2001. Rather, in the decade following WTO accession, economy-wide rules, macroeconomic policies, and non-sector-specific micropolicy levers influenced industrial growth and promoted domestic capacity and upgrading in textiles. To begin, the government's interest rates and fiscal policies, which applied to the entire economy, affected textile development. Low interest rates encouraged infrastructural investment while periodic adjustments curtailed overexpansion. Fiscal policies explicitly favored FDI until 2007, when the State Council reconfigured taxation schemes to increase revenue and strengthen the competitiveness of domestic companies.[6] New legislation standardized corporate income tax at 25 percent for all businesses and the new

---

5. Interview on April 24, 2006, in Beijing with Li Jinbao, vice president of science and technology at CNTAC.

6. Interview on November 11, 2005, in Shanghai with Vivian Jiang, an accountant at Deloitte, Touche, and Tohmatsu. Also see "Ministries Clash over Plan to Raise Income Tax on Foreign Firms," *Nikkei Weekly* (August 8, 2005).

Corporate Tax Law abolished tax incentives for FDI.[7] Moreover, the government periodically adjusted tariffs on textiles at the behest of sector associations or bilateral pressures during periods of economic volatility to address an overheating economy or to soften the blow on domestic companies.

Additionally, to increase exports and attract export-oriented FDI, the government strictly managed its currency regime to maintain a low value for the renminbi. This non-sector-specific policy for currency control disproportionately affected exporters and importers in the value-added segments of the industry. For exporters in the high-end segments, imports of core technology were a significant proportion of production costs. As currency control kept Chinese exports competitive in global markets, this macroeconomic tool led to the adoption of a de facto import substitution policy in technical sectors, which benefited domestic industry and hurt importers. In 2005 the state adopted a slightly more flexible foreign exchange regime. The government released the RMB, previously fixed at a certain rate to the U.S. dollar, to a restricted float of +/- 0.3 percent a day against the dollar and based on a currency basket.[8] Because of the minuscule adjustment, however, most foreign investors have not changed their strategies for expansion in China.[9] During the global economic slowdown in 2008, to alleviate the impact of the collapse and shutdown of small and medium enterprises, the central government temporarily returned to the dollar peg.[10]

Furthermore, exercising macroeconomic levers that increased foreign reserves and monetary policy flexibility, the central government both loosened and tightened restrictions on capital flows to bolster or scale back economic growth and support state-owned financial institutions and domestic industry. It loosened restrictions on select types of capital outflows to boost the competitiveness of Chinese companies overseas. New rules enhanced the oversight of portfolio investment to increase fiscal revenue; for example, the rules cracked down on the "round-tripping" behavior typical of domestic companies incorporated offshore to take advantage of fiscal incentives for FDI. Moreover, the government set bank reserve requirements to reduce overheating and overexpansion in sectors, such as chemical fiber processing; but to encourage exports, it issued guidelines that ordered banks to lend to companies tapping foreign markets.[11] It also applied tariffs and quotas on the trade of specific inputs—such as natural fibers and petrochemicals—and select product

7. See "Mixed Feelings over China's New Tax System," *Asia Times* (March 21, 2007), for details on the Corporate Income Tax Law that took effect on January 1, 2008, and "Beijing Phasing Out Tax Incentives for Foreign Firms under New Strategy," *Nikkei Weekly* (February 18, 2008), on the Corporate Tax Law.

8. See "From T-Shirts to T-Bonds—China and the World Economy," *Economist* (July 30, 2005).

9. "Top Execs Stick to Expansion in China," *Nikkei Weekly* (July 25, 2005), and interviews between 2005 and 2008 with managers of foreign-invested export-oriented manufacturers.

10. See "China Needs to Focus on Job Creation," *Economic Observer* (November 25, 2008).

11. See "Chinese Banks Encouraged to Support Exporters, Processing Abroad," *Xinhua* (August 3, 1999).

categories, such as apparel, to promote domestic producers and encourage industrial upgrading.

Non-sector-specific microeconomic levers also affected the level and direction of FDI and promoted domestic productive capacity and industrial upgrading in textiles. These microeconomic mechanisms included labor market and government procurement policies and non–sector-specific rules for commerce, such as restrictions on wholly foreign-owned enterprises. The Labor Contract Law, promulgated in 2007, covers labor-intensive industries, such as textiles. It made dismissing contracted workers more difficult and gave CCP-controlled trade unions more influence.[12] In response, foreign investors expressed fears of relying on temporary workers in lieu of contracted ones or worker stoppages.[13] Labor clashes following the law's issuance reveal, however, that local authorities often persuaded relevant stakeholders to resolve disputes rather than provide the legal recourse guaranteed by law. Moreover, State Council announcements during the 2008 global slowdown promised employment for the forty million workers in the labor-intensive light and textile industries. New measures required companies to handle migrant-related issues internally, local governments to train and provide employment in destination and homes areas, and company-level communication mechanisms between labor and capital.[14] Measures aimed at protecting employers, including those that delayed setting a minimum wage and relaxed rules on company contribution to insurance funds, offset labor-oriented measures.

The Government Procurement Law indirectly subsidized the technical sectors of textiles that are more strategic to national security and to technological and infrastructural development.[15] For example, the Shenzhou VI spaceship project procured only domestically produced technical fabrics. Moreover, in June 2009, during a global financial crisis, the NDRC ordered government agencies to buy only Chinese-made products with the USD 600 billion economic stimulus. It reinforced the rule in November of that year when it notified domestic and foreign companies that products using technology developed in China and trademarks that registered first

---

12. A survey of 436 companies (97 percent FDI and 3 percent Chinese enterprises), which measured employer reaction to the second draft of the Labor Contract Law, found that more than half believed the law would have a negative or very negative impact. For survey results on particular clauses, see Hewitt Associates and Baker & Mckenzie, *The Hewitt Global Report* (April 2007). For analysis on the impact of the law on FDI, see the 2007 and 2008 issues of the White Paper of the American Chamber of Commerce of the People's Republic of China.

13. "Firms Fear New Chinese Labor," *Nikkei Weekly* (August 6, 2007), and "China's Labor Law Raises U.S. Concerns," *Financial Times* (May 2, 2007).

14. Statements made by the newly created Minister of Human Resources and Social Security (former Ministry of Labor) in a press conference on November 20, 2008.

15. The Government Procurement Law mandated that priority be given to purchasing "local" goods, construction work, and services. Yet to achieve state goals, such as infrastructural modernization, the government exempted SOEs in strategic industries from compliance.

in China would receive preference in procurement.[16] Other non-sector-specific micropolicies with impact on textiles included laws on franchises, foreign investment in commercial services, and the Foreign Trade Law. Additionally, when demand fell due to the global financial crisis, ailing textile manufacturers in overexpanding textile subsectors, such as dye and printing, declared bankruptcy under the Law on Bankruptcy issued in 2007. Because deregulation and decentralization characterized the dominant pattern of state control in textiles, the non-sector-specific rules discussed here became microcontrol levers when local authorities and stakeholders exercised discretionary enforcement that selectively promoted or discouraged local textiles.

TEXTILE MANUFACTURING: DECENTRALIZED REREGULATION

In the post-WTO era, deregulation combined with decentralization in textile manufacturing to undermine state control and enhance the vagaries of the postreform local state. Textile sector associations and local governments exercised discretion in enforcing rules of commerce and wrote new rules and reformulated old ones to promote local industry and maximize local employment and FDI. State-industry relations and control measures across subsectors unraveled according to a strategic value logic; the structuring effects of sectoral characteristics shaped the actual methods employed. Institutional factors and economic conditions explain temporal adjustments in regulation.

LIBERALIZATION PHASE (WTO ACCESSION–2003)

In the period shortly after WTO accession, local governments and branches of the commerce ministry and sector and business associations governed industry developments to achieve local development goals. Textile manufacturing's high labor requirements and, therefore, contributions to local employment augmented the local governments' interests. Local branches of the Communist Party maintained political influence through state-controlled labor unions.[17] Moreover, textile associations functioned as arenas for companies and other organizations to network and build relationships with each other and the relevant bureaucracies. Through sector and business associations, companies established relationships with suppliers, potential customers, local governments, and provincial branch officials of central-level ministries, which regularly gave special treatment in product quality inspections and

---

16. See "Google Is Not Alone in Discontent, but Its Threat to Leave Stands Out," *New York Times* (January 14, 2010).

17. The Labor Contract Law of 2007 reiterated the union requirement.

export quota allocations. For example, local customs routinely waived the export inspections of politically favored companies.[18] These associations, in turn, charged companies for consulting services, which provided opportunities through supplier roundtables and trade fairs to connect with potential domestic and foreign clients.

Sector associations also coordinated industrial and professional development for its members. The CNTAC operated testing and quality inspection labs and proposed the China Corporate Social Compliance 9000 Textiles (Ch 9000T), a China-specific standard for corporate social responsibility in the textile industry. This standard did not prove particularly popular, however, since garment manufacturers typically aimed to meet global industry standards at the behest of brand marketers and foreign retailers.[19] Sector associations, along with the Ministry of Commerce, the AQSIQ, and other relevant government departments, further supported garment, furniture textile, and fabric manufacturers through an award system, including special recognition and inspection exemptions and tariff discounts, to produce, brand, and market value-added products. For example, the China Textile Information Center awarded "Fabrics China" certification, similar to the Lycra certification, to qualifying enterprises. In addition, manufacturers, such as Bosideng, received export inspection and tariff exemptions for its efforts to brand globally. By the same token, the Ministry of Commerce, the Ministry of Finance, and the National Development and Reform Commission, at the initiative of the CCC-T, sponsored a "Going Out Fund" that encouraged domestic textile mills to tap markets and establish production lines overseas.[20]

The state retained the discretion to intervene in issue areas that affect strategic state imperatives, such as social stability and foreign economic relations. Textiles' labor intensity, highly polluting production, and ease of market entry, as well as local rents and the decentralized enforcement of business, environmental, and labor regulations, often led to labor and other business disputes concerning factory closures and violations of environmental and labor regulations and other corrupt practices.[21] The central government rarely intervened, doing so only when incidents jeopardized party legitimacy and other political or economic goals.[22] Through the assistance of CCC-T and local commerce departments, the state also retained over-

---

18. Factory visits and interviews between 2005 and 2008 with managers of garment manufacturers operating in greater Shanghai and Guangdong, Jiangsu, and Zhejiang provinces.

19. Gu interview (March 8, 2006).

20. The 2006 Circular on Relevant Policies to Promote Chinese Textile Industry to Shift to New Ways of Growth in Foreign Trade and Support Chinese Textile Enterprises to Go Global allocated RMB 560 million to projects related to technology innovation and restructuring and RMB 800 million for "going global," which provincial governments were to distribute.

21. "Liaoyang Petrochemical Commences Construction of 10 MLN TIA Refinery," *China Chemical Reporter* (August 2, 2009), is representative of protests against chemical fiber processors in northeast China, and "Chinese City Suspends Work on Chemical Plant after Pollution Complaints," *Associated Press* (May 31, 2007), of such protests in southern China.

22. Interviews with industry insiders between 2005 and 2008.

sight of textile trade to ensure it did not exceed quantitative restraints imposed by international agreements. The actual exercise and implementation of discretionary authority, however, varied according to local conditions and the decentralized actors involved.

Industrial and Technical Textiles

The Ministry of Commerce cautioned that the development of the global textile industry and competition revealed that no country can dominate textiles for long and, thus, the Chinese industry needed to constantly reinvent and pursue industrial upgrading.[23] The central government also extensively liberalized market entry in technical and industrial textiles, but it more deliberately promoted domestic industry in these subsectors because of their strategic value to national security and technological development. The central government earmarked subsidies and grants for R&D, industrial upgrading, and technical standards setting. An informant explained, "*Guobiao* [national standards] deals with more important, security related issues whereas industrial or company standards govern most of textiles."[24] Moreover, fiscal and investment incentives encouraged market entry in high-tech, value-added textile subsectors. Policies on the procurement of raw materials and energy resources also indirectly promoted the growth of these textile subsectors. Actual control outcomes varied according to the decentralized actors involved, which responded to central initiatives with their own rules and regulations.

Central policies included the 2004 Catalogue for the Guidance of Foreign Investment Industries ("2004 Catalogue"), which listed the production of special textiles for engineering use, weaving, dyeing, and post dressing of high-grade loomage face fabric as encouraged sectors; it removed the treatment and production of urethane elastic fiber and polyester from the encouraged category because of those subsectors' tendency to overheat.[25] In 2005, the Ministry of Science and Technology added high-performance chemical fiber processing to the eight areas designated for development under the 863 Program. The Eleventh Five-Year Plan (2006–10) further promoted technological upgrading in textile machinery and R&D in textile and clothing sectors.[26] The 15-year Medium-to-Long-Term Plan for Science and Technology (2006–20) also included funding lines for technical textiles. The plan called for special funding for producers of industrial fabric with applications for airplanes and other aviation equipment for civilian use. Even before the Sichuan

---

23. See Zhao (2005b).

24. Li Jinbao interview (April 24, 2006).

25. Other overheating sectors the government tried to control via policy included the manufacturing of galvanized boards, the smelting and rolling of ferrous metal, and the processing of scrap metal.

26. See European Commission (2005), 15.

earthquake in early 2008, the central government earmarked company-level funding for the commercialization of high-performance fiber.[27]

The 863 Program, which funded R&D involving high-tech materials, routinely
sponsored collaborative efforts between chemical fiber processors, technical textile manufacturers, and universities and research institutes.[28] For example, Donghua University in Shanghai has twenty-one ongoing technical innovation projects
with the Shanghai Textiles Holding Group, an SOE and the city's largest textile
conglomerate.[29] The 863 Program also supported basic research, such as the development of Bt cotton strands, whose commercialization the government funded
through farms owned and operated by the People Liberation Army's Xingjiang
Productions and Construction Corps.[30]

The central government also indirectly subsidized technical sectors by securing raw material inputs through foreign economic bargains and by calibrating fiscal
policies on income, trade, energy, and high-tech content. The central government
ensured that chemical fiber processors obtained stable and inexpensive access to raw
material inputs.[31] These raw material inputs included oil procured from countries
in the Middle East, Central Asia, Latin America, Africa, and Southeast Asia that
China befriended through investments, loans, concessions, and aid.[32] Fiscal methods also included levying an export tax on energy and metal products and raw materials to discourage the growth of energy-intensive and pollution-prone exports,
and reducing import fees to ensure domestic access to critical production inputs.[33]
Moreover, the central government, and some local ones, periodically awarded tax
breaks to companies that satisfied indigenous intellectual property thresholds.

Heeding central government calls for industrial upgrading, technical and industrial textile associations, in conjunction with government departments in charge of
high-tech and raw material inputs, viewed their primary role as sponsors and pro-
moters of industrial upgrading in subsectors with construction, military, shipbuild-

27. Y. M. Wang interview (September 25, 2008).

28. Y. M. Wang interviews (April and September 2006).

29. During the Mao era, at least a dozen colleges and engineering institutes focused primarily
on disciplines related to apparel and textiles. They have changed their names and merged with other
colleges as the government shifted away from a sector-specific strategy toward textiles. East China
Textiles Science and Technology was renamed Textile University in the 1970s and Donghua in the
1980s.

30. Chinese scientists engineered Bacillus thuringiensis (Bt) crops to resist insects while posing
limited threats to other organisms. Interview in Beijing with a MOST official on March 2, 2006. See
also Rozelle et al. (2002), Wu (2007), and Roisli (2006).

31. Y. M. Wang interviews (September 7 and 8, 2006) and Hongjian Sha interview (September 9,
2006). See also "The Halo Effect," *Economist* (October 2, 2004), on how increases in global prices on
raw materials and commodities offset China's comparative advantage in the global economy.

32. A growing literature on China's cultivation of authoritarian allies to secure raw materials for the
purpose of industrial development and its impact has emerged.

33. "Beijing Raises Tax on Energy and Metals Products," *South China Morning Post* (October 28,
2006).

ing, aviation, and other industrial applications. Inside the halls of the dilapidated building that formerly housed the Ministry of Textile Industry, the pervasive conviction among former textile bureaucrats, now heads of sector associations, is that China relied too much on imports of manufacturing equipment and high-tech fabrics and that when Chinese companies produced high-value fabrics, they relied too heavily on expensive raw material imports. CNTAC officials also expressed concern that FDI and foreign-invested JVs dominated the domestic production of equipment components and spare parts. Export restrictions of high-tech industrial fabrics imposed by advanced industrialized countries justified calls to substitute imports.[34]

"To alleviate China's indigenous high-tech deficiency," the CNTAC also released five-year development plans.[35] The CNTAC's five-year plan released in 2005 echoed the Eleventh Five-Year Plan, which listed industrial textiles as an industry to be encouraged, and the MOST's emphasis on indigenous technological innovation. To support this plan, the CNTAC released a package of nonfinancial incentives, dubbed the "Direction 28 Plus 10," to promote R&D and domestic supply chain capacity in twenty-eight areas and ten processes. Yet the CNTAC did not have the resources or the political urgency needed to supervise this initiative; two years after the program's commencement, it had not produced reports or company case studies to track the program's progress.[36]

Politics of Decentralization

The decentralized nature of textile governance shaped the nature of central and local promotion of technical textiles. Local governments and business associations distributed and allocated resources based on local criteria. In this context, local authorities reformulated old rules, created new ones, and entered into formal and informal arrangements that favored local industry. Domestic companies established patronage relationships with local governments eager to enhance local development and maximize employment and FDI. Developments in chemical fiber processing illustrate how central edicts enacted on the local level led to overexpansion in less-capital-intensive subsectors with low-tech requirements.

Moreover, local distribution of central and local funds reserved for high-value, high-tech projects occasionally led to misappropriation. For example, faked R&D proposals ran rampant.[37] "Because the government isn't so concerned about taxpayers' money, it gives away money in R&D funding; as long as you can make up a good reason for the money, projects are awarded. As a result, there is a lot of waste and a lot of money goes to power interests," explained Wang Yimin, professor of

34. Interview in Beijing on September 14, 2006, with Baiyi Wang, High Technology R&D Center, MOST.

35. Interview with Zhao Hong (March 1, 2006).

36. Interview with Zhao (September 23, 2008).

37. Interviews in Beijing, Guangdong, Jiangsu, Shanghai, and Zhejiang with industry experts, industrial and technical textile manufacturers, and sector associations between 2005 and 2008.

material science at the Shanghai Modern Institute of Textiles, Donghua University.[38] At other times, funding criteria eschewed national imperatives to benefit local development. For instance, in 2008, in response to China's participation in several environmental agreements, Shanghai earmarked funding for industrial textiles with energy-saving and recycling applications as much to support local industry as to promote green energy. Relatedly, local stakeholders, to protect local markets, often colluded to set technical standards in more capital-intensive subsectors with high-tech requirements.

Chemical Fiber

Beginning in the late 1980s, as multinationals, such as Dupont, exited heavily polluting subsectors of technical and industrial textiles, central policies began to encourage investments in chemical fiber processing, hoping to fill market gaps and increase China's capacity in these areas.[39] In this context, China-specific sectoral characteristics, incomplete and ambiguous rules on environmental and labor standards, and the decentralized nature of regulatory governance influenced the development of chemical fiber processing. In 1995, when U.S.-invested Performance Fibers entered China, the Chinese chemical fiber industry was in its infancy.[40] A decade later, overcapacity characterized the subsector as companies rushed to produce for domestic and export markets.[41]

Market entry proved easy. Rules on manufacturing and quality control were incomplete, easy to dodge, and frequently went unenforced. To maximize job creation and maintain local tax revenue, localities generously granted licenses and investment incentives. Companies wishing to enter the market easily obtained loans from local banks or informal financial institutions, purchased extruder machines, recycled chemical fiber and other regenerated and inorganic materials, hired labor eager to work, and began operation. Newly corporatized SOEs and quasi-private companies flooded the highly polluting and technologically less complex subsectors of chemical fiber as Dupont and other companies entered biotechnology and other new industries. Kingring Group, one of China's largest neon sign manufacturers, produced popcorn prior to entering chemical fiber processing. The constant infusion of credit allowed factories to keep machines running, and the substitution of inorganic materials artificially inflated quality and allowed companies to compete furiously by cutting prices. An industry insider remarked, "It's like drugs because the government can't leave, banks can't leave, and enterprises can't leave. Those

---

38. Interview with Y. M. Wang (September 25, 2008).

39. When Performance Fibers' former parent, Honeywell, exited chemical fibers, it chose to keep Spectrum, the business that produced bulletproof vests.

40. Interview with Sha (September 9, 2006).

41. The handbook on investments designated chemical fiber processing as a "discouraged sector," but the state did not enforce market entry restrictions because of its low strategic value. Sector associations also indirectly promoted market saturation through encouraging the modernization of textile equipment.

who suffer are the workers because their salaries become lower and lower as these companies recklessly produce despite losing money."[42]

The newly corporatized state-owned oil and petrochemical companies, eager to profit, also rushed to invest in chemical processing and downstream sectors, such as polyester and polyester fibers. Similar to their private counterparts, state-owned companies, such as the petrochemical monopoly Sinopec Yizheng Chemical Fibre Company, did not invest in high-tech development and innovation; rather, they relied on a business strategy that increased production without industrial upgrading.[43] "Sinopec should take responsibility for why China's chemical fiber industry is doing so poorly," explained an industry expert.[44]

State-owned and private companies alike crowded the sectors that did not produce tires, sectors that had less technical barriers to entry and less stringent customer requirements. In contrast, high technological requirements and customer demands for production consistency and reliability in the tire segment of chemical fibers, where Performance Fibers found its market niche, presented entry barriers for many Chinese companies in spite of government subsidies and technical and market guidance from sector associations.[45] To survive market saturation, domestic chemical fiber processors entered raw material sectors to lower input costs or went downstream to produce low-tech applications. They also collaborated with one another and sector associations to set technical standards, which presented market barriers. But few foreign-invested manufacturers joined sector associations and technical committees because they felt these organizations protected domestic sector interests and "besides, their products outcompeted domestic counterparts by quality."[46] These local efforts to promote tire and other subsectors increased domestic capacity; in 2009, the United States filed a safeguard action before the WTO and increased tariffs to 39 percent from 4 percent on China-made tires for three years.[47]

Setting Technical Standards in Nonstrategic Sectors

"The lowest tier of companies focuses on production, the second tier focuses on marketing and branding, and the highest tier companies focus on setting standards,"

---

42. Interview on April 15, 2006, in Shanghai with a contractor for chemical fiber processors. State-owned financial institutions bankrolled manufacturers because their survival depended on these companies staying afloat. The vicious cycle stifled private industry as banks loaned only to politically favored firms.

43. Yizheng Chemical Fibre Company, a subsidiary of Sinopec, did not produce high-value differentiated fiber because of reluctance to exit its top spot globally in the production of PET fiber.

44. Interview with Y. M. Wang (September 7, 2006).

45. Still, between 2004 and 2008 the number of Chinese tires imported to the United States more than tripled, and their share of the U.S. market rose from 5 to 17 percent. In September 2009, the U.S. government filed a "safeguard" action before the WTO against the surging (dumping) of tire imports (and oil well pipes) into the United States.

46. Sha interview (September 9, 2006).

47. See "U.S. to Impose Tariff on Tires from China," *Washington Post* (September 12, 2009).

remarked Polo He, the CEO of Ocean Power.[48] Located in the Tianan Cyber Park Customs Zone in Shenzhen, Ocean Power, a developer of production processes for geosynthetics, fiber processing, and fabric dyes, dominated internal markets by setting local and national technical standards.[49]

The setting of technical standards to increase domestic market share in the context of market liberalization became the nonofficial market-building policy across many industries in China in the 2000s. In strategic industries, such as telecommunications, the central government led the way. In extensively liberalized industries, such as technical textiles, local stakeholders initiated standards setting, with the assistance of sector associations and relevant central-level ministries. These attempts to control technology barred foreign enterprises with few local connections from "open" procurement of infrastructural materials for the construction of roads, expressways, and highways. Standards setting is based on technology and market criteria in a liberal economic context; in China, however, the interests of local and national powerbrokers dominated, whether in the decentralized regulatory context of nonstrategic sectors or in the centralized one of the strategic industries.

The varying experiences of Ocean Power, named for the idea of infinite possibilities as reflected in the company's mottos of "all rivers go to the ocean" and "open minded is great," and Polyfelt, a foreign retailer of nonwoven fabric examined in more detail in the trade and distribution section, illustrate how government-company bargains in the setting of technical standards favored the domestic sector.

Ocean Power actively set technical standards because it specialized in applying foreign technology to develop "indigenous innovations" across various, unrelated industrial sectors. The company's foray into vastly different sectors and market segments harks back to its storied history. It also represents the China-specific sectoral characteristics of comparatively low-tech, low-value-added industries. Ocean Power began business as a TVE that distributed globally branded products for foreign manufacturers in the food, chemical, pharmaceutical, and automotive industries; it also periodically engaged in contract manufacturing.[50] As Ocean Power helped multinationals develop China-specific products and establish trade and distribution channels, it learned engineering and manufacturing processes through technology and knowledge-transfer agreements and reverse engineering.[51] Ocean Power steadily moved up the value chain: from producing mixes for soft serve ice cream,

---

48. Interview on April 20, 2006, in Shenzhen, Guangdong, with Polo He, CEO, Ocean Power.

49. Factory visit and interviews on April 20, 2006, in Shenzhen with He; Great Xu, vice director of Ocean Power R&D Institute; Sophie Dragon, manager of International Business Development; and Jonson Wang, business representative.

50. These companies included Henkel, Sumitomo Chemical, Dunlop, Hoechst AG, General Motors, Bayer, Ranpak, CPS Color, and Iterchimica Srl.

51. Murky supply chains prevent copying and stealing technology from being prosecutable in China. In 2006, a Dutch company, Dyneema, filed a case against a foreign-invested Chinese company in the Court of Paris for exporting and distributing products using stolen technology. Interview on September 8, 2006, in Shanghai with an industry insider involved in the investigation of the case.

it expanded into manufacturing ice cream machines and eventually the dyes for ice cream. The companies that made ice cream for McDonald's in China, for example, paid Ocean Power for special color dyes. Right around when it began making dyes, Ocean Power also became a representative for foreign companies importing technical fibers into China. From there, Ocean Power moved to producing fibers and construction textiles and setting national standards for the manufacturing processes of dyes, fibers, and geotextiles, as well as for wastewater treatment.[52] Ocean Power drafted and participated in creating more than fifteen national and professional standards, four of which have been commercialized, and became the first to draft national standards in the field of color. In 2003, it ranked twenty-fifth in patents nationally, fifth in Guangdong Province, and fourth in the city of Shenzhen.

Ocean Power's efforts "to become a leader in international global research and development for the domestic market" and adeptness at navigating the terrain of domestic standards setting cannot be disconnected from its involvement in sector associations. Polo He served as the vice director of the China National Color Technical Standardization Committee and participated in the All China Federation of Industry and Commerce, the All China National Distributors Conference, and other industry associations. He's status as an important businessman and leader in standards setting garnered him membership in the National People's Congress as a delegate and good *guanxi* with the central government.

He's ambition to set national standards dovetailed with the central government's calls for industrial upgrading across the economy. His activism in business associations provided him the critical introductions to related central ministries, which granted requisite approvals and funded and sponsored Ocean Power's R&D labs.[53] Ocean Power has received funding and awards from CNTAC, MOST, the Chinese Academy of Science, the Ministry of Construction, and other central bureaucracies. Among its many standards setting honors, in February 2004 the MOST, the Standardization Administration of China, and the AQSIQ selected Ocean Power as one of twenty-two enterprises to participate in the national key standardization program.[54] It was named one of China's top one hundred science and technology enterprises in 2006 and, a year later, the Manual for Construction and Science Technology of the Eleventh Five-Year Plan incorporated Ocean Power's products.

---

52. These included research projects that involved novel polymer and macromolecule material and application technologies in civil engineering.

53. The process for setting standards and obtaining intellectual property rights contains many loopholes, leading to frequent approval of inferior technologies. Patents with abstract and ambiguous explanations regularly received approval; applicants must explain how their patent or innovation contributes to society. Interview on March 14, 2006, in Beijing, with James Haynes, lawyer, Tee & Howe.

54. Ocean Power also operates a postdoctoral program authorized by the ministries of Personnel and Construction, in collaboration with several SOEs and research institutes. For its efforts, the Ministry of Construction awarded Ocean Power a "certificate of enterprise qualification in the architecture industry."

In 2008, a standards association in cement production designated Ocean Power as a final arbiter.

Ocean Power's success exhibits Polo He's ability to take advantage of China's market reforms (which gave birth to the recognition of de facto property rights), the liberalization of market entry in technical textiles, and the decentralization of licensing powers and regulatory enforcement. It also exhibits how standards setting, compliance testing for complex technological processes, and local content policies became chaotic sites of contention where conflicts of interest abound and local power brokers, including powerful domestic companies, hijack theoretically juridified processes. As Polo He explained, "The norm [of standards setting] in China is not that work is under the table, but that it is underground. In fact, it is virtually 'government law' to pay government officials to set standards," which Ocean Power considered a "tax" on its efforts to promote scientific standards.

Reregulation Phase (2004–2006)

In the post-WTO period, the state provided only lackluster response to overexpansion and market saturation in select textile subsectors; this was a regulatory departure from the spindle-cutting campaign of 1998 to 2001. The elimination of a central-level textile bureaucracy and the lower strategic value of technical textiles—chemical fiber processing in particular—to national security and technological development shaped the central government's response. Lacking regulatory capacity and without the will to commit more bureaucratic resources, the central government could neither quash rising demand fueled by the construction of roads and infrastructure nor control local regulators and stakeholders who collaborate to favor local interests and achieve local goals.

The central government did, however, regularly set quantitative floors on bank reserves to tighten credit, issue edicts to commerce departments to limit license approvals in discouraged sectors, and tinker with export and import tariffs to encourage high-value-added technical sectors and discourage low-end, low-value-added sectors. Importantly, between 2004 and 2006, when skyrocketing oil prices hit upstream sectors of chemical fiber processing particularly hard, the central government encouraged local governments, many of which heeded the call, to restructure companies to produce high-value differentiated fiber and, on a larger scale, to compete with foreign overseas fiber giants.[55] During that time, global oil prices increased the cost of raw material inputs, and many Chinese manufacturers of PET chips operated at near zero profit margins. CNTAC and other sector associations

---

55. Y. M. Wang interview (September 7, 2006). See also "Fiber Company Weaves Way into Overseas Markets," *Business Daily* (November 15, 2004).

also encouraged mergers and acquisitions, targeting state-owned or affiliated enterprises under their spheres of influence.[56]

TEXTILE TRADE AND DISTRIBUTION:
STRATEGIC REREGULATION

The trade-offs that China made in its WTO accession protocol show that it viewed textiles to be of less strategic value than other industries that make a larger contribution to national security and the national technology base. The Chinese government agreed to constrain apparel exports to the quotas mandated by the fifth Sino-U.S. Textiles Agreement, which covered the period between 1997 and 2008. It also committed to removing product-specific import restrictions (including chemicals, processed oil, and crude oil) five years after WTO accession. Several rounds of textile negotiations with the United States and the European Union in 2005 further imposed voluntary export restraints.

To fulfill WTO commitments and at the same time enhance state management of trade to achieve state imperatives, whether promoting domestic industry or engaging in foreign economic relations, the Chinese government restructured its trade administration in 2003 and issued new rules that nominally acknowledged trading rights. The actual regulation of textile trade varied across subsectors according to a strategic value logic. The government tolerated the entry of FDI in apparel retail and released rules legalizing their presence, on the one hand, and micromanaged the trade of raw materials and high-tech contents, on the other hand. All the same, the decentralized nature of regulatory governance in textiles influenced the effectiveness of internal and external trade regulation.

A Consolidated Commerce Ministry

In 2003, the State Council established the Ministry of Commerce, a merger between the Ministry of Foreign Trade and Economic Cooperation and the departments related to internal trade under the State Economic and Trade Commission. In forming the Ministry of Commerce, it sought to better coordinate the regulation of internal and external markets to minimize the costs that liberalization imposed on domestic retailers and distributors. Soon after consolidating the administration of internal and external trade, the government issued rules in 2004 that legalized FDI participation in retail and distribution. It also promulgated the Foreign Trade Law, which streamlined licensing procedures and inspections and liberalized external trade. While meeting WTO commitments, these laws also enhanced state control and favored domestic industry.

---

56. See "Oil Price Surge Casts Great Cost Pressure on Chemical Fiber Makers in China," *Xinhua Economic New Service* (September 16, 2005). Also Chen and Zhao (2005).

Until the promulgation of new rules on internal trade, regulations formally barred FDI from the internal retail and distribution of products not manufactured domestically. A few foreign brand marketers, including Bestseller and Esprit, distributed domestically by circumventing entry rules (see chapter 6). The first set of the new rules regulated businesses engaged in franchise relationships.[57] The Administrative Measures on Commercial Franchise Business stipulated cumbersome qualifying requirements and increased the commerce ministry's supervisory and discretionary powers. Prerequisites for application included that the franchisor (or its subsidiary) must have operated at least two company-owned franchises in China for more than twelve months and that it had already registered and obtained approval of its business scope from the appropriate governmental regulator. Other rules, which favored the domestic contracting parties, included the full disclosure of the franchised business within twenty days after execution of an agreement and any information requested by the franchisee (both before the sale and during the term of the franchise agreement); franchisor liability for certain actions of its suppliers; and a three-year minimum on all franchise agreements. They also included annual reporting requirements by the franchisor and monetary and other penalties for regulatory infractions. Taken together, these rules disproportionately affected new and existing foreign franchisors. Many de facto franchisors opted not to restructure to comply with these new rules.[58]

The second set of rules released in 2004 regulated FDI wishing to set up retail, wholesale, or franchise spaces and distribute goods that the company did not manufacture.[59] The 2004 Administrative Measures on Foreign Investment in the Commercial Sector and the April 2005 MOFCOM circular on business scope expansion and holding companies required that foreign-invested distributors present local governments and licensing authorities with documentation and environmental impact assessments explaining how new stores suited the urban and commercial development plans of the location selected, a catalog of imported and exported merchandise, and detailed business plans and leases. These qualifying requirements empowered local governments with broad, subjective standards (e.g., the condition of the local economy and the market), which provided opportunities for local protectionism. The MOFCOM and its branch offices could reject applications based on the types of merchandise specified. Foreign-invested commercial enterprises could only distribute products in the same "category," which various licenses defined inconsistently, as those that they produced.[60] Additionally, these regulations

57. See Ross and Zhou (2005) and Nixon Peabody LLP, "New Franchise Regulations in China," *Franchise Law Alert* (April 22, 2005).

58. Allan Warburg interview (April 27, 2006).

59. See American Chamber of Commerce of People's Republic of China (2004, 2005, and 2006).

60. In April 2005, MOFCOM and the State Administration of Taxation stipulated that a manufacturer would lose its tax incentives if it sold goods or services that it did not manufacture if they exceeded 30 percent of total sales. This rule departed from the preexisting SAT rule of a 50 percent threshold.

prohibited a headquarters holding company, the typical offshore enterprise structure for many current WFOEs, from distributing goods not in the same category
as those produced by their parent company. In the end, the central government
approved commercial licenses for foreign-invested apparel retailers, but they were
limited in scope.

Finally, the Foreign Trade Law released in 2004 to comply with WTO commitments erected nontariff barriers even as it permitted foreign companies that
did not manufacture in China to trade in all goods throughout the country. The
new law eliminated previously cumbersome and bureaucratic licensing procedures,
which required central-level examination and approval, and replaced it with registration; however, only PRC residents could register for oversees trading.[61] "Notwithstanding the definition's inclusion of individuals, foreign individuals may
only engage in foreign trade in the PRC through the establishment of a foreign-
invested enterprise," explained Neal Stender, Matthew McConkey, and Bi Xing
of the China-based Coudert Brothers.[62] Moreover, provisions in the law enhanced
the MOFCOM's authority to prohibit trade that "harmed" national security and
public interests. The government could impose restrictions or prohibit trading
even if the goods and services were included in the WTO accession agreements.
Other sections enhanced the MOFCOM's discretionary authority on a number
of issues to ensure the orderly growth of domestic industries, including clamping
down on monopoly and unfair trade practices via antidumping, countervailing, and
safeguard measures. It could also interfere on intellectual property licensed as a
package in a contract or in an exclusive grant-back license. Finally, violations could
lead to punitive action on administrative, criminal, and legal fronts. A license cancellation could entail a ban on the right to trade for several years.

The Actual Administration of Textile Trade

The government formally liberalized FDI in retail by 2004, but as early as 1998 foreign apparel retailers tapped the domestic market via special contractual arrangements and bargains with local stakeholders (see chapter 6). Upon market entry, the
decentralized governance of textiles structured their experiences with regulatory
authorities. Other distributors of textile products also confronted local variation,
structured by China-specific and universal sectoral attributes, in regulatory enforcement.

In external trade, the government instituted a reformed quota allocation
system in apparel textiles, but the enforcement of export restraints also varied
on the local level. Moreover, sector and business associations empowered by

---

61. Walton (2004).
62. "China's Foreign Trade Law Revised for WTO Era," *China Law & Practice* (May 30, 2004).

decentralization represented industry interests to advocate for incremental fiscal protection from global competition. Taking a more deliberate orientation and retaining more centralized supervision, the central government issued import licenses and implemented the tariff rate quota regime for raw materials and high-tech content to favor large state-owned trade corporations and domestic manufacturers with political connections.

Regulation of Internal Trade

Foreign-invested retailers, before and after rules that liberalized internal retail and distribution, had to contend with subjective inspections and with delays or postponements in the issuance of licenses and certifications as local authorities balanced their interests with that of local businesses. Once a retailer obtains the requisite permissions to operate, it must submit a quality report, which requires detailed information on fabric content, including dyes and chemicals, in order to certify each piece of clothing. After product certification, retailers confront local inspection bureaus with discretionary authority to demand quality reports and conduct spot-checks. For example, the Beijing quality and inspection bureau tested Danish-invested Bestseller China's apparel products for market; however, spot-check inspections regularly occurred in its stores across the country. "Local inspection bureaucrats enter shops to cause trouble and to be taken out for a 'free lunch,'" explained Allan Warburg, CEO of Bestseller China. "Chinese competitors have ways of getting around this type of harassment, but we do not want to get involved. In fact, Bestseller China uses our multinational status to argue that it can't get involved in corruption."[63] To help Bestseller resolve problems in its stand-alone stores, the Danish government intervened on behalf of Bestseller to ensure property rights and to exert pressure on business bureaus. In one instance, the Danish government helped Bestseller connect with MOFCOM in Beijing to pressure local bureaus to crack down on fake stores.

In industrial and technical textiles, even after the State Council liberalized internal trade and distribution and issued the Foreign Trade Law, foreign-invested companies found that local stakeholders, from local commerce and construction bureaus to local companies, designers, planners, and sector associations, regularly erected nontariff trade barriers. In geotextiles, designers and architects had great influence over the vendors chosen to supply construction projects. They wrote specifications in their designs, proposals, and plans that included or excluded certain grades of materials that could favor or disfavor particular vendors or sets of vendors. They also colluded with manufacturers to set technical standards, often written to exclude certain players in the market. Local manufacturers and vendors regularly lobbied designers to the detriment of foreign distributors, even those with the best technology. "Too often designers don't want to stick out their heads

---

63. Warburg interview (April 27, 2006).

to defend better quality materials and standards," explained a former Beijing-based representative of Polyfelt, now Royal Tencate, a manufacturer of woven and non-woven geosynthetic fabrics. "This behavior happens in the construction industry everywhere, but this type of corruption, with designers and manufacturers becoming bedfellows, is especially rampant in China."[64] Moreover, local authorities cooperated with foreign manufacturers and distributors only to renege on business plans once the technology and knowledge transfer concluded. In such cases, foreign-invested factories, such as Royal Tencate's Zhuhai factory, stood underutilized while their foreign owners relied on factories in other countries to supply the Chinese market.[65]

Taking the market entry path most common among manufacturers of high-tech fabrics wishing to internally distribute their products, Polyfelt entered the Chinese market in 2004 by forming alliances with local manufacturers with an established domestic clientele.[66] Upon market entry, Polyfelt immediately experienced the "unregulated collusion between architects, developers, and trade associations that set technical standards for bridges, roads, and buildings" and "engage in *peibiao*," a form of collusive price fixing. After Polyfelt submitted a bid to supply geotextiles for the construction of an underwater facility in Shanghai, project leaders decided against procuring foreign-manufactured products. Nonetheless, the project leaders (including designers and other stakeholders in the city) invited Polyfelt and other foreign companies, under the pretense that the project had chosen their products, to introduce their products at meetings where the project leaders peppered Polyfelt with detailed questions about the production of geo-synthetics.[67] Since the project leaders and other bidders had already decided who would win the bid and arrived at payoffs that satisfied all parties involved, the inexpensive technology transfer "surely will contribute to the safety of those who transverse the Yangtze."[68]

Regulation of External Trade

The central government employed voluntary export restraints in response to foreign bilateral demands to restrain exports and to prevent the triggering of WTO safeguards. These measures included an export licensure regime, fiscal

---

64. Interview on February 9, 2006, in Beijing with the former general manager of the Beijing office of a foreign geotextile manufacturer.

65. Interview on September 21, 2008, with former general manager for PolyFelt/Royal Tencate.

66. Tencate purchased PolyFelt, a global market leader in geotextiles, in December 2005.

67. The strategy of obtaining "inexpensive" technology transfer is not atypical. After dissolving their business relationship, a domestic company, which had retained the consulting services of Donghua professor Yimin Wang, continued using his technology without paying licensing fees. The company stole Wang's technology by taking photos during a presentation. They escaped prosecution even after the court ruled in favor of Professor Wang. Y. M. Wang interviews (September 7 and 8, 2006).

68. Interviews in Beijing between February and June 2006 with the former general manager of Polyfelt China.

adjustments, and industry self-discipline.[69] Because the textile sector is ultimately a nonstrategic one, however, the government devoted limited resources to enforce these control mechanisms, and locally led reregulation limited the state's enforcement capacity. The export licensure regime was more cumbersome than effective. The Chinese manager of a Hong Kong trading company explained that the licensing regime reflected the Communist legacy of "obsession with process and little else."[70] To ensure Chinese exports did not exceed allotted quotas, the government required export licenses for more than two hundred textile products, shirts, underwear, trousers, and children's clothing. The licensure regime required detailed contract information for each export shipment but placed no limits on the number of licenses granted by each of the forty-six MOFCOM-designated licensing centers. Moreover, because of uneven enforcement, only low-end textiles heading to sensitive regions actually required export licenses.[71] The regime did not enforce licenses for products bound for nonsensitive regions such as Southeast Asia and Japan.

The CCC-T and the CNTAC supervised the textile industry's self-discipline system to stem production in prenegotiated categories of textiles and coordinated a lowest selling price.[72] The industry self-discipline system included such mechanisms as an industry self-monitoring system, which comprised a precaution system and a self-discipline agreement whereby enterprises that ran counter to trade laws and regulations and disturbed the export order had their import and export rights suspended. Exporters complained that this system of self-discipline created a bureaucracy without an observable increase in state capacity to regulate export volume.

The decentralized nature of state control in textiles complicated the effectiveness of the central government's efforts to enhance its authority to manage apparel exports. Local MOFCOM branches, local governments, and nonstate stakeholders, including sector and business associations, mobilized to promote the domestic export industry. To encourage export-oriented manufacturing and achieve other local goals, they gave special treatment in inspections and license and quota allocations to favored companies. Large brand marketers routinely received preferential treatment because of their contribution to the local garment industry. For example, the Customs Administration and the MOFCOM routinely waived export inspections for Bosideng, a manufacturer and brand marketer profiled in chapter 6.

---

69. Bilateral frustration with Chinese exports extended to product categories outside of low-end, low-value apparel and textiles. In June 2006, the United States attempted to prevent one hundred Chinese companies from exporting differentiated fiber.

70. Interview on September 7, 2006, in Shanghai with Jeff Chen, Suntor & Blooming.

71. Those regions covered in China's bilateral textile agreements are deemed sensitive. Interview on September 8, 2006, in Shanghai with Enock Mundia, former general manager for Liz Claiborne China.

72. See "Measures to Stop Disorderly Competition in China's Apparel and Textile Industry," *China Daily* (February 3, 2005), and Brown, Waldron, and Longworth (2005), 110.

Chenfeng Apparel, a domestic manufacturer also profiled in chapter 6, regularly received quality inspection exemptions and export licenses for categories of goods that fell under the export restrictions set by bilateral trade agreements.[73] Chenfeng aggressively lobbied local customs bureaus for these quotas. Allocation officially depended on a manufacturer's "performance" and customer record; thus, "the better you do, the more quotas you get," one manager explained. To ensure that it received adequate quotas, Chenfeng, which already was a prolific local exporter, diligently categorized and recorded by article number each piece of clothing and garment bound for the U.S. and European markets. The special attention Chenfeng paid to cumbersome and arbitrary allocation rules, combined with its contribution to the local economy and good *guanxi*, routinely garnered dividends.

Market liberalization in textiles, combined with the decentralized nature of textile regulation, produced a textile industry with limited political influence. Since the expiration of the Multi-Fiber Agreement, the central government has frequently adjusted taxation in response to the interests of the textile industry. For example, garment manufacturers continue to receive fairly high tax rebates despite a quota regime, reflecting the growing power of sector associations. In February 2007 the United States filed a complaint with the WTO alleging that China used export subsidies to promote domestic industries, citing garment manufacturing as one such industry. The CNTAC proudly proclaimed that sector associations had lobbied effectively to maintain export rebates. A CNTAC vice president Li Jinbao remarked, "It's ridiculous that the global industry wants China to be more marketized when it at the same time wants China to control export volume!"[74] In 2007, the government reduced tax rebates by 4 percent in garments.[75] But a year later, in response to industry-wide protests led by the CNTAC during slowing global demand, the central government adjusted textile export rebates back to the 2006 level to stem industry-wide business failures. "The CNTAC first observed the economic slowdown and hardship experienced by textile manufacturers through a comprehensive survey of more than thirty-three thousand companies. Then, taking the CNTAC's report seriously, the State Council and the NDRC pursued their own investigations, leading them to readjust export rebates," explained CNTAC vice president Zhao Hong.[76]

In contrast to the incidental orientation taken by the central government toward the management of apparel trade, despite WTO commitments to liberalize the internal distribution of raw material inputs, such as cotton and petrochemicals, the government continued its strict management of the textile supply chain for raw

73. Interviews on May 16, 2006 (in Jintan, Jiangsu) and on September 8, 2006 (in Shanghai) with general managers of Chenfeng Apparel.

74. Li Jinbao interview (April 24, 2006).

75. "China to Lower Tax Rebate for Textile Exports to Reduce Trade Surplus," *Xinhua* (April 13, 2007).

76. Zhao interview (September 23, 2008).

materials and high-tech inputs. The state indirectly restricted the level of raw material imports critical to subsectors up and down the textile supply chain. Moreover, the higher the technology content and value-added potential of a material input, the more the state controlled the import of that input. But it shifted from imposing quantitative restrictions to imposing tariff and nontariff trade barriers. In doing so, the government favored state-owned companies and domestic industry and limited the extent of foreign participation in the retail and distribution of what it viewed as strategic assets.

To begin, the government established a tariff rate quota regime for imports of major bulk commodities upon China's WTO accession. Foreign-invested cotton importers argued that the associated tariff for textile inputs, such as cotton, violated China's WTO accession agreement because of the use of a price benchmark.[77] Moreover, the government managed the allocation of import licenses and the distribution of quotas among processing mills with a murky, nontransparent set of criteria. Technically, a textile manufacturer could obtain an import license if the enterprise operated fifty thousand or more spindles and had a "good" record of value-added exports within the last year, the measure of which the government did not publicize. In practice, the "good" record requirement meant that the NDRC, which allocated the quotas, gave priority to state-owned trading groups and producers with a record of import utilization and political connections.[78] Even with additional quotas added in 2004, the Chinese government remained ambiguous about how the MOFCOM allocated the TRQ. China's top four cotton consumers, dominated by trading companies, automatically obtained import licenses. From there, good *guanxi* was a prerequisite for import licenses. Notably, with a gap of four million tons of cotton between what China produced and what China imported and a very low import quota level, most companies did not receive licenses to import within the TRQ. This created a situation where companies sought rents by selling quotas. Even with rents, imports were cheaper than domestically produced cotton.[79] This was in part a consequence of foreign cotton distributors and their representatives, such as Cotton Inc., working closely with Chinese fiber processing mills, garment manufacturers, and foreign brand marketers and retailers to increase cotton imports even if their consumption did not fall within the TRQ regime.

To promote the domestic oil and petrochemical industries, the government indirectly controlled the level of petrochemical imports critical to chemical fiber

77. "Cotton Industry Mulls Challenge to China's Tariff Rate Quota," *Inside US-China Trade* (October 22, 2007), and "Serious Concerns Raised over Some Chinese WTO Compliance," *Washington File: The State Department* (March 19, 2003).

78. Interview on September 8, 2006, in Shanghai with Sherry Wu, executive account manager for Global Account Management, Cotton Inc. China.

79. Prices for domestically produced cotton remained high because of low supply; also, the state did not directly subsidize cotton production in the post-WTO era. Qingliang Gu interview (September 8, 2006).

processing and the production of technical textiles, including geosynthetics. The government limited the number of import licenses granted to nonstate companies, which enhanced local protectionism in the distribution of petrochemicals.[80] By the end of 2005, in addition to state-owned trading and oil and petrochemical companies, only forty-eight private enterprises had obtained the right to import oil products. With few chemical fiber companies authorized to import, they instituted rents, such as monthly service fees, in collaboration with local governments. But because domestically produced petrochemicals were more expensive, most companies with *guanxi* imported.[81] To affect market developments, the government raised the domestic content requirement of major oil and petrochemical products when domestic productive capacity increased in 2005.[82] It also instituted taxes on imported inputs and export taxes on domestic production to ensure that domestically processed inputs remained in China and at a price competitive with imports.

REREGULATION TO RELINQUISH STATE CONTROL IN TEXTILES

By WTO accession in 2001, more than a decade of market reform had greatly diminished or eliminated bureaucratic control in textile manufacturing. Administrative restructuring, decentralization, and reregulation emphasizing liberalization had introduced competition, easing market entry and exit for private companies and FDI (see table 7.2). In the post-WTO era, *decentralized engagement* emerged as the dominant pattern of state control as the state devoted few resources to enforce central rules and completely devolved regulatory authority to local governments. Incidental control governed labor-intensive, low-value-added manufacturing sectors; government authorities intervened only when labor conflicts threatened social and political stability. In contrast, local governments, related ministries, and sector and business associations promoted technical textiles through standards setting, subsidies for value-added production, and other nontariff barriers.

The central government consolidated the management of internal and external textile trade to achieve its WTO and subsequent bilateral commitments and regulate the trade of raw materials and high-tech inputs. Employing export restraints, discretionary quota allocation, and macroeconomic measures, the government sought to appease its trade partners, on the one hand, and it sought to control the inflows and outflows of strategic assets, on the other hand. Several decades of decentralization, however, affected the implementation of trade rules. The dominant pattern of state control in textiles illustrates the relinquishing of central control

---

80. See case study on energy in chapter 8 for discussion of state control in petrochemicals.

81. Y. M. Wang interviews (September 8 and 9, 2006).

82. For example, the domestic content requirement for synthetic resin was raised to 50 percent; terylene, from 88.7 percent to 98.7 percent; and synthetic rubber, from 56 percent to 62 percent.

TABLE 7.2. STATE CONTROL IN TEXTILES

Pattern of control	Decentralized Engagement			
Timing of control	Pre–WTO Accession (1993–2001)		Post–WTO Accession (2002–10)	
Subsector	Manufacturing	Trade and distribution	Manufacturing	Trade and distribution
Type of control	Decentralized reregulation	Delegated reregulation	Decentralized reregulation	Strategic reregulation
Scope of control (central government's goals)	Introduce competition and relinquish regulation to local authorities	Promote external trade and manage internal trade of raw materials	Local authorities promote local industry and maximize FDI and employment	Promote external trade and domestic consumption to support domestic industry
Extent of control (central government's relationship with industry)	Demoted textile bureaucracy and related central ministries regulate textile supply chain.	Foreign trade ministry regulates external trade and distribution.	Quasi-government business and sector associations represent domestic industry and related central ministries intervene in technical sectors.	Locally enforced trade administration favors domestic producers and brand marketers.
	Local governments enforce central policies and regulate local industry.	Local governments and internal trade bureaucracy regulate internal trade and distribution.	Local governments enforce central policies and regulate local industry.	Quasi-government sector associations represent domestic manufacturers and importers and exporters.
Methods (nature of state control) *Macroeconomic levers*	Low interest rates; foreign exchange and currency control; quantitative measures (on loans, reserves, quotas and tariffs, fiscal incentives, and so forth); economy-wide rules (on labor, consolidation, bankruptcy, and so forth)	Low interest rates; foreign exchange and currency control; quantitative measures (on loans, reserves, quotas and tariffs, fiscal incentives, and so forth); economy-wide rules (on labor, consolidation, bankruptcy, and so forth)	Low interest rates; foreign exchange and currency control; quantitative measures (on loans, reserves, quotas and tariffs, fiscal incentives, and so forth); economy-wide rules (on labor, consolidation, bankruptcy, and so forth)	Low interest rates; foreign exchange and currency control; quantitative measures (on loans, reserves, quotas and tariffs, fiscal incentives, and so forth); economy-wide rules (on labor, consolidation, bankruptcy, and so forth)
Methods (nature of state control) *Micro (sector) levers*	Liberal entry; state sector restructuring (privatization and consolidation); central intervention to encourage industrial upgrading and product diversification; local fiscal and infrastructural incentives	Rules prohibited FDI in internal trade (but de facto liberalization) and liberalized export-oriented FDI; local enforcement of commerce; export rights for domestic industry and FDI; nonmarket allocation of trade quotas	Liberal entry; local regulatory enforcement and sector restructuring; global standards in garments and locally led standards setting in technical sectors	Rules on internal trade liberalize market entry but expanded bureaucratic control and favored domestic sector; voluntary export restraints; nonmarket allocation of trade quotas; tariffs on raw materials and high-tech contents

in (1) industries that are unimportant to national security; (2) that do not contribute to the national technology base, and (3) where the domestic sector is globally competitive.

TEXTILES AND THE DEVELOPMENTAL STATE

Japan and the East Asian NICs, during a comparable stage of industrial development, treated their domestic textile industries quite differently. In contrast to China's relinquishing of state control, tolerance toward extensive and intensive market competition, and courting of FDI for this industry with its globally integrated supply chain and production systems, the developmental state intervened to actively promote the development of and cushion the structural adjustment of textiles. Textiles served as the leading sector for these economies from the 1950s through the 1970s. With some variation, the developmental state in Japan, South Korea, and Taiwan, working closely with domestic capital, protected the domestic market from foreign competition; manipulated credit systems to give textile subsectors and companies a comparative advantage; and promoted textiles as, first, an industry critical for import-substitution and, later, as being key for export-oriented industrialization. As the developmental state directed industrial development, it used market and nonmarket methods to achieve its goals.

Japan

In postwar Japan, national reconstruction rebuilt textile mills with new machinery and quickly restored production. By the 1950s and 1960s, the Japanese textile industry was a major producer of synthetic fibers and engaged in full-scale production of vinylon and nylon. Textiles had fewer ties to the government through loans and preferential financing compared to other industries; raw cotton and wool imports were freed from government restrictions at the end of 1959 and faced export-restraint agreements with the United States. Yet protective measures in the face of growing global competition permitted the formation of cartels for retrenchment during recession and the discarding of excess facilities under protection of law whenever small and medium manufacturers suffered from excess supply.[83] "Administrative guidance" included setting up industry cooperation discussion groups, ordering mergers or "cooperation" and production reduction, imposing production quotas, and creating cartels to allocate the reduction of market share and the number of employees to be retrained or pensioned.[84]

---

83. See Matsuzaki (1982).
84. Johnson (1982), 224–25 and 264–65, 267, 278, and 303.

In 1971, after two years of trade disputes with the United States and currency realignment after the Nixon Shock (a series of economic measures, which included the unilateral cancellation of the direct convertibility of the U.S. dollar to gold, in response to deficits in balance of payments and trade), the Japan-U.S. textile agreement imposed voluntary export restraints that the Japanese government believed would "stall the Mills bill," the measure before U.S. Congress that sought quotas on American imports of textiles and shoes.[85] Notwithstanding what the Japanese textile industry believed was its sacrificial status, the Japanese government secured a relatively high base level growth rate of 5 percent; moreover, the accord provided controls for three years in contrast to the five-year bilateral accords the United States negotiated with South Korea, Taiwan, and Hong Kong.[86] The Chinese government, in contrast, later sacrificed the textile industry during trade negotiations in favor of more strategic industries, such as telecommunications.

From the 1970s, structural adjustment policies enabled Japan to retain a share of around 25 percent of total global cotton yarn production in the mid-1970s and above 20 percent in the mid-1980s in world exports of more capital-intensive synthetic fibers and fabrics.[87] The Law for Extraordinary Measures for the Stabilization of Recession-Hit Industries helped the industry survive by discarding production facilities and reducing daily output in the period after the Japan-U.S. textile agreement of 1971, the founding of the Multi-Fiber Agreement in 1974, and the 1974 and 1979 oil shocks. Other measures to sustain "appropriate competition" and "assurance of suitable profits" included an equipment registration system, which was designed to restrain expansion and prevent new entries and based on a Smaller Industries Organization Law that exempted select industries from the Anti-Trust Law.[88]

Moreover, in 1976 the Ministry of International Trade and Industry (MITI)— prompted in part by the rising strength of the textile industrial alliance and the increasing concern of Diet officials over MITI policies that increasingly favored new high-tech sectors over "smokestack" industries—issued Textile Policy Guidelines. These included overt forms of import relief (though devoid of quantitative or price-based restrictions), such as import surveillance, administrative guidance on the pace of import contracts, unofficial bilateral talks with trading partners, and temporary restrictions based on GATT rules.[89] The Japanese government also used the MFA to restrict textile and apparel imports from its low-wage and increasingly technologically sophisticated neighbors.[90]

---

85. "Caught in a Bind: Under Fire in U.S., Japan Textile Makers Are Hit by Woes, Including Imports, at Home," *Wall Street Journal* (November 17, 1970).

86. Aggarwal (1985), 123.

87. Macnaughtan (2005), 14, for former figure, and Park and Anderson (1991), 545, for latter figure.

88. Johnson (1982), 225–26, and McNamara (1995), 3.

89. Friman (1988).

90. Aggarwal (1985), 128 and 147.

In the post–1980s period, "the survival of Japan's larger textile mills owes less to the market and more to corporatist strategies of adjustment worked out by capital, labor, and the state," which did not significantly alter the leadership of the textile industry established by the "big ten" spinners and the "big nine" synthetic-fiber makers.[91] Rather, through the Industrial Restructuring Council for Textiles, government and corporate stakeholders used strategies of adjustment and mediation that encouraged competitive interests to find common cause, moderated decline, and maintained market hierarchy in the industry.

Korea

Japanese textile companies began to lose world market share to the East Asian NICs in the 1960s. By 1970, the combined textiles exports of Korea, Taiwan, Singapore, and Hong Kong exceeded those of Japan by 82 percent.[92] State intervention also served as a hallmark of textile development in these other countries. The developmental state in Taiwan and Korea supported textiles first as import-substitution and later as a leader in exports from the 1960s through 1980s. "The evolution of integrated, Korean-based export operations" served as "part of the national drive to acquire the individual and organizational skills necessary for rapid development."[93] Strong exports and relatively low levels of consumer imports translated into huge trade surpluses, making Korean textiles an export powerhouse, a state priority as a source of foreign exchange, and a significant regional employer.

The textile industry in Korea grew out of the acquisition of confiscated Japanese property, and in the 1950s and 1960s it received a large share of government subsidies.[94] These included price controls on yarn and fabric, exemptions for imports serving as inputs for exports, and foreign loans that financed investments in modern plants and equipment. In addition, the government made it a priority starting in the 1960s to extend a line of serial export production in textiles, from the upstream subsectors of synthetics and natural fibers through the midstream processes of weaving, cutting, and dyeing, and then to the actual sewing of garments downstream. The state not only established a highly integrated export production line but also oversaw and intervened to ensure adequate supplies and reasonable prices among various segments.[95] This departed from the Chinese experience, where FDI relocating manufacturing to China assisted in establishing modern production lines for most textile subsectors, from apparel to chemical fiber processing.

---

91. McNamara (1995), xiv.
92. Amsden (1989), 247.
93. Mody and Wheeler (1987), 1270.
94. Amsden (1994).
95. McNamara (2002), 48.

Other export promotion measures included preferential loans, tax and tariff exemptions, and social overhead and administrative supports, such as prioritizing yarn supplies for downstream weavers and garment makers and maintaining the artificially higher prices of local supplies of polyester until synthetic plants, and then petrochemical plants, could succeed. Moreover, export performance determined import quotas for raw cotton critical for competition in the highly protected and lucrative domestic market."[96] Government-subsidized profits were invested in modernized plant and equipment, new synthetic fiber capacity, and improved production techniques.

In the 1970s, Korea endured the longest "knock-down drag-out fight" of those "put up by all four East Asian textile-exporting countries."[97] This, and the advent of a multilateral quota system on textile exports, spurred the establishment of textile associations, both sector-specific and industry-wide, under tight government control. State and industry cooperated to coordinate textile plans, which identified goals along the textile production line and targets for exports. The symbiotic relationship between state and industry led to the emergence of a small number of major players in competition with one another in times of growth and decline.

To reverse the decline of the industry, the Interim Measures for Textile Industry Equipment of 1968 was replaced in 1980 by the Textile Industry Modernization Promotion Law. Moreover, the Textile Modernization Fund, Structural Adjustment Fund, Rationalization Fund, and other distributions of cheap credit and patient capital, and the designation of textiles as a "depressed industry" under the Industrial Promotion Law in 1986, supported industrial upgrading and expansion into value-added subsectors. The government, through industry associations, also instituted capacity controls. Additionally, it worked closely with companies to reach compromises to keep wage growth low in the face of the labor unrest, particularly intense in textiles, that swept over Korea beginning in the late 1970s.[98] Furthermore, the Textile Vision included goals of increasing textile and apparel exports and improvements in dyeing and fashion design. Through these efforts, textiles remained Korea's single most important export and made up a significant share of all large size firms through the 1980s.[99]

In the 1990s and 2000s, through the 1997 financial crisis and beyond, the Korean government played a "mediator" role in the cooperation between public and private sectors to coordinate structural adjustment. It coordinated mediation "with multiple sources in finance and policy instruments."[100] For example, the $680 million Milano Project pushed for higher value-added production and saved the

---

96. Amsden, quoted in Evans (1995), 89.

97. Woo-Cumings (1991), 126.

98. Amsden (1989), 252.

99. In 1983, textiles accounted for 13 percent of big Korean enterprise, compared with 5.5 percent in Japan, 2.0 percent in Germany, and 1.7 percent in the United States (Chandler 1990).

100. McNamara (2002), 131.

jobs and investments of the Taegu textile area. Other state interventions included government-sponsored warehouses to keep tabs on inventories and destinations to check overexpansion. The relationship between state and industry in financing and managing the fate of industry in Korea differs markedly from the dominant Chinese approach of decentralized industrial governance and limited central resources.

Taiwan

The textile industry in Taiwan grew out of factories equipped with Japanese textile machinery left behind after World War II, and those of relocated mainlanders, who put their machines abroad ships as the Nationalist regime on the mainland crumbled and retreated to Taiwan.[101] The émigré KMT government named the textile industry a "strategic import substitution sector" in the First Four-Year Economic Development Plan of 1953, and beginning in the early 1950s it employed a battery of market-distorting and market-replacing methods to establish the industry quickly and promote local production. It was a "self-conscious policy of import-substitution" that included tariffs and quantitative restrictions on imports of yarn and finished products, restrictions on the entry of new producers to prevent "excessive" competition, and controlled access to raw materials.[102] Across subsectors, a government agency replaced market allocation. For example, the textile entrustment scheme supplied raw cotton, which arrived in the form of U.S. aid, directly to the spinning mills, advanced working capital requirements, and bought up all production.[103] By the mid-1950s, Taiwan was more than self-sufficient in yarn and cloth; from there, the government granted cheap credit to existing textile firms to expand their equipment, but it restricted the entry of new firms or factories. By 1958, Taiwan was a net textile exporter; the textile industry remained the largest exporter until 1984 when electrical and electronic goods overtook it.[104]

The public-private ties between the KMT government and the native Taiwanese private sector operated at a further distance and were less dense than the Korean and Japanese versions of the developmental state. Still, state managers from Taiwan's extensive set of SOEs, each with its own set of relations with private companies, cultivated close interaction with private capital. Moreover, many industrial associations acted "as the arms and legs of the government."[105] They collected data on the production capabilities of members, helping the Industrial Development Bureau locate a weak link in the production structure and find firms willing to invest in the gap. They also assisted in creating linkages between different textile

---

101. Stubbs (2005), 42, on the Japanese connection, and Wade (1990), 79, on the PRC connection.
102. Quotes from Haggard (1990), 89.
103. Gold (1986).
104. Wade (1990).
105. Haggard (1990), 89.

subsectors and segments, including allocating raw cotton and yarn and guaranteeing repurchases.

The development of synthetic fibers, which began in the late 1950s, represented import-substitution aimed at the upstream end of export industries.[106] In addition to tariffs, import controls, and multiple exchange rates, the state also influenced investment decisions and stimulated the supply of entrepreneurs. It took the lead in bringing together foreign companies and local producers to start a new industry; in this way, the original synthetic fiber and related petrochemical companies were the creation of the state, under close government supervision and with much public ownership. But foreign-invested JVs did not bring in foreign technology, as witnessed in the Chinese case. Rather, the government helped companies to negotiate technology-licensing agreements.[107] Foreign assistance was also obtained through U.S. military aid as a function of the cold war strategy; it helped to "make better military uniforms."[108] The government also became involved in negotiations between upstream suppliers and downstream buyers. "Government rationing of credit, foreign exchange, and raw materials, and licensing control over the investment decision-making itself" together consisted what K. Y. Yin, the head of the Industrial Development Commission in the 1950s, described as government caution not to overlook "the possibility of . . . a free market being taken advantage of by speculators and profiteers."

In the export-led growth phase in the 1960s and onward, the Taiwanese government, with the assistance of trade cartels sponsored by sector associations, allocated export targets and penalized those firms that fell short. In cotton and woolen textiles, for example, only 40 percent of total output could be sold on the home market, with excess sales subject to penalties.[109] The Taiwanese state also exposed its nurtured capitalists to the rigors of the market, making export quotas dependent on the quality and price of goods and diminishing protection over time. The establishment of the first export processing zone in 1966 facilitated the inflow of textile-related foreign investment and technology, in the form of joint ventures. By 1981, Taiwan had become the fourth largest producer of synthetic fibers in the world.

To maintain Taiwanese textiles' global competitiveness, the Ten Year Textile Industry Revitalization Plan of 1980 sought to promote vertical reorganization, industrial upgrading to value-added products with a high technology content, and equipment modernization with a package of comprehensive financial, tax, investment, and administrative incentives. Such comprehensive industrial promotion packages simply did not exist in the Chinese regulatory approach toward textiles. Although some experts believe that implementation fell short of the plan due to

---

106. Gold (1986), 72; Wade (1990), 79–81; and Stubbs (2005), 102.
107. Wade (1990), 91.
108. Wade (1990), 83, and Stubbs (2005), 100.
109. Haggard (1990), 94.

the fragmented nature of Taiwanese textiles (as compared to Japanese and Korean industries, which are dominated by larger firms), the industry "managed to sustain its performance through increasing value-added" production despite upward pressure on wage costs and stagnating sales value.[110] Moreover, despite the dramatic appreciation of the Taiwanese currency in 1987 and changes in the labor standards law, which saw the shift of production, particularly in the low-value, labor-intensive subsectors, to lower-cost countries, Taiwan became number one in synthetic fibers by the second half of the 1990s, falling only to China in the 2000s.[111]

In the post-MFA era, to promote diversification as textile factories moved to China and other lower-cost countries, Taiwan's China Textile Institute recruited several hundred engineers to engage in research in industrial textiles, the results of which it planned to transfer to domestic manufacturers.[112] Moreover, many large textile combines diversified into other sectors, including real estate, retail, and telecommunications.[113]

---

110. "Promotion and Development of the Textile and Garment Industry in Asia and the Pacific: Prospects and Challenges." *Industrial Development News for Asia and the Pacific* 22 (1993): 13–35.

111. According to Thun (2000), despite shifting production to China, Taiwanese textile companies have retained overall control of the manufacturing process in what Gereffi and Pan (1994) characterize as the "triangular manufacturing process," which involves global sourcing in Taiwan, manufacturing via offshore factories, and shipping of final goods to international buyers.

112. "Taiwan Business: Textile Makers Move Upmarket," *Topics* 35:6 (2005).

113. Amsden and Chu (2003), 144–47.

PART IV

THE EMERGENCE OF CHINA'S REGULATORY STATE

8

DELIBERATE REINFORCEMENT
IN STRATEGIC INDUSTRIES

In the preceding chapters, I systematically mapped sectoral and cross-time variation in how the Chinese government reregulated after economy-wide liberalization. In the next two chapters, I will survey other industries to test, extend, and
refine the broader applicability of the strategic value framework developed in earlier chapters. The following mini case studies contribute methodologically (more
cases) and empirically (broadening the scope) to the story told in this book: the
transformation of Chinese statecraft toward the economy, more broadly, and the
differentiated relationship between government and business across strategic and
nonstrategic industries in the post-Deng era, more specifically. The cross-sector
survey also reinforces how China has pursued a separate path from the East Asian
developmental state. Japan, South Korea, and Taiwan restricted FDI, managed
competition, and worked closely with domestic private industry to coordinate technological and industrial development through market-conforming policies; this
dominant pattern of government-business relations applied across industries. In
contrast, this book's main case studies and the next two chapters show that China
has liberalized FDI on the macro-level and permitted fierce competition among
market players. But depending on the strategic value of the sector in question, the
Chinese government strictly manages ownership structures, market entry, and business scope, or deregulates markets and relinquishes regulation to local authorities.

The remainder of this chapter surveys strategic industries (financial services,
energy, and automotives), and the next chapter surveys nonstrategic industries
(consumer electronics, foodstuffs, and paper). Each case study is organized according to the industry's strategic value and distinctive features, state goals and
methods, narrative of regulatory change, and subsectoral variation. The dominant

pattern of state control in strategic sectors is *deliberate reinforcement*, comparable to the approach taken in telecommunications. These industries make a major contribution to the national technology base; in most cases they are considered important to national security; and they comprise a domestic sector that is less competitive than foreign companies (see figure 2.4). They involve complex, interactive technology, connect to producer-driven commodity chains, and require high capital/knowledge intensity. During economy-wide liberalization, the state separated regulation from ownership and introduced competition. Yet, to achieve national security imperatives, develop physical or service infrastructure, and promote industrial development, the separation of state assets from regulation involved corporate restructuring and reorganization, not full-scale privatization or the relinquishment of state control. Moreover, managed entry and exit accompanied the introduction of competition.

In the most strategic subsectors, after business units and companies legally separated from the bureaucracy and underwent corporatization, they retained strong links with state agencies. Central government departments governed markets by limiting the number of players and restricting FDI to equity investment or minority shares in JVs. The central government delegated economic decision making to local branches of central bureaucracies in the less strategic subsectors. Foreign and domestic private companies entered and exited without interference so long as they satisfied China-specific rules on conformity compliance and product or service inspections. The politics of decentralization governed until central imperatives necessitated intervention. The increasingly competitive domestic sector voiced policy preferences through state-controlled sector associations.

FINANCIAL SERVICES

Among the strategic industries surveyed, the state exercised the most deliberate control in financial services. Figure 2.4 shows that financial services scores high on our measures of strategic value (importance to national security broadly defined and contribution to national technology base) but low in domestic sector competitiveness. Since the Mao era, the state has retained its monopoly of the financial industry to finance economic reform. It required state-owned banks, disconnected from international markets, to lend in their respective policy areas to state-owned enterprises. Economy-wide liberalization in the 1990s introduced foreign investment but the state did not relinquish its control. Rather, reregulation designed to enhance state control and develop and diversify financial services orchestrated reform, which accelerated in the mid-2000s. Notwithstanding strict controls in the most strategic subsectors, a growing nonstate sector, including informal banking, which addressed the credit scarcity faced by private domestic industry, flourished outside of regulatory boundaries.

State Goals and Methods

To achieve economic and national security imperatives, the state calibrated regulatory reform in ways that introduced competition, promoted the development of sophisticated financial services, and retained state control of the money supply. To develop financial services, the state selectively introduced competition across subsectors in the 1990s, committed to further liberalization in its WTO accession agreement, separated the central bank from regulation in 2003, and restructured the top national banks in the mid-2000s and beyond. It also managed banking restructuring, created functional line regulators, strictly regulated the market entry and business scope of nonstate financial institutions, strategically utilized foreign investment, and purposively timed the introduction of new financial services. The Big Four banks (Agricultural Bank of China, Bank of China, China Construction Bank, and Industrial and Commercial Bank of China) underwent corporatization, assets reorganization, and international public offerings typical of national champions in strategic industries. To control the money supply, including inflation and credit overexpansion, the state employed administrative measures and macroeconomic instruments. These control mechanisms also diversified financial markets and enhanced the state's control of financial infrastructure, allowing it to institute capital controls, manage inflation, allocate capital, rescue SOEs, raise domestic consumption, and ensure social stability. The prevailing practice of capital allocation, which favored SOEs and government imperatives, however, gave rise to parallel financial institutions disconnected from the state, which reregulation sought to incorporate under state control.

Regulatory Change

The Chinese government regulated financial services and the money supply through administrative decrees until 2003. That year, it separated regulation from the central bank. Throughout the 1980s until the mid-1990s, the central bank issued nonnegotiable loan ceilings to regional branches and channeled loans only to recipients approved by state planners. Moreover, a national credit plan quantitatively managed national, provincial, and sectoral lending. In this context, national state-owned banks formed along policy jurisdictions and came to dominate financial services.

China's national banks were established during the first decade of reform.[1] The People's Bank of China (PBOC) gained ministerial status in 1978 and became the central bank charged with the foreign currency portfolio in 1984. The Agricultural

---

1. In addition to the Big Four, the State Development Bank of China, Agricultural Development Bank of China, and China Import and Export Bank were created to finance policy initiatives.

Bank of China (ABC) established in 1979 to handle the financing of grain procurement and rural development. In 1984, the Industrial and Commercial Bank of China (ICBC) took over the PBOC's previous deposit-and-lending functions to finance SOEs. Around the same time, the China Construction Bank (CCB) separated from the Ministry of Finance and came under the State Council's administration. To formalize foreign financial exchange, China joined the World Bank and the International Monetary Fund in 1980 and created the China Investment Bank. The bank assumed responsibility for development funds when China joined the Asian Development Bank in 1986.

Provincial-level banks, including national bank branches, developed in parallel. The Notice on the Method of Controlling Loan-to-Deposit Difference granted provincial branches the authority to distribute a part of their respective credit quotas to local development projects. Local party committees also obtained the authority to jointly appoint local Big Four bank managers and central bank officials, the local party groups within these financial institutions, and local disciplinary and inspection networks. Moreover, large state-owned regional banks received licenses to operate in the 1980s. For example, the Shanghai-based Bank of Communication received its license to operate in 1987. Until the late 1990s, however, rules restricted private ownership of local banks. The Minsheng Bank, China's first private bank, received its license to operate without geographical restrictions in 1996.[2]

In the late 1980s and early 1990s, the central bank experimented with asset-liability management as a replacement of the credit plan. The State Council introduced asset-liability management in commercial banks in 1993, and five years later a guidance plan replaced the credit plan. But even earlier, given administrative decentralization in the 1980s, the credit plan and reserve requirements did not completely constrain local lending. Responding to central and local development goals, provincial and local governments pressured state bank branches and other financial institutions into extending loans. Corruption and collusion ran rampant as local politics governed lending decisions and bank managers siphoned off funds, often without detection or with political protection.[3]

Though local governments possessed the authority to lend, ordinary citizens and nonstate and small businesses had little access to formal financial institutions; local banks served predominantly state-owned companies and local political interests. Moreover, a fragmented regulatory regime governed secured transactions or loans based on collateral, making it confusing and inefficient for borrowers to qualify for business loans. Laws allowed tangible moveable property only to be used as collateral; this meant a majority of TVEs could not borrow because they lacked the requisite secured property for collateral. Also, without a centralized

---

2. See Zheng (2004), 121–28, for a history of banking restructuring from 1979 through 1998.

3. Remarks by David Wu, a partner at PriceWaterhouseCoopers Beijing and participant of the recapitalization and IPO of the Bank of China, at a UC Berkeley workshop on February 21, 2007.

property registration system, borrowers often ran into difficulty providing proof of their qualifications. Some scholars argue that the Property Rights Laws of 2007 recognized and provided security for more property, prompting banks to lend more to small and medium enterprises.[4] In response to capital scarcity, small business owners created a variety of informal financing mechanisms, including rotating credit associations and private banks disguised as other types of organizations.[5] Urban and rural credit cooperatives, the more formal of these local institutions, began converting into urban commercial banks and rural commercial banks in the mid-1990s.

The 1986 Provincial Banking Regulations established the basis for a national commercial banking system, including financial services, such as securities, to serve specific developmental objectives and market niches.[6] During the 1980s through the 1990s, financial services were diversified and conventional methods for financial intermediation were created through the establishment of trust and investment corporations, including the China International Trust and Investment Corporation (CITIC); insurance companies, such as the People's Insurance Company of China (PPIC); fund management corporations to assist ailing SOEs; and the Shanghai and Shenzhen stock markets to raise capital. The securities and insurance sectors developed slowly. For example, the stock exchanges began operation in 1990 and the government established the China Security Regulatory Commission in 1992 but the regulatory commission did not have much authority until 1998 or attain legal status until 1999 under the Securities Law. Moreover, banking dominated financial services despite the entry of brokerages, such as Anshan Securities, established in 1988 by a local branch of the central bank.[7]

The Central Bank Law and the Commercial Bank Law of 1994 began the transformation of the Big Four into commercial banks. To set the stage, between 1994 and 1996, the central government unified the official and market exchange rates and allowed current accounts to convert (but it forbade capital account convertibility and exerted other capital controls). The state also created a ten-year plan for reforming financial services; consolidated central authority over a fragmented system of financial market supervision; and prepared domestic industry for competition ahead of WTO accession.[8] As a first step, to centralize market supervision and at the same time develop and diversify financial services, the State Council created three regulators to oversee banking, insurance, and securities in 1998. The State Council further created the Central Finance and Economics Leading Group

---

4. Marechal, Tekin, and Guliyeva (2009) presented data that suggest that banks lend more to small and medium enterprises in the post–Property Rights Law era.
5. See Tsai (2002) for more on the informal financial sector.
6. See Xu (1998) for a discussion of China's financial reforms between 1979 and 1991.
7. See Walter and Howie (2001) for a history of the Chinese securities industry.
8. Interview on September 22, 2008, in Beijing with Joshua Kurtzig, director, DAC Management Ltd.

(CFELG) to make policy. The Communist Party also formed the Central Financial Work Commission (CFWC), charged with installing new CCP organs and centralized party hierarchy in the regulators and the twenty-seven most important national financial companies. The CFELG and CFWC functioned essentially like a shadow central bank.[9] What is more, the CFELG mirrored the function of the State Office of Informationization in telecommunications; it brought together top leadership to set sector-specific policy, and through the CFELG, the central leadership consolidated control of financial sector personnel.[10] Once the state enhanced regulatory authority and installed leadership discipline, the State Council dismissed the CFWC in 2003.

That year, the PRC Banking Law eliminated the central bank's jurisdiction over the regulatory commissions and formally granted the Big Four banks permission to engage in commercial activities. The regulatory commissions also gained ministerial status.[11] Notwithstanding their new status, a complex web of regulators with competing agendas—including the line regulators, the finance and commerce ministries, the NDRC, the State Administration of Foreign Exchange, and the central bank—slowed policy developments and regulatory enforcement. Moreover, even while the March 2008 administrative and industrial restructuring eliminated overlapping jurisdictions and consolidated state control in many strategic industries, the regulatory landscape in financial services remained the same. "Financial services remain separately regulated and, without further institutional reform, personnel problems and competing local and national interests will continue to plague the industry," economics professor Deming Huo of Peking University explained.[12]

Subsectoral Variation

Imperatives to prepare the banking sector for international competition and to diversify financial services, and to retain state control of the money supply to finance development priorities, motivated the state's approach to the reregulation typical of strategic sectors. Reregulation enhanced state control, and state goals, government-business relations, and state methods varied across banking, securities, and insurance. Bargains between local and national banks and foreign ones tested and stretched the scope of rules even before formal market liberalization. The stra-

9. The central bank governor served as deputy secretary of the CFWC.

10. The creation of the CFWC represented the CCP's attempt to arrest the breakdown of hierarchies in financial services and restore central policy decisiveness (Heilmann 2005). Some believe that centralization failed because it constrained inflation but precluded fundamental banking reform (Shih 2008).

11. Administrative reforms in financial services varied subtly from telecommunications. One central ministry, but not an independent regulator, consolidated state control of subsectors in telecommunications.

12. Interview on September 23, 2008, in Beijing.

tegic value of subsector and political imperatives arising from the organization of state institutions and economic conditions shaped the nature of company-level bargains and other market and nonmarket measures that controlled market developments across subsectors.

Banking

To rid the Big Four banks of nonperforming loans (NPL) and attract foreign investment, the state created four asset management companies (AMCs) in 1999, before WTO accession.[13] The Ministry of Finance injected billions of dollars into the AMCs and issued bonds to purchase bad loans. The AMCs also began selling distressed assets to foreigners that year. Foreign activity in the NPL market slowed, however, when the shift from closed negotiations to open auctions in 2004 favored well-funded domestic institutions. In 2005, foreign investors boycotted the Xinda auction to protest NPL sales by the AMCs to one another at unrealistic prices. In 2006, foreign participation returned when the State Council pressured AMCs to meet recovery quotas.

At the end of 2003, the state created Central Huijin Investment, a subsidiary of the sovereign wealth fund, China Investment Corporation (CIC), to transfer funds, supervise investment, and institute corporate governance reform.[14] This commenced the typical process of China's "privatization" of strategic assets. Through Huijin, the state injected USD 100 billion to strengthen the Big Four and enlisted foreign experts and bankers to help institute corporate governance reform. By mid-2010, the Big Four's most competitive assets became listed on the Hong Kong and Shanghai exchanges.[15] The newly raised cash from global listings allowed the "reformed" banks to make acquisitions overseas.[16] "The government owns 80 percent of the financial industry but calls them 'privatized' because they trade in international stock exchanges," explained Jack Wadsworth, former chairman of Morgan Stanley Asia and China International Capital Corporation.[17]

Through the 2000s, the AMCs had limited success in recovering or selling off bad assets, and Huijin moved slowly in corporate governance, transparency, and risk management reform. Experienced mainly with loaning to SOEs as a matter of policy, state banks struggled with managing risk and pricing capital. Further

---

13. Government estimates placed bad debts at 25 percent of total loans, but private estimates doubled that amount and placed bailout costs at almost 25 percent of China's 2003 GDP (Lo 2004). Another estimate placed NPLs at 50 percent of GDP in 2001 (Shih 2008).

14. Huijin's board members included officials from the Ministry of Finance, the State Administration of Foreign Exchange (SAFE), and the central bank.

15. The ABC went public in July 2010, the last of the Big Four to do so. The state retained overall control of these banks' listed arms through Huijin.

16. To name some of the more high-profile acquisitions, ICBC invested 20 percent in Standard Bank of South Africa and Minsheng invested 10 percent in Overseas Chinese Bank.

17. Conversation on March 12, 2007, in San Francisco with Jack Wadsworth, the brainchild behind China International Capital Corporation, a JV between Morgan Stanley and CCB.

frustrating reforms were strict controls on interest rates, weak independent credit rating agencies, a feeble corporate bond market, inadequate regulatory capacity, political relationships, poor management, and a huge default risk. Not to be overlooked, the employment of tens of millions of people by state banks and their branches made social stability also a concern. In late 2008, in the midst of a global financial crisis, the CIC announced it would purchase stakes in commercial banks to further reform. Industry insiders interpreted this as the state's readiness to bail out financial services when it saw fit. This initiative was part of a government stimulus package worth USD 645 billion, which helped China weather the economic slowdown. In remarks in January 2010, central bank governor Zhou Xiaochuan of the People's Bank of China vowed to "keep a good handle on the pace of monetary and credit growth, guiding financial institutions toward balanced release of credit and avoiding excessive turbulence."[18]

Foreign banks invested in China as local governments, empowered by decentralization, lured FDI through bargains that stayed within the investment ceiling and business scope allowed by the central government in its WTO accession agreement. The WTO accession protocol committed China to liberalizing market entry in banking from a 15 percent foreign equity ceiling in 2001 to 20 percent in 2006, when geographic restrictions were lifted. Moreover, the government began permitting wholly foreign-owned branches, limited to the foreign currency business, in 2001. Despite the gradual relaxation of the FDI ceiling, market-access barriers persisted, including high working capital requirements for bank branches and a limit of one branch expansion per year.[19] To obtain market foothold, some foreign banks targeted smaller regional banks in exchange for bigger shares while other banks targeted large national banks in exchange for smaller shares. In 2008, no foreign valuation reached the legal ceiling in the Big Four, but foreign equity in smaller banks came close. In 2009, HSBC (China) Company Limited, the locally incorporated foreign subsidiary of HSBC, became the first bank to underwrite an RMB-denominated bond issued by the Bank of Shanghai.

Securities

The Commercial Banking Law of 1995 separated securities from other forms of banking and enacted strict rules to regulate this subsector.[20] China's WTO commitments limited FDI to a 33 percent equity ceiling in brokerage JVs with domestic partners and 49 percent in domestic fund management firms. These minority-

---

18. See "Special Report: Global Financial Outlook: Economic Stimulus a Mixed Blessing for China," *New York Times* (January 21, 2010).

19. Working capital requirements exceeded EU requirements by fifteen times. See "White Paper: Coming of Age Multinational Companies in China," *Economist Intelligence Unit* (June 2004), 70.

20. Laylois (2001), 611.

owned JVs were prohibited from directly trading A shares and were limited to underwriting and trading government and corporate debt and B and H shares.[21]

China International Capital Corporation (CICC), the foreign-invested investment banking JV between majority owner CCB and U.S. financial services provider Morgan Stanley, represented a state-FDI bargain that exceeded China's WTO commitment. Morgan Stanley owned 35 percent of CICC when it formed in 1995, at a time when rules prohibited FDI. But from the beginning the government did not strictly enforce the contract between the partners, which covered personnel issues to investment projects. Politics and mistrust between employees separately appointed by the partners further strained the partnership. In a sign of Morgan Stanley's falling out with CICC, in 1997 the central leadership chose Goldman Sachs to partner with CICC in managing China Telecom's first IPO in Hong Kong and New York.[22] After losing management control and becoming a passive investor, Morgan Stanley sold its stake in CICC to an investor group led by equity investors in 2010.

Since CICC, FDI-state bargains in investment banking approved by the China Security Regulatory Commission have not exceeded China's WTO commitments. Goldman Sachs, Credit Suisse, and Deutsche Bank hold 33 percent stakes in their brokerage JVs with Gao Hua Securities, Founder Securities, and Shanxi Securities, respectively. Morgan Stanley, along with JPMorgan Chase, entered China again in 2011, when they gained approval in January 2011 to form JVs with Huaxin Securities and First Capital Securities, respectively. The only global investment bank to hold a 49 percent stake is UBS, in its fund management JV with the State Development Investment Corporation, approved in 2005.

In addition to rules on ownership and business scope, other rules, such as a high fixed minimum capital requirement, dissuaded smaller entrants in securities and reduced the overall attractiveness of the JV vehicle. What is more, in late 2006 the government announced a moratorium on FDI in securities and increased the investment required from qualified foreign institutional investors from $10 billion to $30 billion. Industry insiders attributed these actions to the state's fear of FDI dominating a domestic sector teetering on bankruptcy. "Between 2006 and 2008, the Chinese government launched full-scale sector reform to get the house in order. In 2008, it lifted the moratorium and approved two JVs to underwrite mergers and acquisitions," explained a principal at a foreign-invested securities company.[23] During this period, securities reform, including liberalizing the convertibility of trade-

---

21. Only domestic investors, foreign financial firms with qualified foreign institutional investor status, and foreign strategic investors were permitted to invest in RMB-denominated A shares. Investment parameters for foreign-currency-denominated B shares and Hong Kong-listed H shares were less restrictive.

22. See McGregor (2005), chapter 2.

23. Interview on September 22, 2008, in Beijing.

able and nontradeable shares, diversified ownership in securities, but state-affiliated agencies and management teams represented a majority of the owners. The banking regulatory commission also issued a rule in December 2006 that required that senior executives pass a Chinese financial knowledge test. This barred Goldman Sach's top choice to run its JV from taking the position the following year.

The government also regularly intervened with non–market-based mechanisms to manage the stock market. It adjusted taxation involved with stock trading as it responded to domestic and global economic conditions. For example, to provide incentives for stock purchases during the 2008 global financial crisis, the government eliminated the two-side collection of the stamp tax on stock purchases and replaced it with single-side collection from the seller only.[24] The 0.1 percent tax remained at the same rate as it was in April 2008, when it was reduced from a threefold hike in 2007 to cool down the domestic economy. The government also regularly purchased stock in SOEs and permitted them to buy back stocks as assurance against company failure. In another response to global conditions, the CIC announced in September 2008 that it would purchase stock from China's Big Four banks. Moreover, to maintain a "healthy" stock market, practices common in Western stock markets, such as short selling, were made illegal.

Ambiguous rules, such as those on corporate stock disclosures, allowed the government to exercise discretion in suspending corporate trading and allowed local companies to conceal negative news. For example, in November 2008 the government suspended trading in shares of Gome Electrical Appliance Holdings because of an investigation into a sudden percentage jump in mid-2007 in shares of the medical company SD Jintai, owned by Huang Junqin, the brother of Gome CEO Huang Guangyu. In 2010, it fined and sentenced Huang Guangyu to fourteen years in prison for insider trading and bribery involving another company, Beijing Centergate Technologies.[25] Murky corporate stock disclosure rules also helped companies when negative factors led to uncertain financial prospects.[26] Yunnan-based Yuntianhua, a producer of fertilizer, suspended shares for nearly eight months, until an asset injection by its state-owned parent in late 2008.

The actual level and scope of foreign equity investment that brokerages were permitted to invest and that companies were permitted to attract varied according to the strategic value of a sector logic and the extent of global and domestic attention paid to particular bargains. When U.S. Treasury Secretary Henry Paulson began the U.S.-China Strategic Economic Dialogue, the Chinese government approved UBS's purchase of a 20 percent share of Beijing Securities in 2006, allowing the Swiss Bank to hold the biggest quota among foreign groups to invest in onshore stocks.[27] This came shortly after licensure delays to protect the domes-

24. See "China Looks to Stamp Duty Cut," *Asia Times* (March 7, 2008).

25. "Chinese Business Mogul Sentenced to Prison," *New York Times* (May 18, 2010).

26. See "Gome Affair Shows Risks of Wealth," *Financial Times* (November 24, 2008).

27. "UBS May Be First Allowed to Buy Out China Brokerage," *International Herald Tribune* (March 6, 2007).

tic securities sector. All the same, local lobbying regularly vetoed foreign equity arrangements in extensively liberalized industrial sectors. In those sectors where the central government possessed less nonnegotiable imperatives, it more readily responded to "popular" opinion. For example, after two and a half years of aggressive lobbying by sector and business associations and domestic competitor Sany Heavy Industry, the National Development and Reform Commission, in mid-2008, vetoed on "national economic security" grounds the attempt by Carlyle, a U.S.-based securities firm, to purchase a minority share of Xugong Heavy Machinery in Xuzhou, Jiangsu Province.[28] Other cases where similar concerns came into play included Pepsi's thwarted attempt to purchase Wahaha and Coke's quest for Huiyuan, which failed in 2009 after the Ministry of Commerce concluded that the acquisition would adversely affect competition. This came after an Internet survey launched by Sina.com and letters issued by Chinese scholars protested the acquisition in the name of national brand and industry protection. Danone's existing JV with Wahaha and 22.98 percent stake in Huiyuan did not jeopardize national interests since these were not controlling stakes and presumably transferred technology and know-how.

As a consequence of protectionist practices, sector-specific restrictions, and economy-wide rules such as the Anti-Trust Law looming on the horizon, large and small investors and funds targeted smaller deals or routinely broke large investments into chunks to escape central-level scrutiny.[29] The Mergers and Acquisitions Law, recalibrated in 2006, spurred local governments in Shanghai, Shenyang, and Chongqing, which traditionally have been strongholds of the state sector, to court foreign securities to assist in sectoral development.[30] The central government granted approvals by case based on structure, target type, and transaction value; the two-year moratorium against foreign investment further slowed market activity. Localities, however, possessed approval authority for equity investment in the nonstrategic sectors and for smaller deals. Until 2008, foreign securities companies routinely circumvented rules to participate in primary and secondary equity and debt markets through offshore vehicles, which became popular in the 1990s.[31] Even after the government relaxed or lifted rules against foreign entry, the use of these

28. See "Beijing Casts Cloud on Carlyle's China Deal," *International Herald Tribune* (June 30, 2006), and "China's Xugong Drops Equity Sale to Carlyle," *China Daily* (July 23, 2008).

29. An investment of 300 million RMB or more required central government approval; for investments of 100 million RMB or less, local governments had final approval authority. In September 2008, several government agencies circulated a draft of the Anti-Trust Law to a select group of foreign companies.

30. Interview on September 28, 2008, in Beijing with Zhou Bing, government relations, GE Capital.

31. Chapters 4 and 5 on state control of telecommunications examine the "Sina.com Model" in detail.

offshore holding companies remained the most popular market entry model in sectors where strategic imperatives delayed the issuance of operation licenses and for foreign equity investors weary of confronting regulatory barriers.

Many Chinese companies without genuine foreign investment also adopted this model of entry. In the absence of vibrant domestic financial markets and with financial controls that restricted consumer finance and prohibited domestic companies from making loans to one another, domestic companies participated in underground banking and turned to offshore vehicles to enjoy incentives granted FDI and to raise funds at home and abroad.[32] The government began cracking down on this "round-tripping" strategy in 2005. Circular No. 75, issued by the State Administration of Foreign Exchange, required that PRC corporate and individual residents register their offshore vehicles, though it set no clear review standards, nor did it indicate the time frame required to register. The rule also required repatriation of foreign exchange received by PRC residents from offshore dividends or income.[33] Many foreign venture capitalists viewed the reregulation as harmful for the venture capital industry and believed that it would dramatically slow down FDI while proving no solution for stopping Chinese companies from taking advantage of FDI status.[34] Others viewed this phenomenon as a clear signal of "growing demands of a domestic constituency in equity investment."[35]

After a series of implementing rules restricted round-tripping between 2006 and 2008, the government proposed the Regulation for Lenders. This law would allow private companies and individuals to lend to one another, widen access to capital, and increase RMB investment. It would also regulate underground banks and strengthen the imperative for foreign equity investors to partner with local investors to structure equity deals.[36] Importantly, it represented government efforts to enhance its control of money supply and financial services and to promote domestic sector development. By bringing underground banking, which some studies reported comprised as much as 20 percent of total lending in the economy, under the regulatory regime, the government also aimed to bolster lending to small and medium enterprises hit hard by the 2008 economic downturn and narrow the gap between rural and urban incomes.[37] Rural Zhejiang and other localities experi-

---

32. The 1994 General Principle of Understanding banned companies from lending to each other. Tsai (2002) finds that Maoist legacies and entrepreneurs' identities affected how informal finance varied across localities.

33. "The PRC State Administration of Foreign Exchange Issues Circular No. 75—A New Chapter Begins?" *Lovells Beijing Corporate Bulletin* (October 2005). See also footnote 20 in chapter 6.

34. Conversations between October and December 2005 in Beijing with Rocky Lee, DLA Piper UK LLP.

35. Interview on October 10, 2005, in Beijing with Mary Yu, general manager, Walden International China.

36. Zhou interview (September 18, 2008). See also "Beijing to Legalize Private Lenders," *South China Morning Post* (November 18, 2008).

37. "China Allows Lending by Informal Bankers," *International Herald Tribune* (November 24, 2008).

mented with permitting nonfinancial businesses to lend to other businesses, and Citigroup received state approval in October 2008 to set up two lending institutions in rural China.[38] However, rules that prohibit deposit taking by nonbank-run entities and control rights to nonbanks, require high registered capital, and restrict interest rates and loan amounts made these nascent efforts to formalize underground banking. According to Stephen Green of Standard Chartered China, "So far there has been no breakthrough."[39]

Insurance

Relative to banking and securities, the government liberalized insurance and permitted high FDI ceilings, making it one of the more liberal financial services. Moreover, in 2003 FDI in all market segments except life insurance and fund management could register as WFOE. Rules on business scope, however, restricted underwriters of policies other than for life insurance to insuring master policies and large commercial risks nationwide; they were also restricted to a 15 percent reinsurance floor until 2005, when the floor dropped to 5 percent. Rules further restricted foreign fund management companies to a 33 percent ownership ceiling, which rose to 49 percent at the end of 2004 (see discussion in above section on securities). To tap more market segments, foreign insurers routinely entered into JVs with domestic insurers. For example, AIG purchased a 9.9 percent stake in People's Insurance Company of China to access the accident and health insurance markets.

Individual deals varied according to company-level factors, and government backing continued to play an important role, especially because several agencies possessed the authority to approve licenses. The German Industry and Commerce in Beijing believed that because China did not want German companies to dominate the insurance industry, the government routinely delayed granting licensure approvals to GIC's members. Attempts by the GIC to contact the China Regulatory Insurance Commission on behalf of these companies went unanswered. These companies could not go straight to the WTO because the Chinese government had not formally rejected their applications. Moreover, since the EU possessed jurisdiction over European cases, whether the EU would pursue WTO arbitration remained unclear.[40]

---

38. See Tsai (2002) on the development of informal banking in Fujian, Wenzhou, and Henan.

39. November 25, 2008, electronic mail comments by a China-based banker, who spoke with finance industry experts, practitioners engaged in underground lending in Zhejiang, and NGOs promoting microfinance.

40. Interview on November 1, 2005, in Beijing with Holger Hanisch, GIC Beijing.

Other Financial Services

The Chinese government permitted foreign-invested JVs to operate credit card and other fee-based income businesses (such as trust and wealth management). However, competing bureaucratic agendas delayed the issuance of rules, such as the Credit Card Law, to promote the development of universal banks. Moreover, although the Chinese government committed to removing market barriers and national treatment limitations in electronic payment by the end of 2006, China Union Pay (CUP), the only domestic credit card organization, monopolized the handling of domestic-currency payment card transactions. In September 2010, the U.S. government requested consultations from the WTO alleging that the People's Bank of China, the regulator of electronic payment services, favored CUP with a series of measures dating back to 2001, which excluded other potential suppliers, including U.S. credit and debit card companies.

Leasing and credit financing (in transportation, including in automobiles and aircraft), however, remained the one subsector in financial services free of entry restrictions. What is more, the Chinese government aggressively courted FDI to expand the underdeveloped domestic sector. The government also used money from the stimulus package introduced in 2008 to stave off a sharp economic slowdown to encourage consumer finance companies to subsidize purchases of private cars and large appliances.[41] But "the word on the street," according to one industry insider, "is the government is starting to write regulations in this area. As a result, lots of foreign companies are rushing to this market, so they can be grandfathered in."[42]

ENERGY

The energy sectors score medium high to high in degree of strategic value, and domestic firms are not as competitive as foreign companies in the energy industry (see figure 2.4). In energy, more than in other industries, the state has sought to balance China's resource requirements for industrialization, which it strived to address through indigenous development, with concerns for internal stability and energy security. During the reform era, energy requirements soared, but although China possessed some capabilities in conventional oil and gas, it did not have the technical expertise or manufacturing capacity in many value-added subsectors. Comparable to energy market infrastructures around the globe, which in recent years experienced at least partial privatization while China's did not, state-owned companies dominated the oil and petrochemical sectors, and state-owned grid companies monopolized electricity and other power distribution. In contrast, quasi-private and foreign companies competed in renewable sectors; the state strategically utilized

---

41. See "Special Report: Global Financial Outlook: Economic Stimulus a Mixed Blessing for China," *New York Times* (January 21, 2010).

42. Interview with Kurtzig (September 22, 2008).

FDI to develop domestic capacity. Similar to what occurred in other strategic industries, reregulation, favoring domestic industry and enhancing state control, soon followed.

State Goals and Methods

Securing sources of energy tops China's priorities. From gas to electricity to renewable energy, the state sought to develop and control China's energy infrastructure and resources; to promote technological upgrading and the competitiveness of the domestic sector; and to decrease reliance on fossil fuels and limited natural resources, such as coal. To achieve these goals, the state liberalized and courted FDI in those subsectors not directly linked to the energy infrastructure and where China possessed less technological and infrastructural capacity. It limited nonstate investment in oil and gas distribution and forbade FDI in electricity retail and distribution, but decentralization led to a proliferation of quasi-private players in power generation. To create more competitive players, reregulation restructured and corporatized state-owned oil companies and power distributors and calibrated market liberalization in oil and gas exploration and refining and renewables. Moreover, although the state dismantled subsectoral ministries in the 1990s, various rounds of reregulation enhanced state control in strategic subsectors.

Regulatory Change

The state retained central regulatory discretion over the energy sectors because of their importance to national security but introduced structured nonstate competition to develop infrastructure, maximize competitiveness of domestic industry, and enhance the national technology base. In the 1998 round of administrative restructuring, instead of consolidating regulatory control with the creation of a supraministry, as it did in telecommunications, or creating separate regulatory commissions to supervise subsectoral development, as it did in financial services, the State Council dismantled several ministries formerly responsible for the oil, gas, petrochemical, coal, and electricity sectors.[43] To facilitate its goal of relinquishing control in less strategic areas while retaining control in the most strategic subsectors, the state created bureau-level government offices under the State Economic and Trade Commission to replace these sector-specific ministries. In 2003, these bureau-level energy offices, along with other SETC industry planning and management offices

---

43. After the state dismantled the Ministry of Energy, it established subsector-specific ministries. For a review of administrative restructuring in 1993 and 1998, see Zheng (2004). Zheng interprets the 1993 creation of separate ministries as an expansion of the political power of Li Peng, viewed as the patron of the energy industry. For pre-1993 developments, see Wirtshafter and Shih (1990), 505–12.

and the State Development and Planning Commission, came under the supervision of the NDRC.

By the mid-2000s, administrative and corporate reforms in the 1990s generated what the central leadership viewed as administrative and policy fragmentation. To enhance state authority in energy sectors, the State Council created the Leading Group on Energy, an interagency task force. The Leading Group was headed by the premier and its members included two vice premiers and leaders from thirteen other government agencies. It coordinated the many different institutions that governed energy and helped formulate subsectoral regulation.[44] The Leading Group also supervised the NDRC's Energy Bureau, which regulated electricity and set energy prices. Between 2005 and 2008, rumors circulated that administrative restructuring in March 2008 would create a supraministry to regulate energy sectors and eliminate bureaucratic fragmentation. Ultimately, the State Council did not create a supra-ministry. Instead, it created an administrative body outside of NDRC control, which "paves the way for cabinet development of the energy sector," according to Zhang Libin, chief representative of Baker Botts LLP in Beijing.[45] The State Council created the National Energy Administration (NEA), merging the Leading Group on Energy, the NDRC's Energy Bureau, other NDRC energy offices, and the nuclear power administration of the Commission of Science, Technology, and Industry for National Defense. It also formed the State Energy Commission, a high-level discussion and coordination body.[46] The State Council empowered NEA with a broad mandate, including managing energy sectors, drafting energy plans and policies, negotiating with international energy agencies, and approving foreign investments. Li Junfeng, a member of the NEA, expects the People's Congress to adopt an energy law in 2011 embodying the concept "'that energy supply should be where you can plant your food on it,' meaning that as much energy as possible should come from within China."[47]

Subsectoral Variation

Through administrative restructuring, the state attempted to enhance its regulatory authority in energy writ large while relinquishing some control to achieve state goals. Subsectoral variation in the extent and scope of state control reveals the government's strategic orientation and approach in energy at the same time that it illustrates how the organization of institutions influenced bureaucratic politics,

---

44. Related bureaucracies included the Ministry of Water Resources, Ministry of Land and Resources, and the State Administration of Coal Mine Safety, an office under the State Administration of Work Safety.

45. See "Energy Bureau Gets Nod to Increase Size," *Xinhua* (June 28, 2008).

46. See Downs (2008).

47. "Security Tops the Environment in China's Energy Plan," *New York Times* (June 17, 2010).

which prevented a coherent energy policy in practice. The government courted FDI with fiscal policies and attractive production-sharing contracts to develop high-tech, value-added subsectors. Moreover, market liberalization in less strategic subsectors attracted quasi-private enterprises to growing markets in oil exploration and refining, power generation, and renewable energy. In contrast, the state limited market competition in strategic energy subsectors to SOEs, which underwent the corporatization process typical of strategic state assets. National oil and power companies formally separated from government offices, but corporate restructuring did not undermine state control; rather, ownership restructuring to establish a centralized corporate shareholder model, similar to the experience of the telecommunications carriers, enhanced state authority over sectoral developments.[48]

Oil and Petrochemicals

In oil and petrochemicals, to increase efficiency and profit, the State Council established national oil corporations along functional lines when it dismantled the Ministry of Petroleum Energy in 1988.[49] A decade later, the state introduced competition when it restructured the national oil corporations to create vertically integrated regional monopolies. This restructuring of state monopolies is similar to that of state-owned telecommunications carriers that occurred during the same period and in 2008. In restructuring along regional lines, the state hoped to better utilize and employ resources, including foreign investment, to develop particular oil fields and build infrastructural capacity.[50] The national oil and petrochemical companies also underwent Chinese-style corporatization, similar to that experienced by the telecommunications carriers and the Big Four banks. The State-Owned Assets Supervision and Administration Commission held their assets, with the core competitive ones issued as shares on the Hong Kong and New York capital markets.

The extent of decentralization and rules on market access, business scope, and FDI varied across oil and petrochemical subsectors according to a strategic value logic. Eager to obtain technology and knowledge transfers and at the same time retain ownership and control, the state permitted foreign equity investment as minority stakeholders without board participation in listed stock and foreign minority partners in JVs to develop crude and refined oil with the national oil companies. Moreover, a generous fiscal policy attracted FDI in high-tech, value-added upstream subsectors where national oil companies were less competitive.

---

48. See Lin (2006 and 2008) for details of this process in oil and petrochemicals. The SASAC managed assets of state-owned power and energy companies.

49. The national oil corporations operated as functional monopolies: upstream (China National Petroleum Corporation), refineries (China Petroleum and Chemical Corporation, also known as Sinopec), offshore (China National Offshore Oil Corporation), and international trading (Sinochem).

50. For example, CNPC became dominant in northern and western China and Sinopec in the east and south. CNPC retained more than two thirds of China's crude oil production capacity, while Sinopec controlled more than half of the refining capacity and crude oil imports.

Production-sharing contracts, similar to global industry standards with minor variances, governed typical project collaborations with national oil companies. All the same, the State Council possessed final authority in approving energy projects, budget allocations, and financing arrangements, and the Ministry of Land and Resources became involved in issues related to oil exploration and greenfield natural gas reserves. Moreover, FDI faced limits on choices in suppliers and JV partners, restrictions on business scope and market access, and cumbersome licensing and import procedures that required minimum capitalization and earnings, storage capacity, and port infrastructure.[51] The government controlled its take through a windfall tax, which adjusted profit levels, and an export tax, which it levied to encourage domestic sales.

To protect and promote the domestic sector in downstream sectors, the government channeled the bulk of imported refined and processed oil through four designated state-trading companies.[52] Furthermore, the state subsidized petroleum producers at the pump through retail price regulation. This produced a major gap between domestic and international prices, forcing the national oil companies to self-correct through increased exports, which led to shortages at home. Actual retail prices varied according to location and China-specific sectoral attributes, such as consumer type. In this regulatory environment, foreign companies with first-mover advantage, such as Shell and Exxon, collaborated with national or local retailers with strong connections to local authorities. But delivery via a lower cost base, with little concern for safety, too often motivated these authorities. In 2003, Total, a French oil giant, won a bid against Shell in a project that eventuated in three hundred deaths and the evacuation of ten thousand people when a well exploded.[53] Other FDI opted out of retail. For example, Chevron invested predominately in upstream subsectors, including offshore exploration with China National Offshore Oil Corporation, a government-encouraged collaboration, because China lacked expertise in this area.[54]

The state took a mixed orientation toward the regulation of petrochemicals. It combined central-level discretion in high-value projects with decentralized regulatory authority and a more liberalized FDI regime. Petrochemicals is an applications subsector rather than one with infrastructural implications within energy, yet it serves as value-added input for strategic subsectors of nonstrategic industries. In its WTO protocol, the state committed to removing restrictions on the import,

---

51. Interview on September 22, 2009, in Beijing with Isikeli Taureka, president of Chevron Asia Pacific Exploration and Production.

52. They were the China National Chemical Import and Export Co., China International United Petroleum and Chemicals Co., China National United Oil Co., and Zhuhai Zhenrong Co.

53. See "China Buys 1.6 Percent Stake in Total," *Financial Times* (April 3, 2008), for more on SAFE's investment in Total, the world's fourth largest oil group.

54. Chevron operated a lubricant WFOE and a JV with a small Chinese company to engage in retail operations in Macau, Guangdong, and Hong Kong.

resale, and distribution activities of existing foreign-invested petrochemicals; to permitting the provincial approval of FDI projects with less than $30 million in total investment; and to enacting no restrictions on foreign ownership. The state dismantled the Ministry of Chemical Industry in 1998 along with the Ministry of Power and Coal Industry, and in 2001 it downgraded residual government offices to sector associations.[55] In this regulatory environment, FDI in petrochemicals operated at the whim of local governments and group companies, which were spin-offs of former chemical industry bureaus or subsidiaries of national petrochemical companies. A crowded market, with roots in a Mao-era policy of localized production of critical commodities that was augmented by the decentralization of regulatory enforcement of petrochemicals in the reform era, pitted foreign-invested JVs against their Chinese parents. Many Chinese competitors were able to produce serviceable products and sophisticated copies of foreign products.

All the same, because petrochemicals serve as upstream inputs for strategic subsectors of nonstrategic industries, such as technical textiles, the central government retained its licensure authority in certain market segments, such as ethylene cracker and its derivatives, that produce commodity plastics. Moreover, new tariff structures favored domestic refiners that supplied raw materials. The government reduced tariffs on raw feedstock for cracker producers but not those for the downstream inputs of their foreign-invested competitors.[56]

Electricity

Compared to oil and petrochemicals, the state regulated the power industry in a less centralized manner and less strictly regulated the market entry of nonstate companies. Through the mid-2000s, the government experimented with relinquishing regulatory enforcement in power sectors during several rounds of administrative restructuring. In 1988, the electric power bureaucracy merged with other energy bureaucracies to create the Ministry of Energy. Centralization under the Ministry of Energy between 1988 and 1993 created provincial power companies that formed power groups. In 1993, the government created the Ministry of Electric Power, which supervised provincial power companies. In 1998, the government demoted the Ministry of Electric Power to a bureau-level office, and power companies merged and corporatized to form the State Power Corporation.[57] In 2002, the state introduced state-owned competition when it separated State Power's generation, transmission, and service units.[58] The state also separated policy and regulatory

---

55. The State Administration of Petroleum and Chemical Industries under the SETC became the China Petroleum and Chemical Industry Association in 2001.

56. Floyd (2002).

57. See Yan and Yu (1996), 735–57, for the state's management of the power industry between 1988 and the mid-1990s and figure 3 for an organization chart of the Ministry of Electric Power.

58. In 2002, the State Power Corporation separated into eleven regional transmission and distribution companies and five power generators, which managed more than 80 percent of China's power generation. See Pearson (2005).

functions with the creation of the State Electricity Regulatory Commission, which regulated the power sector from the plant to the consumer. In March 2008, after a decade without a centralized bureaucracy, the creation of the National Energy Administration represented the state's attempt to increase regulatory capacity in a decentralized and conflict-ridden institutional terrain.

State control varied across subsectors of electrical power. The state strictly controlled and managed electricity grids, mindful of the importance of an efficient electricity infrastructure to national security and ultimate control over the more liberalized energy equipment and generation subsectors.[59] The linking of regional grids to create two state-owned regional grid monopolies in 2005 served this purpose.[60] Moreover, provincial utilities routinely joined forces with the regional grid monopolies to tender bids for power stations and substations.[61] The government forbade FDI in distribution, but in its effort to interconnect regional grids, the Chinese government elicited foreign equipment makers, including ABB, a Swedish power equipment maker, to help with systems engineering.[62] In 2004, FDI obtained loan financing for some power transmission projects.[63] Foreign companies, however, were excluded from contract bids for ultra-high-voltage power transmission schemes after participating in research and development. As in telecommunications networking equipment, the Chinese government aimed to master the technology that runs the infrastructure; in this case, to develop ultra-high-voltage transmission lines. Hoping to leverage its good will, ABB, in a JV with Xian High Voltage Switchgear, submitted a proposal to the State Grid Corporation to develop the Shanxi-Hubei transmission project.[64]

The NDRC's energy and pricing bureaus set and regulated electricity prices to balance affordability and industrial goals.[65] In practice, the decentralized nature of regulatory enforcement and the type of user (commercial, industrial, or residential)

---

59. Between 2002 and 2003, the Circular on Promulgation of the Plan for Electric Power System Reform and Circular on Promulgation of the Electric Power Tariff Reform Plan presented reregulation plans.

60. The government aimed for an integrated national electricity grid by 2020. In 2005, the State Grid Corporation covered most of the country, and the Southern Power Grid Corporation covered the rest. China had previously relied upon local and regional grids. See Wirtshafter and Shih (1990), 505–12.

61. Interview on April 10, 2006, in Chongqing with Alan Chan, financial controller, ABB Transformer Co.

62. See "Grid United," *ABB Review* (2003), 22–24, for more on the collaboration between ABB's corporate research center and the Tsinghua-run State Key Lab of Power Systems.

63. The Catalogue of Foreign Investment encouraged investment in coal-gas–integrated gasification combined cycle plant technology and equipment and the construction and management of power stations.

64. See "Foreign Firms Feel Left Out in Cold," *South China Morning Post* (November 7, 2005).

65. The 2005 NDRC Circular No. 514 presented base prices for three stages of power. In the first stage, the set price, which was applied to every generator in the same region, reflected the generators' average fixed cost and market demand. In the second, the state permitted distribution and transmission

and their importance to local interests affected how actual prices varied across localities. The large number of regulatory and market stakeholders fighting for influence disallowed prices from conforming to official prices.[66] The State Council created the NEA, according to an industry insider, to enhance state control of energy infrastructure and other energy subsectors.[67] In 2010, to improve energy efficiency, the NDRC forced twenty-two provinces to halt the practice of providing electricity at discounted prices. The two thousand–plus factories on a government list would be barred from obtaining bank loans, export credits, business licenses, and land, and have their electricity shut off, if necessary. The prolonged decentralized nature of electricity regulation left open the question of enforcement.[68]

As early as the 1980s, the central government shifted the responsibility of building electricity capacity to the provincial and local levels and liberalized competition in power generation. Although approval for projects resided initially in the planning commission, in practice local governments approved and regulated small independent power producers, often quasi-private companies. Well-connected local entrepreneurs began to build electricity capacity, often turning to hydropower and coal, commencing the problem of small polluting coal power plants, which dot China's immense rural countryside.[69] Coal-fired power stations, a consequence of deregulation and decentralization, generate 75 percent of electricity.[70]

The government also courted FDI in electricity generation. As early as the mid-1980s, to generate capital, local power generators lured foreign investment with power purchasing agreements that promised generating hours and generous electricity rates.[71] Through 1997, during a period of de facto liberalization much like that experienced by telecommunications carriers during the same period, FDI flooded power generation and signed build-operate-transfer agreements with local power operators. Since 1998, however, a series of broken contracts (which the central government refused to honor), rising coal prices, fixed electricity tariffs, state

---

companies to incorporate more of the electricity cost into their pricing. In the third, the NDRC set electricity prices based on an undisclosed mechanism to ensure that the end user price floated with what grid companies paid to generators.

66. According to Cunningham (2007), decentralization and partial deregulation created independent corporate actors unknown and unguided by central regulators; they operated obscured from official view and selectively tapped state resources to pursue energy provision.

67. Interview on September 18, 2008, in Beijing with Troels Beltoft, senior strategy manager, Vestas Corp.

68. "In Crackdown on Energy Use, China to Shut 2,000 Factories," *New York Times* (August 9, 2010).

69. A 2008 study found new coal plants had been built to high technical standards, using the most modern technologies available. Rather, the type and quality of coal consumed and interactions between new market forces, commercial pressures, and regulation proved problematic. See Steinfeld, Lester, and Cunningham (2008).

70. "Despite Its Problems, Coal Is Here to Stay," *South China Morning Post* (November 4–7, 2005).

71. "Foreign Firms Quit Power Sector," *China Daily* (January 20, 2005).

subsidies to state-owned power groups, and overinvestment by local governments forced existing FDI to withdraw as their build-operate-transfer agreements expired and slowed FDI in general.[72] American Electric Power, Siemens, and Hew (a unit of the Swedish electricity firm Vattenfall) separately decided to exit the market when their contracts expired in 2005 because of profit shortfalls.[73] The regulatory environment led to overinvestment in power infrastructure, fast and unsustainable economic growth, and, ultimately, energy shortages.

Renewables

Even as FDI decreased in electrical power generation, FDI increased in renewable energy. The state promoted the development of renewable energy sectors through installation-based fiscal incentives and procurement policies. The policies were aimed at subsidizing local and provincial utilities that controlled generation and distribution, grid companies that controlled transmission infrastructure, and energy farm developers that sold power to grids. It also supported domestic equipment makers technically unable to produce equipment that connected successfully to grids.[74] Regulatory initiatives in hydropower and wind power, the fastest renewable sources to deploy technologically and with low barriers of entry, provide a good case study.[75] In late 2001, the NDRC introduced a Wind Power Concession approach, a tendering procedure aimed at bringing down the cost of wind-power generation. This empowered local governments to invite international and domestic investors to develop 100 megawatt wind farms on potential wind sites. In 2002, the Ministry of Finance and the State Duty Bureau implemented a new tax policy that reduced the value-added tax for wind generation from 17 percent to 8.5 percent.

Starting in the mid-2000s, government policies shifted to promoting an emerging domestic sector in renewables. In 2005, the government mandated the newly created grid companies to deploy wind power and the NDRC began awarding contracts to local wind power manufacturers without tender. Goldwind, a domestic company that licensed technology from German companies and whose first product copied an earlier product of Vestas, a Danish wind turbine company and global leader in the industry, routinely received lucrative government contracts outside of a formal procurement process.

Moreover, high local content requirements, which violate the WTO rules, favored domestic companies over foreign ones. In July 2005, the NDRC replaced

---

72. Most industry analysts attributed the state's unwillingness to intervene to Li Peng's efforts to restrict FDI in power generation. Interview on October 10, 2005, in Shanghai with Bill Savadove, journalist, *South China Morning Post*, and on October 30, 2005, in Beijing with Patrick Powers, U.S.-China Business Council.

73. "Foreign Power Firms Leaving China," *Agence France-Presse* (February 1, 2005).

74. In the mid-2000s, 20 to 25 percent of installed wind power infrastructure never connected to a grid.

75. Beltoft interview (September 18, 2008).

the existing 50 percent local content requirement on certain wind power projects with a 70 percent floor, which forced foreign vendors of domestic generators and distributors and state-initiated projects to produce domestically.[76] In an effort to meet the local content requirement, Vestas began operations at a wholly foreign-owned factory in Tianjin in mid-2006.[77] Meeting the 2005 NDRC requirement also entailed instructing domestic contractors in the manufacturing processes involved in steel forgings and castings and fabricating complex electronic controls. By the time the Chinese government dropped this particular local content requirement in November 2009, in response to foreign motions to challenge the rule in front of the WTO, most foreign wind turbine makers' domestic inputs far exceeded the 70 percent obligation.

In hydropower, ABB established a JV in 1998 with Chongqing Transformer, an SOE, to produce power transformers, which move energy from power stations to grids, to service the Three Gorges infrastructure.[78] Transformers assembled at the plant included up to 46 percent domestic content, which satisfied the localization rule at the time and avoided high import duties.[79] In the first round of procurement, ABB did not win contracts; Chinese hydro equipment maker Baoding received all the left bank bids. In the second round of procurement, however, "ABB's 'made in China' efforts won twelve contracts to power the right bank."[80]

The Renewable Energy Law of 2006 further incentivized investment in high-tech, value-added energy sectors. It spurred the development of the domestic sector as well as increased investment and market opportunities for foreign equipment makers.[81] "After the promulgation of the Renewable Energy Law, Vestas gained twenty-five competitors overnight," exclaimed Troels Beltoft, senior strategy manager for Vestas. Similar to the pattern witnessed in technical textiles, existing industrial equipment producers, with part of their supply chain already in place, tweaked

---

76. Conversations on October 11 and December 13, 2005, in Beijing with Eugenia Katsigris, consultant on energy projects between the World Bank and the NDRC.

77. Conversations in October and November 2005 and September 2006 in Beijing with Lilli-Anne Suzuki, sales and marketing manager, Vestas China.

78. ABB previously owned a 49 percent share in ABB Chongqing, the largest of its twenty-seven companies in China. Subsequent capital infusions raised ABB's share to 62 percent.

79. Interview on April 10, 2006, in Chongqing with Charlie Yang, director of supply management, ABB CQ. For example, the Chinese government imposed import duties on grain-oriented flat-rolled electrical steel (GOES) used in transformers, reactors, and other large electrical equipment. Beginning in April 2010 it imposed antidumping and countervailing duties, alleging that subsidized American steel was being dumped in the Chinese market. Five months later, the U.S. government requested dispute settlement consultations by filing a case against China at the WTO. The U.S. government, for its part, also imposed high tariffs on steel products from China on the grounds that unfair pricing and subsidies received by Chinese counterparts harmed U.S. steelmakers.

80. Chan interview (April 10, 2006).

81. China's wind turbine market has exploded so much that foreign equipment makers experience growth even as the domestic sector dominates "more than 85 percent" of the market. See "China Wins in Wind Power, by Its Own Rules," *New York Times* (December 14, 2010).

their equipment to enter wind power. Other domestic companies purchased technology from less successful European and other Western companies or partnered with FDI eager to enter the Chinese market. The domestic wind power sector took off so fast that foreign securities companies began to invest in Chinese wind power equipment makers.[82]

Other regulatory interventions to promote the domestic sector and accelerate R&D efforts in wind power included prioritizing the sector in the 2007 update of the Foreign Investment Catalogue and in the fifteen-year Medium-to-Long-Term Plan for Science and Technology (2006–20). Moreover, the government gave foreign turbine manufacturers of 1.5 megawatt turbines three weeks to register before they had to form JVs with Chinese partners, a rule effective November 2007. The National Debt Wind Power Program subsidized domestic turbine manufacturers; favorable national debt interest subsidy programs made possible wind farms supplied with domestically produced turbines. Furthermore, the State Council released a white paper on energy in December 2007, and starting in 2008, the domestic manufacturers received a 10 percent subsidy per megawatt and the Special Fund for Wind Power Manufacturing awarded grants ranging from USD 6.7 million to USD 22.5 million to wind turbine and components manufacturers. "These initiatives are in line with the shift from the 'Made in China' to the 'Created in China' strategy announced at the October 2007 meeting of the National People's Congress" and exemplify how "the Chinese government maps out industry and releases regulations accordingly in a systematic and proactive manner," explained Beltoft. In December 2010, claiming that the Special Fund violates WTO policy because grants awarded appear to be tied to a local content policy and that Chinese policies lack transparency and are released only in Chinese, the U.S. government requested dispute settlement consultations through the WTO.[83]

AUTOMOTIVES

China overtook the United States as the world's top automotive market in November 2009, according to figures from the China Association of Automobile Manufacturers.[84] The development of the Chinese automotive industry cannot be

---

82. Interview with Zhou (September 28, 2008). The development of a coherent renewable energy agenda and policy regime in wind power, moving away from bureaucratic fragmentation, is consistent with the strategic value framework introduced in this book as well as with the findings of Lema and Ruby (2007).

83. The U.S. government took action in response to a petition filed by the United Steelworkers, which also cited other support programs that China has since discontinued. "WTO Wind Industry Throwdown: U.S. vs. China: The U.S. Trade Representative Cries Foul on China's Wind Subsidies," *Greentech Media* (December 28, 2010).

84. See "China Could Learn from Henry Ford," *New York Times* (January 20, 2010).

disconnected from the government's priority in increasing its technological and infrastructural base or the deliberate orientation of its policies and interventions toward developing indigenous capacity. But as the Chinese automobile sector had few national security implications and infrastructural assets that required central coordination, the state delegated industrial management to provincial governments. Decentralization and market liberalization created a domestic market made up of more than one hundred automakers under provincial ownership and management and thousands more state-owned and nonstate producers of auto parts. Among domestic automobile producers, overcapacity and underutilization reigned as an onslaught of them completed only a few thousand units per year with outmoded plants and equipment. Fewer in numbers, foreign-invested automobile joint ventures made up 75 percent of the domestic market in sales in the mid-2000s. Foreign component manufacturers tended to adopt wholly foreign-owned structures and competed with a domestic sector subsidized by localities.

State Goals and Methods

The state's primary goal in the automotive industry is the development of indigenous capacity to dominate domestic markets and compete internationally. The state separated state-owned manufacturers from ministerial ownership and supervision, introduced subsectoral competition, and decentralized administrative supervision of market developments. On the one hand, it facilitated the entry of FDI to increase technology and knowledge acquisition, especially in passenger car production. On the other hand, it restricted the market access, investment level, and business scope of FDI, and central measures and local initiatives promoted domestic manufacturers. Provincial and local governments implemented industrial policy; and sector-specific rules on imports, exports, and local content subsidized the domestic sector.

Regulatory Change

The development of the Chinese automotive industry began when the government collaborated with the Soviet Union in the 1950s and 1960s to build trucks. The need for trucks and buses for freight, passenger, and military transport overshadowed passenger car production; through the 1960s, the state relied on Eastern European imports to supply its minimal needs. During the Cultural Revolution, only top leadership had access to passenger cars. After the economic opening in 1978, imports surged as demand skyrocketed. By the mid-1980s, nearly all provinces operated plants, which built a variety of commercial vehicles, including trucks, buses, and special utility vehicles. Empowered by the general trend of decentralization, provincial governments and provincial-level municipalities, such as Shanghai and

Beijing, became especially active in promoting local state-owned automakers, a pattern that continued in the 2000s.[85] The 124 state-owned automakers that operated in 1993 reflected the decentralized nature of the market. Local authorities formed automotive leading groups that drafted industrial plans; they also incorporated industrial groups that connected suppliers to manufacturers.

Since the early 1990s, administrative restructuring formally delegated economic decision making concerning domestic sector entry and exit to lower levels of government and production to corporatized companies separated from the ownership and daily management of a bureaucracy. Moreover, a State Council–level leading group staffed by NDRC bureaucrats and consisting of members from multiple ministries, such as those found in telecommunications, financial services, and energy today, had not presided over industrial developments for more than twenty years.

A central-level office last officially regulated automotives between 1987 and 1993. After realizing that China could not depend on domestic manufacturers producing outdated models to satisfy growing demand, the Chinese government under the leadership of Li Peng recentralized during that period to coordinate cooperation with foreign investors to use their technology, capital, and management skills to foster large-scale manufacturing. In 1987, the State Council created the Automobile Leading Group, which it dismantled two years later after the merger of the State Machinery Industry Commission and the Ministry of Electronic Industry created the Ministry of Machinery and Electronic Industry. In a further attempt to enhance central control of domestic sector developments, the China National Automotive Industry Corporation (CNAIC), founded in 1982 by the machinery bureaucracy and given the responsibility for automotive planning, project approval, and technology acquisition, regained bureaucratic status.[86]

During administrative restructuring in 1993, however, the central government relinquished central supervision of automotive sectors. The CNAIC became a sector association, and the State Council reorganized the Ministry of Machinery and Electronic Industry. The reestablished Ministry of Electronic Industry and newly created Ministry of Machinery held peripheral responsibility for the automotive industry. In 1997, the MEI merged with the Ministry of Post and Telecommunications to form the Ministry of Information Industry and the Ministry of Machinery was downgraded to a bureau-level office. In 2003, reduced to a single office, the automotive planning bureaucracy folded into the NDRC when the industrial planning offices of the SETC merged with the NDRC.

Yet sector-specific rules and policies, such as the 2004 Policy on the Development of Automotive Industry and the Planning on Restructuring and Revitalization of Auto Industry issued in 2009, promoted the development of the domestic

---

85. For regional variation in development outcomes and local state-industry relations in the automotive industry, see Thun (2004 and 2006) and Segal and Thun (2001). For firm-level variation in state-FDI bargains in the 1980s, see Harwit (1992).

86. See Harwit (1992), 142–44, for historical background on the Chinese automotive industry.

industry and managed market developments. Import tariffs and domestic content policies subsidized domestic automakers and auto parts manufacturers.[87] Moreover, to stem overexpansion and ensure the competitiveness of the domestic sector, the central government retained the discretion to veto new operation licenses, regularly forced smaller, uncompetitive domestic companies to shut down, and merged the remaining companies with large manufacturers.[88] Importantly, the state also strategically utilized FDI to deepen industrialization and promote domestic sector competitiveness at home and abroad. For example, Zhejiang Geely, whose development benefited from the mechanisms of FDI utilization described in this case study, exported around 5 percent of its compact cars annually and further expanded globally with its acquisition of Volvo from Ford Motor Company in March 2010.[89] Thus, even while decentralization and liberalization introduced competition, the government strictly managed the investment level, ownership structure, and business scope of FDI. Between the 1980s and 1997, the "Big Three, Small Three, and Mini Two" policy limited FDI to eight automobile joint ventures. Ownership shares and technology transfers varied among these foreign-invested JVs. FDI has increased considerably since the late 1990s, but a "two-plus-two" rule restricted the number of JVs a foreign automaker could operate to two passenger and two commercial productions.

Subsectoral Variation

Bargains between foreign automakers and local governments illustrate how a strategic value logic influenced subsectoral variation in government control of automotives. To develop competitive automakers, the central government assigned local partners to foreign automakers of commercial and passenger vehicles from a small coterie of SOEs.[90] Law limited each foreign automaker to two 50-percent-equity JVs and each JV to one plant producing a single model based on a local sourcing requirement of 40 percent. "Without economies of scale and fierce competition from all the major global players also in China, the costs of locally produced cars made of locally procured components are much higher than they need to be," explained the general manager for a foreign-invested automaker.[91] Moreover, local partners and their local government owners supervised daily operations. Since China's WTO accession, foreign automakers shared control of domestic distribution. "While the

87. "Car Firms in China Look Locally for Parts," *Nikkei Weekly* (September 4, 2006).

88. See "White Paper: Coming of Age; Multinational Companies in China," *Economist Intelligence Unit* (June 2004), 54–65.

89. "China's Lucky Man Bags Volvo," *Economist* (August 7, 2010).

90. In 2009, thirteen foreign automakers had Chinese JVs. Most of them had little choice in their partners, and some shared the same Chinese partner.

91. Interview on October 13, 2008, in Beijing with Constanze Picking of government relations, Daimler.

ownership share is 50–50, different incentives motivate the partners—market profits drive foreign partners while Communist Party reward systems motivate local partners," the manager elaborated.[92] Moreover, the Opinion on Promoting Auto Consumption issued in 2009 explicitly stated that future revisions of the rules on Branded Auto Sales would encourage various sales models to balance the market power of automobile suppliers (manufacturers and general distributors) vis-à-vis brand dealers restricted to a single brand under current rules.

Commercial and Passenger Vehicles

China's explicit strategy toward automotives favored domestic automakers and promoted the development of domestic producers of automotive parts. Among recent rules, the Policy on Development of Automotive Industry (Order No. 8), issued in 2004 by the NDRC, outlined government objectives for building the local automotive industry. It included a 50 percent market share for domestic automakers by 2010, and stipulated tariffs on imported parts and subassemblies as part of a domestic content strategy.[93] Measures for the Administration of Import of Automotive Parts and Components for Complete Vehicles (Decree 125) and Rules for Determining Whether Imported Automotive Parts and Components Constitute Complete Vehicles (Customs Announcement No. 4), also issued in 2004, specified that in order to be taxed at the completely knocked down (CKD) subassembly rate, four out of seven categories (totaling 57 percent) of a completely built up (CBU) vehicle, exceeding the original 40 percent local content requirement, must contain local contents. These rules required every CBU to pay a deposit and register sensitive information until submission of proof that the complete vehicle contained the mandated level of local content.[94]

The international community rose in uproar in response to the 2004 measures. They claimed that these regulations breached WTO rules prohibiting discriminatory taxation and subsidies contingent on local content. A 2006 request for consultation with China filed by Canada, the European Community, and the United States, and joined by Australia, Brazil, Mexico, Japan, Thailand, and Argentina, eventuated in the WTO Appellate Body issuing a ruling in the claimants' favor on December 15, 2008.[95] The Appellate Body "recommends that the [Dispute Settle-

---

92. Interview in May 2005 in Shanghai with the manager of a foreign-invested automotive JV.

93. The 2009 Planning on Restructuring and Revitalization of Auto Industry eliminated this and other market-share requirements but not without setting new objectives on creating a competitive domestic automotive industry and promoting high-tech and environmental friendly technology.

94. Interview on May 22, 2006, in Beijing with Bengti Tan, accountant, Ernst & Young. See also "Customs & Trade Alert: China Automotive Industry," *Ernst & Young Trade Services* (March 2005).

95. The ruling affirmed a July 18, 2008, report by a WTO panel established by the WTO Dispute Settlement Body. Also see WTO DS339, DS340, and DS342 requests for consultations filed with the WTO Dispute Settlement Body by the European Communities, the United States, and Canada, respectively.

ment Body] request China to bring its measures into conformity" with its General Agreement on Tariffs and Trade (GATT) and WTO obligations.

Whispers among foreign investors and along the halls of the newly created Ministry of Industry and Information Technology, which the State Council assigned to regulate the automotive industry, indicated that in light of the WTO ruling, the Chinese government planned to revise Order No. 8.[96] The revised policy would eliminate Decree 125 but create new rules to maximize technology and knowledge transfers and encourage industrial upgrading. For example, the two-plus-two rule would be loosened, but the JV rule would stay in place. Permitting more JVs would increase technology transfers and continue local oversight of daily operations. In 2007, the NDRC linked subsidies for entry into high-tech, value-added areas, such as alternative fuel vehicles, to a local procurement requirement.[97]

The Planning on Restructuring and Revitalization of Auto Industry issued in March 2009 by the State Council and the Opinion on Promoting Auto Consumption jointly issued by the MOFCOM and the MIIT, among other government agencies, stated the government's intent to promote domestic demand through a variety of methods, such as the elimination of a tax loophole that benefited importers, the enactment of new traffic laws by local governments, and the development of legal and financial support systems for consumption; encourage industry consolidation by domestic automakers, including identifying potential mergers and acquisitions, setting an investment floor for new entrants, and restricting the acquisition of failing producers; and promote the development of high-tech and environmentally friendly cars through subsidies to taxi fleets and local governments and directions to state electricity grids to establish electric car charging stations.

In addition to rules on market entry and exit and local content policies, the central government employed company-level intervention, the nature of which varied across subsectors according to a strategic value logic. To promote technological upgrading in passenger cars, the government regularly participated in negotiations with foreign automakers on behalf of domestic partners. For example, in 2006, a senior Chinese Communist party official on the legal team of the National People's Congress participated in contract negotiations with DaimlerChrysler and BMW on behalf of Lifan Group, a quasi-private producer of motorcycles and passenger cars. Lifan had sought to purchase the Campo Largo factory in Brazil, which combined the latest U.S. and German technology to produce the 1.6-liter, 16-valve Tritec engine. It planned to "take it apart, piece by piece, transport it halfway around the globe and put it back together again" in China.[98] Despite initial reluctance to issue

---

96. Interviews in September 2008 with MIIT bureaucrats and China managers of foreign automakers.

97. This rule was aimed partly at Toyota, which assembled Prius gasoline-electric hybrid cars in China but shipped critical components in sealed boxes from plants in Japan. "G.M. Will Build Its Own Research Center in China," *New York Times* (October 30, 2007).

98. See "China Seeking Auto Industry, Piece by Piece," *New York Times* (February 16, 2006).

another production license, the Ministry of Commerce granted Lifan a license after Bo Xilai, then commerce minister and, beginning in 2007, the general secretary of the CCP in Chongqing, visited Lifan's new Chongqing factory.[99] Moreover, despite strict controls on FDI entry and exit, the government willingly struck company-level bargains with FDI in exchange for terms that increased its strategic goals. It relaxed the 50 percent ownership threshold when it permitted Honda to own two-thirds of its assembly plant in Guangzhou after Honda promised to export production to Europe.[100]

In contrast, the central government delayed or resisted cracking down on the counterfeiting of vehicles and automotive parts. For example, in an old Volkswagen factory purchased from a Mexican group, Chery, a subsidiary of Shanghai Automotive Industry Corporation (SAIC), VW's domestic partner, copied VW's Jetta model in 2000 and priced the counterfeits 20 percent cheaper. VW's Chinese parts partners supplied some of the components, and the high tolerances and quality of the new car surprised even VW. The central government's promises to VW to intervene went unrealized even while Chery increased its production volume and launched another counterfeit modeled after a design of GM, another of SAIC's foreign partners.[101] In two other cases in 2007, China National Machinery & Equipment Import & Export Corporation and Shuanghuan Automobile introduced Electric City and Noble, respectively, both extremely sophisticated copies of Daimler's smart fortwo car. "Though the new IPR [intellectual property rights] law is quite good, implementation has been very slow," explained Constanze Picking, the government relations officer for Daimler in Beijing.[102]

All the same, Picking worried more about the Chinese government's technology transfer policy than counterfeits. Despite lenient IPR enforcement, the government did not actively support fakes. However, the difficulty of enforcing patents in China augmented "the requirement that FDI give away technology." Yet, foreign automakers feel "obliged to open R&D centers" to signal their commitment to share technology and innovate based on Chinese consumer needs.[103] Moreover, eager to gain market share, they continued to aggressively expand production despite barriers on market entry, business scope, and operations.

---

99. Interview on April 12, 2006, in Shanghai with Jeff Albright, general manager of Briggs & Stratton China.

100. "China Looms as the World's Next Leading Auto Exporter," *New York Times* (April 22, 2005).

101. VW and GM were not alone. For similar stories, see "White Paper: Coming of Age; Multinational Companies in China," *Economist Intelligence Unit* (June 2004), 51 and 60.

102. Picking interview (October 13, 2008).

103. Picking interview (October 13, 2008) and "G.M. Will Build Its Own Research Center in China," *New York Times* (October 30, 2007).

Automotive Components

The production of automotive components contributed less to the industrial base for an indigenous automotives industry, which is considered critical for China's technology infrastructure. Thus, less concerned about the competitiveness of domestic players, the government did not directly control market entry, business scope, and production volume in automotive parts. The government lifted a JV requirement for FDI in the late 1990s and relinquished regulatory authority of this subsector to lower levels of government in early rounds of reform. All the same, local content policies in automobile assembly promoted and sustained the development of domestic capacity in automotive components. Though domestic production relied on imports of high-strength grades of steel and manufacturing equipment, which increased the costs of locally produced components, local content policies and tariff regimes in vehicle production and assembly guaranteed ready markets. Moreover, localization rules also governed components production. In a 2006 study on policy choices, the State Council incorporated the strategic utilization of FDI in auto parts as part of an industrial policy in automotives.[104] That the automotives industry accounted for half of the output value and profit of equipment manufacturing in China revealed the impact of such localization policies.[105] By 2006, close to 70 percent of the world's top one hundred suppliers of automotive parts and components had invested in manufacturing capacity in China, and the number of foreign-funded production enterprises on the mainland exceeded twelve hundred.[106]

Mechanisms of control in auto parts typified those in other less strategic subsectors of strategic industries. Trade regulations typically combined cumbersome certification procedures and China-specific standards to limit imports. Although no industry-specific ministry supervised standards development, and foreign-invested companies participated in technical standards committees on a case-by-case basis, standards and certification processes and procedures favored the domestic sector. The government published the First Catalogue of Import Commodities subject to the Safety License System in automotives in 1989, but this was poorly enforced throughout the 1990s. Beginning in 2000, immediately before WTO accession, the central government began to enforce related laws and integrate enforcement into the customs system. In 2002, the Chinese government centralized the certification process with a new system, which required manufacturers in 132 product categories, many of which are automotives, to obtain the China Compulsory Certification

---

104. See Li and Qiang (2006).
105. Chen (2006).
106. This compares to the more than eight thousand domestic enterprises. "Competition Intensifies for Automobile Parts and Components Industry," *China Economic News* (September 4, 2006).

Mark before entering Chinese markets.[107] Moreover, as in telecommunications equipment, central-level government bodies collaborated with sector associations, which replaced former state- or provincial-level offices and competed with each other to set technical standards. Through standards committees, quasi-government bodies attempted to internationalize China-specific standards via active involvement in international standards and sector associations. Rockwell Automation, a U.S. manufacturer of automotive engines and parts, and a leader in standards setting globally, regularly confronted Chinese standards setting efforts in the automotive and electronics sectors. To expand its influence and protect its global standards, Rockwell successfully secured seats on technical standards committees by "exploiting the Chinese desire to learn from foreigners."[108]

The relinquishing of more regulatory control in automotive parts meant foreign market entrants interacted regularly with local authorities possessing discretionary authority. Whether enforcing national laws or local ones, local authorities worked to benefit local interests. In an example involving labor protests at Honda-invested parts factories in 2010, industry insiders suspected that mediation by local authorities, including the local All-China Federation of Trade Unions, to stem further unrest had led to wage increases and arrests of protest leaders. The labor disputes did not reach the arbitration committees or courts guaranteed by the 2007 Labor Contract Law. The investment trajectory of Cummins Inc., a U.S.-based company, also exemplifies local governance at work. In 1995, Cummins established a 50–50 JV with Chongqing Heavy-Duty Truck Corporation (CHTC).[109] Between the JV's inception and 1999, Cummins and CHTC struggled in their collaboration to manufacture heavy-duty and HHP diesel engines. When the central government lifted the JV requirement in 1999 and profit was at zero for the JV, Cummins debated exiting the partnership. Cummins retained the JV after workforce cuts, and the reduction of Chongqing Cummins's social responsibilities, including the operation of a restaurant and school, and Western corporate governance standards helped bring the JV to profitability. Retaining the JV structure had its costs, however. Because Cummins chose to remain in collaboration with CHTC, the Chinese partner had to review and approve each introduction of technology and product mix before Chongqing Cummins could amend its business license. This process entailed obtaining final approval from Chongqing's vice mayor, the head of the local State-owned Assets Supervision and Administration Commission, which owned CHTC. Moreover, Chongqing

---

107. Equipment makers from strategic to nonstrategic industries reported the cumbersome nature of the CCC process, which they viewed as a nontariff barrier to entry.

108. Interview on March 9, 2006, in Shanghai with Kaitai Chen, senior consultant, Standards and Technologies, Rockwell Automation, and professor emeritus at Fudan University.

109. Cummins also operated WFOEs and JVs in Hubei with Dongfeng, producing heavy-duty machinery, and Beijing with Foton, producing automotive components.

Cummins reported to the local CCP central committee and operated an active party branch and labor union.[110]

Briggs & Stratton (B&S), a maker of motorcycle engines, also retained its JV partnership in Chongqing, though it established a wholly foreign-owned factory in Shanghai's Qingpu Industrial Zone when it became legal to do so.[111] Despite B&S's 95 percent stake, its Chinese partner held jurisdiction and approval rights over four key issues: changes in registered capital, business license, sale of assets, and dissolution of business. According to Jeff Albright, B&S's general manager in China, even while connections to distribution networks skewed its short list of benefits, the decentralized nature of machinery sectors and the central government's unwillingness and lack of capacity to enforce juridical rules inadvertently promoted local protectionism and exacerbated logistical problems for FDI. For example, when B&S caught a Chongqing-based supplier selling component parts with its logo, Chongqing authorities refused to enforce B&S's intellectual property because the sale occurred in Sichuan Province. As a solution to such counterfeiting, B&S molded its logo so suppliers could not easily ship components out the backdoor.[112] In another case related to B&S's WFOE, in 2006 the safety bureau in Qingpu contradicted policy by initially holding B&S responsible for the death of its subcontractor's employee despite evidence showing the contractor's negligence. Furthermore, B&S regularly faced district bureaus whose decisions conflicted with one another. In 2006, the Chongqing factory could not issue VAT invoices and bills because one district refused to transfer taxes out of its jurisdiction.

CONCLUSION

The industries surveyed in this chapter are critical for China's national security broadly defined and contribute greatly to the national technology base and the competitiveness of other sectors in the economy. The deliberate orientation taken by the state in their reregulation upon market liberalization explains similarities in government goals, state-industry relations, and methods of state control exhibited across these industries. Table 8.1 shows how financial services, energy, and automotives fit into the broad pattern of state control in strategic industries.

The details of reregulation in these industries and subsectors were shaped by their varying strategic value, sector-specific characteristics, and the organization of state institutions. The Chinese government courted nonstate investment and FDI to develop infrastructure but restricted their ownership share and/or their business

---

110. Factory visit and interviews on May 18, 2006, in Chongqing with Kirpal Singh, the general manager appointed by the foreign partner, and Gang Jin, a Chinese manager of Chongqing Cummins.

111. B&S established its JV in Chongqing in the early 1980s to produce for the Philippines market. In 2003, it increased its stake from 52 to 95 percent. Interview with Albright (April 12, 2006).

112. In another case, Linhai, Yamaha's partner in Nanjing, operated a plant in Yangjing, which produced exact replicas of B & S's products.

TABLE 8.1. DELIBERATE REINFORCEMENT IN STRATEGIC SECTORS

Dominant Pattern of State Control	Deliberate Reinforcement		
	Financial Services	Energy	Automotives
State goals	Enhance state control of money supply and modernize and diversify financial services	Modernize energy infrastructure and control the utilization and management of raw material resources	Create indigenous automotive industry and promote domestic manufacturing capacity
State-industry relations	Enhanced state control with central ministry, subsector regulators, and state ownership of banks but liberalized calibrated private entry of financial value-added services	Enhanced state control with state ownership and control of oil and petrochemical monopolies and transmission grids; liberalization of private and foreign entry in power generation and equipment	Enhanced central control of industrial developments but decentralized regulatory enforcement and ownership of automobile manufacturers; liberalization of entry in automotive parts
State methods	Sector-specific rules, regulations, and technical standards; restrictions on FDI ownership and business scope; macroeconomic measures and economy-wide rules	Sector-specific rules, regulations, and technical standards; restrictions on FDI ownership and business scope; macroeconomic measures and economy-wide rules	Sector-specific rules, regulations, and technical standards; restrictions on FDI ownership and business scope; macroeconomic levers and economy-wide rules

scope to control the industrial base and market developments. It also took steps to reform regulatory institutions and restructure SOEs to create competitive national champions. Nonstate enterprises enjoyed market share in less strategic subsectors, though the state managed the number of new entrants and calibrated their business scope to benefit the development of new technologies and markets and promote domestic industry. The state delegated regulatory control of these subsectors and issue areas to lower levels of government.

The developmental state in East Asia also took a deliberate approach to develop high-tech, capital-intensive industries that tended to have complex transactions. Rather than calibrating the extent and manner of state control according to a strategic value logic, however, the Japanese, Korean, and Taiwanese governments mobilized investment and industrial coordination through a much closer relationship with domestic private industry, promoting their development to achieve industrialization and global integration.

9

DECENTRALIZED ENGAGEMENT IN NONSTRATEGIC INDUSTRIES

This chapter applies the strategic value framework to mini case studies of non-strategic industries (consumer electronics, foodstuffs, and paper) to show that *decentralized engagement* is the dominant regulatory pattern in low-tech, labor-intensive industries.

These industries score low in their contribution to the national technology base and their importance to national security, and consist of relatively competitive local companies (see figure 2.4). Manufacturing involves linear technology, connects to buyer-driven global commodity chains, and requires low capital but high labor inputs; moreover, quasi-state–quasi-private companies dominate markets. Thus, according to the strategic value logic, the state takes an incidental orientation toward market players and seldom intervenes in industrial activities. The central government extensively liberalized market entry, eliminated a central-level bureaucracy, decentralized regulatory authority, and created sector associations. Macroeconomic measures and economy-wide rules governed markets; occasionally, administrative measures spurred or stemmed consumption and expansion and local and provincial commerce bureaus encouraged industry consolidation in oversaturated sectors. These methods reveal a market-oriented approach aimed at supporting modernization and domestic competitiveness in nonstrategic industries.

Local government imperatives, including maximization of FDI and local employment, became important in this decentralized regulatory environment. To achieve local economic and political goals, local authorities exercised discretion to approve business licenses and, along with other local stakeholders, governed local markets with local rules. Government-business relations and control mechanisms favored local interests despite China's WTO commitment to provide national treatment to all market players. The enforcement of nominally juridical rules varied across locality, reinforced by local state-business bargains.

Notwithstanding deregulation and local enforcement, the central government retained the discretion to intervene when social stability became a concern in a labor-intensive industry. It also worked with lower levels of government, sector and business associations, and quasi-private companies to promote subsectors where applications contributed to infrastructural and military uses and the national technology base. Moreover, it more strictly regulated retail and trade and distribution to promote service industries, control internal markets, and conduct foreign trade relations.

CONSUMER ELECTRONICS

Among the nonstrategic sectors surveyed, consumer electronics ranks the highest in strategic value. As an important part of the global supply chain, domestic manufacturers of consumer electronics had become highly competitive by the early 2000s in low-value-added production and increasingly competitive in the manufacturing of more high-tech and value-added electronic components and home appliances. Though consumer electronics has low strategic value for national security applications and ranks medium in contribution to the national technology base, the most high-tech subsectors, including microelectronics, produce inputs and have applications for strategic industries, including telecommunications and transportation. The state adopted a more deliberate orientation toward the development of indigenous technologies and domestic industry in these subsectors. It exerted incidental control in the rest of the industry. Market liberalization empowered local governments to support a domestic sector marked by overexpansion in low-tech, low-value-added market segments, increasingly competitive contract manufacturers, and the emergence of national brand marketers. In 2003, China had become the fastest-growing chip market in the world, accounting for nearly 11 percent of global demand in semiconductors, up from just 3 percent in 1998.[1]

State Goals and Methods

The central government directed high-tech policy but delegated industrial management and control of market developments in consumer electronics to provincial branches of central ministries and local governments. When the central government intervened, it focused on the most high-tech subsectors with the goal of increasing the national technology base and deploying technology to satisfy national

---

1. See "White Paper: Coming of Age: Multinational Companies in China," *Economist Intelligence Unit* (June 2004), 14.

security concerns. It shifted from a strategy of importing technology, to absorbing it through foreign-invested JVs and facilitating FDI in microelectronics, to subsidizing domestic research and development through investment in industrial infrastructure and designated topic areas. In the rest of the industry, decentralization and state-sector reform produced a domestic industry dominated by quasi-state-quasi-private small and medium enterprises, restructured and formally separated from national and local government research institutions.

Regulatory Change

At the beginning of the reform era, the Chinese electronics industry served mainly military purposes and operated manufacturing plants, much like automotives, imported from Russia and Eastern Europe. Developments throughout the 1980s and 1990s, however, reveal a pattern of reregulation that more resembled the control of a nonstrategic industry, where the central government relinquished control of industry during each phase of reform. The Chinese government's national security orientation toward electronics shifted in the late 1970s and early 1980s just as the civilian-led microelectronics revolution in the advanced industrialized countries, which yielded semiconductors and integrated circuits, reversed what had become prevalent thinking about the relationship between defense and civilian sectors.[2]

Each successive phase of liberalization and reregulation in consumer electronics undermined state control. In the early 1980s, the government decentralized the management of electronics imports under a certain financial ceiling to local governments and SOEs.[3] SOEs began to import foreign technology to produce consumer products, such as televisions and refrigerators. Between 1978 and 1986, local governments imported more than 124 production lines, mainly from Japan, with limited technological assistance.[4]

Production grew in the mid-1980s, but SOEs had difficulty accumulating technological capabilities. Around that time, the *South China Morning Post* quoted Jiang Zemin, who served as the minister of electronic industry before becoming mayor of Shanghai and later the premier of China, as stating that China "must develop electronics as eagerly as we developed atomic bombs." After explicitly connecting electronics to the development of national security, the government shifted its FDI strategy from importing technology to absorbing technology through foreign-invested JV that produced for the domestic market. In an effort to benefit from foreign technology transfers and increase domestic productive capabilities, from the mid-1980s through the 1990s the state liberalized market entry and courted FDI through a mix of regulations from investment incentives, to a reorganized science

---

2. Feigenbaum (1999), 98.
3. Naughton and Segal (2003), 181.
4. Huchet (1997), 257–60.

and technology policy, to market access through JVs with domestic companies. The Leading Group for the Revitalization of the Electronics Industry, established in 1984, focused on technology-importing programs and FDI liberalization to develop large-scale integrated circuits, computers, software, and telecommunications.[5] Key policies included the 1985 Decision Concerning the Reform of Science and Technology Management System and the 1988 Torch Program.[6] In spite of these central policy initiatives, the state did not micromanage market developments.

Japanese company Matsushita's experience typified China's shift in FDI strategy from importing foreign technology to liberalizing FDI in order to absorb foreign technology through foreign-invested JVs.[7] Between 1980 and 1987, Matsushita collaborated with six SOEs on 150 different areas of home appliances through exchanging technology for market access.[8] In 1987, after two years of contract negotiations, Matsushita established Beijing · Matsushita Color CRT Co. The 50–50 joint venture shipped a CRT TV production line, components, and assembly kits from Japan, and Chinese trained in Beijing by Matsushita on how to dissemble, clean, wash, and reassemble the equipment put the production line back together. Beijing · Matsushita produced 50–50 for the domestic and the export markets; strict capital controls meant profits obtained foreign exchange to purchase imported components and parts. Despite market reverberations, such as fierce price competition from Chinese companies and the global industry's shift to LCD plasma displays, Beijing · Matsushita, joined later by Toshiba, operated with a profit through the late 2000s.[9] Philips of the Netherlands also experienced a similar investment trajectory. It entered China in 1993 through a partnership with Suzhou's Peacock TV, a top-ten TV producer at the time. Contract negotiations lasted from 1989 to 1993 and the detailed contract stipulated conditions for technology transfers.[10]

By 1993, the MEI, which oversaw the computer and electronics industries and had become increasingly focused on high-tech, high-value-added equipment in telecommunications, devolved decision-making powers in consumer electronics to provincial branches. Moreover, government offices and research institutes previously under the supervision of the MEI, Ministry of Machinery Industry, and the Chinese Academy of Sciences (CAS) separated from the state to become corporatized SOEs and sector and business associations. The 1993 Decision on Several

---

5. Mueller and Tan (1997), 55–56.

6. Naughton and Segal (2002).

7. Interviews on March 13 and April 27, 2006, in Beijing with Toshihiko Shibyua, general manager of Matsushita China.

8. Panasonic built China's first color TV assembly line and supplied technology for washing machine motor production and assembly.

9. Beijing · Matsushita-Toshiba ranked number one within Matsushita Group for lowest cost and highest margin, and ranked number two globally in the CRT market segment for profit margin.

10. Interview on May 17, 2005, in Suzhou, Jiangsu, with Peter Lee, former general manager of Philips-Peacock JV.

Problems Facing the Enthusiastic Promotion of Nongovernmental Technology Enterprises further empowered quasi-government organizations and state-funded research institutes to establish nongovernmental enterprises that existed between "private" and "public" ownership. The 1995 Decision on Accelerating Science and Technology Development and a late 1999 State Council decision on technology policy advocated market development of applied technologies and encouraged JVs between foreign companies and domestic high-tech nongovernmental companies run by scientific research institutes.

The state created the Ministry of Science and Technology in 1998 to promote and consolidate supervision of science and technology matters. The MOST did not possess or enforce licensure or registration approval authority for the actual conduct of industrial business. Rather, the MOST had the power of the purse, which it used to fund domestic manufacturing capacity in consumer electronics (and the initial incubation of more sensitive high-technology projects, such as those with national security and infrastructure development implications) specified by several national plans, including the 1988 Torch Program and the more recent 863 and 973 plans.[11] The MOST directly and through the sponsorship and distribution to high-tech enterprises of local branch offices, research centers, institutes, and sector associations financed high-tech enterprises. In the mid-1980s, a group of scientists from CAS's Institute of Computer Technology, early beneficiaries of the Torch Program, founded Legend, the predecessor to Lenovo, one of the world's largest personal computer manufacturers after its 2005 acquisition of IBM's personal computer unit.[12] Ren Zhengfei, former director of the Information Engineering Academy of the People's Liberation Army, founded Huawei, a quasi-private telecommunications manufacturer, in 1988.[13]

Subsectoral Variation

By the mid-1990s, deregulation and the decentralization of regulatory governance produced a quasi-private sector not only in clothing and technical textiles but also in electronics assembly and other production associated with consumer-oriented high technology, surging FDI in medium- to high-technology sectors, and regional and firm-level variation in industrial outcomes. The private sector grew as thousands of SOEs liquidated or substantially restructured, and local commerce bureaus

---

11. The Torch Program also funded local industrial parks, and the 863 plan targeted biotechnology, new materials, lasers, energy, information, robotics, and space. Interview on September 23, 2008, in Beijing with Wang Baiyi, director of High Technology R&D Center, MOST.

12. In 2000, when it registered as a joint-stock company, Legend listed the Institute of Computing Technology as one of its largest shareholders. In 2010, CAS remained the largest shareholder of Lenovo's unlisted parent company. See Ling (2005) for a history of the development of Legend/Lenovo.

13. The Information Engineering Academy oversaw telecommunications. See Medeiros et al. (2005).

licensed thousands of TVEs and other quasi-private companies.[14] From the mid-1980s through the 1990s, this path of privatization in a nonstrategic industry gave birth to commercial giants in consumer electronics, such as Haier, China's premier major and home appliance manufacturer, and electronics producer Stone.[15] These two manufacturers, now brand marketers, traveled the same development trajectory as many quasi-private enterprises in textiles. Similar to Chenfeng's founding, which was profiled in chapter 6, Haier began as Qingdao Refrigerator Co., a substantially restructured SOE shepherded from bankruptcy to success by Zhang Ruimin, then a manager in charge of Qingdao's city-owned appliance companies. In 1984, it partnered with the German Liebherr Group to produce home appliances under the brand Qingdao-Liebherr. In 1986, the Stone Group, which began as a TVE, similar to the founding of Bosideng and Ocean Power examined in chapters 6 and 7, respectively, teamed with Japanese equipment maker Mitsui to design and produce an integrated Chinese word processor. Alps Electronics, a contract manufacturer for Mitsui, further tweaked the word processor to develop hardware for printing Han characters.[16]

The importation of foreign technology, the devolution of economic decision making to localities and market liberalization, and the influx of foreign-invested JVs and direct investments contributed to the development of a growing nonstate sector in consumer electronics. Because the government deemed consumer electronics a nonstrategic sector, it allowed domestic market forces to compete and take the lead in setting technical standards in most subsectors—unlike its approach in telecommunications but not dissimilar to its approach toward technical textiles.[17] Haier and Lenovo's battle to develop digital home network standards exemplifies domestic competition in consumer electronics.[18]

Export-Oriented Manufacturers

Market reform and liberalization of FDI in consumer electronics in the 1990s paralleled the regionalization of production networks in Asia. The decentralized approach toward controlling FDI in this industry attracted unprecedented FDI inflows oriented toward taking advantage of China's extremely open export-processing regime, under which imported inputs were duty-free. Cheap labor and supplier clusters that formed up and down China's eastern coastline further attracted FDI.[19] Export-

---

14. See chapters 6 and 7 on the development of private industry in textiles and Steinfeld (2004).

15. See Kennedy (1997) for a history of the development of Stone Corporation.

16. Xi interview (May 19, 2006); he worked for Stone-Mitsui in the 1980s. See also Lu (2000), 25–46.

17. For more on technical standards setting in telecommunications, see Chapter 5.

18. See Suttmeier, Yao, and Tan (2006) for variation in standards setting across high-technology sectors.

19. Scholars, including Hatch and Yamamura (1996), Naughton (1997), and Yusuf, Altaf, and Nabeshima (2004), have produced a rich literature on Asian FDI, in particular, overseas Chinese FDI.

oriented FDI in electronics manufacturing dominated domestic-machinery purchases and emerged as the major consumers of technology imports through 1997.[20] These inflows of FDI tended to be by Japanese and other Asian companies and proliferated across subsectors, including integrated circuits, as many Asian subcontractors and original equipment manufacturers (OEMs) of global technology companies shifted production to China.[21] Large multinationals, producing products such as computer hardware and consumer telecommunications equipment, also invested in productive capacity in China. Local governments responded to the influx of Asian and other FDI with industrial parks that facilitated company clusters based on national origin, similar to the experience of foreign-invested textile producers. Japanese companies clustered around Dalian and Hangzhou, the Taiwanese dominated economic and industrial zones in the Pearl River and Yangtze River deltas, and the Koreans operated factories on the Bohai Peninsula.[22]

The industrial expansion ushered in by FDI and domestic production gave birth to competition strategies that involved cost cutting and price wars. Companies that engaged in these strategies benefited from localities that leniently enforced technical compliances and granted licenses based on political and unscientific economic criteria. Few local companies designed parts for foreign customers, and many used trading companies to handle interactions with the broader customer base, leading some scholars to describe this as the "relative shallowness with which Chinese firms integrate into global supply chains."[23] Industry experts lamented this phenomenon, which occurred in the context of FDI liberalization, investment from foreign equity partners, foreign ownership stakes that averaged 50 percent, and collaborations as contract manufacturers producing parts or final products to the specifications of foreign partners or customers.[24]

Other scholars argued that some domestic companies with ties to regional governments and research centers moved gradually but steadily into higher technology stages of the complex electronics production chains.[25] These firms found niches in which they could cooperate with multinationals. Success varied by region and sector because variation in local state–private sector relationships predisposed par-

20. Naughton and Segal (2003), 171–76.

21. Hong Kong and Taiwan FDI comprised the majority operating in electronics. See Naughton (1997).

22. Factory visits and interviews in July and August 2003 and April and May 2005 in Guangdong and Jiangsu provinces with managers of Amertek Computer, Prime Technology, Danriver, and 3CEMS Group of First International Computer, Taiwanese-invested producers of laptops and other consumer electronics.

23. Steinfeld (2004).

24. A 2001 World Bank survey found 41 percent of firms sampled produced based on specifications set by foreign firms, 21 percent produced parts for foreign firms, 25 percent produced final products for such customers, and 25 percent had foreign equity partners with ownership stakes at an average of 50 percent. See Steinfeld (2004).

25. Naughton and Segal (2003), 181–82.

ticular regions to the development of certain types of industries.[26] For example, the Shanghai government nurtured SOEs and adopted an interventionist mode of governance because as a Special Administrative Region, it had to remit local revenue to the center. This mode of governance proved critical for the development of a successful capital-intensive automotive sector. In contrast, with fewer revenue-sharing burdens, Beijing had more leeway to experiment with market forces, which stimulated the development of nongovernmental organizations and the private sector. The resulting horizontal ties and innovation proved instrumental in the development of a successful IT industry.

Market-Pursuing Retailers

Among the FDI in consumer electronics were those that localized to pursue Chinese markets. They found well-established distribution networks because the central government previously had placed electronics in the domain of military legacy companies.[27] Because the state had relinquished regulatory control of consumer electronics for two decades meant, however, that the politics of decentralization affected the competitive dynamics of China's consumer electronics retail market. Rampant price wars caused by overcapacity squeezed the profit margins for manufacturers to some of the lowest levels in the world. A handful of domestic players controlled 40 percent of sales in first-tier cities, such as Beijing and Shanghai. Local government–led efforts to consolidate domestic electronics retailers, such as the 2006 acquisition of China Paradise Electronics Retail by Gome Electrical Appliances Holding, a leading electronics specialty chain, reinforced the politics of local interests, including the goal of creating competitive local champions and the power dynamics surrounding it. After the Gome and Paradise merger, the consolidated company controlled 60 to 70 percent of TV sales in Shanghai.[28] Local government–affiliated stakeholders, such as sector and business associations, also intervened on behalf of manufacturers to "force profitable retailers to take responsibility for failing manufacturers."[29] For example, shortly before Gome's acquisition of Paradise, a business association formerly under the now-defunct Ministry of Internal Trade orchestrated the collaboration between Dazhong Electrical Appliance and Yolo, a consumer electronics manufacturer owned by Paradise.

FDI entered this market milieu with different entry models. Taking advantage of the Mergers and Acquisitions Law, which allowed FDI in nonstrategic sectors to participate, foreign retailers, such as the U.S.-based Best Buy, acquired domestic ones. More often, manufacturers and brand marketers, such as Sony and Apple,

---

26. Segal (2002) and Segal and Thun (2001).

27. Interview with Anne Stevenson-Yang, former manager director of U.S. Information Technology Organization (USITO) based in Beijing, on December 12, 2005.

28. "The Great Electronic Wars," *South China Morning Post* (September 1, 2006).

29. Interview with Stevenson-Yang on September 15, 2006.

teamed with local partners to establish stand-alone stores or vied for shelf space, as did Dell, in national and local chains. The politics of decentralization made retail licenses difficult to secure despite WTO commitments.

Semiconductors and Microelectronics

The central government retained a more deliberate orientation to developing indigenous productive capacity in the most strategic subsectors, such as semiconductors and microelectronics. But the more market-oriented nature of consumer electronics shaped the nature of control mechanisms in even the most strategic subsectors. As foreign firms increasingly reoriented their strategies from efficiency- to market-pursuing in the mid-1990s, the central government reasserted some of its regulatory authority and took measures to maximize domestic sector returns and enhance indigenous capacity, including the acquisition of foreign technologies expected to flood into China. A bureau within the telecommunications authority regulated the licensure and certification of electronics products.[30] Moreover, blaming slim profit margins on the royalty fees of licensed technology, the state shifted to promoting the "indigenization" of technological competencies in response to miniscule technological spillovers. The central government also shifted toward targeted promotion of microelectronics subsectors, namely, the fabrication of semiconductor chips and the design of integrated circuits (ICs). These subsectors are strategic because they produce high-tech inputs for and contribute to the competitiveness of downstream subsectors of consumer electronics, and their high-tech content has potential national security implications. The government imposed tariffs and duties on imported components, including ICs, key inputs for the downstream computer assembly subsectors. In practice, the tariffs acted as a tax on downstream sectors but provided little protection for or promotion of sectors further upstream. Rather, they proved to be strong disincentives for including Chinese firms in IT production networks.[31]

China's signing of the Information Technology Agreement in lieu of WTO membership ended some of these tariff-based barriers. Instead, the Chinese government accelerated the deliberate utilization of FDI to develop domestic microelectronics, which began in the mid-1990s. The Ninth Five-Year Plan's 909 Project gave birth to Shanghai Huahong NEC Electronics, a collaboration between Chinese and Japanese companies, in 1996.[32] In 1998, the government included in the

---

30. All the same, industry insiders did not expect the dominant pattern of incidental control in consumer electronics to change despite the enhancement of regulatory authority in telecommunications. Interviews in Beijing with Ted Dean, managing partner at BDA Consulting, on September 23, 2008, and John Chiang, director of Global Innovation Research Center, Peking University, and vice chair of the China Association of Standards, on September 29, 2008.

31. Borrus and Cohen (1998).

32. China Huajing Electronic Group's metal-oxide semiconductor line, which was composed of technology from Toshiba and Siemens, became China's first foundry; and Shenyang Beiling became the first to list in 1998.

Catalogue for the Guidance of Foreign Investment Industries the manufacturing of large-scale ICs with lines less than 0.35 microns and lifted the shareholding requirement of FDI in microelectronics. In 2000, the government lifted restrictions on domestic IC firms seeking venture capital and other sources of funding, and the State Council promulgated Policies to Encourage the Development of Software and IC Industries, which promised to streamline approval processes for JVs and WFOEs. The State Council also lowered the value-added tax that domestic and foreign manufacturers had to pay.[33] Furthermore, the government added IC design and production to the list of sectors promoted by the 863 Plan and the Tenth Five-Year Plan. Around the same time, the MOST, in collaboration with the Shanghai government, established the Zhangjiang High Technology Park, China's first formal industrial base for IC design and microelectronics. The park attracted Semiconductor Manufacturing International Corporation (SMIC) as a major investor in 2000.[34] In 2001, the Ministry of Information Industry explicitly linked the fate of Chinese telecommunications to capabilities in IC design and production, and the State Council announced plans to protect intellectual property in IC design and layout.[35] These and other national and local efforts drew FDI to build IC production lines in other localities, including Chengdu, where SMIC and Intel built assembly factories in 2003.[36]

As a result of these deliberate attempts by the government to promote domestic industry and attract FDI in microelectronics, domestic companies coexisted with foreign ones and advanced technologies coexisted with outdated ones. Foreign investors, including American and European IC manufacturers and Taiwanese foundries facing restructuring at home—in part a function of the reconfiguration of global production networks—responded to these policies by making significant direct investments, especially in assembly and testing.[37]

Notwithstanding the state's more deliberate orientation toward microelectronics—unlike in telecommunications and other strategic industries that this book

---

33. Instead of a 17 percent VAT, IC manufacturers would be responsible for only 6 percent, and companies both designing and producing chips would pay 3 percent. Foreign manufacturers selling products that competed with China-made products viewed this as a nontariff barrier instituted after WTO commitments. See "Chip Group Seeks China, U.S. Reforms," *CNET News* (October 28, 2003). International sector associations, such as the U.S.-based Semiconductor Industry Association, lobbied to remove this rebate.

34. Factory tour and interviews on November 9 and December 12, 2005, in Shanghai with SMIC employees and founder Richard Chang. Before SMIC, China had twenty-five IC production lines producing older technology.

35. Wu Jichuan, then minister of MII, made these remarks in a series of workshops and conferences, including a seminar on microelectronics and IT and the National Integrated Circuit Work Conference.

36. "Developing the West: Building It—But Will They Come?" *Far Eastern Economic Review* (September 4, 2003).

37. See Simon (2001).

surveys—the government did not restrict ownership to the state, limit the number of market players, restrict business scope, selectively license technology, or seek to control industrial infrastructure in the high-tech subsectors of consumer electronics. The state consistently and extensively liberalized FDI and relied on a mix of market mechanisms, investment promotion, and state intervention to promote strategic subsectors of consumer electronics.

FOODSTUFFS

From the Mao period through almost thirty years of economic reform, the state had not prioritized the regulation of foodstuffs. In the mid-2000s, however, food product safety became an issue of strategic concern due to the severe acute respiratory syndrome (SARS) crisis and to highly publicized domestic and international cases of food-related poisoning injuries and deaths involving China-produced foodstuffs. International scrutiny, augmented by China's deepening participation in the global food supply chain, shaped the nature of reregulation after years of decentralization. That food production is a buyer-driven commodity chain also influenced the nature of state intervention in response to the potential of food safety problems to disrupt social stability. Still, foodstuff's low strategic value ultimately affected the nature and enforcement of reregulation in the aftermath of the food scandals. In a decentralized environment, subsectors that traditionally received more intervention included grain processing, which the state claimed was a matter of food security; genetically modified foods, which contribute to the national technology base; and food retail and distribution, which involved local politics.

State Goals and Methods

Up until the food safety scandals of the 2000s, which prompted reregulation that temporarily enhanced central control, the state had extensively liberalized market entry and business scope in foodstuffs. It eliminated central administration of food production in the 1980s, decentralizing regulatory authority to local governments, which routinely exercised regulatory authority to protect local producers and retailers. In the post-WTO era, the state imposed nontariff barriers on agricultural imports to achieve food self-sufficiency and retained central authority in the regulation of biotechnology to promote indigenous technological development. Moreover, to better regulate the food processing supply chain, the state created the State Food and Drug Administration. It subsumed the SFDA under the control of the Ministry of Health after global scrutiny of food safety scandals. The low strategic value of foodstuffs and the politics of decentralization, however, continued to drive the actual details of reregulation.

Regulatory Change

The Chinese government first experimented with market reforms in the agricultural sector, an industry closely related to foodstuffs.[38] In the early 1980s the household responsibility system decollectivized agricultural and food production supervised by communes and work teams. It empowered individual households to work the land and exercise discretion in the disposal of any surplus after tax and grain obligations. The new system rapidly increased food production efficiencies and household income.[39] In 1982, the government demoted and subsumed the Ministry of Food and the National Supply and Marketing Cooperative within the Ministry of Commerce.[40] The state also dismantled communes and work teams and replaced them with townships. A decade later, sector-specific bureaucracies previously under the Ministry of Food became sector associations.[41]

In the mid-1980s, the state experimented with abolishing mandatory grain purchases. When prices fell as a result, causing farmers to cut production, the state, which prioritized food security, halted reforms in grain production, pricing, and distribution. To sustain food subsidies for urban workers, the central government reinstated stringent grain production and delivery quotas, sown-area targets, political rewards for high grain output, subsidies to producers, and increased investment in infrastructure.[42] The state did not free prices of grain and certain staples until 1992, but it freed prices on most food products and abolished food rationing at the onset of urban industrial reforms in the mid-1980s.[43]

Subsectoral Variation

The government liberalized food production and decentralized its regulation in the 1980s; yet a strategic value logic influenced how it intervened in retail and distribution until the early 1990s and more strictly regulated related agricultural subsectors.

---

38. Scholars debate why the state launched market reform in the agricultural sector. Some argue the Great Leap Forward and the resulting famine delegitimated communes; others argue that stagnation in productivity and per capita income in rural areas convinced authorities to dismantle the communes. See Wen (1998).

39. Smil (1986).

40. Several reorganizations occurred before the most recent Ministry of Commerce was established in 2003.

41. "China Food Industry Reports Health Progress," *Beijing Youth Daily* (December 5, 2001).

42. For a history of the liberalization of the grain economy, see Rozelle (1994) and Rozelle et al. (2000).

43. Prior to 1992, the government forced farmers to sell to the state at below market prices. Some left to work in the rural industrial sector, where private entrepreneurs exercised informal property rights to operate in liberalized industries, including foodstuffs, and others migrated to the cities in search of work.

Manufacturing of Food

The launching of urban reforms in 1984 and the dismantling and decentralizing of central-level bureaucracies that supervised food manufacturing led to a boom in factory-manufactured foodstuffs as the production of traditional staple crops gave way to more profitable agricultural and nonagricultural pursuits. Growing demand for a greater variety of food in cities and the countryside further propelled growth in the production of foodstuffs.[44] The government experimented with market incentives, such as managerial autonomy for enterprises and monetary incentives for workers and staff, and separated state-owned food processing factories from government supervision through corporatization or quasi privatization in early rounds of SOE reform.[45] In 1993, local government-run farm bureaus restructured into vertically integrated agribusinesses called agriculture, industry, and commerce operations, some of which diversified into supermarkets and pharmaceuticals. In 1995, at the request of the Chinese government, the World Bank helped commercialize state farms, facilitated technology transfers, and loaned $200 million to provincial, prefecture, and county bureaus and participating SOEs to establish, expand, or renovate primary, secondary, and tertiary industries.[46] The Ministry of Agriculture's State Farms Department also shifted from direct involvement in enterprise operations to overall planning and policy guidance.[47]

Moreover, economic liberalization, coupled with decentralization, encouraged local governments to create large-scale, vertically integrated companies that merged local government-run food companies with small-scale livestock and agricultural farms.[48] Decentralization of food production also gave rise to the provincial "governor responsibility system" of the mid-1990s, which promoted regional self-sufficiency in ways that reduced interprovincial transfers of grain, exerted pressure on local authorities to sustain grain output, and distributed central government funding to lower-level administrative units to promote the development of specific agricultural and livestock sectors. For example, the Straw for Beef program provided incentives for localities to develop beef and cattle industries.[49] Food industry experts predicted that the expansion of the livestock sector would turn China into a net importer of corn and soybeans by 2010.[50]

The government also extensively liberalized FDI in food processing. According to the State Administration for Industry and Commerce, in 2007, of China's 25,570

---

44. Jing (2000), 24.
45. See Mok (2002), 423–31.
46. See Hill (1994) for a list of sectors.
47. Hill (1994).
48. Helsell (1997).
49. Brown, Waldron, and Longworth (2002) maintain that the beef sector developed in parallel with market regionalization.
50. Boosted by subsidies prior to WTO accession, China became a net exporter of corn. See Gale (2002).

foreign-funded food enterprises and branch offices, 45.5 percent produced food, 21.1 percent engaged in transport of food, and 33.3 percent operated restaurant services.[51] Foreign food production and restaurant chains entered China through JVs in the mid-1980s. As early as 1984, American food giant H.J. Heinz Co. established a JV with United Food Enterprise of Guangdong to produce dry baby cereals from various grains.[52] The Heinz-UFE JV engaged mainly in market research, testing, and quality control in the beginning, but by the late 1980s it had established full-scale production. In another example, in 1990 Nestlé invested in ice cream and other dairy production in the northeastern city of Harbin.[53]

Beginning in the 1990s, Asian-invested capital dominated FDI in food processing and much of China's agro-food exports were destined for Japan, Hong Kong, South Korea, North Korea, and Taiwan.[54] Market entry models and the business scope of FDI varied. Japanese FDI formed JVs, invested equity, and produced predominately for export to Japan. Japanese partners typically provided capital, seeds, technology, and management skills to domestic partners. For example, Japanese firms owned approximately 40 percent of Wanfu Food Group, an agriculture, industry, and commerce operation in Qingdao, Shandong Province. Another example is Shandong Longda Enterprise Group (SLEG), a TVE in Yantai and one of China's largest fruit and vegetable processing groups. SLEG operated JVs with FDI, including Mitsubishi and McDonalds, to produce for export and domestic distribution by foreign-invested retailers. In 2001 alone, SLEG signed three thousand contracts with Japanese companies; such strong ties rewarded SLEG with a Japanese import permit, which waived inspections for its products entering Japan.[55] In contrast, Taiwanese companies tended to operate small- to medium-sized, wholly foreign-owned processing facilities.

China-based production's growing significance in the international food supply chain, and food safety scandals involving Chinese production, influenced the nature of state intervention in the mid-2000s. The SARS crisis in 2003, though not directly related to food production, also raised awareness of food safety.[56] Concerns about domestic political legitimacy and international scrutiny regarding the safety of Chinese food exports compelled the government to enhance regulatory authority at least temporarily, and, in cases concerning enforcement corruption, swiftly and harshly. Although the State Council enacted the Product Quality Law and the

---

51. "China Has More Than 25,000 Foreign-Invested Food Companies," PRC Ministry of Commerce, http://ccbu2.mofcom.gov.cn/aarticle/chinanews/200710/20071005170577.html.

52. "Heinz in Pact on China Venture," *Associated Press* (September 1, 1984).

53. See Jing (2000), 18–20.

54. See Hisano et al. (1998). American and European producers also invested, but in lower numbers.

55. Conversations in July 2002 in Yantai, Shandong, with a general manager and a public relations manager of one of SLEG's processing facilities.

56. Tam and Yang (2005) connected the SARS crisis to China's food safety regulations.

Food Hygiene Law in 1993 and 1995, respectively, fragmentation of regulatory functions among six agencies produced incompatible regulations and standards adopted by different agencies, bureaucratic competition, and corruption. Furthermore, local officials, empowered by the devolution of economic decision making during early rounds of administrative reform, routinely participated in, and profited from, counterfeiting activities and bribery related to cases of improper licensure. In this institutional landscape, enforcement loopholes developed up and down the industry supply chain, leading to thousands of cases of food- and drug-related injuries and deaths.[57]

To enhance the regulation of food safety, the State Council created the State Food and Drug Administration (SFDA), an autonomous bureaucracy outside of the control of the ministries of health, agriculture, and other foodstuffs bureaucracies, in 2003. From the beginning, conflicts between government offices charged with the regulation of food safety and corruption within the ranks plagued the SFDA. In an ironic twist, the state executed Zheng Xiaoyu, the first head of the SFDA, in July 2007 for approving substandard pharmaceuticals, including an antibiotic blamed for at least ten deaths, after taking bribes.[58] What is more, after dominating domestic news for years, food and drug safety issues made global news in the mid-2000s; poorly regulated companies produced and distributed substandard, tainted, and poisonous foods and chemical and drug inputs, which caused illnesses and deaths in Asia, Europe, North America, and Latin America.[59]

The Chinese government denied globally that its food exports, which caused some of the largest food recalls in history, were hazardous and responded to global scrutiny by seizing U.S. and European imports.[60] Nevertheless, to alleviate international pressure and stave off potential domestic instability, the National People's Congress announced at its 2008 annual meeting that the Ministry of Health would supervise the State Food and Drug Administration.[61] In November of that year, the government tightened food inspection processes and permitted the United States to open branches of the U.S. Food and Drug Administration in Beijing, Shanghai, and Guangzhou after a contaminated milk supply caused by poor regulation of suppliers along the production chain tainted infant formulas and other products, sickening ten of thousands in China.[62]

---

57. Heinz became an early victim of counterfeit: a Chinese food processor copied thirty-six Heinz food products. See Weldon and Vanhonacker (1999).

58. See "China Ex-Food and Drug Chief Executed," *Associated Press* (July 10, 2007).

59. In 2007, contaminated vegetable protein in Chinese exports led to the largest pet food recall in U.S. history. Tainted foods also leaked into meat and fish supplies there and in Europe and Asia, and China-produced cough syrup and toothpaste marketed in Australia and Latin America contained a toxic chemical. See "China Sentences Former Drug Regulator to Death," *New York Times* (May 29, 2007).

60. See "China Blocks Some Imports of U.S. Chicken and Pork," *New York Times* (July 15, 2007).

61. See Tam and Yang (2005) for more on the creation in 2003 of the SFDA.

62. See "F.D.A. Opens Inspection Office in China," *New York Times* (November 19, 2008). At least four children died from drinking contaminated formula, thousands were hospitalized, and fifty thousand were sickened.

Food Retail and Distribution

Until the early 1990s, state-run distribution groups set up under different ministries that were responsible for a certain category of foodstuffs monopolized food retail and distribution.[63] Local branches of central-level ministries managed urban retail outlets, the central government set prices for processed foods, and the purchase of staple products, such as meat and rice, required ration coupons. Regulatory reforms and the rapid development of varied marketing channels in the 1980s gave distributors at every level of the system freedom to buy from any supplier and sell to any customer.

The national distribution system gradually gave way to a local one, with wholesalers previously belonging to the same group but at different points along the chain competing with one another. By 1993, a fragmented system of small-scale local traders with limited geographic scope replaced and/or competed with state-owned monopolies and other SOEs under the China National Cereals, Oils, and Foodstuffs Import and Export Corporation and the ministries of Internal Trade and Agriculture and their bureaus throughout the country. In the urban areas, grain outlets commercialized, and when the government granted retail outlet managers and other personnel informal control of their outlets, they established marketing networks. In the rural areas, grain bureaus were converted into commercial trading companies. Local food markets emerged comprising quasi-private companies and corporatized SOEs previously owned and operated by food bureaucracies.[64]

Due to China's self-professed goal of grain self-sufficiency, however, the NDRC maintained a State Administration of Grain to exert "macrocontrol of national grain distribution [and to provide] guidelines for the development of grain industry and administrating national grain reserves."[65] Through centralized supervision of grain distribution, the state retained the authority to intervene when it saw fit. For example, in 1994, concerned about soaring inflation rates, it reinstituted the fixed quota purchase system for select grains and oilseeds.[66]

In the retail of other foods, the growing number of domestic chains tended to be small and locally based. Regulations issued in 1992 sanctioned foreign-invested JVs in eleven cities but under highly restrictive terms to protect the retail sector. The government did not lift the rule requiring JVs until 2005 as per its WTO commitments. Rules also prohibited foreign-invested JVs from acting as wholesalers and

---

63. For example, the agriculture ministry's Grain Bureau distributed rice, wholesalers under the commerce ministry carried meats and processed foods, and the Ministry of Light Industry distributed sweets, tobacco, and alcohol.

64. McNiel et al. (1994).

65. Rozelle et al. (2000), 230–36.

66. To offset the burden on farmers, the central government raised state purchase prices to improve peasant incomes and give them the means to purchase inputs, which were no longer priced at fixed rates. Quota prices varied by province because decentralization allowed localities to retain considerable authority over quota purchases. See Crook (1994).

import-export agents and mandated that imported goods consist of no more than 30 percent of inventory. Regulations promulgated in 1996, however, relaxed FDI regulations in trading, wholesaling, and distribution. Moreover, the 1998 to 2001 phase of reregulation, which separated SOEs in nonstrategic sectors from the bureaucracy and merged or divested them to create stronger enterprises, relinquished overall state control. Thus, despite restrictions on FDI, the number of foreign-invested retail outlets grew to 2,785 and the government had approved more than eighty foreign-invested projects and licenses in food retailing by 1996.[67] Since that time, foreign-invested retail JVs formed in markets of upscale department stores, modern supermarkets, and hypermarkets, such as France's Carrefour. Carrefour entered China in 1995 and has since become the largest foreign investor in hyper-markets with seventy-three stores in twenty-nine cities.[68] But the central government halted Carrefour's expansion for eighteen months in 2001 when Carrefour violated the rule concerning foreign investment levels in food retailing and failed to obtain the requisite operation licenses for some of its retail outlets. Having experienced state intervention, Carrefour retained two-thirds of its local partners— even after the government lifted the prohibition against wholly foreign-owned food retailers in 2005—with the express purpose of learning about China's complex and varied local markets and how to deal with local governments, distributors, and suppliers.

Among domestic retailers, Hualian, owned by China Commerce Enterprises Group, previously under the Ministry of Internal Trade, which the government demoted in 1998, and Lianhua, which was established under the Shanghai government in 1991, represented two state-owned chains with national presence that utilized competitive pricing techniques and adopted competitors' management methods. Both companies have collaborated extensively with FDI. Hualian's development benefited from JVs with foreign food retailers, such as the Japanese firm Daiei Convenience, and from a merger with three domestic operators as part of the 1998 economy-wide restructuring of SOEs. Mitsubishi Corporation owns a 6.74 percent share of Lianhua.

Agriculture and Livestock
Though the central government traditionally had intervened more in the retailing and distribution of food and advocated self-owned marketing channels "to achieve macroeconomic development, enhance quality of human resources, and support the development of service industry," it had, for the most part, respected WTO commitments made in this subsector.[69] In contrast, the government enhanced its

---

67. Bowles (1998).
68. Child (2006). Carrefour also operated the Champion supermarkets and Dia convenience stores.
69. See Zhao (2005a).

control of agricultural subsectors of foodstuffs despite WTO commitments; it liberalized agricultural import only to reregulate it. On the one hand, it substantially reduced the number of products subject to import licensing requirements in the 1990s, and it began to lift restrictions on foreign grain, citrus, and meat imports following the signing of bilateral treaties, such as the U.S.-China Agricultural Cooperation Agreement in 1999. Moreover, it decreased tariff rates and eliminated some trade barriers when China joined the WTO.

On the other hand, to ensure agricultural self-sufficiency and protect domestic industry, the government expanded bureaucratic authority over agriculture and livestock trade. The tariff rate quota system on commodities and unnecessarily burdensome licensing procedures and requirements—including registration, labeling, and overlapping import permit systems administered by different bureaucracies—favored state trading enterprises.[70] Other measures included "one-license-per-shipment" and JV requirements for FDI in agricultural biotechnology; protectionist sanitary and phytosanitary rules imposed on agricultural and livestock products, such as bovine products and soybeans, and unequally applied to foreign and domestic suppliers; and differential value-added-tax rates for domestic and foreign products.[71] The government also regularly delayed approval of import applications and biosafety certificates for transgenic crops.

The state strictly calibrated FDI in biotechnology to promote domestic capacity in value-added subsectors. The 2004 Catalogue for the Guidance of Foreign Investment Industries prohibited FDI in biotechnology seed projects, which contradicted the government's stated commitment to support R&D in agricultural biotechnology.[72] The following also restricted foreign entry: lax rules on the counterfeiting of agricultural chemical products; nondisclosure concerning outside panel safety reviews for genetically modified products; and the sample seed deposit requirement, which potentially exposed foreign companies to violations of intellectual property rights.[73] Moreover, the ministries of Science and Technology, Agriculture, and Health, and the State Environment Protection Authority adopted overlapping biosafety rules and inconsistently enforced them. For example, they failed to enforce the Seed Law of 2000, which would have protected seed variety and quality through strict registration procedures.[74]

---

70. See "Gain Report Number CH7403," *USDA Foreign Agricultural Service* (June 13, 2007), for more detail on these and other measures.

71. Administrative measures, which became effective in 1992, required importers to obtain an inspection permit prior to signing contracts for all traded commodities.

72. The 1997 foreign investment catalogue prohibited seed business dealings in major grain and fiber crops. See *AmCham White Paper* (2004).

73. See "Enhancing Dialogue, Moving Forward," American Chamber of Commerce *White Paper* (2006).

74. American Chamber of Commerce (2004).

To protect and develop domestic industry in the name of food security, the government also restricted FDI in grain processing. Soybean processing serves as a good case study of how reregulation upon liberalization protected strategic subsectors in a nonstrategic industry. In 2008, China became the largest importer of U.S.-produced soybeans, and high domestic demand, three-quarters of which were met by imports, drove soybean prices to 40 percent above international prices. Though the domestic sector invested in production capacity, it processed only 40 percent of the demand due to inefficient and outdated operations. Proclaiming the danger of foreigners gaining control of import price and volume on such a highly desired commodity and claiming responsiveness to consumer protests, the government limited FDI in soy processing to JVs with Chinese partners.[75] In 2004, it briefly liberalized foreign entry when the profit margins of Chinese crushers collapsed, but the door shut when "crush margins" quickly recovered.[76] No matter, a group of four large foreign-invested agricultural concerns controlled 45 percent of soy processing in China.[77] The Mergers and Acquisitions and Bankruptcy laws helped foreign companies acquire, expand, and re-outfit crushing factories, and begin operations with domestic partners, such as the state-owned COFCO, China's largest oils and food importer and exporter.[78] Other foreign investors, such as U.S. agribusiness firm Continental Grain, sought to take advantage of the liberalization of foreign equity investment in food production to partner with COFCO to create an onshore fund to invest in agricultural and food production.[79]

Reregulation in foodstuffs contradicted scholastic projections by both international and Chinese food security experts on consumption demand versus production supply. Though they disagreed on solutions, most studies agreed that China would remain a significant net importer of grains and shift toward a net importer of processed food products without more public policy attention. All the same, "grain reserves at central and provincial levels exceeded the UN standard of 18 percent of its annual needs," according to Nie Zhenbang, a former director of the State Grain Administration.[80] Rather than adhering to scientific estimations, the govern-

---

75. Interviews on September 22, 2008, in Beijing with Phillip Laney, China director, American Soybean Association and United Soybean Board, and Zhang Xiaoping, his deputy. See "Notice on the Health and Development of the Soybean Processing Industry," NDRC Guidance Paper (August 22, 2008).

76. Two foreign-invested soy processers, Noble, owned by a Hong Kong shopping and commodities group, and Wilmar, owned by a Malaysian Chinese tycoon, entered China during this time. See "The Noble Art of a Commodity Pipeline," Financial Times (August 21, 2008).

77. The "ABCD" companies dominated soy processing despite restrictions against FDI. They are U.S.-based Archer Daniels Midland, Bungee, and Cargill, and the French company Dreyfus.

78. Laney and Zhang interviews (September 22, 2008).

79. Interview on September 19, 2008, in Beijing with Eugenia Katsigris, principal, Kamksy Associates.

80. China relaxed national grain self-sufficiency standards in 1993 (Crook 1997), but it remained a goal. See "Grain Self-Sufficiency Still Key for Nation," China Daily (March 7, 2005).

ment chose to implement policies according to a strategic value logic. It regulated nongrain food production in the decentralized and incidental pattern characteristic of nonstrategic sectors, despite warnings from both international and domestic experts on food security and safety. Relative to its population and limited land base, China's imports were miniscule. Agricultural products accounted for a declining share of China's imports—from about one third in 1980 to less than 10 percent in 2000.[81] Nevertheless, the government devolved regulatory authority in foodstuffs so much that investments in public infrastructure, such as irrigation, and the enforcement of food safety were less productive than reactive in increasing production to meet the projected demand based on existing production.[82]

PAPER

China had an early comparative advantage in paper; the Chinese invented paper as early as 200 BC.[83] In 2008, China ranked number two in paper production and consumption, and with the exception of the most high-tech subsectors, the domestic sector outcompeted the global industry.[84] The central government took an incidental orientation toward paper because paper production has miniscule applications for national security and makes a small contribution to China's national technology base. But because the paper industry contributes to the local GDP and industrial base, local governments, empowered by decentralization, regularly intervened to promote local producers. In 2010, the Chinese paper industry was made up of highly modern paper mills and quasi-state–quasi-private local companies producing low-end and low-value-added products. Domestic consumption dominated paper production but exports expanded rapidly due to local subsidization.[85] Moreover, the central government's strategic orientation toward developing a raw material resource base prompted national and local measures to court FDI in wood fiber production. With the exception of high-tech, value-added subsectors, local subsidies contributed to FDI's uncompetitive position. Rising costs in labor, raw materials, and energy and trade tariffs further aggravated FDI's position.

State Goals and Methods

The state liberalized market entry and business scope in the mid-1980s and by the early 1990s had separated the regulation of paper production from printing and

---

81. See Gale (2002).

82. Southern provinces imported corn even while northeastern provinces exported corn.

83. For a history of the Chinese invention of paper, see Gunaratne (2001).

84. In 2004, China's thirty-five hundred paper manufacturers produced 49.5 million tons of paper products, 10 percent of the world's total. See "Pulp Fiction," *Straits Times* (May 4, 2004).

85. Beginning in the early 1980s, to satisfy domestic demand, China imported more than one million tons of paper pulp annually. See Feldman (1986), 523, and Flynn (2006).

publishing; these were more strategic areas because of their close connection to information control. The dismantling of the Ministry of Light Industry in 1993 transferred the governance of paper production and distribution to local governments and sector associations. Since then, the central government has exerted only incidental control and used occasional macroeconomic levers to regulate the paper industry. Decentralization empowered local stakeholders to license and subsidize a proliferation of low-end, highly polluting paper mills. To increase the local revenue base, local measures also promoted high-end, value-added production and industrial upgrading. To stem overexpansion in low-end sectors, local governments consolidated or shut down paper mills and courted FDI to assist in industrial upgrading. In the 2000s, to create an indigenous raw materials base because of rising input costs, national and local measures promoted the development of tree plantations, including courting FDI for technology transfers and technical support.

Regulatory Change

Until 1985, the Ministry of Light Industry controlled paper mill production through quotas and monopoly purchasing, and the China National Publishing Administration (CNPA), under the Ministry of Culture, supplied paper and machinery to printing houses owned and managed by different ministries supervised by the CNPA. The CNPA also set prices for books according to page number and book type.[86] By the early 1980s, shortages in print and paper capacity became common, further exacerbated by a black market that appeared when many paper mills switched to a "guideline plan" system, which based production on customer contracts. Black market publishers purchased paper at prices far higher than those paid by state publishing houses, contributing to the publishing sector's paper shortage.[87]

In the late 1980s, the state freed quotas and monopoly purchasing. The liberalization of market entry and decentralization of regulation soon followed. By 1992, government offices responsible for paper production became quasi-government sector associations, nearly a decade earlier than counterparts in other nonstrategic industries, such as textiles. The elimination of the Ministry of Light Industry in 1993 officially granted localities licensure and business scope approval authority. Since the early 1990s, the central government exercised incidental control over the paper industry. It infrequently intervened in low-end, low-value-added sectors, which are dominated by labor-intensive and injury-prone production. Local governments intervened when labor issues arose and enforced health and safety guide-

---

86. For example, only prices for full color books factored in production costs, making them very expensive.

87. Feldman (1986), 519.

lines, which in principle were applied initially only to SOEs since no law governed occupational health and safety in the rest of the economy.

Notwithstanding the dominant pattern of incidental control, immediately prior to WTO accession the central government directed local governments to restructure the less competitive subsectors of paper. Those efforts, however, did not lead to direct state intervention on the company or aggregate industry level. The central government pressed local governments to shutter heavy producers of wastewater, such as non–wood pulp mills, but did not enforce such mandates. Moreover, even while the central government encouraged investment in high-tech production, central subsidies did not always arrive. For example, in 2001 state-owned Shandong Quanlin had to put its plans to build a pulp base sponsored by the central government on hold when Quanlin Bank failed to meet requests for improved guarantees.[88] Not surprisingly, local governments did not always respond to central pronouncements, or they responded in ways that favored local interests. To promote industrial upgrading, the center relied instead on macroeconomic measures, such as import duties on high-tech subsectors.

Subsectoral Variation

The devolution of economic powers to local levels created a fragmented domestic paper industry consisting of large modern mills and a large number of low-end, highly polluting small paper mills.[89] Local governments invested excessively in low- and mid-range paper mills, which were constrained by outdated equipment and high costs in raw materials.[90] According to the China Paper Industry Association, in 2004 over thirty-five hundred paper mills operated in small polluting plants built before 1996.[91]

Newsprint

Eager to restructure the newsprint subsector but at the same time unwilling to invest state resources in a nonstrategic industry, the state extensively liberalized foreign entry in paper in the 1990s, encouraged local paper mills to engage in property swaps, and invited FDI to merge with and acquire paper plants. Multinationals

---

88. See Yu et al. (1999) and "Quanlin Orders Pipeline," *Pulp and Paper International* (November 2001).

89. These paper mills produced fewer than sixty-five hundred tons a year, compared to the global average of more than forty thousand tons and developed countries' one hundred thousand tons and more. See "Defining the China Market for Pulp, Paper and Board: A Multi-Client Report," *Hawkins Wright* (2006); for more information, http://s288964693.websitehome.co.uk/hawkinswright/multi-client-reports/china-market.html.

90. Many of China's paper mills operated equipment at the technical level of the 1950s or 1960s. Chinese mills used considerably more tons of coal and water than the global average.

91. See "Newsprint Sector Forced into Changes," *Standard* (March 25, 2004).

responded enthusiastically to relaxed capital controls by entering into JVs. For example, in 1995 the world's largest paper producer, Jefferson Smurfit Group, began paper production through a JV with China Industry Management and Investment Company, a Chinese holding company.[92] In 2010, Jefferson Smurfit operated JVs in Zhejiang, Shanghai, and Qingdao, and wholly foreign-owned factories in Dongguan.

In 1997, to ensure competitive domestic industries upon China's WTO accession, the central government ordered the closure of more than three hundred state-owned and controlled newspapers, a sixth of those circulating domestically.[93] The restructuring of newspapers that took place between 1997 and 2001 resulted in a surge in paper exports as paper producers turned to foreign markets when they lost a significant domestic market.

During that period before WTO accession and low demand due to the Asian financial crisis, the government also imposed higher import tariffs on newsprint than on household and sanitary paper to protect the high number of low-tech, out-of-date paper mills. In the post-WTO era, to stem overexpansion of the domestic sector in low-end newsprint and stave off rising prices of raw materials, in 2004 the government levied antidumping duties for five years on newsprint imported from Canada, Korea, and the United States. The central government also continued to encourage localities to consolidate or shut down low-end, low-value-added paper mills, which regularly overexpanded, consumed tremendous amount of water and pulp fiber, and generated waste. Moreover, it encouraged mills to relocate to low-cost western interior provinces, where they would be closer to wood resources and cheaper labor. To protect its domestic industry, China prohibited FDI in various subsectors, and to reduce reliance on paper imports, a "paper substitution policy" established in 2005 encouraged the use of other materials in place of paper, as well as more reliance on information shared on computers and other electronic devices.[94]

Upstream Material Processing Sectors

In addition to utilizing FDI to restructure its large newsprint mills and consolidate small mills, to meet the high demand for raw materials the government courted FDI in chemical and mechanical wood pulp as China faced a shortage of wood pulp and recovered paper used as basic fiber inputs.[95] Macroeconomic levers also facilitated the import of raw material inputs in high demand as these upstream sec-

92. "Smurfit Forms Joint Venture Linerboard Project in China," *Irish Times* (May 24, 1995).

93. Hao, Yu, and Zhang (1998).

94. Phone interview on October 7, 2008, with Tate Miller, former trade policy advisor based in Beijing for the American Forest and Paper Association.

95. According to the China Paper Industry Association, 80 percent of pulp produced in China contained bamboo, wheat straw, and other nonwood sources, yielding low-quality products relative to those produced from wood pulp. See "Pulp Fiction," *Straits Times* (May 4, 2004).

tors fed into other industries, such as chemical fiber processing of industrial and technical textiles.

By 2002, China imported twice as much pulp as paper and paperboard, allowing it to achieve a number-two position as a global leader in the production of paper.[96] To meet demand, the government laxly enforced the import of wood fiber from illegal logging in Russia. In the third Strategic Economic Dialogue between the United States and China in December 2007, however, it signed a memo on climate change, which forbade the support of unsustainable forestry.[97] In the 2000s the state encouraged local governments to develop tree plantations to establish a raw materials resource base to meet the growing paper demand. In 2002, the central government approved Finnish-Swedish Stora Enso's plan to build a paper mill as part of an agreement for sustainable development that began with the planting of 120,000 hectares of eucalyptus trees. Stora Enso also signed a memorandum with the United Nations Development Program, which focused on the conservation of biodiversity and community projects involving health, water, hygiene, education, and skills development for up to one hundred thousand households in the vicinity of the paper mill.[98]

Value-Added Paper

Local government efforts to support and subsidize industrial upgrading since the mid-1990s increased investments in value-added subsectors, such as paper manufacturing from recycled paper and paper refuse imported from abroad. Macroeconomic levers also promoted industrial upgrading and the growth of high-end subsectors.[99] According to the United Nations Food and Agricultural Organization, between 1997 and 2001 China accounted for more than 12 percent of the total world imports of paper and paperboard. Since 2001, the share of Chinese imports has declined to around 9 percent.[100] In 2003, in China's first antidumping investigation since joining WTO, the government imposed antidumping duties for five years on high-end paper products, including coated wood-free and linerboard paper, from Japan and Korea.[101] It took similar steps against Taiwanese and Korean imports of synthetic fibers and imports of unbleached Kraft Liner and Kraft Top Liner from the United States, Korea, Thailand, and Taiwan.

But in an apparent tactical change, in late 2007 the MOFCOM decided to reevaluate the antidumping duties imposed on coated art paper imported from Japan

---

96. Canada, Indonesia, Russia, Chile, and the United States are major suppliers of China's wood pulp imports. See Katsigris et al. (2004) for PRC Customs and State Forestry Administration statistics.

97. Miller interview (October 7, 2008).

98. "Paper Mill Agrees to Protect Environment," *China Daily* (April 1, 2006).

99. See Li (2006).

100. Statistics cited in Li (2006).

101. See "China Reviews Antidumping Duties on Coated Art Paper from Japan, ROK," *Xinhua* (November 6, 2007).

and Korea after a request from Japan Oji Paper Co. Ltd. Industry insiders believed the Chinese government did so in response to the Bush administration's threat to impose duties on high-end glossy paper, which the United States claimed the Chinese government subsidized through antidumping duties between 112 percent and 267 percent on certain imports of crepe paper and tissue paper.

Such efforts led to the growth of a vibrant domestic industry in high-end paper. China's richest woman, Yin Zhang, owned and managed America Chung Nam, China's number-one recovered paper importer, and JVs in drywall, plasterboard, and special grade papers. She also operated Nine Dragons, one of China's three biggest paper producers and its largest containerboard producer, which listed internationally in 2005.[102] Large, high-speed, and efficient machines, using imported pulp and recovered paper as inputs, dominated expansion in the 2000s.[103] This led global equipment makers Metso and Voith to invest in production in China. "The birthplace of paper is now the site of the world's fastest and biggest paper machines," exclaimed the *Montreal Gazette* on Canada's role as a major pulp supplier for China.[104] Labor costs became increasingly a minor consideration in the competitiveness of the Chinese pulp and paper industry.[105] But ironically, as factories invested in advanced machines, newsprint production skyrocketed, exacerbating already saturated markets.[106] The proportion of loss-making companies between 2003 and 2005 jumped significantly.[107] Notwithstanding the paper industry's industrial upgrading achievements, in a decentralized and deregulated market environment paper producers regularly entered in large numbers with local sponsorship and subsidy but exited in failure. This proved commonplace in nonstrategic industries, where the government liberalized market entry and relinquished regulation to local authorities.

CONCLUSION

The Chinese government took an incidental orientation and a decentralized approach toward the regulation of nonstrategic industries, which tend to be low-tech and labor-intensive industries that score zero to low in complexity of transactions

---

102. See "Blazing a Paper Trail in China: A Self-Made Billionaire Wrote Her Ticket on Recycled Cardboard," *New York Times* (January 16, 2007).

103. See "Into the Mix: Driven by Market Demand, Mixed Paper Is Coming into Its Own in the Recovered Fiber Market," *Recycling Today* (May 2005).

104. "China's Fast-Growing Paper Industry Needs Pulp," *Montreal Gazette* (January 24, 2004).

105. For example, by 2000, Nanping Paper Mill and Pan Asia Mill operated the world's fastest newsprint machines, and Shandong Bohui operated the largest folding boxboard machine. See Flynn (2006).

106. Phone interview on September 19, 2008, with Frank Rexach, vice president and general manger of Haworth Asia Pacific, Middle East, and Latin America.

107. Statistics cited in Li (2006).

TABLE 9.1. DECENTRALIZED ENGAGEMENT IN NONSTRATEGIC SECTORS

Dominant Pattern of State Control	Decentralized Engagement		
	Consumer Electronics	Foodstuffs	Paper
State goals	Enhance national technology base and promote domestic industry; local interests shape local goals	Regulate the supply chain and production of foodstuffs; local interests shape local goals	Develop raw material base for paper production; local interests shape local goals
State–industry relations	Undermined state control with local branches of central ministry and local governments	Undermined state control with local branches of central bureaucracy and local governments except in food safety, where government enhanced bureaucratic authority	Undermined state control with quasi-government business associations and local governments
State methods	Macroeconomic measures and economy-wide rules; local rules and regulations; subsidies for domestic sector in value-added sectors, such as semiconductor chip design and fabrication	Macroeconomic measures and economy-wide rules; local rules and regulations; licensure approvals favored domestic sector in retail and distribution and agricultural biotechnology; import duties on agricultural staples	Macroeconomic measures and economy-wide rules; local rules and regulations; import duties on high-end paper products and subsidies for raw material processors

and security implications. This dominant pattern of state control contrasts with the deliberate and interventionist approach of the developmental state toward both light and heavy industries during import-substitution and export-oriented industrialization. The Chinese government did not limit the number of market players and allowed the nonstate sector to flourish under the governance of local governments and private actors. Moreover, save for the most sensitive subsectors, which the government viewed as related to national security, including social stability, and the development of the national technology base, it neither intervened nor regulated these nonstrategic industries with a central bureaucracy. Sector and business associations replaced government offices, and local governments and local branches of the commerce ministry approved licenses and certifications. In all three industries surveyed, the state extensively liberalized market entry, promoted the indigenous development of high-tech, high-value-added subsectors through macroeconomic measures, supported domestic companies in standards setting (as opposed to taking the lead), and issued nonbinding directives to localities to intervene with nontariff barriers. Table 9.1 shows how consumer electronics, foodstuffs, and paper fit into the broad pattern of state control in nonstrategic industries.

10

CHINA'S DEVELOPMENT MODEL
A New Strategy for Globalization

A front-page editorial in the *People's Daily* on January 5, 2010, read, "When the financial crisis forced the neoliberal economic system into a dead end, the shortcomings of the capitalist system were exposed for all to see. . . . But a China that was pushed to a crossroads proved its 'national capabilities' in taking on a crisis by answering with the advantage of the socialist system with Chinese characteristics." Notwithstanding the Chinese leadership's desire to characterize the Chinese development model as a "socialist system with Chinese characteristics," China today is not a socialist system.[1] In the transformation of state-society relations in the last thirty years, China has categorically departed from its Communist past. But our task "is neither to clear the Chinese Communists of charges of heresy nor to deride their claims of innovation," as French historian Lucien Bianco aptly stated when describing Mao's innovations to socialism, "but to establish exactly where their originality lies." Bianco further explained, "The novelty lay in the facts, not in the professions of faith."[2] In the same spirit of understanding, the case studies detailed in the preceding chapters reveal a more rational, efficient, and strategic Chinese state, which engages with society in ways that it had not in the past. Yet China's new political-economic model does not conform to a liberal economic model, coordinated market economy, or state-led development, as illustrated by the mini case studies of Japan, South Korea, and Taiwan in the main case chapters. Rather, the Chinese example shows that a country could mobilize limited resources

---

1. Quote cited in "China on Path to Become Second-Largest Economy," *New York Times* (January 21, 2010).

2. Bianco (1967), 77, for first quote, and 78 for the second one.

and enhance administrative capacity in ways that adeptly adopt market instruments of liberal economic and state interventionist varieties and apply them selectively across industrial sectors and subsectors. China does so all the while inviting foreign capital and influence into the domestic economy.

My initial skepticism about the diminishing role of the state during the reform era requires revision. China's economic power and political authority have increased, but it has become so because the state selectively relinquished state control in nonstrategic areas and enhanced its role in strategic ones. But the Chinese state is not everywhere; a regulatory state has emerged to achieve its goals. It has liberalized and reregulated across industries based on a strategic value logic. This bifurcated strategy has not, however, guaranteed effective regulatory or industrial outcomes. In this concluding chapter, we evaluate the evidence presented to distinguish overall sectoral patterns, specific sector and subsector cases, and development over time. In doing so, I am able to assess China's new development model based on actual economic outcomes and political change. I also consider how these findings add to existing debates on the relationship between markets and states in the international and comparative political economy literature.

THE NEW REGULATORY STATE: SECTORAL PATTERNS
AND PATTERNS OVER TIME

"China is very marketized in some aspects, but it won't let go of many areas. There's a saying that government can only govern macro issues, but the reality is government continues to intervene in micro issues to retain power," explained an official in the Division of Information Technology at the Ministry of Science and Technology.[3] At the level of overall patterns, evidence from strategic industries (automobiles, energy, financial services, and telecommunications) and nonstrategic industries (consumer electronics, foodstuffs, paper, and textiles) confirm how the strategic value of a sector shapes the basic direction of state control. The state adopts a deliberate orientation to introduce market competition in ways that reinforce the state's control of industries important to national security, which contribute to the national technology base, and where domestic companies are less competitive. The state may have permitted foreign capital to penetrate these industries, but it has done so to achieve industrial goals and strategically utilize FDI to benefit the development of the domestic industrial base. To balance bureaucratic conflicts and retain its authority to manage sectoral developments, including leveraging FDI and technology and knowledge transfers and retaining control over strategic assets, the state typically consolidates control over industry through administrative and corporate restructuring. To retain or enhance central authority over industry, the state man-

---

3. Interview on September 23, 2008, in Beijing.

ages competition to limit the number and type of market players and reformulates old rules and writes new ones concerning market entry and business scope with sector-specific goals in mind. Departing from the developmental state model, the Chinese government ensures the enhancement of state authority in these industries first and foremost, and from there it pursues industrial development that achieves security and economic goals.

In contrast to deliberate control in strategic industries, the state introduces competition in ways that relinquish control over industries that are less important to national security, that make little contribution to the national technology base, and where the domestic industry is more competitive. The state's goals take on an incidental orientation, and it liberalizes market entry to domestic players and FDI. It decentralizes or delegates economic and regulatory authority to lower levels of government and sector and business associations, disengages from sector-specific developments, and rarely distributes central resources to subsidize these industries. Local governments and their goals become important as they engage with industry through their enforcement of economy-wide rules and the creation of local rules. The developmental state never relinquished its regulatory control of any of its industries in ways that China has in its extensively liberalized and decentralized industries. The following list illustrates the bifurcated nature of China's market reform trajectory, which varies by industry according to a strategic value logic:

STRATEGIC INDUSTRIES
- Separation of enterprise from government bureaucracy, corporatization, business restructuring, and/or creation of SOE groups (and public listing)
- Introduction of competition between SOEs and sometimes the nonstate sector
- Strict rules on entry (no nonstate entry, domestic sector only, and/or foreign investment through joint ventures)

NONSTRATEGIC INDUSTRIES
- Divestment of state assets to former managers, corporatization, and/or business restructuring (and public listing)
- Liberalization of market entry
- Vibrant private sector, comprising quasi-state–quasi-private firms and FDI
- Local approval of market entry and licensure of business scope

Strategic Value Logic at the Subsector Level

These broad patterns cannot account for differences across subsectors within the same industry. The strategic value framework, nevertheless, continues to have utility at the subsectoral level of analysis. On the one hand, the state exerts less control in subsectors, including those of strategic industries, that have less application for national security and where less infrastructural assets are involved. These include equipment subsectors that manufacture products that are incorporated into infrastructure already controlled by the state, such as telecommunications terminal equipment and wind turbines that power electricity grids. Rather than restrict market entry and ownership structure, the government introduces nonstate and foreign competition in order to maximize technology transfer and diffusion in equipment production. At the same time, to promote domestic industry, government procurement balances market share among domestic and foreign equipment makers. Bureaucracies also work with government-controlled sector associations and the domestic sector to initiate and set technical standards.

On the other hand, in the more strategic subsectors of nonstrategic industries, the state takes a deliberate orientation to assert subsector-specific control. This is particularly salient in subsectors with high-tech content, where raw materials are in short supply, and/or which contribute to military applications. For example, FDI in construction fabric contends with limited government intervention in the setting of technical standards, and FDI in agricultural biotechnology endures cumbersome licensing and registration processes designed to protect the domestic sector. The government also strictly regulates raw material inputs of high-tech fibers and fabrics in order to spur the consumption of domestic upstream sectors and promote value-added production.

Specific Sector and Subsector Case Studies

In-depth and mini case studies demonstrate variation in the actual type and methods of reregulation across strategic and nonstrategic sectors. They also show that the exercise of state control does not fall neatly under incidental or deliberate control. Obvious and subtle differences in perception of strategic value, sectoral attributes, and level of domestic sector competitiveness influence whether state control in each sector or subsector is incidental, deliberate, or mixed. In strategic industries, the actual details and substance of state control reveal that the state more closely regulates telecommunications services, which have a higher strategic value, and relinquishes more central control in the production of automobiles, which have a lower strategic value. The state employs different control methods to achieve sector-specific goals and enhance its regulatory authority in these industries.

In telecommunications, the state retains central control of services and equipment subsectors with one overarching ministry. To retain control of the telecommunications infrastructure, the central government limits the number of state-owned carriers and the type of networks they operate and restricts FDI to equity investment. To encourage the development of value-added services, which run on state-controlled networks, the government liberalizes domestic entry but formally restricts FDI to JVs without cracking down on illegal ownership vehicles. It also liberalizes the equipment industry, which plugs into state-controlled infrastructure, to maximize technology transfers but controls technology through state-led standards setting.

The state separated centralized control of financial services along subsector lines due to competing bureaucratic interests, but similar to telecommunications, it retains ownership and management of the Big Four banks and restricts FDI to minority foreign equity investment. It does so to ensure state control of the national money supply, exchange rate, and other macroeconomic tools. Moreover, similar to the less restrictive regulation of value-added services in telecommunications, the state has permitted an increasingly pluralistic political-economic landscape across subsectors of financial services.

While the state consolidated central control in telecommunications and financial services, the energy bureau of the National Development and Reform Commission directed energy policy and attempted to coordinate what had become chaotic sites of contention under bureaucratic fragmentation. The State Council attempted to centralize state control when it merged energy bureaucracies under a national energy administration and created a central-level energy commission to make policy. Notwithstanding bureaucratic contention, the state has retained control of power infrastructure, including corporatized national and local state-owned energy distributors, in domestic hands by forbidding nonstate and foreign entry in power transmission and retail. But to modernize infrastructure and maximize sources of renewable energy, the state liberalizes FDI in power equipment and generation. To retain control of oil resources, the state limits exploration and refining to SOEs, permitting only foreign equity and foreign collaboration in value-added sectors.

Among strategic industries, the state exercises the least central authority over automotives because it is less strategic to immediate national security imperatives. Thus, the state delegates intervention and regulatory authority to provincial governments. However, because the automotive industry contributes to the development of the national technology base, and the domestic automobile manufacturers are less competitive than foreign ones, the central state directs local governments to strategically promote and subsidize automakers owned and operated by the provinces. Moreover, the central government has final approval concerning market entry and limits FDI to JVs in automobile assembly and production. Furthermore, it regulates automotive parts with tariffs and nontariff barriers to promote and subsidize domestic sector development.

The details and substance of reregulation also vary among nonstrategic industries, but the strategic value framework works less well to explain actual particulars because the decentralized nature of state control has produced diverse and empowered market actors whose responses to contingencies vary. The state implements mostly corollary measures created for functional and political reasons, not sector-specific ones, to facilitate the implementation of macroeconomic measures and economy-wide rules. All the same, the strategic value framework sheds light on the basic direction of government intervention in strategic subsectors of nonstrategic industries.

Among the nonstrategic industries surveyed, the state exercises the most central control in consumer electronics and appliances. Technically, the Ministry of

Industry and Information Technology approves licenses issued by the local commerce bureaus, but the state has fully embraced private entry and FDI to develop and promote the domestic industry. Moreover, the central government has relinquished industrial regulation to local authorities. The central government retains regulatory discretion, which it seldom exercises, in only the most strategic subsectors and issue areas. In foodstuffs, the government extensively liberalized competition in food processing and distribution, but, to appease local stakeholders, FDI is limited to JVs in retail and trade. Due to inherent features of food services, including the proximity of local markets, local governments regularly intervene to control distribution in favor of local interests. In the mid-2000s, the state recentralized the regulation of the foodstuffs supply chain as a result of food safety scandals, which raised global scrutiny and state fears of disruptions to internal stability. Food security concerns also affect state control of agricultural inputs and biotechnology.

In textiles, the state has fully liberalized private and foreign entry in manufacturing, trade, and distribution, but different central bureaucracies promote technical sectors, which have infrastructural, military, and aeronautic applications and produce high-tech inputs for strategic industries. Moreover, as a matter of foreign economic relations, the state regulates textile trade and distribution with discretionary licensing and quota regimes. To promote value-added sectors, it uses a tariffs regime for raw material imports that favors domestic industry. The decentralized nature of regulation means that local governments and stakeholders exercise discretion at all points along the supply chain and production process, and the central state increasingly responds to the growing domestic sector in its calibration of trade tariffs and fiscal incentives.

The paper industry is the most extensively liberalized and decentralized sector. Unlike the other nonstrategic industries, it does not have at least one subsector that involves licensing approvals beyond that of registration with a central-level ministry. Moreover, because of the growing number of domestic, private players in the industry, the central government makes laws that most clearly adhere to political interests rather than a strategic logic. For example, import tariffs protect select paper sectors because of the growing political voice of an increasingly globally competitive industry. Table 10.1 presents the strategic orientation and type of control in the surveyed sectors.

TABLE 10.1. MAPPING SECTORS TO STATE CONTROL		
Strategic Value of Sector	Domestic Sector More Competitive	Foreign Sector More Competitive
High	Foodstuffs; textile trade and distribution • Mixed orientation	Telecommunications; energy; financial services • Deliberate control
Low	Garment manufacturing; paper • Incidental control	Automobiles; consumer electronics • Mixed orientation

Variation over Time and Other Logics

In the strategic and nonstrategic industries surveyed, within dominant patterns and subsectoral variation, each phase of de jure or de facto liberalization is followed by reregulation. The competitiveness of the domestic sector during its exposure to the international economy and the organization of state institutions of a given sector elucidate the actual substance and details of state control across time. For example, the faltering competitiveness of the domestic newsprint sector became salient when overexpansion in 1997, exacerbated by the state-directed closure of three hundred state-owned and controlled newspapers, induced the government to encourage exports through fiscal incentives. All the same, the dominant pattern of reregulation held sway; the regulatory tools available had less force because the government had previously relinquished the regulation of entry and exit and business scope to local authorities. In another example, the organization of state institutions in 1998 became salient when bureaucratic conflict between the four regulatory commissions in financial services delayed banking reform. The government had to first create a special Communist Party working group to consolidate its authority. From there, reregulation conformed to that of the telecommunications carriers and oil companies. To restructure the Big Four banks, the state retained central-level managerial control and strategically utilized FDI to modernize and enhance its control of the financial industry.

ECONOMIC OUTCOMES AND POLITICAL CHANGE

By pursuing a strategy of economy-wide market liberalization and sector-specific reregulation, China has managed to obtain technological know-how, foster domestic champions, and retain an upper hand over foreign forces even in a more liberal environment. By liberalizing market entry and strategically utilizing FDI at the sectoral and subsectoral level, the Chinese government has modernized domestic infrastructure, maximized the domestic technology base, and promoted the competitiveness of domestic industry. At the same time, it has enhanced control of the most sensitive and strategic assets and restricted the business scope and market share of foreign companies in the most sensitive industrial sectors. Yet not all regulatory manifestations and sectoral outcomes point to economic success and industrial transformation. Moreover, although the introduction of economic competition and tolerance, if not also in deliberate invitation, of private and foreign ideas and norms ushered in political changes, they are not necessarily democratic ones.

Competitive Performance of Industries

In terms of real world outcomes, what are the implications of China's bifurcated strategy for the competitive performance of these sectors? What are the implications for global market competition? In general, our main and mini case studies illustrate that, among strategic industries, the Chinese government has been more successful in developing an autonomous technological base in high-technology sectors than in service industries. China has taken steps to develop a successful domestic industry in telecommunications and automobiles but has struggled in developing the financial and power energy sectors. On the one hand, China's state-owned telecommunications carriers operate networks at home, and the government has sought to limit foreign access to domestic equipment markets by managing technical standards setting and delaying the licensing of new generation telecommunications technology. The internationally listed arms of the state-owned carriers have expanded into Africa and the Middle East, where they collaborate with local operators to provide services. Chinese telecommunications equipment makers sell equipment in the United States and Europe as well as in developing countries, where they help build telecommunications infrastructure to serve the goals of nondemocratic governments. In automotives, technology and knowledge transfers from multinational JV partners have enabled Chinese automakers to export cars to Africa, Latin America, and the Middle East. They also assemble cars with JV partners in developing countries, including India, and have plans to sell cars in Europe. At the same time, foreign automakers are barred from independently producing cars in China.

On the other hand, less well-coordinated bureaucracies with overlapping responsibilities and conflicting local and central state goals disrupt the state's deliberate orientation toward electricity and financial services. The electricity distribution regime remains in state and quasi-state hands in such an institutional context. All the same, China's energy infrastructure has modernized. Foreign equipment makers serve as suppliers, and domestic ones, which have benefited from foreign technology transfers through JVs, are gaining market share in state-controlled procurement for wind farms and other renewable energy infrastructure. Domestic manufacturers of wind power turbines and solar power systems, with government coordinated export strategies and technical assistance, have filled orders from abroad. Moreover, state-owned oil monopolies through foreign-invested JVs are refining and exploring resources at home and have expanded abroad. For example, CNOOC, China's offshore oil monopoly, attempted to acquire a top multinational, which ultimately failed due to national security intervention by the U.S. government. In financial services, provincial and local banks and the nonlisted arms of the national banks are saddled with nonperforming loans and bad debt, problems exacerbated by murky corporate governance and nontransparent policy lending. Yet since deliberate reregulation in the mid-2000s and beyond checked bureaucratic wrangling, the Big Four listed internationally, and during the 2008 financial crisis China's sovereign wealth fund rescued global financial institutions by purchasing stakes worth billions of dollars.

Among the nonstrategic industries, de facto and formal market liberalization and reregulation encouraged the emergence of domestic companies. Hypercompetition reigns; thus many businesses emerge and quickly fail. Those that survive dominate local markets regulated by local rules and local enforcement of economy-wide rules. Extensive market liberalization and non-sector-specific economy-wide and macroeconomic rules attract FDI, benefiting the domestic sector through technology and knowledge transfers. Domestic companies have also benefited from subsidies targeted at strategic subsectors along the supply chain that contribute to the development of infrastructure, that have military applications, and that contribute to the competitiveness of other sectors and the rest of the economy. In 2006, of the top polyester fiber manufacturers large enough to receive PCI Fibers ranking, China ranked number one among countries, with ten domestic Chinese companies. Moreover, several of the top global producers of household appliances and consumer electronics are Chinese brands. Significantly, in addition to manufacturing garments, China now exports tires around the world, and its food products are becoming accepted internationally because foreign countries have deemed Chinese food imports acceptable for consumption.

Figure 10.1 shows that between 1992 and 2005 the makeup of China's manufacturing exports moved toward high technology.[4] Data also show that much of the high skill content of China's exports arises from imported inputs with high skill content (figure 10.2). This disparity continues to motivate the Chinese government to combine market liberalization with reregulation according to a strategic value logic to achieve its economic and political goals.

Economy-wide Consequences

China's bifurcated approach toward FDI and industrial development has produced unintended consequences. Premier Hu Jintao acknowledged at a government meeting in November 2008 that "China is under growing tension from its large population, limited resources, and environmental problems, and needs faster reform of its economic growth pattern to achieve sustainable development."[5] In sectors and issue areas in which the Chinese government has relinquished control, the lack of rules and lackluster enforcement of regulations have created economic, social, and political problems that challenge China's political regime. These problems include, on the one hand, deficient regulatory capacity to enforce rules concerning human and animal health and safety and the environment. This is prevalent in industrial sectors, such as food production and distribution and energy generation, where the state had previously decentralized regulatory control. Likewise, strict regulation of

---

4. This figure is adapted from Amiti and Freund (2007). A sector is defined as "major" if its trade is above 3 percent of total trade in 1992 and 2005. Major sectors account for 70 percent of manufacturing exports.

5. Quoted from "Chinese President Warns Hurdles Ahead," *Wall Street Journal* (November 30, 2008).

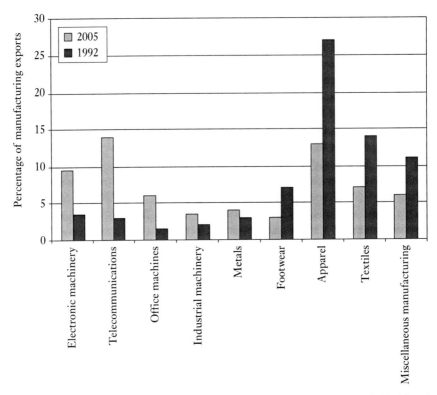

Figure 10.1. Movement toward high technology. Customs Administration of China, 2007. Adapted from Amiti and Freund (2007).

strategic sectors stifles domestic innovation and the market viability of indigenous technologies, including TD-SCDMA, China's homegrown telecommunications standard.

Moreover, the Chinese government has concentrated much of its macro- and micro-level measures on promoting export growth. Many of these measures encourage manufactured exports at the expense of the service sector, depressing job growth and cramping spending power when wages are already low, thereby dampening domestic consumption. In the Eleventh Five-Year Plan issued in 2006, the Chinese government switched its focus to promoting indigenous production and domestic consumption, relying on administrative and macroeconomic measures to do so. But to the chagrin of its trade partners, the Chinese government has not increased the value of the renminbi to a satisfactory level. What is more, the central government's efforts to address the unintended consequences of China's development model never stray too far from its bifurcated strategy of reregulation. For example, during the global economic slowdown in 2008, the Chinese government announced an economic stimulus plan that allocated nearly USD 600 billion to infrastructure and social programs. Provincial governments followed suit with their

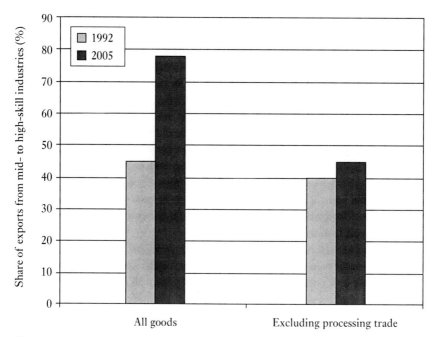

Figure 10.2. Increasing skill content. Customs Administration of China, 2007. Adapted from Amiti and Freund (2007).

own stimulus packages. Central and local stimulus plans, however, were not necessarily conceived in response to the financial crisis. The Eleventh Five-Year Plan had already included many of the projects, and provincial governments revived previously defunct projects "in the hopes difficult financial times would persuade Beijing to fund them."[6] Unsurprisingly, Beijing has paid special attention to strategic sectors with the goals and methods delineated in this book and left the rest of the economy to the localities.

No Liberal Convergence Yet

The case studies of telecommunications and textiles presented in their full complexity and the mini case studies of other strategic and nonstrategic sectors reveal that China has not become a liberal market economy. They also shed light on the prospects of political liberalization. Administrative restructuring, regulatory reinforcement, and de jure and de facto restrictions on the ownership structure and business scope of economic actors in the context of market liberalization con-

6. Quoted from "Chinese Provinces Propose $14 Trillion Yuan Stimulus," *Yomiuri Shimbun* (November 23, 2008).

firm, at least in the short term, that international economic integration and China's strong linkages to the global economy will not lead to liberal policy convergence. Although China has extensively liberalized on the aggregate level, it strictly regulates markets and economic actors in select industrial sectors, using market and nonmarket mechanisms to achieve state goals. In fact, by understanding China's bifurcated strategy, media headlines, such as *Forbes* magazine's "China Reorganizes Aerospace Industry" on December 4, 2008, no longer surprise us. The state dismantled the aerospace monopoly and introduced managed competition when it created two state-owned companies in 1997; a decade later, it again reorganized the aerospace industry to increase efficiency and take on more challenging collaborative programs with FDI. We witness a similar approach in the strategic industries studied in this book. The institutional landscape in nonstrategic sectors, in contrast, is more liberal because the Chinese state designed its bifurcated strategy to use more liberal instruments there.

Various dynamics at different levels of government have emerged in the regulatory transformation entailed in China's bifurcated strategy of market reform. The administrative and ownership restructuring witnessed in the different phases of liberalization and reregulation in the industries surveyed illustrate the growing diversity in function and form of government agencies and quasi-state organizations from the center to the locality. In strategic industries, central ministries have a mandate but it does not mean that central bureaucrats always agree on actual policy details. In nonstrategic ones, provincial and local branches of central ministries wrestle for influence in regulatory enforcement and local rulemaking. In these contexts, actual details of regulatory and market restructuring and new and reformulated rules to enhance or relinquish central authority are often products of much protracted bureaucratic conflict or fierce bargaining between relevant political and economic stakeholders.

Market liberalization and increasing pluralization in policymaking raise questions concerning the Chinese state's role in managing the social ramifications of economic liberalization with changing labor laws and social policy. But at least in the short term, the distinct path-dependent patterns of state control presented in this book disincentivize both bottom-up democratic mobilization and political reform from above. The nature of government-business coordination and market governance in telecommunications provides a case in point. The liberalization and subsequent reregulation of telecommunications has, in fact, enhanced state control of information dissemination to ensure social stability and political regime resilience. By introducing competition, the Chinese government modernized network infrastructure, diversified value-added services, promoted the development of domestic equipment makers, and thereby created a new business class of high-tech entrepreneurs. But by consolidating regulatory control over the equipment and service sectors, carefully regulating the business scope of market players and trading market share for self-censorship, the state enhances its ability to direct the development of the entire industry and monitor information dissemination to achieve security imperatives. It deliberately regulates the technology that runs the networks, works closely with domestic companies to exploit technology, and employs sophisticated instruments developed by foreign and domestic equipment makers to control the direction of infrastructural development and detect and halt political dissent and "illegal" activity when and where it sees fit.[7]

Granted, even as government control of telecommunications mediates and delays exposure to information, these rules and practices might prove less effective in controlling the effects of the information revolution on ordinary citizens and the prospects for grassroots political mobilization.[8] The reinforcing patterns of economic control studied in this book and their implications for social control, however, do not suggest that economic liberalization will be followed by political liberalization in China's foreseeable future. As the late eminent Chinese historian Frederic E. Wakeman contended, the transformation from a centrally planned economy to a regulated one "gave the authoritarian services of the state a much more important role than they had enjoyed when Mao's ideological campaigns inspired autarkic collective behavior."[9] In other words, social control in China today is the not so benign, Chinese-style manifestation of the reality of "free markets, more rules."[10]

STATES AND MARKETS: CHINA'S NEW CAPITALISM

This book's case studies show that today's China is not Communist China.[11] China today is a one-party dominant state that does not use ideologically driven control over its economy. Rather, it bases its control of the economy and markets on a strategic value logic, which varies by sector. The departure from Marxism-Leninism is exemplified in the distribution of de facto property rights across the political economy. While state-owned national champions in strategic industries receive preferential treatment from government financial and administrative bureaucracies, foreign and quasi-private and de facto private companies fiercely compete with

---

7. Google's allegations of Chinese government involvement in cyberattacks to steal intellectual property and restrain communication by human rights activists, made on January 28, 2010, exemplify Chinese government initiatives to use technology obtained through market liberalization to control information and dissent. See "Google, Citing Attack, Threatens to Exit China," *New York Times* (January 13, 2010), and "Chinese Attack on Google Seen as Cybertheft," National Public Radio (January 18, 2010).

8. See Zheng (2008) and Harwit (2008) on the ways in which the proliferation of Internet and mobile users in China poses to change the political landscape.

9. Quote from Wakeman (1991)'s fascinating case study of the institutional development of the modern police in twentieth-century China.

10. The quote is the title of Vogel (1996), which argues that the introduction of competition is inevitably followed by the rewriting of old rules and the creation of new ones.

11. Janos Kornai's (2000) differentiation of a market economy from a command one along four institutional dimensions begins our consideration of China's regulatory model.

one another in nonstrategic industries. Moreover, whereas bureaucratic coordination dominated Mao's China, today central bureaucracies preside over less than half of the economy. Decentralized bureaucratic and market governance dominate industries nonessential to national security, the national technological base, and the competitiveness of the rest of the economy. As for the typical behavior of economic actors, despite the fact that some national and local SOEs enjoy soft budget constraints, most state-owned companies have instituted reforms to operate on hard budgets, especially ones operating in industries considered strategic by the government. Additionally, cost-cutting competition to increase market share directs much of the economy; this reflects deregulated markets rather than ones constrained by a central plan. The typical economic phenomena in the new China are chaotic and saturated markets and business cycle fluctuations, not chronic shortages and seller's markets.

Moreover, China has not experienced the economic trajectory of its post-Communist neighbors. In the reform era, in lieu of embracing the "rationalism" espoused by the Washington Consensus, China relied first on empiricism in introducing markets and then embarked on a bifurcated strategy in its reregulation upon economy-wide liberalization. Many of China's post-Communist neighbors implemented "shock therapy" reforms; in contrast, the Chinese government gradually, over three decades, liberalized and reregulated to achieve state goals. Instead of comprehensive market liberalization upon the breakdown of Communist regimes, China shifted away from ideologically driven economics and introduced carefully calibrated competition in strategic industries and reorganized and/or privatized the state sector and permitted the emergence of private industry. Furthermore, China never adopted the laissez-faire orientation toward industry of many post-Communist countries guided by the liberal economic model. Rather, the Chinese government selectively and deliberately intervened to enhance state control in sectors and subsectors and issue areas with application for external and internal security and contribution to the national technology base and competitiveness of other industries.

Importantly, the post-Deng Chinese model departs from the East Asian developmental state. China has done so through the introduction of competition, including unprecedented liberalization of FDI; the careful calibration of ownership structures to retain state control and regulate the number of market players in strategic industries; and extensive deregulation in nonstrategic ones. The developmental state, on the contrary, undertook import-substitution and export-oriented industrialization through promoting and subsidizing domestic private industry, prohibiting FDI, distributing foreign aid from the United States to favored economic players, and coordinating foreign investment and collaboration. The mini case studies of the developmental state's treatment of telecommunications and textiles in Japan, South Korea, and Taiwan illustrate how the developmental state model differs from China's bifurcated strategy. In spite of actual policy differences across these countries, the developmental state actively promoted the development and cushioned the structural adjustment of textiles, a pillar industry when Japan, South Korea, and Taiwan were at a stage of economic development similar to China's. They coordinated domestic competition, worked closely with private industry to develop production lines and market segments, negotiated foreign technology transfers, and restricted FDI to joint ventures. Likewise, despite introducing competition across service and equipment sectors to promote indigenous development, the developmental state modernized communications infrastructure largely with domestic capital and protected incumbent telecommunications companies through cumbersome rules and regulations, including restricting foreign market share and favoring domestic technology.

The Chinese government, on the contrary, relinquished market control of textiles, perceived as a nonstrategic industry, and deregulated production and trade. Decentralized bureaucrats, working closely with domestic and global market actors, dominate market governance in textiles. Moreover, instead of privileging the incumbent, after dismantling the telecommunications monopoly the Chinese government licensed basic and value-added service providers outside of the traditional telecommunications regime and allowed FDI to participate in value-added services and equipment to modernize communications infrastructure. At the same time, to enhance state control of network infrastructure and create competitive state-owned operators, it undertook administrative and ownership restructuring. To promote domestic technology, it liberalized equipment markets but delayed licensing foreign network technology. In short, China departs from the developmental state by embracing foreign competition and know-how, rather than protecting domestic private industry; pursuing sectoral reregulation based on a strategic value logic, rather than working closely with private industry to achieve national development goals; and privileging bureaucracies and state-owned companies over private actors when strategic assets are at stake.

Lessons for Development

The Chinese model, which represents a radical break from the developmental state, shatters some basic assumptions on internal growth and trade in the study of development.[12] The diverse economic and industrial outcomes of China's bifurcated strategy of macro-liberalization and sectoral reregulation challenge the Keynesian notion that the state has the capacity and can be good for industrial planning purposes, personified by the phenomenal growth of the developmental state in the 1960s and 1970s. At the same time, they also defy the neoliberal view that interventionism produces inefficiencies and inefficacies, which adherents claimed was

---

12. See Ocampo and Johnson (1972) and Bell (1987) for summation narratives on the liberal and radical critiques of development economics and the literature on the developmental state cited elsewhere in this book on its challenge to both linear growth and structural change theories of development.

shown by the apparent cronyism and feeble responses of some of the NICs to the Asian financial crisis in the 1990s. Furthermore, China's pursuit of industrialization of the entire economy by liberalizing foreign direct investment on the macro-level rather than focusing on foreign aid and protectionism calls into question the dependency paradigm that direct foreign investment is necessarily exploitative and leads to dependent development; and that only aid can get societies out of the cycle of poverty when savings cannot.

On the flip side, the development of high-tech, high-value-added products, such as telecommunications and wind power equipment, from scratch through FDI and exposure to technology and knowledge transfers in exchange for market access, questions the neoclassical view that countries should focus on apparent absolute strength to obtain optimal efficiency. Yet China's continued strength in low-end, low-value-added production, such as those in undergarments and newsprint, forces a reexamination of the idea that countries should emphasize competition in the production of higher value goods by producing better and more efficient ones. China's pursuit of both comparative and competitive advantage shatters the notion that countries should focus energies and resources on only leading sectors because growth is significantly faster in some segments of the economy. And that pursuit appears to resolve, along with a strictly regulated currency regime, the gap between imports and exports, which plagues many developing countries.

What then does China's development model imply for developing countries seeking to fast-track industrialization even while opening up to the outside world? Can these countries succeed if they pursue a bifurcated strategy of growth and development, or, at the very least, get policies just right?[13] I would argue that the mixed industrial and economic effects witnessed in China's strategic and nonstrategic industries force us to move away from simplistic ideas of the mutual benefits of liberal markets and trade and the macro-level economic indicators that measure them. Yet sequencing or combining strategies of import-substitution and export-orientation or specifying the optimal relationship between government and business might not do the trick either. Rather, at least for China's integration into the international economy, the internal and global contexts in which the Chinese government balances country-specific and structural sectoral characteristics and national security and development imperatives deserve some consideration.

The structural contexts in which the Chinese model has defied conventional wisdom on the promises and pitfalls of both state intervention and deregulation cannot be disconnected from China's recent economic success. China opened its door to the world as the cold war came to an end. It integrated into the international economy in a context of neoliberal ascendance, which replaced cold war

---

13. To maximize the benefits of economic globalization, Rodrik (2007) suggests solutions to get out of poverty "usually requires following policies that are tailored to local economic and political realities" and Harrison and Rodríguez-Clare (2010) call for a soft industrial policy, "whereby government, industry and cluster-level private organizations can collaborate on interventions to increase productivity."

politics when the Soviet Union and its satellites collapsed. During this period of transnational rule-making by multilateral organizations, such as the WTO and the IMF, and global sectoral alliances, such as the International Telecommunications Union, China joined the game and adopted the prevailing norms rather than turn the other way. In this effort, China has welcomed foreign influences and joined regional and transnational forums, even while maintaining control of its economy through a bifurcated strategy of market liberalization and reregulation. In parallel, many developing countries have experienced less than desirable side effects from the internationalization of finance and neoliberal policies.

Still, the industrial and economic effects of China's liberalization two-step reveal uneven development. Not all deliberate utilization of market-oriented or interventionist methods or combinations thereof have generated industrial success. Moreover, China is more affected by boom-bust cycles because of the extensiveness, intensity, and speed of capital flows in the neoliberal era. Internal dissent and social unrest, by-products of post-Mao reforms, have also cast doubt on the legitimacy of the transforming Chinese political-economic system. All the same, China perceived the end of the cold war as the dawn of American military leadership in East Asia, targeting regional security against China and exerting ideological if not also political supremacy elsewhere. With the backdrop of a divided Korea, a solid U.S.-Japan alliance, a de facto independent Taiwan, and social protests and political dissent against the less savory effects of market liberalization and unabating state authority, China's security orientation has only reinforced the strategic value logic of sectoral reregulation rather than undermined it.

A National Model of Sectoral Integration

In response to the global forces of change outlined above, reregulation has happened in many countries. Scholars have found that political, economic, and social institutions, and the ideas that shape how these institutions emerge, affect a country's economic growth and market developments; the nature of the international economy, in turn, is affected by these national developments. But what China is doing differs from reregulation elsewhere. This book's case studies show that China's bifurcated strategy in response to economic globalization signifies a distinctive national model of sectoral integration into the international economy. This distinctive model of economic integration questions conventional wisdom on liberalization's implications for state strength, capacity, and autonomy in the developing world. The Chinese government's perception of the strategic value of industrial sectors has driven the bifurcated nature of its international integration. But sectoral attributes also shape the actual details of regulatory reform. Moreover, the organization of state bureaucracies and the competitiveness of domestic industry during critical junctures in China's exposure to the international economy explain temporal variation within dominant patterns of reregulation. No doubt China's authoritarian government has facilitated this bifurcated approach toward government-business relations. Insulated from domestic political pressures, the Chinese government liberalizes market competition without upsetting an electoral constituency. It also intervenes in strategic sectors and issue areas when it sees fit without having to face political retaliation or opposition.

How does China's national sectoral model of integration compare to that of other developing countries, especially ones of comparable geographical size and population? How does China's model compare to that of India, a democracy with a large domestic market and growing capabilities in high-tech services? Or Russia? India extensively liberalized in the 1990s after balance of payment and currency crises, and the former Soviet Union underwent substantial political centralization in recent years after it launched economy-wide liberalization upon Communist collapse. Have India and Russia pursued different models of sectoral integration based on a national logic of perceived strategic value and institutional and ideological legacies? How would variation in strategies toward FDI and industry translate into effective development models in the twenty-first century? Which model of international integration will become best practice now that the United States' liberal economic model has lost traction, along with the diminished appeal and influence of American power and might in the post–Iraq War era and in light of the 2008 financial crisis?

China's new model of development also raises theoretically and empirically relevant questions for economic development in the global South and South-South linkages. Chinese companies, with the assistance of Chinese financial institutions and diplomatic backing, have successfully secured contracts to build infrastructure and provide equipment and services in developing countries. The practical implications for economic development are important and so is the relevance of such South-South linkages on how we think about globalization and the state. For example, what impact does China's growing presence in Africa and the Middle East have on the relationship between state-building and market-building in developing countries with traditionally weak regulatory capacity? Moreover, what impact might China's ostensible political-economic ascendance have on global order (and disorder) in the twenty-first century?

REFERENCES

Abdelal, Rawi. 2001. *National Purpose in the World Economy: Post-Soviet States in Comparative Perspective.* Ithaca: Cornell University Press.

Abernathy, Frederick, John T. Dunlop, Janice H. Hammond, David Weil, eds. 1999. *A Stitch in Time: Lean Retailing and the Transformation of Manufacturing—Lessons from Apparel and Textile Industries.* Oxford: Oxford University Press.

Abernathy, Frederick, Anthony Volpe, and David Weil. 2005. *The Future of Apparel and Textile Industries: Prospects and Choices for Public and Private Actors.* Cambridge: Harvard Center for Textile and Apparel Research.

Aggarwal, Vinod. 1985. *Liberal Protectionism: The International Politics of Organized Textile Trade.* Berkeley: University of California Press.

Aldrich, Michael. 2006. "The MII VAS Circular: A Summer of Uncertainty to Be Followed by a Winter of Discontent." *Lovells Brief Bulletin*, September.

Alpermann, Bjorn. 2006. "Wrapped Up in Cotton Wool: Political Integration of Private Entrepreneurs in Rural China." *China Journal* 56: 33–61.

———. 2010. *China's Cotton Industry: Economic Transformation and State Capacity.* New York: Routledge.

American Chamber of Commerce of People's Republic of China. Various Years. *White Paper: American Business in China.* 2004, 2005, 2006 editions. Beijing.

Amiti, Mary, and Caroline Freund. 2007. "China's Export Boom." *Finance and Development* 44(3): 10–14.

Amsden, Alice. 1989. *Asia's Next Giant: South Korea and Late Industrialization.* New York: Oxford University Press.

———. 1994. "The Textile Industry in Asian Industrialization: A Leading Sector Institutionally?" *Journal of Asian Economics* 5(4): 573–84

Amsden, Alice, and Wan-Wen Chu. 2003. *Beyond Late Development: Taiwan's Upgrading Policies.* Cambridge: MIT Press.

Anchordoguy, Marie. 2005. *Reprogramming Japan: The High-Tech Crisis under Communitarian Capitalism.* Ithaca: Cornell University Press.

Balassa, Belas. 1981. *The Newly Industrializing Countries in the World Economy.* New York: Pergamon Press.

———. 1988. "The Lessons of East Asian Development: An Overview." *Economic Development and Cultural Change* 36(2), supplement 1: S273–S290.

Barnett, A. Doak. 1985. *The Making of Foreign Policy in China: Structure and Process.* SAIS Papers in International Affairs, No. 9. Boulder: Westview Press.

Bean, Willam Bao. 2005. "China Internet Wireless VAS: The Second Coming." Hong Kong: Deutsche Bank AG.

Bell, Clive. 1987. "Development Economics." In *The New Palgrave: A Dictionary of Economics*, edited by John Eatwell, Murray Milgate, and Peter Newman. Volume 1, 818–26. London: Macmillan.

Bianco, Lucien. 1967. *Origins of the Chinese Revolution*. Translated from French by Muriel Bell. Stanford: Stanford University Press.

Blecher, Marc J., and Vivienne Shue. 1996. *Tethered Deer: Government and Economy in a Chinese County*. Stanford: Stanford University Press.

——. 2001. "Into Leather: State-Led Development and The Private Sector in Xinji." *China Quarterly* 166: 368–93.

Borrus, Michael, and Stephen S. Cohen. 1998. "Building China's Information Technology Industry: Tariff Policy and China's Accession to the World Trade Organization." *Asian Survey* 38(11): 1005–17.

Boulton, William R. 2002. "Taiwan's Telecommunications Industry." In *Asian Telecommunications Update*, edited by Magdy Iskander, William Boulton, Y.T. Chien, Wayne Stark, Keith Warble, and Jack Winters. Baltimore, Md.: Internatioanl Technology Research Institute.

Bowles, Richard. 1998. "Food Retailig Takes Off." *China Business Review*, September–October.

Brandt, Loren, and Xiaodong Zhu. 2000. "Redistribution in a Decentralized Economy: Growth and Inflation in China under Reform." *Journal of Political Economy* 108(2): 422–51.

Breznitz, Dan. 2007. *Innovation and the State: Political Choice and Strategies for Growth in Israel, Taiwan, and Ireland*. New Haven: Yale University Press.

Brodsgaard, Kjeld Erik, and Zheng Yongnian, eds. 2004. *Bringing the Party Back In: How China Is Governed*. Singapore: Eastern Universities Press.

Brown, Colin G., Scott A. Waldron, and John W. Longworth, eds. 2002. *Regionalization and Integration in China: Lessons from the Transformation of the Beef Industry*. Hampshire, England: Ashgate Publishing.

——. 2005. *Modernizing China's Industries: Lessons from Wool and Wool Textiles*. Cheltenham: Edward Elgar.

Brown, Lester. 1995. *Who Will Feed China? Wake-Up Call for a Small Planet*. New York: W. W. Norton.

Bruins, Hendrik, and Fengxian Bu. 2006. "Food Security in China and Contingency Planning: The Significance of Grain Reserves." *Journal of Contingencies and Crisis Management* 14(3): 114–24.

Cammett, Melani. 2007. *Globalization and Business Politics in Arab North Africa: A Comparative Perspective*. Cambridge: Cambridge University Press.

Campbell, John L., J. Rogers Hollingsworth, and Leon N. Lindberg, eds. 1991. *Governance of the American Economy*. Cambridge: Cambridge University Press.

Campbell, John L., and Leon N. Lindberg. 1990. "Property Rights and the Organization of Economic Activity by the State." *American Sociological Review* 55(5): 634–47.

Cao, Cong, Richard Suttmeier, and Denis Fred Simon. 2006. "China's 15-Year Science and Technology Plan." *Physics Today* 59(12): 38–43.

Chan, Che-Po, and Gavin Drewry. 2001. "The 1998 State Council Organizational Streamlining: Personnel Reduction and Change of Government Function." *Journal of Contemporary China* 10(29): 553–72.

Chan, Jeanette, and Charles F. Goldsmith. 1999. "The Regulatory Game." *China Business Review*, May–June: 16–19.

Chandler, Alfred D. Jr. 1990. *Scale and Scope: The Dynamics of Industrial Capitalism*. Cambridge: Belknap Press of Harvard University.

Chang, Sea-Jin, and Dean Xu. 2008. "Spillovers and Competition among Foreign and Local Firms in China." *Strategic Management Journal* 29(5): 495–518.

Chaudhry, Kiren Aziz. 1993. "The Myths of the Market and the Common History of Late Developers." *Politics & Society* 21(3): 245–74.

———. 1997. *The Price of Wealth: Economies and Institutions in the Middle East.* Ithaca: Cornell University Press.

Chen, Changnian. 2006. "Analysis of China's Auto Manufacturing Equipment Market." *Chinamac Journal,* June.

Chen, Paul. 2003. "Special Report Standards: The Ins and Outs of CCC Marks." *China Business Review,* May–June.

Chen, Shin-Horng. 2000. "Telecommunications Liberalization: A Taiwanese Perspective." In *Deregulation and Interdependence in the Asia-Pacific Region,* edited by Takatoshi Ito and Anne O. Krueger. Chicago: University of Chicago Press.

Chen, Wenjing, and Yumin Zhao. 2005. "A Faster Speed of Greenfield Investment and M&As: The Effects Analysis and Expansion Tendency of Foreign Investment in China's Retail Industry." *Intertrade,* March. (In Chinese.)

Cheung, Carmencita. 2004. "Technology Transfer and Competition: The Mobile Handset Industry in Post-WTO China." University of Hamburg manuscript.

Child, Peter N. 2006. "Carrefour China: Lessons from a Global Retailer." *McKinsey Quarterly,* June.

China Business Review. 2000. "WTO Special Report: The Real Work Begins." *China Business Review,* January–February.

China National Textile and Apparel Council. 2004. "2003–2004 Report on China Textile Industry Development." In *Report on China Textile Industry Development.* Beijing: China National Textile and Apparel Council (CNTAC).

Chou, Yuntsai, and Kung-Chung Liu. 2006. "Paradoxical Impact of Asymmetric Regulation in Taiwan's Telecommunications Industry: Restriction and Rent Seeking." *Telecommunications Policy* 30(3–4): 171–82.

Chung, Inho. 2006. "Broadband, the Information Society, and National Systems: The Korean Case." In *Global Broadband Battles,* edited by Martin Fransman. Stanford: Stanford University Press.

Chung, Jae Ho. 2001. "Vertical Support, Horizontal Linkages, and Regional Disparities in China: Typology, Incentive Structure, and Operational Logic." *Issues & Studies* 37(4): 121–48.

———. 2003. "China's Reforms at Twenty-five: Challenges for the New Leadership." *China: An International Journal* 1(1): 119–32.

Central Intelligence Agency. Various Years. *World Fact Book.*

Clarke, Donald. 2003. "Economic Development and the Rights Hypothesis: The China Problem." *American Journal of Comparative Law* 51: 89–111.

Clarke, Donald, Peter Murrell, and Susan Whiting. 2006. "The Role of Law in China's Economic Development." George Washington University Law School Public Law Research Paper No. 187.

Clissold, Tim. 2005. *Mr. China.* New York: HarperCollins.

Cohen, Benjamin J., and Charles Lipson, eds. 1999. *Issues and Agents in International Political Economy: An International Organization Reader.* Cambridge: MIT Press.

Collier, Ruth B., and David Collier. 1991. *Shaping the Political Arena.* Princeton: Princeton University Press.

Crook, Frederick. 1994. "Seeds of Change." *China Business Review,* November–December.

———. 1997. "Grain Galore." *China Business Review,* September–October.

Cunningham, Edward. 2007. "China's Energy Governance: Perception and Reality, Audit of the Conventional Wisdom Series." Cambridge: MIT Center for International Studies.

Dean, Ted. 2001. "The Data Communications Market Open Up." *China Business Review,* May–June: 22–49.

———. 2003. "The Fight for China's Handsets." *China Business Review,* November–December: 28–31.

Dehousse, Franklin, Katelyne Ghemar, and Tsonka Iotsova. 2000. "Market Access Analysis: To Identify Barriers in China and in Russia Affecting the EU Textiles Industry." Centre d'Etudes Economiques et Institutionnelles: Commission of European Communities.

DeWoskin, Kenneth J. 2001. "The WTO and the Telecommunications Sector in China." *China Quarterly* 167: 630–54.

Dittmer, Lowell, and Yu-Shan Wu. 2006. "Leadership Coalitions and Economic Transformation in Reform China: Revisiting the Political Business Cycle." In *China's Deep Reform: Domestic Politics in Transition,* edited by Lowell Dittmer and Guoli Liu. Lanham, Md.: Rowman and Littlefield.

Dollar, David, and Aart Kraay. 2006. "Neither a Borrower Nor a Lender: Does China's Net Zero Foreign Asset Position Make Economic Sense?" *Journal of Monetary Economics* 53(5): 943–71.

Doner, Richard F., Bryan K. Ritchie, and Dan Slater. 2005. "Systemic Vulnerability and the Origins of the Developmental States: Northeast and Southeast Asia in Comparative Perspective." *International Organization* 59(2): 327–61.

Downs, Erica S. 2008. "China's Energy Policies and Their Environmental Impacts." U.S.-China Economic and Security Review Commission. Washington, D.C.: Brookings Institution.

Etchemendy, Sebastian. 2001. "Constructing Reform Coalitions: The Politics of Compensations in Argentina's Economic Liberalization." *Latin American Politics and Society* 43(3): 1–35.

———. 2004. "Revamping the Weak, Protecting the Strong, and Managing Privatization: Governing Globalization in the Spanish Take-off." *Comparative Political Studies* 37(6): 623–51.

European Commission. 2005. "Study on Chinese Textiles and Clothing Industry and Its Market Expansion Strategy," January.

Evans, Peter B. 1979. *Dependent Development: The Alliance of Multinational, State, and Local Capital in Brazil.* Princeton: Princeton University Press.

———. 1995. *Embedded Autonomy: States and Industrial Transformation.* Princeton: Princeton University Press.

Evans, Peter B., and John D. Stephens. 1988. "Development and the World Economy." In *The Handbook of Sociology,* edited by Neil Smelser. Newbury Park, Calif.: Sage Publications.

Fan, Frank Xing. 2000. "Foreign Investment in China's Internet Business: Forbidden, Forgiven, Forced Open?" Washington, D.C.: Center for Strategic and International Studies.

———. 2001. *Communications and Information in China: Regulatory Issues, Strategic Implications.* Lanham, Md.: University Press of America.

Feigenbaum, Evan A. 1999. "Who's Behind China's High Technology 'Revolution'? How Bomb Makers Remade Beijing's Priorities, Policies, and Institutions." *International Security* 24(1): 95–126.

———. 2003. *China's Techno-Warriors: National Security and Strategic Competition from the Nuclear to the Information Age.* Stanford: Stanford University Press.

Feldman, Gayle. 1986. "The Organization of Publishing in China." *China Quarterly* 107: 519–29.

Fewsmith, Joseph. 2001. "The Political and Social Implications of China's Accession to the WTO." *China Quarterly* 167: 573–91.

Fleisher, Belton M., Keyong Dong, and Yunhua Liu. 1996. "Education, Enterprise Organization, and Productivity in the Chinese Paper Industry." *Economic Development and Cultural Change* 44(3): 571–87.

Floyd, Sigmund. 2002. "Special Report: Chemicals; Cracking the Chemical Sector." *China Business Review*, March–April: 32–39.

Flynn, Robert. 2006. "China's Pulp and Paper Industry: What Low Cost Labor Advantage? China's Boom: Implications for Investment and Trade in Forest Products and Forestry." Vancouver, B.C., Canada: Wood Resources International.

Foster, Kenneth W. 2001. "Associations in the Embrace of an Authoritarian State." *Studies in Comparative International Development*. 35(4): 84–109.

Fransman, Martin. 1995. *Japan's Computer and Communications Industry: The Evolution of Industrial Giants and Global Competitiveness.* Oxford: Oxford Uniersity Press.

——, ed. 2006. *Global Broadband Battles: Why the U.S. and Europe Lag While Asia Leads.* Stanford: Stanford University Press.

Friman, H. Richard. 1988. "Rocks, Hard Places, and the New Protectionism: Textile Trade Policy Choices in the United States and Japan." *International Organization* 42(4): 689–723.

Fu, Jun. 2000. *Institutions and Investments: FDI in China during an Era of Reforms.* Ann Arbor: The University of Michigan Press.

Funk, Jeffrey L. 2006. "The Mobile Phone Industry: A Microcosm of Deregulation, Globalization, and Technological Change in the Japanese Economy." In *Japanese Telecommunications: Market and Policy in Transition*, edited by Ruth Taplin and Masako Wakui. New York: Routledge.

Gale, Fred. 2002. "Will China's Food Imports Rise?" *China Business Review*, March–April.

Gallagher, Mary E. 2002. "'Reform and Openness': Why China's Economic Reforms Have Delayed Democracy." *World Politics* 54: 338–72.

——. 2005. *Contagious Capitalism: Globalization and the Politics of Labor in China.* Princeton: Princeton University Press.

Garrett, Geoffrey, and Peter Lange, 1995. "Internationalization, Institutions and Political Change." *International Organization* 49(4): 627–55.

Gereffi, Gary. 1989. "Industrial Restructuring and National Development Strategies: A Comparison of Taiwan, South Korea, Brazil and Mexico." In *Taiwan: A Newly Industrialized State*, edited by Hsin-Huang Michael Hsiao, Wei-Yuan Cheng, and Hou-Sheng Chan. Taipei: Department of Sociology, National Taiwan University.

——. 2001. "Shifting Governance Structures in Global Commodity Chains." *American Behavioral Scientist* 44: 1616.

——. 2009. "Development Models and Industrial Upgrading in China and Mexico." *European Sociological Review* 25(1): 37–51.

Gereffi, Gary, John Humphrey, and Timothy Sturgeon. 2005. "The Governance of Global Value Chains." *Review of International Political Economy* 12(1): 78–104.

Gereffi, Gary, and Olga Memedovic. 2003. "The Global Apparel Value Chain: What Prospects for Upgrading by Developing Countries?" Vienna: Sectorial Studies Series, United Nations Industrial Development Organization.

Gereffi, Gary, and Mei-Lin Pan. 1994. "The Globalization of Taiwan's Garment Industry." In *Global Production: The Apparel Industry in the Pacific Rim*, edited by Edna Bonacich,

Lucie Cheng, Norma Chinchilla, Nora Hailton, and Paul Ong. Philadelphia: Temple University.

Gereffi, Gary, and Donald L. Wyman, eds. 1990. *Manufacturing Miracles.* Princeton: Princeton University Press.

Gerschenkron, Alexander. 1962. *Economic Backwardness in Historical Perspective.* Cambridge: Harvard University Press.

Gibbons, Russell. 1996. *Joint Ventures in China: A Guide for the Foreign Investor.* South Melbourne: MacMillan Education Australia.

Gilboy, George. 2004. "The Myth behind China's Miracle." *Foreign Affairs* 83: 33–48.

Gilpin, Robert. 1975. *U.S. Power and the Multinational Corporation: The Political Economy of Foreign Direct Investment.* New York: Basic Books.

———. 2001. *Global Political Economy: Understanding the International Economic Order.* Princeton: Princeton University Press.

Gold, Thomas B. 1986. *State and Society in the Taiwan Miracle.* Armonk, N.Y.: M.E. Sharpe.

———. 1989. "Urban Private Business in China." *Studies in Comparative Communism* 22: 187–200.

Gorham, Sid, and Achmad M. Chadran. 1993. "Telecom Races Ahead." *China Business Review,* March–April: 18–25.

Gourevitch, Peter A. 1978. "The Second Image Reversed: The International Sources of Domestic Politics." *International Organization* 32(4): 881–912.

———. 1986. *Politics in Hard Times: Comparative Responses to International Economic Crises.* Ithaca: Cornell University Press.

Graham, John M., and Chaoyi Zhao. "The PRC's Evolving Standards System: Institutions and Strategy." *Asia Policy* 2: 63–88.

Gregory, Neil, Stoyan Tenev, and Dileep Wagle. 2000. *China's Emerging Private Enterprises: Prospects for the New Century.* Washington, D.C.: International Finance Corporation.

Gu, Qingliang. 1999. "The Development of the China Apparel Industry: China." Cambridge: China Textile University and Harvard Center for Textile and Apparel Research.

Guillen, Mauro F. 2001. *The Limits of Convergence: Globalization and Organizational Change in Argentina, South Korea, and Spain.* Princeton: Princeton University Press.

Gunaratne, Shelton A. 2001. "Paper, Printing, and the Printing Press: A Horizontally Integrative Macrohistory Analysis." *International Communication Gazette* 63(6): 459–79.

Guthrie, Doug. 1999. *Dragon in a Three-Piece Suit: The Emergence of Capitalism in China.* Princeton: Princeton University Press.

———. 2006. *China and Globalization: The Social, Economic, and Political Transformation of Chinese Society.* New York: Routledge.

Haggard, Stephan. 1990. *Pathways from the Periphery: The Politics of Growth in the Newly Industrializing Countries.* Ithaca: Cornell University Press.

Haggard, Stephan, and Tun-jen Cheng. 1987. "State and Foreign Capital in the East Asian NICs." In *The Political Economy of the New Asian Industrialism,* edited by Frederic Deyo. Ithaca: Cornell University Press.

Haggard, Stephan, and Robert Kaufman. 1992. *The Politics of Economic Adjustment: International Constraints, Distributive Conflicts, and the State.* Princeton: Princeton University Press.

Hall, Peter A., and David Soskice, eds. 2001. *Varieties of Capitalism: The Institutional Foundations of Comparative Advantage.* Oxford: Oxford University Press.

Hao, Xiaoming, Huang Yu, and Kewen Zhang. 1998. "Free Market vs. Political Control in China: Convenience or Contradiction?" *Media Development* 1: 35–38.

Harrison, Ann, and Andrés Rodríguez-Clare. 2010. "Trade, Foreign Investment, and Industrial Policy for Developing Countries." In *Handbook of Development Economics*, edited by Dani Rodrick and M.R. Rosenzweig, 4039–4214. Amsterdam: North-Holland.

Harwit, Eric. 1992. "Foreign Passenger Car Ventures and Chinese Decision-Making." *Australian Journal of Chinese Affairs* 22: 141–66.

——. 1995. *China's Automobile Industry: Policies, Problems, and Prospects.* Armonk, N.Y.: M. E. Sharpe.

——. 1998. "China's Telecommunications Industry: Development Patterns and Policies." *Pacific Affairs* 71(2): 175–93.

——. 2004. "Spreading Telecommunications to Developing Areas in China: Telephones, the Internet and the Digital Divide." *China Quarterly* 180: 1010–30.

——. 2005. "Telecommunications and the Internet in Shanghai: Political and Economic Factors Shaping the Network in a Chinese City." *Urban Studies* 42(10): 1837–58.

——. 2008. *China's Telecommunications Revolution.* New York: Oxford University Press.

Harwit, Eric, and Duncan Clark. 2001. "Shaping the Internet in China: Evolution of Political Control over Network Infrastructure and Content." *Asian Survey* 41(3): 377–408.

Hatch, Walter, and Kozo Yamamura. 1996. *Asia in Japan's Embrace.* Cambridge: Cambridge University Press.

Heilmann, Sebastian. 2005. "Regulatory Innovation by Leninist Means: Communist Party Supervision in China's Financial Industry." *China Quarterly* 181: 1–21.

Helsell, Tina. 1997. "Turning Farmers into Entrepreneurs." *China Business Review,* September–October.

Henisz, Witold J., Bennet A. Zelner, and Mauro F. Guillén. 2005. "Market-Oriented Infrastructure Reforms, 1977–1999." *American Sociological Review* 70(6): 871–97.

Hill, Kay. 1994. "China's State Farms Go Corporate." *China Business Review,* November–December.

Hisano, Shuji, Raymond A. Jussaume Jr., Chul-Kyoo Kim, Philip McMichael, Shigeru Otsuka, Yoshimitsu Taniguchi, and Lin Zhibin. 1998. "The Role of Asian Transnational Corporations in Evolving Asian Agri-Food Systems." In *The Global Agri-Food Sector and Transnational Corporations Conference, Research Committee on Agriculture (RC-40).* Montreal: International Sociological Association.

Ho, Samuel, and Ralph W. Huenemann. 1984. *China's Open Door Policy: The Quest for Foreign Technology and Capital.* Vancouver: University of British Columbia Press.

Hollingsworth, J. Roger, Philippe C. Schmitter, and Wolfgang Streeck. 1994. *Governing Capitalist Economies.* Cambridge: Cambridge University Press.

Hope, Nicholas, Dennis Tao Yang, and Mu Yang Li, eds. 2003. *How Far across the River: China Policy Reform at the Millennium.* Stanford: Stanford University Press.

Horsley, Jamie P. 2001. "PRC Regulation of Foreign Telecom Equipment and the WTO." *China Business Review,* September–October: 66–68.

Hsing, You-tien. 1998. *Making Capitalism in China: The Taiwan Connection.* Oxford: Oxford University Press.

Hsu, C. Stephen, ed. 2003. *Understanding China's Legal System.* New York: New York University Press.

Hsueh, Roselyn. 2008. "Crossing the River by Feeling for Stones: Conducting Resaerch in Varying Contexts in China." Paper presented at the Annual Meeting of the American Political Science Association, Boston.

Hu, Albert G. Z., and Gary H. Jefferson. 2002. "FDI Impact and Spillover: Evidence from China's Electronic and Textile Industries." *World Economy* 25: 1063–76.

Huang, Yasheng. 1996. *Inflation and Investment Controls in China.* Cambridge: Cambridge University Press.

———. 2003. *Selling China: Foreign Direct Investment during the Reform Era.* Cambridge: Cambridge University Press.

Huchet, Jean-Francois. 1997. "The China Circle and Technological Development in the Chinese Electronics Industry." In *The China Circle: Economics and Electronics in the PRC, Taiwan, and Hong Kong,* edited by Barry Naughton. Washington, D.C.: Brookings Institution Press.

Institute of World Economics and Politics, Chinese Academy of Social Sciences. 2006. *China and World Economy* 14(1–3). (In Chinese.)

International Monetary Fund. Various Years. *World Economic Outlook database.* Accessed online.

———. Various Years. *Direction of Trade Statistics Yearbook.* Accessed online.

Jacobs, Brenda. 1997. "Talking Textiles." *China Business Review,* March–April: 30–37.

Jacobson, Harold, and Michel Oksenberg. 1990. *China's Participation in the IMF, World Bank, and GATT.* Ann Arbor: University of Michigan Press.

Jia, Liangding, Junjun Zhang, Haiyan Qian, Rongjun Cui, and Yongxia Chen. 2005. "A Study on the Comparison between the Cognitions of Western Theories and Chinese Enterprises." *Management World,* August. (In Chinese.)

Jing, Jun, ed. 2000. *Feeding China's Little Emperors.* Stanford: Stanford University Press.

Johnson, Chalmers. 1982. *MITI and the Japanese Miracle: The Growth of Industrial Policy, 1925–1975.* Stanford: Stanford University Press.

———. 1995. *Japan: Who Governs? The Rise of the Developmental State.* New York: W. W. Norton.

Kahler, Miles, and David Lake, eds. 2003. *Governance in a Global Economy: Political Authority in Transition.* Princeton: Princeton University Press.

Kang, Chao-Chung. 2009. "Privatization and Production Efficiency in Taiwan's Telecommunications Industry." *Telecommunications Policy* 33(9): 495–505.

Katsigris, Eugenia, Xiufang Sun, Nian Cheng, Andy White, and R. Anders West. 2004. "China's Forest Product Import Trends: 1997–2002." A Joint project between Forest Trends, Chinese Center for Agricultural Policy, Chinese Academy of Science, and Center for International Forestry Research, Indonesia.

Katzenstein, Peter. 1978. *Between Power and Plenty: Foreign Economic Policies of Advanced Industrialized States.* Madison: University of Wisconsin Press.

Kennedy, Scott. 1997. "The Stone Group: State Client or Market Pathbreaker?" *China Quarterly* 152: 746–77.

———. 2005a. "China's Porous Protectionism: The Changing Political Economy of Trade Policy." *Political Science Quarterly* 120(3): 407–32.

———. 2005b. *The Business of Lobbying in China.* Cambridge: Harvard University Press.

———. 2006. "The Political Economy of Standards Coalitions: Explaining China's Involvement in High-Tech Standards Wars." *Asia Policy* 2: 41–62.

Keohane, Robert O., and Helen V. Milner, eds. 1996. *Internationalization and Domestic Politics.* Cambridge: Cambridge University Press.

Kitschelt, Herbert. 1991. "Industrial Governance Structures, Innovation Strategies, and the Case of Japan: Sectoral or Cross-National Comparative Analysis?" *International Organization* 45(4): 453–93.

Kitschelt, Herbert, Peter Lange, Gary Marks, and John D. Stephens, eds. 1999. *Continuity and Change in Contemporary Capitalism.* Cambridge: Cambridge University Press.

Kornai, Janos. 2000. "What the Change of the System from Socialism to Capitalism Does or Does Not Mean." *Journal of Economic Perspectives* 1(14): 27–42.

Krasner, Stephen. 1991. "Global Communications and National Power: Life on the Pareto Frontier." *World Politics* 43(3): 336–66.

Ku, Cheng-Yuan, Yi-Wen Chang, and David C. Yen. 2009. "National Information Security Policy and Its Implementation: A Case Study in Taiwan." *Telecommunications Policy* 33(7): 371–84.

Kuhn, Dieter. 1988. "Chemistry and Chemical Technology Part IX Textile Technology: Spinning and Reeling." In *Science and Civilization in China,* edited by J. Needham. Cambridge: Cambridge University Press.

Kurth, James. 1979. "The Political Consequences of the Product Cycle: Industrial History and Political Outcomes." *International Organization* 33(1): 1–34.

Kushida, Kenji. 2009. "Inside the Castle Gates: How Foreign Companies Navigate Japan's Policymaking Processes." PhD dissertation, Department of Political Science, UC Berkeley.

Kushida, Kenji, and Seung-Young Oh. 2007. "The Political Economies of Broadband in Japan and South Korea." *Asian Survey* 47(3): 481–504.

Lam, Alex. 1995. "Tapping the Retail Market in China." *China Business Review,* September–October: 23–28.

Lampton, David, ed. 1987. *Policy Implementation in Post-Mao China.* Berkeley: University of California Press.

Laperrouza, Marc. 2006. "China's Telecommunication Policy-Making in the Context of Trade and Economic Reforms." PhD thesis, Department of Information Systems, London School of Economics and Political Science.

Lapres, Daniel Arthur. 2000. "The EU-China WTO Deal Compared." *China Business Review* (July–August): 8–14.

Lardy, Nicholas. 1998. *China's Unfinished Economic Revolution.* Washington, D.C.: Brookings Institution Press.

——. 2002. *Integrating China in the Global Economy.* Washington, D.C.: Brookings Institution Press.

Lau, Lawrence J., Yingyi Qian, and Gerard Roland. 2000. "Reform without Losers: An Interpretation of China's Dual-Track Approach to Transition." *Journal of Political Economy* 108: 120–43.

Lawrence, Susan V. 1998. "Silver Lining." *Far Eastern Economic Review* 161(36): 18–19.

Laylois, John D. 2001. "The WTO and China's Financial System." *China Quarterly* 167: 610–29.

Lee, Hong Yung. 2000. *Xiagang, the Chinese Style of Laying Off Workers. Asian Survey* 40(6): 914–37.

Lema, Adrian, and Kristian Ruby. 2007. "Between Fragmented Authoritarianism and Policy Coordination: Creating a Chinese Market for Wind Energy." *Energy Policy* 35: 3879–90.

Levi-Faur, David. 2004. "Comparative Research Design in the Study of Regulation." In *The Politics of Regulation: Institutions and Regulatory Reforms for the Governance Age,* edited by Jacint Jordana and David Levi-Faur. Cheltenham, U.K.: Edward Elgar.

Levy, Jonah. 1999. *Tocqueville's Revenge: State, Society, and Economy in Contemporary France.* Cambridge: Harvard University Press.

———, ed. 2006. *The State after Statism: New State Activities in the Age of Liberalization.* Cambridge: Harvard University Press.

Li, Haizheng. 2006. "Pulp and Paper Industry in China: Current Status, Trends, and Implications for International Products." Atlanta: Center for Business and Industry Studies, School of Economics, Georgia Institute of Technology.

Li, Shen, and Mei Qiang. 2006. "A Study of the Policies We Should Adopt in China's Automobile Spare Parts Industry—When Foreign Funds Directly Enter China for Investment." *Management World,* January. (In Chinese.)

Lieberthal, Kenneth G., and David M. Lampton, eds. 1992. *Bureaucracy, Politics, and Decision Making in Post-Mao China.* Berkeley: University of California Press.

Lieberthal, Kenneth, and Michel Oksenberg. 1988. *Policy Making in China: Leaders, Structures, and Processes.* Princeton: Princeton University Press.

Lin, Kun-Chin. 2006. "Disembedding Socialist Firms as a Statist Project: Restructuring the Chinese Oil Industry, 1997–2002." *Enterprise and Society* 7(1): 59–97.

———. 2008. "Macroeconomic Disequilibria and Enterprise Reform: Restructuring the Chinese Oil and Petrochemical Industries in the 1990s." *China Journal* 60: 49–79.

Lin, Yi-Min. 2001. *Between Politics and Markets: Firms, Competition, and Institutional Change in Post-Mao China.* New York: Cambridge University Press.

Lindberg, Leon N., John L. Campbell, and J. Rogers Hollingsworth, eds. 1991. *Governance of the American Economy.* New York: Cambridge University Press.

Lindblom, Charles E. 1977. *Politics and Markets: The World's Political-Economic Systems.* New York: Basic Books.

Ling, Zhihun. 2005. *The Lenovo Affair: The Growth of China's Computer Giant and Its Takeover of IBM-PC.* Translated by M. Avery. Singapore: John Wiley and Sons (Asia).

Liu, Guy S., Pei Sun, and Wing Thye Woo. 2006. "The Political Economy of Chinese-Style Privatization: Motives and Constraints." *World Development* 34: 2016–33.

Liu, Manqiang. 2006. "Broadband Access Development in China." In *Global Broadband Battles: Why the U.S. and Europe Lag While Asia Leads,* edited by Martin Fransman. Stanford: Stanford University Press.

Liu, Shouying, and Luo Dan. 2004. *Can China Feed Itself? Chinese Scholars on China's Food Issue, Focus on China Series.* Beijing: Foreign Languages Press.

Lo, Chi. 2004. "Bank Reform: How Much Time Does China Have? *China Business Review,* March–April.

Lu, Ding. 1994. "The Management of China's Telecommunications Industry: Some Institutional Facts." *Telecommunications Policy* 18(3): 195–205.

Lu, Ding, and Chee Kong Wong. 2003. *China's Telecommunications Market: Entering a New Competitive Age.* Cheltenham, U.K.: Edward Elgar.

Lu, Feng. 1998. "Grain versus Food: A Hidden Issue in China's Food Policy Debate." *World Development* 26(9): 1641–52.

Lu, Qiwen. 2000. *China's Leap into the Information Age: Innovation and Organization in the Computer Industry.* Oxford: Oxford University Press.

Luo, Yadong. 2000. *How to Enter China: Choices and Lessons.* Ann Arbor: University of Michigan Press.

Macnaughtan, Helen. 2005. *Women, Work, and the Japanese Economic Miracle: The Case of the Cotton Textile Industry.* London: Routledge.

Marechal, Valerie, Pelin Tekin, and Humay Guliyeva. 2009. "China's New Property Rights Law: An Important Step towards Improving Access to Credit for Small and Medium Enterprises." Celebrating Reform 2009 Case Studies—Doing Business. World Bank.

Martin, Dan. 1994. "Mending the Textile Rift." *China Business Review,* May–June: 9–14.

Matsuzaki, Masahiro. 1982. "Textiles—Probing the Way to Revitalization." *Japan Quarterly* 29: 205–11.

McGregor, James. 2005. *One Billion Customers: Lessons from the Front Lines of Doing Business in China.* New York: Wall Street Journal Books.

McMillan, John, and Barry Naughton. 1992. "How to Reform a Planned Economy: Lessons from China." *Oxford Review of Economic Policy* 8(1): 130–43.

McNally, Christopher, and Peter Nan-shong Lee. 1998. "Is Big Beautiful?—Restructuring China's State Sector under the Zhuada Policy." *Issues & Studies* 34(9).

McNamara, Dennis. 1995. *Textiles and Industrial Transition in Japan.* Ithaca: Cornell University Press.

——. 2002. *Market and Society in Korea: Interests, Institutions, and the Textile Industry.* London: Routledge.

McNiel, Theresa, and Kerstin Nilsson. 1994. "The Food Chain." *China Business Review,* November–December.

Medeiros, Evan S., Roger Cliff, Keith Crane, and James C. Melvenon. 2005. "A New Direction for China's Defense Industry." Santa Monica, Calif.: Project AIR FORCE, Rand Corporation.

Meisner, Maurice. 1999. *Mao's China and After: A History of the People's Republic.* 3rd ed. New York: Free Press.

Mertha, Andrew C. 2005a. "China's 'Soft' Centralization: Shifting Tiao/Kuai Authority Relations." *China Quarterly* 184: 792–810.

——. 2005b. *The Politics of Piracy: Intellectual Property in Contemporary China.* Ithaca: Cornell University Press.

Mody, Ashoka, and David Wheeler. 1987. "Towards a Vanishing Middle: Competition in the World Garment Industry." *World Development* 15: 1269–84.

Mok, Vincent Wai-Kwong. 2002. "Industrial Productivity in China: The Case of Food Industry in Guangdong Province." *Journal of Economic Studies* 29(6): 423–31.

Montinola, Gabriella, Yingyi Qian, and Barry R. Weingast. 1995. "Federalism, Chinese Style: The Political Basis for Economic Success in China." *World Politics* 48(1): 50–81.

Moore, Thomas G. 2002. *China in the World Market: Chinese Industry and International Sources of Reform in the Post-Mao Era.* Cambridge: Cambridge University Press.

Mueller, Milton, and Peter Lovelock. 2000. "The WTO and China's Ban on Foreign Investment in Telecommunication Services: A Game-Theoretic Analysis." *Telecommunications Policy* 24: 731–59.

Mueller, Milton, and Zixiang Tan. 1997. *China in the Information Age: Telecommunications and the Dilemmas of Reform.* London: Praeger.

Murillo, María Victoria. 2002. "Political Bias in Policy Convergence: Privatization Choices in Latin America." *World Politics* 54: 462–93.

National Bureau of Statistics, People's Republic of China. Various Years. *Trade and External Economic Statistical Yearbook of China.* Beijing: China Statistics Press.

Naughton, Barry. 1995. *Growing Out of the Plan: Chinese Economic Reform, 1978–1993.* Cambridge: Cambridge University Press.

——, ed. 1997. *The China Circle: Economics and Technology in the PRC, Taiwan, and Hong Kong.* Washington, D.C.: Brookings Institution Press.

——. 2002. "China's Economic Thinktanks." *China Quarterly* 171 (September): 625–35.

Naughton, Barry, and Adam Segal. 2003. "China in Search of a Workable Model: Technology Development in the New Millennium." In *Crisis and Innovation: In Asian Technology,* edited by William Keller and Richard Samuels. New York: Cambridge University Press.

Naughton, Barry, and Dali Yang, eds. 2004. *Holding China Together: Diversity and National Integration in the Post-Deng Era.* Cambridge: Cambridge University Press.

Nee, Victor. 1989. "A Theory of Market Transition: From Redistribution to Markets in State Socialism." *American Sociological Review* 54(5): 663–681.

Newman, Abraham, and John Zysman, eds. 2006. *How Revolutionary Was the Digital Revolution? National Responses, Market Transitions, and Global Technology.* A BRIE/ETLA Project. Stanford: Stanford Business Books.

Ngo, Tak-Wing, and Yongping Wu. 2009. *Rent Seeking in China.* New York: Routledge.

Nolan, Peter. 2001. *China and the Global Business Revolution.* New York: Palgrave.

Nolan, Peter, and Fureng Dong, eds. 1989. *Market Forces in China: Competition and Small Business.* New Jersey: Zed Books.

Ocampo, Jose, and Dale Johnson. 1972. "The Concept of Political Development." In *Dependence and Development,* edited by James Cockcroft, Andre Gunder Frank, and Dale Johnson, 399–424. Garden City, N.Y.: Anchor Books.

OECD, ed. 2002. "China in the World Economy: The Domestic Policy Challenges." Paris: Organisation for Economic Co-operation and Development.

Oi, Jean. 1992. "Fiscal Reform and the Economic Foundations of Local State Corporatism in China." *World Politics* 45: 1.

——. 1999. *Rural China Takes Off: Institutional Foundations of Economic Reform.* Berkeley: University of California Press.

Oksenberg, Michel, and Elizabeth Economy, eds. 1999. *China Joins the World: Progress and Prospects.* New York: Council of Foreign Relations Press.

Oksenberg, Michel, and James Tong. 1991. "The Evolution of Central-Provincial Fiscal Relations in China, 1971–1984." *China Quarterly* 125: 1–32.

Paul, T.V., G. John Ikenberry, and John Hall. 2003. *The Nation-State in Question.* Princeton: Princeton University Press.

Pan, Suwen, Mark Welch, Samarendu Mohanty, Mohamadou Fadiga, and Don Ethridge. 2005. "Chinese Tariff Rate Quota vs. U.S. Subsidies: What Affects of the World Cotton Market More?" Lubbock: Department of Agricultural and Applied Economics, Texas Tech University.

Park, Young-il, and Kym Anderson. 1991. "The Rise and Demise of Textiles and Clothing in Economic Development: The Case of Japan." *Economic Development and Cultural Change* 393: 531–48.

Parris, Kristin. 1993. "Local Initiative and National Reform: The Wenzhou Model of Development." *China Quarterly* 134: 242–63.

Pearson, Margaret. 1991a. "The Erosion of Controls over Foreign Capital in China, 1979–1988: Having Their Cake and Eating It Too?" *Modern China* 17(1): 112–50.

——. 1991b. *Joint Ventures in the People's Republic of China.* Princeton: Princeton University Press.

——. 1994. "The Janus Face of Business Associations in China: Socialist Corporatism in Foreign Enterprises." *Australian Journal of Chinese Affairs* (31): 25–46.

——. 1997. *China's New Business Elite: The Political Consequences of Economic Reform.* Berkeley: University of California Press.

——. 1999. "China's Integration into the International Trade and Investment Regime." In *China Joins the World: Progress and Prospects,* edited by Michel Oksenberg and Elizabeth Economy. New York: Council on Foreign Relations Press.

——. 2001. "The Case of China's Accession to GATT/WTO." In *The Making of Chinese Foreign and Security Policy in the Era of Reform,* edited by David M. Lampton. Stanford: Stanford University Press.

———. 2005. "The Business of Governing Business in China: Institutions and Norms of the Emerging Regulatory State." *World Politics* 57: 296–322.

———. 2007. "Governing the Chinese Economy: Regulatory Reform in the Service of the State." *Public Administration Review* 67(4): 718–30.

Peerenboom, Randall. 2001. "Globalization, Path Dependency, and the Limits of Law: Administrative Law Reform and Rule of Law in the People's Republic of China." *Berkeley Journal of International Law* 19: 161–264.

Perkins, Dwight. 1986. *China: Asia's Next Economic Giant.* Seattle: University of Washington Press.

Perry, Elizabeth J., and Mark Selden, eds. 2000. *Chinese Society: Change, Conflict, and Resistance.* London: Routledge.

Pickles, John. 2006. "Guest Editorial: Trade Liberalization, Industrial Upgrading, and Regionalization in the Global Clothing Industry." *Environment and Planning* 38: 2201–06.

Pierson, Paul. 1994. *Dismantling the Welfare State? Reagan, Thatcher, and the Politics of Retrenchment.* Cambridge: Cambridge University Press.

———. 2004. *Politics in Time: History, Institutions, and Social Analysis.* Princeton: Princeton University Press.

Pirie, Iain. 2008. *The Korean Developmental State: From Dirigisme to Neo-Liberalism.* New York: Routledge.

Polanyi, Karl. 1944. *The Great Transformation: The Political and Economic Origins of Our Time.* Boston: Beacon Press.

Pomfret, Richard. 1991. *Investing in China: Ten Years of the Open Door Policy.* Ames: Iowa State University Press.

Potter, Pitman B. 2001. "The Legal Implications of China's Accession to the WTO." *China Quarterly* 167: 592–609.

People's Republic of China, Ministry of Commerce. *Intertrade.* Monthly publication. Multiple issues. (In Chinese.)

People's Republic of China, National Development and Reform Commission. *Macroeconomics.* Monthly publication. Multiple issues. (In Chinese.)

People's Republic of China, State Council. *Management World.* Monthly publication. Multiple issues. (In Chinese.)

Qian, Yingyi. 2003. "How Reform Worked in China." In *Search of Prosperity: Analytic Narratives on Economic Growth,* edited by Dani Rodrik. Princeton: Princeton University Press.

Qian, Yingyi, and Barry Weingast. 1997. "Federalism as a Commitment to Market Incentives." *Journal of Economic Perspectives* 1(4): 83–89.

Qian, Yingyi, and Jinglian Wu. 2003. "China's Transition to a Market Economy: How Far across the River." In *How Far across the River: Chinese Policy Reform at the Millennium,* edited by Nicholas C. Hope, Dennis Tao Yang, and Mu Yang Li. Stanford: Stanford University Press.

Rawski, Thomas G. 1999a. "China's Move to Market: How Far? What Next?" Unpublished paper. Department of Economics, University of Pittsburgh.

———. 1999b. "Reforming China's Economy: What Have We Learned?" *China Journal* 41: 139–56.

Reich, Simon. 1989. "Roads to Follow: Regulating Direct Foreign Investment." *International Organization* 43(4): 543–84.

Remick, Elizabeth. 2002. "The Significance of Variation in Local States: The Case of Twentieth-Century China." *Comparative Politics* 34(4): 399–418.

Rodrik, Dani. 1999. *Making Openness Work: The New Global Economy and the Developing Countries.* Washington, D.C.: Overseas Development Council.

——. 2007. *One Economics, Many Recipes: Globalization, Institutions, and Economic Growth.* Princeton: Princeton University Press.

Rodine, Kirsten. 2008. "Global Telecom Regulatory Reform." PhD dissertation, Department of Political Science, UC Berkeley.

Røisli, Kjell. 2006. "Development or Marginalization? Xinjiang Bingtuan and State-Run Development in China's Wild West." *Internasjonal Politikk* 64(4): 511–32.

Rosen, Daniel H. 1999. *Behind the Open Door: Foreign Enterprises in the Chinese Marketplace.* New York: Institute for International Economics.

Rosen, Stanley. 1995. "Women and Political Participation in China." *Pacific Affairs* 68(3): 315–41.

Ross, Adam. 2005. "Bursting at the Seams." *China Business Review,* September–October.

Ross, Lester, and Kenneth Zhou. 2005. "Trading and Distribution in China." In *Global Competition Review.* Hong Kong: Wilmer Cutler Pickering Hale and Dorr.

Rozelle, Scott. 1994. "Rural Industrialization and Increasing Inequality: Emerging Patterns in China's Reforming Economy." *Journal of Comparative Economics* 19(3): 362–91.

Rozelle, Scott, Albert Park, Jikun Huang, and Hehui Jin. 2000. "Bureaucrat to Entrepreneur: The Changing Role of the State in China's Grain Economy." *Economic Development and Cultural Change* 48(2): 227–52.

Rozelle, Scott, Jikun Huang, Ruifa Hu, Cuihui Fan, and Carl E. Pray. 2002. "Bt Cotton Benefits, Costs, and Impacts in China." *AgBioForum* 5(4): 153–66.

Rudolph, Matthew. 2006. "Diversity amid Convergence: State Authority, Economic Governance, and the Politics of Securities Finance in China and India." PhD dissertation, Department of Political Science, Cornell University.

Saich, Tony. 2001. *Governance and Politics of China.* New York: Palgrave.

Schiller, Dan. 2005. "Poles of Market Growth? Open Questions about China, Information, and the World Economy." *Global Media and Communication* 1(1): 79–103.

Schurmann, Franz. 1968. *Ideology and Organization in Communist China.* Berkeley: University of California Press.

Segal, Adam. 2002. *Digital Dragon: High-Technology Enterprises in China.* Ithaca: Cornell University Press.

Segal, Adam, and Eric Thun. 2001. "Thinking Globally, Acting Locally: Local Governments, Industrial Sectors, and Development in China." *Politics and Society* 29(4): 557–88.

Serger, Sylvia Schwaag, and Magnus Breidne. 2007. "China's Fifteen-Year Plan for Science and Technology: An Assessment." *Asia Policy* 4: 135–64.

Shafer, Michael. 1994. *Winners and Losers: How Sectors Shape the Developmental Prospects of States.* Ithaca: Cornell University Press.

Shen, Xiaobai. 1999. *The Chinese Road to High Technology: A Study of Telecommunications Switching Technology in the Economic Transition.* New York: St. Martin's Press.

Sheng, Yumin. 2007. "Global Market Integration and Central Political Control: Foreign Trade and Intergovernmental Relations in China." *Comparative Political Studies* 40(4): 405–34.

Shih, Victor. 2008. *Factions and Finance in China.* Cambridge: Cambridge University Press.

Shih, Victor, and Louie Huang, 2006. "China's NPL Market, Revealed." *China Business Review,* May–June.

Shirk, Susan L. 1993. *The Political Logic of Economic Reform in China.* Berkeley: University of California Press.

Shonfield, Andrew. 1965. *Modern Capitalism: The Changing Balance of Public and Private Power*. London: Oxford University Press.

Shue, Vivienne. 1988. *The Reach of the State: Sketches of the Chinese Body Politic*. Stanford: Stanford University Press.

Simon, Dennis. 2001. "Microelectronic Industry Crosses a Critical Threshold." *China Business Review*, November–December.

Simmons, Beth, and Zachary Elkins. 2004. "The Globalization of Liberalization: Policy Diffusion in the International Political Economy." *American Political Science Review* 98(1): 171–89.

Skocpol, Theda. 1979. *States and Social Revolutions: A Comparative Analysis of France, Russia, and China*. Cambridge: Harvard University Press.

Skocpol, Theda, and Margaret Somers. 1980. "The Uses of Comparative History in Macrosocial Inquiry." *Comparative Studies in Society and History* 22(2): 174–97.

Smil, Vaclav. 1986. "Food Production and Quality of Diet in China." *Population and Development Review* 12(1): 25–45.

——. 1995. "Who Will Feed China?" *China Quarterly* 143: 801–13.

Snyder, Richard. 2001. *Politics after Neoliberalism: Reregulation in Mexico*. Cambridge: Cambridge University Press.

Solinger, Dorothy J. 1984. *Chinese Business under Socialism: The Politics of Domestic Commerce in Contemporary China*. Berkeley: University of California Press.

——. 1991. *From Lathes to Looms*. Stanford: Stanford University Press.

Sprafkin, Jeffrey, and Ross O'Brien. 1989. "Keeping Telecom on Hold." *China Business Review*, November–December: 24–28.

Steinbock, Dan. 2003. *Wireless Horizon: Strategy and Competition in the Worldwide Mobile Marketplace*. New York: American Management Association.

Steinfeld, Edward S. 1998. *Forging Reform in China: The Fate of State Industry*. Cambridge: Cambridge University Press.

——. 2002. "Moving Beyond Transition in China: Financial Reform and the Political Economy of Declining Growth." *Comparative Politics* 34(4): 379–98.

——. 2004. "China's Shallow Integration: Networked Production and the New Challenges of Late Industrialization." *World Development* 32(1): 1971–87.

Steinfeld, Edward, Richard K. Lester, and Edward Cunningham. 2008. "Greener Plants, Grayer Skies: A Report from the Frontlines of China's Energy Sector." Cambridge: China Energy Group, MIT Industrial Performance Center.

Sterling, Darryl. 1999. "Paging the PRC." *China Business Review*, July–August.

Stiglitz, Joseph. 2001. *Globalization and Its Discontents*. London: W.W. Norton.

Stoner-Weiss, Kathryn. 2001. "The Russian Central State in Crisis: Center and Periphery in the Post-Soviet Era." In *Russian Politics: Challenges of Democratization*, edited by Robert Moser and Zoltan Barany. New York: Cambridge University Press.

——. 2006. *Resisting the State: Reform and Retrenchment in Post-Soviet Russia*. New York: Cambridge University Press.

Strange, Susan. 1996. *The Retreat of the State: The Diffusion of Power in the World Economy*. Cambridge: Cambridge University Press.

Streeck, Wolfgang, and Kathleen Thelen, eds. 2005. *Beyond Continuity: Institutional Change in Advanced Political Economies*. Oxford: Oxford University Press.

Stubbs, Richard. 1999. "War and Economic Development: Export-Oriented Industrialization in East and Southeast Asia." *Comparative Politics* 31: 337–55.

——. 2005. *Rethinking Asia's Economic Miracle: The Political Economy of War, Prosperity and Crisis*. Basingstoke: Macmillan.

——. 2009. "What Ever Happened to the East Asian Developmental State? The Unfolding Debate." *Pacific Review* 22(1): 1–22.

Sun, E-tu Zen. 1990. "Review of 'Science and Civilization in China' by Joseph Needham in *Chemistry and Chemical Technology Volume 5, Textile Technology Spinning and Reeling Part 9*, by Dieter Kuhn." *Technology and Culture* 31(4): 865–67.

Sun, Huaibin, and Hong Zhao, English ed. 2005. *China Textile & Apparel* 1: 1–60.

Suttmeier, Richard. 2004. "China's Techno-Warriors: Another View (Review Article)." *China Quarterly* 179 (September): 804–10.

Suttmeier, Richard. 2005. "A New Technonationalism? China and the Development of Technical Standards." *Communications of the ACM* 48(4): 35–37.

Suttmeier, Richard P., Xiangkui Yao, and Alex Zixiang Tan. 2004. "China's Post-WTO Technology Policy: Standards, Software, and the Changing Nature of Techno-Nationalism." Washington, D.C.: National Bureau of Asian Research.

——. 2006. "Standards of Power? Technology, Institutions, and Politics in the Development of China's National Standards Strategy." Washington, D.C.: National Bureau of Asian Research.

Tam, Waikeung, and Dali Yang. 2005. "Food Safety and Development of Regulatory Institutions in China." *Asian Perspective* 29(4): 5–36.

Tan, Zixiang. 1994. "Challenges to the MPT's Monopoly." *Telecommunications Policy* 18 (3): 174–81.

——. 1999. "Regulating China's Internet: Convergence toward a Coherent Regulatory Regime." *Telecommunications Policy* 23: 261–76.

——. 2002. "Product Cycle Theory and Telecommunications Industry—Foreign Direct Investment, Government Policy, and Indigenous Manufacturing in China." *Telecommunications Policy* 26: 17–30.

Tang, Harina Suk-Ching, and Paul S.N. Lee. 2003. "Growth on Adversity: Non-Economic Factors in Telecommunications Development in China." *Telematics and Informatics* 20: 19–33.

Tanner, Murray Scot. 1999. *The Politics of Lawmaking in Post-Mao China: Institutions, Processes and Democratic Prospects*. Oxford: Clarendon Press.

Tao, Yi-Feng. 2005. "A Catch-Up Strategy? China's Policy toward Foreign Direct Investment." In *Japan and China in the World Economy*, edited by Saadia Pekkanen. London: Routledge.

Thelen, Kathleen. 2004. *How Institutions Evolve: The Political Economy of Skills in Germany, Britain, the United States and Japan*. New York: Cambridge University Press.

Thompson, Edmund R. 2002. "Clustering of Foreign Direct Investment and Enhanced Technology Transfer: Evidence from Hong Kong Garment Firms in China." *World Development* 30(2): 873–89.

Thun, Eric. 2000. "Growing Up and Moving Out: Globalization in the Taiwanese Textile/Apparel and Automotive Sectors." Working paper. Cambridge: MIT Industrial Performance Center.

——. 2004. "Keeping Up with the Joneses: Decentralization, Policy Imitation, and Industrial Development in China." *World Development* 32(8): 1289–1308.

——. 2006. *Changing Lanes in China: Foreign Direct Investment, Local Governments, and Auto Sector Development*. Cambridge: Cambridge University Press.

Tilly, Charles. 1975. *The Formation of National States in Western Europe*. Princeton: Princeton University Press.

——. 1985. "War Making and State Making as Organized Crime." In *Bringing the State Back In*, edited by Peter B. Evans, Dietrich Rueschemeyer, and Theda Skocpol. Cambridge: Cambridge University Press.

Tilton, Mark, and Hyeonjung Choi. 2007. "Legacies of the Developmental State for Japan's Information and Communications Industries." In *Competitiveness of New Industries*, edited by Cornelia Storz and Andreas Moerke. New York: Routledge.

Torbert, Preston M. 1994. "Broadening the Scope of Investment: China's New Company Law Codifies Investor Protection." *China Business Review*, May–June.

Tsai, Kellee. 2002. *Back-Alley Banking: Private Entrepreneurs in China*. Ithaca: Cornell University Press.

——. 2003. "Locating the Local State in Reform-Era China." *Politilogiske Studier 6(2): 71–82.*

——. 2007. *Capitalism without Democracy: The Private Sector in Contemporary China*. Ithaca: Cornell University Press.

Tsai, Kellee, and Saadia M. Pekkanen, eds. 2005. *Japan and China in the World Political Economy*. London: Routledge.

Unger, Jonathan, and Anita Chan. 1999. "Inheritors of the Boom: Private Enterprise and the Role of Local Development in Rural South China Township." *China Journal* 42: 45–74.

United Nations Conference on Trade and Development. 2009. "Major FDI Indicators." *World Investment Report Database*. Accessed online.

United States Government Accountability Office. 2005. "U.S.-China Trade: Textile Safeguard Procedures Should Be Improved GAO-05-296." Washington, D.C.: USGAO.

United States Information Technology Office. 2003. *Catalog of Telecommunications Service Categories (PRC)*. Beijing: USITO.

United States Information Technology Office, Telecom Policy Committee. 2005. *White Paper on China's Telecommunications Market Policy and Regulation*. Beijing: USITO.

United States Trade Representative. 2006. *Report to Congress on China's WTO Compliance*. Washington, D.C.: Department of Commerce.

Urata, Shujiro, Chia Siow Yue, and Fukunari Kimura, eds. 2006. *Multinationals and Economic Growth in East Asia: FDI, Corporate Strategies and National Economic Development*. London: Routledge.

Vernon, Raymond. 1966. "International Investment and International Trade in the Product Life Cycle." *Quarterly Journal of Economics* 80: 190–207.

Vogel, David. 1986. *National Styles of Regulation*. Ithaca: Cornell University Press.

Vogel, Ezra F. 1991. *The Four Little Dragons: The Spread of Industrialization in East Asia*. Cambridge: Harvard University Press.

Vogel, Steven K. 1996. *Freer Markets, More Rules: Regulatory Reform in Advanced Industrial Countries*. Ithaca: Cornell University Press.

——. 2006a. *Japan Remodeled: How Government and Industry Are Reforming Japanese Capitalism*. Ithaca: Cornell University Press.

——. 2006b. "Why Freer Markets Need More Rules." In *Creating Competitive Markets: The Politics of Regulatory Reform*, edited by Marc Landy, Martin Levin, and Martin Shapiro. Washington, D.C.: Brookings Institution Press.

Wade, Robert. 1990. *Governing the Market: Economic Theory and The Role of Government in East Asian Industrialization*. Princeton: Princeton University Press.

Wakeman, Frederic E. 1991. "Models of Historical Change: The Chinese State and Society, 1939–1989." In *Perspectives on Modern China: Four Anniversaries*, edited by Thomas Bernstein et al. Armonk, N.Y.: M. E. Sharpe.

Walder, Andrew. 1995. "Local Government as Industrial Firms: An Organizational Analysis of China's Transitional Economy." *American Journal of Sociology* 101(2): 263–301.

Walter, Carl E., and Fraser T. J. Howie. 2001. *To Get Rich Is Glorious: China's Stock Markets in the '80s and '90s*. New York: Palgrave.

Walton, Julie. 2004. "At Your Service: Foreign Service Providers Are Starting to Make Inroads in the China Market—with Some Exceptions." *China Business Review,* September–October.

Wang, Baiyi. 2005. "Report on the Technological Progress of India's Information Industry." Beijing: Beijing University of Post and Telecommunications. (In Chinese.)

Wang, John. 1999. "Signs of Opening in Telecom." *China Business Review,* May–June.

Wang, Yong. 1999. "Why China Went for WTO." *China Business Review,* May–June.

Wank, David. 1999. *Commodifying Communism: Business, Trust, and Politics in a Chinese City.* Cambridge: Cambridge University Press.

Warwick, William. 1994. "A Review of AT&T's Business History in China: The Memorandum of Understanding in Context." *Telecommunications Policy* 18 (3): 265–74.

Wedeman, Andrew. 2003. *From Mao to Market: Rent Seeking, Local Protectionism, and Marketization in China.* Cambridge: Cambridge University Press.

Wei, Yuwa. 2003. *Comparative Corporate Governance: A Chinese Perspective.* The Hague: Kluwer Law International.

Weinstein, Michael M., ed. 2005. *Globalization: What's New.* New York: Columbia University Press.

Weiss, Linda. 1998. *The Myth of the Powerless State.* Ithaca: Cornell University Press.

——, ed. 2003. *States in the Global Economy: Bringing Domestic Institutions Back In.* Cambridge: Cambridge University Press.

Weldon, E., and W. Vanhonacker. 1999. "Operating a Foreign-Invested Enterprise in China: Challenges for Managers and Management Researchers." *Journal of World Business* 34(1): 94–107.

Wen, Guangzhong James. 1998. "Review of *Calamity and Reform in China,* Dali Yang." *Journal of Comparative Economics* 26(1): 204–6.

Whiting, Susan H. 1999. *Power and Wealth in Rural China: The Political Economy of Institutional Change.* Cambridge: Cambridge University Press.

Wilensky, Harold L. 2002. *Rich Democracies: Political Economy, Public Policy, and Performance.* Berkeley: University of California Press.

Wirtshafter, R.M., and E. Shih 1990. "Decentralization of China's Electricity Sector: Is Small Beautiful?" *World Development* 18(4): 505–12.

Woo-Cumings, Meredith. 1991. *Race to the Swift: State and Finance in Korean Industrialization.* New York: Columbia University Press.

Wu, Kong-Ming. 2007. "Environmental Impact and Risk Management Strategies of Bt Cotton Commercialization In China." *Chinese Journal of Agricultural Biotechnology* 4(2): 93–97.

Wu, Shaofan, 2005. "Analysis on the Relationship between the Development of Telecom Enterprises and China Unicom." *Management World,* January. (In Chinese.)

Wu, Yu-Shan. 2003. "Chinese Economic Reform in a Comparative Perspective." *Issues & Studies* 39(1): 93–118.

Wu, Irene. 2009. *From Iron Fist to Invisible Hand: The Uneven Path of Telecommunications Reform in China.* Stanford: Stanford University Press.

Xu, Cheng. 2005. "New Strategy to Reconcile the Needs of Increasing China's Food Production through Agricultural Intensification and Protection of the Environment." *Journal of Sustainable Agriculture* 25(4): 29–47.

Xu, Xiaoping. 1998. *China's Financial System under Transition.* New York: St. Martin's Press.

Xu, Xinwu, and Byung-Kun Min. 1988. "The Struggle of the Handicraft Cotton Industry against Machine Textiles in China." *Modern China* 14(1): 31–49.

Yang, Dali. 1994. "Reform and the Restructuring of Central-Local Relations." In *China Deconstructs: Politics, Trade, and Regionalism,* edited by David Goodman and Gerald Segal. New York: Routledge.

——. 1997. *Beyond Beijing: Liberalization and the Regions in China.* New York: Routledge, 1997.

——. 2004. *Remaking the Chinese Leviathan: Market Transition and the Politics of Governance in China.* Stanford: Stanford University Press.

Yang, Ming and Xin Yu. "China's Power Management." *Energy Policy* 24(8): 735–57.

Yergin, Daniel, and Joseph Stanislaw. 1998. *The Commanding Heights: The Battle between Government and the Marketplace That Is Remaking the Modern World.* New York: Simon and Schuster.

Yeung, Godfrey, and Vincent Mok. 2004. "Does WTO Accession Matter for the Chinese Textile and Clothing Industry?" *Cambridge Journal of Economics* 28(6): 937–54.

Yu, Tak-Sun, Yi Min Liu, Jiong-Liang Zhou, and Tze-Wai Wong. 1999. "Occupational Injuries in Shunde City—a County Undergoing Rapid Economic Change in Southern China." *Accident Analysis and Prevention* 31: 313–17.

Yusuf, Shahid, M. Anjum Altaf, and Kaoru Nabeshima. 2004. *Global Change and East Asian Policy Initiatives.* Washington, D.C.: World Bank; and New York: Oxford University Press.

Yusuf, Shahid, Kaoru Nabeshima, and Dwight H. Perkins. 2006. *Under New Ownership: Privatizing China's State-Owned Enterprises.* Stanford: Stanford University Press.

Zhang, Bing. 2001. "Assessing the WTO Agreements on China's Telecommunications Regulatory Reform and Industrial Liberalization." *Telecommunications Policy* 25: 461–83.

Zhang, Bing, and Mike W. Peng. 2000. "Telecom Competition, Post-WTO Style." *China Business Review,* May–June: 12–21.

Zhang, Yaohuan, and Ling Xiongjiang. 2006. "Policy Choice for China's Telecommunications Industry to Realize an Effective Competition at the Present Time." *Macroeconomics,* January: 17–20. (In Chinese.)

Zhang, Zhiqiang. 2005. "3G Investment Strategy of Telecom Industry and Its Choice of Regulations and Policies." *Macroeconomics,* September. (In Chinese.)

Zhao, Hong, ed. 2006. *China Textile* 1: 1–112.

Zhao, Yumin. 2005a. "Self-Owned Marketing Channels to Be Set Up." *Intertrade,* March. (In Chinese.).

——. 2005b. "The Future Development of China's Textile Industry: Thinking Sparked by the Development of the Global Textile Industry and the Competition Factor." *Intertrade,* June. (In Chinese.)

Zheng, Yongnian. 2004. *Globalization and State Transformation in China.* Cambridge: Cambridge University Press.

——. 2005. "Information Technology, Public Space, and Collective Action in China." *Comparative Political Studies* 38(5): 507–36.

——. 2008. *Technological Empowerment: The Internet, the State, and Society in China.* Stanford: Stanford University Press.

Zhou, Huan. 2006. "On the Strategic Position of TD-SCDMA in the National Information Industry." *Macroeconomics,* January. (In Chinese.)

Zhou, Yu. 2008. *The Inside Story of China's High-Tech Industry: Making Silicon Valley in Beijing.* Plymouth, U.K.: Rowman and Littlefield.

Zita, Ken. 1989. "Telecommunications: China's Uphill Battle to Modernize." *China Business Review,* November–December.

Zweig, David. 1995. "Developmental Communities on China's Coast: The Impact of Trade, Investment, and Transnational Alliances." *Comparative Politics* 27(3): 253–74.

———. 2002. *Internationalizing China: Domestic Interests and Global Linkages.* Ithaca: Cornell University Press.

Zysman, John. 1983. *Governments, Markets, and Growth: Finance and the Politics of Industrial Change.* Ithaca: Cornell University Press.

———. 1994. "How Institutions Create Historically Rooted Trajectories of Growth." *Industrial and Corporate Change* 3(1): 244–83.

INDEX

Page numbers followed by letters *f* and *t* refer to figures and tables, respectively.

CPSIA information can be obtained at www.ICGtesting.com
Printed in the USA
LVOW080836181111

255579LV00006B/1/P